Advances in

THE STUDY OF BEHAVIOR

VOLUME 40

Advances in
THE STUDY OF
BEHAVIOR

Vocal Communication in Birds and Mammals

Chief Editors

MARC NAGUIB

VINCENT M. JANIK

Editors

KLAUS ZUBERBÜHLER

NICOLA S. CLAYTON

Advances in
THE STUDY OF
BEHAVIOR

Edited by

Marc Naguib
Netherlands Institute of Ecology (NIOO-KNAW)
Department of Animal Population Biology
Heteren, The Netherlands

Klaus Zuberbühler
School of Psychology
University of St. Andrews
St. Mary's College
Scotland, United Kingdom

Nicola S. Clayton
Department of Experimental Psychology
Cambridge
United Kingdom

Vincent M. Janik
Sea Mammal Research Unit
School of Biology
University of St. Andrews
United Kingdom

———————————*VOLUME 40*———————————

ELSEVIER

AMSTERDAM • BOSTON • HEIDELBERG • LONDON
NEW YORK • OXFORD • PARIS • SAN DIEGO
SAN FRANCISCO • SINGAPORE • SYDNEY • TOKYO
Academic Press is an imprint of Elsevier

Academic Press is an imprint of Elsevier
32 Jamestown Road, London NW1 7BY, UK
30 Corporate Drive, Suite 400, Burlington, MA 01803, USA
525 B Street, Suite 1900, San Diego, CA 92101-4495, USA
Radarweg 29, PO Box 211, 1000 AE Amsterdam, The Netherlands

First edition 2009

ISBN: 978-0-12-374475-3
ISSN: 0065-3454

For information on all Academic Press publications
visit our website at www.elsevierdirect.com

Printed and bound in United States of America
09 10 10 9 8 7 6 5 4 3 2 1

Contents

Environmental Acoustics and the Evolution of Bird Song
HENRIK BRUMM AND MARC NAGUIB

The Evolution of Song in the *Phylloscopus* Leaf Warblers (Aves: Sylviidae): A Tale of Sexual Selection, Habitat Adaptation, and Morphological Constraints
BETTINA MAHLER AND DIEGO GIL

A Review of Vocal Duetting in Birds
MICHELLE L. HALL

Acoustic Communication in Delphinids

VINCENT M. JANIK

Vocal Performance and Sensorimotor Learning in Songbirds

JEFFREY PODOS, DAVID C. LAHTI,
AND DANA L. MOSELEY

Song and Female Mate Choice in Zebra Finches: A Review

KATHARINA RIEBEL

Plasticity of Communication in Nonhuman Primates

CHARLES T. SNOWDON

Survivor Signals: The Biology and Psychology
of Animal Alarm Calling

KLAUS ZUBERBÜHLER

Contributors

Numbers in parentheses indicate the pages on which the authors' contributions begin.

HENRIK BRUMM (1), *Communication and Social Behaviour Group, Max Planck Institute for Ornithology, 82319 Seewiesen, Germany*

DIEGO GIL (35), *Departamento de Ecología Evolutiva, Museo Nacional de Ciencias Naturales (CSIC), José Gutiérrez Abascal 2, E-28006 Madrid, Spain*

MICHELLE L. HALL (67), *Behavioral Ecology of Sexual Signals Group, Max Planck Institute for Ornithology, Vogelwarte Radolfzell, D-78315, Germany*

VINCENT M. JANIK (123), *Sea Mammal Research Unit, Scottish Oceans Institute, School of Biology, University of St Andrews, Fife KY16 8LB, United Kingdom*

DAVID C. LAHTI (159), *Department of Biology and Graduate Program in Organismic & Evolutionary Biology, University of Massachusetts, Amherst, Massachusetts 01003, USA*

BETTINA MAHLER (35), *Laboratorio de Ecología y Comportamiento Animal, Departamento de Ecología, Genética y Evolución, Facultad de Ciencias Exactas y Naturales, Universidad de Buenos Aires, 4 Piso, Pab. II, Ciudad Universitaria, 1428 Capital Federal, Argentina*

DANA L. MOSELEY (159), *Department of Biology and Graduate Program in Organismic & Evolutionary Biology, University of Massachusetts, Amherst, Massachusetts 01003, USA*

MARC NAGUIB (1), *Netherlands Institute of Ecology (NIOO-KNAW), PO Box 40, 6666 ZG Heteren, The Netherlands*

JEFFREY PODOS (159), *Department of Biology and Graduate Program in Organismic & Evolutionary Biology, University of Massachusetts, Amherst, Massachusetts 01003, USA*

KATHARINA RIEBEL (197), *Behavioral Biology Group, Institute of Biology, Leiden University, Sylvius Laboratory, 2300 RA Leiden, The Netherlands*

CHARLES T. SNOWDON (239), *Department of Psychology, University of Wisconsin, Madison, Wisconsin 53706, USA*

KLAUS ZUBERBÜHLER (277), *School of Psychology, University of St Andrews, St Andrews KY16 9JP, Scotland, United Kingdom*

Preface

Advances in the Study of Behavior is well known for its contributions to animal behavior by publishing influential reviews on key topics in the field. The success of this series in recent years has been so outstanding because of the insightful and professional way it has been handled by Professor Peter Slater, the long-term executive editor of this book serial. Peter Slater became editor with Volume 14 in 1984, and was executive editor for a total of 16 years, being responsible for volumes 19–35. There is no doubt that this series has received its current reputation by benefiting from such a long period of Peter's contribution as an editor. Although he retired from his Chair as Kennedy Professor of Natural History at the University of St Andrews in 2008, he is still very active and continues to play a key role in the field of animal communication. The most recent evidence for Peter's scientific impact is the success of his corner-stone book in birdsong (written together with Clive Catchpole) which has just appeared in a second edition. To celebrate his outstanding contributions to science, a special conference on *Vocal Communication in Birds and Mammals* was organized at the University of St Andrews in 2008 by Vincent Janik, Nicky Clayton, and Klaus Zuberbühler. This conference brought together more than 150 key researchers in the main field that Peter had worked in. This special volume on animal communication was in part inspired by this conference and is dedicated to Peter.

This is the third special volume in this series. Previous special volumes were *Parental Care: Evolution, Mechanisms, and Adaptive Significance* (1996, volume 26) and *Stress and Behavior* (1998, volume 27). The present special volume continues to reflect the diversity of approaches that scientists in this field use and the array of general problems in organismic biology they address by focusing on vocal communication in birds and mammals. The editing of this volume has been helped by many reviewers who are acknowledged in each chapter. Vincent Janik would also like to thank the Royal Society and the Wissenschaftskolleg zu Berlin for their support during the editing of this volume.

The volume includes chapters on birdsong (Brumm and Naguib, Hall, Mahler and Gil, Podos, Riebel), marine mammal communication (Janik), and primate communication (Snowdon, Zuberbühler). The chapter by Brumm and Naguib, "Environmental Acoustics and the Evolution of Birdsong," is a review of adaptation of vocal signals to degradation and communication in noise. A special focus is given to extracting distance cues from signals masked by noise, a problem that is particularly prevalent in territorial long distance signals such as birdsong. The chapter by Mahler and Gil, "The Evolution of Song in the *Phylloscopus* Leaf Warblers (Aves: Sylviidae): A Tale of Sexual Selection, Habitat Adaptation, and Morphological Constraints," provides a phylogenetic analysis of song diversity in warblers and links the findings to natural and sexual selection by evaluating several hypotheses, explaining the diversity of singing in this group of passerines. Hall evaluates duetting in her chapter "A Review of Vocal Duetting in Birds." In recent years, a re-emerging interest in such outstanding vocal performances has generated considerable amounts of new data permitting to evaluate different hypotheses, explaining the evolution of duetting behavior. Podos, Lahti, and Moseley focus on "Vocal Performance and Sensorimotor Learning in Songbirds." Vocal perform-ance is increasingly recognized as an influential factor in song evolution, particularly with respect to vocal output, song consistency, and trill structure. Podos et al. emphasize the importance of considering the developmental history of an individual for understanding the functional implications and evolution of song performance. The chapter by Riebel, "Song and Female Mate Choice in Zebra Finches: A Review," provides an overview of how female song and mate preferences develop and which factors affect female decision making in addition to those traits that can be measured from male behavior. This chapter shows that females play a key role in the evolution of signaling in male songbirds as they are the ones who impose the intersexual selection pressure on these traits.

Dolphins provide an interesting comparison to birds in that they are capable of vocal learning but do not appear to produce song. Janik provides an overview of this group in his chapter on "Acoustic Communication in Delphinids." He shows that a combination of the increased demands on acoustic communication in the marine environment and complex social structures is the most likely cause for the plasticity and flexibility of dolphin communication systems. Whereas learning is well known to play a key role in songbird and marine mammal communication, the evidence for vocal learning in primates has been rather limited. However, Snowdon discusses "Plasticity of Communication in Nonhuman Primates" and argues that they have a higher degree of plasticity than previously recognized. Alarm calls are a feature of communication systems that has been particularly well studied in primates. One of the key questions here is whether animals only signal urgency in alarm calls or also provide referential information, indicating a specific predator type. Zuberbühler's chapter on "Survivor Signals: The Biology and Psychology of Animal Alarm Calling" integrates such studies on alarm calls in primates with those in other taxa and provides new insights into the current state of thinking in this field.

Animal communication is an exciting research topic, and this volume provides key reviews that will inform current debates in this field. Peter Slater's stellar contribution to research on animal communication is very clear and reflected in the number of citations he and his co-workers receive in this volume. We hope that he will continue to contribute to the field for a long time to come. We also hope that this volume will succeed not only in providing comprehensive reviews but also in enticing students to carry this field forward and to become the next generation of animal behavior scientists.

MARC NAGUIB
NICOLA S. CLAYTON
KLAUS ZUBERBÜHLER
VINCENT M. JANIK

Environmental Acoustics and the Evolution
of Bird Song

HENRIK BRUMM* and MARC NAGUIB[†]

*COMMUNICATION AND SOCIAL BEHAVIOUR GROUP, MAX PLANCK INSTITUTE
FOR ORNITHOLOGY, 82319 SEEWIESEN, GERMANY
[†]NETHERLANDS INSTITUTE OF ECOLOGY (NIOO-KNAW), PO BOX 40,
6666 ZG HETEREN, THE NETHERLANDS

I. INTRODUCTION TO COMMUNICATION IN THE WILD

Acoustic signals are widespread among various animal taxa and they are often used as advertisement displays in habitats with dense vegetation and/or over long distances (Bradbury and Vehrencamp, 1998). As a consequence of transmission over long ranges or through dense habitats, acoustic signals inevitably attenuate and degrade on their way to a receiver (Slabbekoorn, 2004; Wiley and Richards, 1978, 1982). Therefore, the signal structure at the position of a receiver differs from the signal structure at the source. In addition, high noise levels in natural and urban habitats limit information transfer over distances over which signals otherwise travel with little degradation. The nature of these environmental factors depends, among others, on the habitat structure, noise sources, and weather conditions. Thus, the acoustic habitat properties are important for the evolution of vocal signals, as certain signal structures will be more effective in long-range communication than others. Over evolutionary time, bird songs will be selected to transmit well over the typical communication distance in a given habitat, provided that the signal structure allows adaptive plasticity. The acoustic habitat characteristics chiefly affecting sound transmission are attenuation, degradation, and masking by ambient noise.

Attenuation of sound in natural environments is affected by frequency-dependent effects such as atmospheric absorption, scattering, and attenuation by the vegetation and the ground (Wiley and Richards, 1982). Ground effects concern mainly frequencies below 1 kHz and thus have only little influence on the propagation of most bird songs. The degree of absorption

1

0065-3454/09 $35.00
DOI: 10.1016/S0065-3454(09)40001-9

and scattering increases with the sound frequency; therefore, lower frequencies attenuate less in all habitats (the exception are frequencies below 1 kHz transmitted near the ground) (Wiley and Richards, 1978). However, the slope of frequency dependence of attenuation is higher in forests because of the high degree of scattering from foliage, that is, high frequencies are attenuated more strongly in forests than in open habitats (Marten and Marler, 1977; Morton, 1975; Wiley and Richards, 1978). The sum of scattering and absorption by the foliage can half the transmission distance of bird songs (Blumenrath and Dabelsteen, 2004), which means that, source level and frequency being equal, songs in deciduous forests will have a four times larger broadcast area before foliation in spring than later in the season when trees are full of leaves.

Degradation refers to the combined effects of reverberation and amplitude fluctuations, as opposed to frequency-dependent attenuation (Wiley and Richards, 1982). Because of reflections from tree trunks and the canopy, there is greater reverberation in dense forests than in less dense forests or open areas (Naguib, 2003; Richards and Wiley, 1980). In open habitats, however, sound transmission properties usually induce greater amplitude fluctuations than in forests, because of stronger winds and thermals that create temporal variation in the propagation of sound (Richards and Wiley, 1980; Wiley and Richards, 1982). On the one hand, degradation impairs long-range signaling and thus birds should avoid signal features that are easily degraded in the respective habitat. On the other hand, birds may use vocalizations that degrade quickly with distance in short-range communication. Moreover, listening birds can use degradation cues to estimate the distance of a singing conspecific, which is particularly important for territorial interactions (Naguib and Wiley, 2001). We will have a closer look at the relation between auditory distance assessment and environmental acoustics in Section III.

In addition to attenuation and degradation, the active space of a sound is also considerably affected by background noise.[1] The degree to which ambient noise interferes with acoustic communication is contingent on the amount of frequency overlap between signal and noise (Dooling, 1982;

---

[1]In terms of Information Theory, noise is any disturbance that affects a signal and that may distort the information carried by it (Shannon, 1948, 1949). Thus, from a receiver's point of view, noise is any factor that reduces the ability of a receiver to detect a signal or to discriminate one signal from another. Considering this perspective, attenuation and degradation would be the particular cases of noise. However, in this review, we will use the term in its more common meaning to describe interfering sounds occurring in the transmission channel during acoustic communication. Thus, the noise we will be looking at here is acoustic background noise, which is a special case of the more general noise concept that is used, for example, in the noisy-channel coding theorem (Shannon, 1949).

Klump, 1996). The actual broadcast distance of a song depends on the relationship between attenuation and the level and spectral characteristics of background noise. Therefore, ambient noise is considered a crucial factor affecting the evolution of bird song characteristics (Brumm and Slabbekoorn, 2005; Ryan and Brenowitz, 1985). The importance of noise for the structure of bird song becomes evident when we consider that all bird habitats are noisy, and—although in many instances we fail to notice it—noise levels are often quite substantial. The major abiotic noise sources include the sounds produced by wind and moving water, such as rain, surf, or the rush of rocky streams. In addition, bird songs can also be masked by the sounds produced by other animals. Thus, the vocalization of one individual can become a masking noise for another's signal. Indeed, biotic noise sources are the major acoustic interference in many habitats; vivid examples are the colonies of many seabirds where thousands of individuals call at the same time (Aubin and Jouventin, 2002) or rainforests with their hubbub of bird songs, frog calls, and insect sounds (Brumm and Slabbekoorn, 2005). It is conceivable that, to reduce mutual masking, the signals of different species may be shifted by selection to different frequency bands, so that species eventually avoid spectral overlap and hence occupy distinct acoustic niches (Nelson and Marler, 1990).

The idea that the acoustic properties of the environment may affect the characteristics of bird songs is not new; one of the first to point it out was the ornithologist Hans Stadler who coined the term voice biotope or melotope (Stadler, 1926). He reckoned that birds in certain habitats use songs of similar structure; specifically, he suggested that birds in areas with low-frequency noise would use particularly high-pitched vocalizations. The more modern Acoustic Adaptation Hypothesis argues that song features get adapted to the sound transmission characteristics of the environment (Morton, 1975), the central prediction being that bird songs will be selected to transmit particularly well in a given habitat across the typical communication distance. So, the Acoustic Adaptation Hypothesis is mainly emphasizing signal transmission and the melotope concept is mainly addressing signal masking. However, the important question is whether a signal can convey information, or in other words, whether a receiver can detect and recognize a signal (Endler, 1993). As both sound transmission and masking play a crucial role for the signal-to-noise ratio at the position of a potential receiver, the Acoustic Adaptation Hypothesis and the melotope idea are simply the two sides of the same coin. Thus, we will use a more generalized Acoustic Adaptation Hypothesis including any environmental source that may decrease signal-to-noise ratios as conceptual framework to investigate how birds have adapted their songs to the environmental acoustics.

To explore this issue, we will take a threefold approach: firstly, we will review the constraints that signalers face and the adaptations they have evolved to cope with unfavorable signaling conditions. Secondly, we will discuss the problems that receivers face and their abilities to extract relevant information from a degraded or masked signal. Thirdly, in the final section, we will integrate effects of communication in noise with the receiver's ability to extract distance information from a signal—which is of particular importance in cases where acoustic signals are used to claim territories, as is the case in most bird songs. Throughout the chapter, our main focus will be on songbirds, but many of the principles we discuss are also relevant for acoustic communication in insects (Römer and Lewald, 1992), anurans (Kime et al., 2000; Wollerman, 1999), and mammals (Brumm et al., 2004; Whitehead, 1987).

II. Signaler Adaptations

In this section, we will investigate the ways in which birds improve signal transmission by increasing the signal-to-noise ratio of their songs and by reducing negative effects of sound degradation during transmission to potential receivers. Such song adjustments can be found on a phylogenetic and, even more so, on an individual level. First, we will look at song structure, that is, phonological and syntactic properties of bird song, and then at performance, that is, aspects of song delivery.

A. Song Structure

One of the first to show that the structure of bird songs appears to be adapted to the acoustic properties of the environment were Jilka and Leisler (1974) who found that the songs of *Acrocephalus* warblers transmit particularly well in their respective habitats. In a comparative study on Central American birds, Morton (1975) reported that the songs of forest species contained more pure tones (whistles) and tended to include fewer trills than those of open grassland species. The latter is in line with predictions from sound transmission experiments, which indicate that rapid trills get easily blurred in forests by reverberation (Naguib, 2003). Moreover, whistle-like vocalizations might also be advantageous in forests, as suggested by some researchers who argue that reverberations can even enhance sound transmission of pure tones by superimposing reflections, which in turn increases signal-to-noise ratios (Nemeth et al., 2006; Slabbekoorn et al., 2002). An effect of the habitat type on the occurrence of rapid amplitude modulations was also demonstrated by Wiley (1991) when he compared the song structures of 120 North American birds. He found that in open habitats most species included trills in their songs and nearly half of them also included notes with sidebands, that is, rapid amplitude modulations. In contrast, most forest species did not sing trills, and only a very small fraction produced sidebands. This suggests that in environments with strong reverberation, selection favors signals that avoid rapid repetitions at a given frequency.

These comparative studies revealed important insights into general patterns in the adaptation of song structure to the acoustics properties of the habitat. However, if adaptation to habitat acoustics is essentially a strong selective force acting upon bird songs, then one has to expect habitat-related variation in song structure also within populations. Indeed, several studies suggest effects within species, and their findings reveal more detailed patterns that cannot appear in an overall comparative analysis. A classic example comes from great tits (*Parus major*), one of the most abundant western Palearctic songbirds. Hunter and Krebs (1979) studied great tit songs in various countries stretching from Norway to Iran. Regardless of the geographical location, forest birds had songs with a lower maximum frequency and less rapidly repeated elements than those in more open woodlands. As discussed above, high frequencies will be attenuated more strongly in forests and rapid element repetitions are vulnerable to blurring through reverberation, so their findings are in line with predictions from sound transmission experiments.

Another species in which the element repetition rate varies with habitat is the rufous-collared sparrow, *Zonotrichia capensis* (Handford, 1981). Males in woodlands were found to sing slower trills than males in more open habitats (Fig. 1).

However, slow trills were also recorded in some open agricultural areas where there was no transmission advantage of low element repetition rates. Handford and Lougheed (1991) discovered that the trill rate in these areas was more strongly related to the original vegetation that had been present before farmland was created rather than the current vegetation. This suggests that the adaptation of song structure to the habitat acoustics shows inertia, either because other conflicting factors prevent fast trills to reoccur or because selection has not had enough time yet to adapt the songs to the new sonic environment.

There are several other examples of habitat-dependent variation of vocal signals within a species (reviewed in Boncoraglio and Saino (2007)); a particularly informative one is that of the satin bowerbird (*Ptilinorhynchus violaceus*). In this species, there is both local and geographical variation in

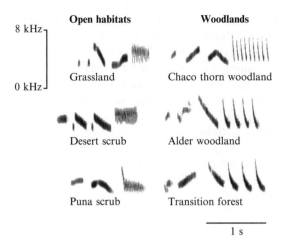

FIG. 1. Habitat-dependent song variation in the rufous-collared sparrow. In northwestern Argentina, this species shows an ecological segregation of song patterns with rapid terminal trills in open habitats and much slower trills in closed woodland and forest habitats. (modified from Handford (2004); used with permission.)

the advertisement call throughout the entire range of the species distribution along the east coast of Australia (Nicholls and Goldizen, 2006). Interestingly, not geographical distance but habitat type was the major correlate of call variation. In line with the acoustic properties of different habitats, in dense forests the calls are lower pitched and show less frequency modulations compared to those in more open areas.

Overall, the current picture suggests that the transmission qualities of different habitats have a major influence on variation in avian vocalizations with selection favoring spectral characteristics and amplitude modulation patterns that are least affected by attenuation and degradation during sound transmission. However, no variation of signal structure with habitat could be found in the song of the chaffinch, *Fringilla coelebs*, (Williams and Slater, 1993) or that of the American redstart, *Setophaga ruticilla*, (Date and Lemon, 1993) or in the calls of chiffchaffs, *Phylloscopus collybita*, (Naguib et al., 2001). This evidence for a lack of a habitat effect does not necessarily disprove the Acoustic Adaptation Hypothesis, but rather indicates that there are also other important factors affecting the structure of bird vocalizations. While the efficiency of signal transmission influences the structure of songs on an evolutionary level, there can also be conflicting social and ecological pressures that act to reduce its importance (Doutrelant and Lambrechts, 2001; Kroon and Westcott, 2006).

Signal-to-noise ratios at the position of the receiver will not only be affected by the changes the signal underwent during transmission but also by the level and spectral characteristics of background noise. Many habitats have their own typical pattern of background noise, due, for instance, to the exposure of wind or a particular set of sound-producing animals. On an evolutionary scale, bird songs will be shaped by selection to stand out before the background of masking noise; in this way, the songs of different species will be fitted into the "symphony of animal sounds" as Krause (1992) phrased it. Indeed, a study of red-winged blackbird (*Agelaius phoeniceus*) songs suggests that these birds use a "silent window" of comparatively low levels of background noise for their songs (Brenowitz, 1982).

Similar to the effect of sound transmission, differences in background noise profiles can also lead to habitat-dependent song differences between populations. Slabbekoorn and Smith (2002) found that there was little low-frequency noise in a rainforest in Cameroon compared with a nearby ecotone forest, and, in line with this, little greenbuls (*Andropadus virens*) in the rainforest used particular low-frequency song elements that are not found in ecotone birds.

In many cases, habitats differ only slightly in their acoustic properties and many studies found only fairly minor differences in song characteristics (Boncoraglio and Saino, 2007; Catchpole and Slater, 2008). However, case studies in habitats exposed to extreme noise intensities provide an excellent opportunity to investigate how bird songs are adapted to the acoustics of the environment and, at the same time, such studies can give us an impression of how powerful background noise can be as a selective force driving the evolution of bird song. For instance, ornithologists have noticed that bird species found close to noisy mountain streams seem to have particular high-pitched songs and it has been speculated that the high song frequencies are an adaptation to the low-frequency noise in their habitat (Brumm and Slabbekoorn, 2005; Dubois and Martens, 1984; Martens and Geduldig, 1990). However, it is quite difficult to show that this is actually the case, because one has to take phylogenetic constraints into account as well as the fact that pitch is limited by body size (Ryan and Brenowitz, 1985; Wiley, 1991). Comparative data from whistling thrushes (*Myophonus* spp.) may help to shed some light on this issue. Whistling thrushes are southeast Asian songbirds that are often found close to noisy mountain streams, usually in riverine forests in ravines and gorges. Species like the Sri Lanka whistling thrush (*Myophonus blighi*) or the Malabar whistling thrush (*Myophonus horsefieldii*), for instance, are often breeding on rock ledges next to waterfalls and rapids (Clement and Hathway, 2000). The sound of running water is concentrated at low frequencies below 2 kHz, but with diminishing amounts of energy at higher frequencies as well. Thus, the higher pitched a song, the less it will be masked in these habitats. On the other hand, high frequencies are less suitable for long-range communication because they get more attenuated. As a result, there is opposite selection on song pitch in whistling thrush habitats. The Javan whistling thrush (*Myophonus glaucinus*) is the only species of the genus that is less tied to water (Clement and Hathway, 2000) and thus also breeding at locations with less intense background noise or noise in other frequency bands. Interestingly, it is this species that produces the songs with the lowest maximum frequencies in relation to the birds' body size (Fig. 2). This finding suggests that the songs of the Javan whistling thrush can be low pitched to benefit from less attenuation because they are not constantly masked by low-frequency noise. In the other species, however, selection has probably pushed song frequencies upward to mitigate signal masking by the noise produced by mountain streams. However, only very few songs from a small number of individuals of each species were available for the analysis and some of the exemplars were recorded in unknown circumstances. Thus, further research is needed to confirm this pattern.

A species that takes the shift of song frequency to an unusual extreme is the rufous-faced warbler (*Abroscopus albogularis*), which, like the whistling thrushes, occurs along noisy streams. Narins et al. (2004) discovered that rufous-faced warbler songs contain prominent harmonics that extend even into the ultrasonic range, suggesting that this shift of song energy may be an evolutionary response to the masking of low frequencies by the stream noise. However, ultrasonic frequencies suffer from high rates of attenuation and scattering and they are also highly directional; all that makes them not very useful for long-range communication. It remains to be shown that rufous-faced warblers actually perceive the ultrasonic components of their songs and use it for communication.[2] By and large, the current evidence suggests that habitat-specific noise may be a powerful selective force, leading to upward shifts of song frequencies among species, or even within species and populations (Brumm and Slater, 2006b; Slabbekoorn and Peet, 2003). In habitats dominated by high-frequency noise (such as the sounds produced by many insect species), the same selective force may theoretically also work in the opposite direction, selecting for a downward shift of vocal frequency.

[2]Extensive research by Narins and coworkers has shown that frogs in the same habitat not only produce ultrasonic sounds but that they indeed use them to exchange information (Arch and Narins, 2008; Feng and Narins, 2008; Feng et al., 2006; Shen et al., 2008). This finding was surprising because the vocal production and perception capacities of the torrent frogs considerably exceed previously posited upper limits for anurans. More research on bird species from habitats with intense low-frequency background noise might reveal that the auditory range of some birds is also much wider than previously thought.

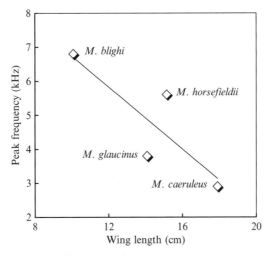

FIG. 2. High-pitched bird songs in habitats with intense low-frequency noise: body size and song frequency in whistling thrushes, genus *Myophonus*. The species of this genus occur along noisy mountain streams with the exception of the Javan whistling thrush, *Myophonus glaucinus*, which is less tied to water. Note that the songs of the Javan whistling thrush are the only to fall considerably below the regression line, that is, in comparison to the other species Javan whistling thrushes have a lower peak frequency in relation to their body size. Wing measures were taken from Delacour (1942). Song frequency measurements are based on recordings from 3 (Sri Lanka whistling thrush, *Myophonus blighi* and Malabar whistling thrush, *Myophonus horsefieldii*) to 5 males (Javan whistling thrush and blue whistling thrush, *M. caeruleus*). The peak frequency is the peak power amplitude in the song spectrum, that is, the loudest, or emphasized, frequency. Song recordings courtesy of Gottfried Bürger, xeno-canto community database (www.xeno-canto.org), and the Tierstimmenarchiv Berlin.

In the recent years, the effect of a particular case of environmental noise has sparked considerable interest among biologists studying bird song, that of anthropogenic noise pollution (Brumm, 2006b; Katti and Warren, 2004; Patricelli and Blickley, 2006; Slabbekoorn and Ripmeester, 2007). In urban habitats, birds of several species have been found to sing at a higher pitch: great tits (Slabbekoorn and Boer-Visser, 2006) and blackbirds, *Turdus merula*, (Nemeth and Brumm, in press) in Europe, and house finches (Bermúdez-Cuamatzin et al., in press; Fernández-Juricic et al., 2005) and song sparrows, *Melospiza melodia,* (Wood and Yezerinac, 2006) in America. This striking variation in vocal frequency has been attributed to anthropogenic noise, and it seems plausible to interpret the higher pitched songs of city birds as an adaptation to the low-frequency traffic noise in urban areas. However, urban and nonurban habitats differ in many more traits than just background noise profiles, and there is no evidence to date that the observed shifts in urban song frequencies are actually adaptive and an evolutionary response to noise. The increase of song pitch could also be an epiphenomenon of the urban ecology of city-dwelling birds (Nemeth and Brumm, in press). For instance, some bird species occur in higher densities in urban areas compared to rural or forest habitats, and as a consequence, they may have more intense territorial interactions with neighboring males. This would change the motivational state of a singer, which can also be reflected in the structure of song. Moreover, urban birds show a different temporal pattern of gonadal development than their conspecifics in forests and as a result city birds breed earlier in the season (Partecke et al., 2004). If song pitch varies over the breeding season, then the higher song frequencies in cities might reflect the advanced breeding stages in urban birds rather than an adaptation to traffic noise. Moreover, the higher pitched songs of city birds could also be a consequence of the Lombard effect: in noisy areas, birds will sing with higher amplitude, and as sound amplitude and sound frequency can be coupled (Beckers et al., 2003), the louder songs could also raise in pitch. Thus, the increase in song pitch would be just a side-effect of the Lombard response and not an adaptation that is driven by the need to reduce signal masking. Therefore, one should be cautious when interpreting the findings from correlational studies on urban bird song as being causally related to ambient noise. Clearly, experimental data are needed to clarify the issue.

Frequency shifts are not the only way in which birds adjust the structure of their songs to counteract noise. Another possible way of mitigating masking is to repeat the message more often so that the receiver is more likely to perceive it, either because one rendition hits a quieter period or because the listener can extract increasing information from each successive song. Such mechanism concerns a higher level of song organization, that is, song sequencing, and thus relates to the serial redundancy of singing. Redundancy is not only a common feature of bird song but also of many animal signals in general (Bradbury and Vehrencamp, 1998). Songbirds with small song-type repertoires typically produce several renditions of each song type before switching to the next, thereby producing highly redundant signal series. Chaffinches are among these species and Brumm and Slater (2006b) found that males close to waterfalls and torrents sing longer bouts of the same song type before switching to a new type than males further away in the same area.[3] The same tactic has been found in

---

[3]These findings suggest that the singing style is a response to noise even though, as in case with the study on urban noise in cities, other factors such as individual spacing or habitat quality may have led to singing with higher redundancy.

calling Japanese quail (Potash, 1972) and penguins (Lengagne et al., 1999b), indicating that an increase in serial redundancy is not a unique feature of songbirds.

To sum up then, environmental acoustics favor certain song characteristics that are suitable for long-range signaling, such as the avoidance of trills in echoic habitats. In general, low frequencies are superior in long-range communication, because they suffer less from attenuation during transmission. However, it is important to be clear that song traits may vary in their ability to respond to selection due to, for instance, physical or phylogenetic constraints (Ryan and Brenowitz, 1985). The production of low song frequencies is, for instance, constrained by a bird's body size. In addition, habitat-specific patterns of environmental noise further constrain the use of certain frequency bands. Thus, the optimal song frequency is, in many cases, much higher than what would be predicted by the patterns of sound attenuation. All in all, the optimal song structure for signal transmission is the result of the interplay between the typical communication distance, the acoustic properties of the habitat, ambient noise profiles, and physical and phylogenetic constraints of the singer.

In contrast to most animal signals, bird song is based on production learning, that is, the modification of song structure as a result of experience with the songs of other individuals (Janik and Slater, 2000). Hence, bird song is more flexible in evolutionary and individual terms compared to the vocal signals of insects and anurans and also the calls of most mammals, except for those that also learn their vocalizations (Janik, 2009). Vocal learning enables birds to adapt their songs more quickly to the acoustic properties of their habitats, because the structure of their vocal signals is shaped by natural and sexual selection including cultural evolution and ontogenetic adaptations. In the next section, we will have a closer look at individual song adjustments on short temporal scales; some of them may involve usage learning.

B. SONG PERFORMANCE

1. Song Amplitude

In the previous section, we saw that the level of masking background noise is crucial for signal reception and, as a result, this may affect the structure of bird songs. The most obvious way to increase the signal-to-noise ratio is to increase song amplitude, and indeed, birds sing more loudly to make themselves heard in noisy environments. This behavior is known as the Lombard effect and it has been shown for a number of songbird species including zebra finches, *Taenopygia guttata*, (Cynx et al., 1998), nightingales, *Luscinia megarhynchos*, (Brumm and Todt, 2002), and Bengalese finches, *Lonchura striata*, (Kobayashi and Okanoya, 2003).[4] In their study on captive zebra finches, Cynx *et al.* (1998) found that males adjusted the amplitude of their courtship songs to the level of masking white noise broadcast to them. When the experimenters increased the noise level, the birds sang louder and when the noise was reduced the birds sang softer again. In a similar experiment with nightingales, Brumm and Todt (2002) showed that it is not noise in general but noise within the frequency band of the bird's own song that is crucial to elicit the Lombard effect. This finding indicates that the spectral overlap between signal and noise is the important feature when it comes to noise-dependent signal plasticity. The Lombard effect has also been found in Japanese quail (Potash, 1972) and domestic fowl (Brumm et al., in press), indicating that noise-induced amplitude modulation has also evolved even in bird species that do not learn their vocalizations. An increase in song amplitude in response to an increase in background noise does not only counteract interference from masking noise for the receiver but also for the sender. Hence, birds may not only increase their vocal amplitude to make themselves heard but, on a proximate level, also to better hear themselves, maintaining a feedback loop between perception and vocal production.[5]

An increase in song amplitude does not only mitigate the masking effects of noise, but can also compensate for an increased communication distance. When addressing a distant receiver, a singing bird could approach the targeted individual or increase the amplitude of its songs—the effect regarding the signal-to-noise ratio at the position of the receiver would be roughly the same. Brumm and Slater (2006a) demonstrated such a behavior in captive zebra finches: males increased the amplitude of their courtship songs with increasing distance of the targeted female, that is, the singing males compensated, at least partly, for the increased transmission loss and maintained a given signal-to-noise ratio at the position of the receiving female. However, none of the birds tested fully compensated for the increased transmission loss of their songs, which may reflect physical limitations of vocal production.[6]

A different case is that of the screaming piha (*Lipaugus vociferans*), a species that is renowned for its remarkably loud songs—hence the name. In this Neotropical rainforest bird, it seems that selection has favored

---

[4]For a more exhaustive review of the literature on the Lombard effect in songbirds and other animals, see Brumm and Slabbekoorn (2005).

[5]Auditory feedback is essential in song ontogeny, learning, and maintenance, as songbirds actively listen to their own song and make adjustments as they produce it (Dooling, 2004).

[6]Similarly, in human speech, speakers do not fully compensate for change of signal amplitude with change in distance (Michael et al., 1995; Traunmüller and Eriksson, 2000).

maximum song amplitude rather than scope for adjustment. Nemeth (2004) reported that screaming piha males produce vocal sound pressure levels of more than 110 dB at 1 m distance, which is about 20 dB higher than what has been recorded for any other bird species. It appears that piha males may produce their songs close to their physical limitations, and thus they would be unable to further increase song amplitude to compensate an increased communication distance or an increase in background noise. Maximization of vocal amplitude is a likely scenario in this species, because males gather in leks to compete for females, and song amplitude may be one component of their competitive mating displays. The example of the screaming piha illustrates the stunning variety in which birds use their vocal signals, and, at the same time, it shall remind us that in addition to environmental acoustics there are also other factors that shape the songs of birds. Obviously, sexual selection is a very powerful one.

2. Song Timing

A way, we have not touched yet, to increase signal-to-noise ratios is the adjustment of song timing. Birds can considerably increase the efficiency of their communication when they shift their vocal output to periods when conditions for signal transmission are favorable. Henwood and Fabrick (1979) suggested that atmospheric conditions for long-range transmission of bird songs are particularly advantageous at dawn, mostly because of reduced wind and air turbulence. This would explain why so many species show a marked peak of singing activity during the early morning hours, a phenomenon known as the dawn chorus. However, other studies could not find a particularly strong sound transmission advantage at dawn (Brown and Handford, 2003; Dabelsteen and Mathevon, 2002) and there may also be other advantages for singing at daybreak, such as feeding conditions (Cuthill and Macdonald, 1990), territory prospecting by nonresident males (Amrhein et al., 2004), and mate guarding (Mace, 1987) (also reviewed in Catchpole and Slater (2008)). Atmospheric conditions are only one reason why birds may adjust their song timing. Another, probably more important one, is again background noise. In fluctuating noise, birds may evade signal masking by singing selectively when background levels are low. A growing body of evidence shows that such adjustments take place on different temporal scales that range from several hours to a few hundred milliseconds.

Urban noise patterns are very predictable on a diurnal scale, as noise levels drop dramatically during the night, when human activities decrease. European robins (*Erithacus rubecula*) in the city of Sheffield sang more often during the night in areas that were noisy during the day (Fuller et al., 2007). The effect of ambient light pollution, to which nocturnal singing in urban birds is often attributed, was much weaker than that of daytime noise levels, suggesting that the robins shifted their song activity to the quieter night time to reduce acoustic interference by environmental noise. In addition to an adjustment of diurnal patterns of singing activity, shifts on shorter time scales can also be adaptive in terms of increased signal-to-noise ratios. In the first section of this chapter, we have discussed acoustic niches in the frequency domain for each species. An adjustment of song timing allows evading signal masking in cases where there is spectral overlap between songs. In contrast to phylogenetic changes in song pitch (see Section IIA), the short-term adjustment of song timing is entirely on the individual level and thus allows dealing with short-term changes in the acoustic environment.

Naturally, short-term adjustments of singing patterns may be used to avoid masking from other species with which a bird shares its habitat. One of the first to show that singing birds can shift their song output in relation to other species were Cody and Brown (1969) with their study on neighboring wrentits (*Chamaea fasciata*) and Bewick's wrens (*Thryomanes bewickii*). These two species appeared to avoid mutual masking by temporal song asynchrony. Both species cycled their song activity, reaching peak values about every 100 min, but the two cycles were out of phase: when one species was at its peak song output the other sang the least. Moreover, birds not only vary their overall singing activity to increase signal-to-noise ratios, but also adjust their song timing on a scale of single song bouts or even single songs. Such behavior would be particularly adaptive in situations such as the dawn chorus, when a multitude of species sing at the same time and their songs may suffer mutual masking.

Planqué and Slabbekoorn (2008) studied the dawn chorus in a Neotropical rainforest and found that several bird species avoided temporal overlap with the songs of other species, especially when they sang in a frequency band that was used by many. Many songbirds have a discontinuous singing style, producing short songs of a few seconds that are separated by silent intervals (Catchpole and Slater, 2008). Therefore, avoidance of temporal overlap is best achieved by starting to sing immediately after the offset of a masking song, since the competing bird is unlikely to start again for a few seconds. Indeed, this is exactly what some birds do. The extent of such precise fine-scale timing of songs has been demonstrated with playback experiments in nightingales (Brumm, 2006a). Males in sound-shielded aviaries avoided temporal overlap with the songs of six sympatric species, and started singing preferentially during the silent intervals between the heterospecific songs. On average, they started to sing 0.8 s after the offset of the preceding heterospecific song. This performance capacity is probably affected by familiarity with the interfering sounds. If a bird could predict the end of a masking song, it could start singing immediately after the offset.

Thus, temporal avoidance may be improved by individual learning. Of course, shifts in the temporal song patterning do not only help to reduce competition for acoustic space between species but also between individuals of the same species (Ficken et al., 1985; Gochfeld, 1978; Smith and Norman, 1979; Wasserman, 1977). However, the timing of bird song sometimes plays a more complicated role than just to avoid acoustic masking, but as an aggressive or dominance signal between rivals (Todt and Naguib, 2000).

3. Singing Position

Several studies suggest that perching higher in a forest reduces song degradation and increases the active space of a song (Barker et al., in press; Dabelsteen et al., 1993; Mathevon et al., 1996; Padgham, 2004). However, birds may not occupy the best position for sound transmission, especially when they become more vulnerable for predators at exposed perches (Krams, 2001). But some species show striking preferences for elevated song posts, for example, corn buntings (*Miliaria calandra*), which have been found to prefer the higher of two singing perches, even if the differences in height was only a few centimeters (Møller, 1986).

In grasslands where there are not many elevated perches, many species use song flights, which increase the active space of their vocalizations (Catchpole and Slater, 2008). One of the most remarkable examples of singing behavior that has evolved in such grassland habitats is that of to the blue-black grassquit (*Volatinia jacarina*). While singing, males of this species jump straight in the air above the grass, and this is probably also an adaptation for sound transmission, as the grassquit songs travel much further above the grass than through it (Wilczynski et al., 1989).

A comparative study of perching heights which suggests that birds position themselves to broadcast songs widely comes from the rainforests of Venezuela, where Nemeth et al. (2001) studied five sympatric antbird species of the family Thamnophilidae. The species examined vary considerably in their singing heights, and Nemeth and his coworkers found that at least in three of the species the song posts were at heights at which the respective songs transmit particularly well. In a forest, the acoustic properties change within different strata because stem and leaf sizes vary with tree height (and as a consequence, rates of reverberation and scattering as well) and atmospheric turbulence are greater in the canopy than at the ground (Wiley and Richards, 1982). Thus, one may well find similar song adaptations between different heights within a forest as those found between forests and open habitat (see Section IIA).

In addition to the position of a bird, also its orientation will affect the transmission of its vocalizations. This is because of the directional sound radiation patterns of bird song, that is, the sound energy is not emitted omnidirectionally but focused in the frontal direction (Brumm and Todt, 2002; Larsen and Dabelsteen, 1990; Patricelli et al., 2007). As expected from predictions, evidence from field observations as well as playback experiments indicate that birds orient themselves toward targeted receivers (Breitwisch and Whitesides, 1987; Brumm and Todt, 2003). By doing so, they exploit the directional sound radiation pattern of their songs and increase the signal-to-noise ratio at the position of the receiver, thus ensuring a most effective signal transmission.

Another, somewhat peculiar, phenomenon of orientation behavior was reported by Hunter (1989), who found that birds of various species on steep slopes in the Himalayas sang preferentially facing uphill. When we consider the directional sound radiation pattern of bird song, then it becomes evident why singing upslope could be adaptive, because more sound energy will be radiated toward other trees (and thus to likely positions of targeted receivers) rather than up into the air. However, there might also be anti-predator advantages to this behavior, as the more camouflaged upper part of a bird's body is most likely less well detectable by predators against the background of trees than the usually lighter breasts.

Data from sound propagation experiments in Australian forests suggest that singing birds can not only decrease the amount of reverberation by moving to elevated perches, but also that attenuation is reduced most effectively by an increase in receiver height (Padgham, 2004). This means that both sender and receiver would benefit from elevated positions. So, do birds use elevated perches as listening posts? This, as well as other possible adaptations that receivers have evolved to increase signal-to-noise ratios, will be investigated in the following section.

III. Receiver Adaptations

The performance of any receiver is considerably affected by the presence of noise and by degraded signal features. Perceptional adaptations to noise and sound degradation are similar but not identical. They involve behavioral changes, such as to move toward a position of better signal reception and special peripheral as well as cognitive processes. Origins of noise and signal degradation differ as the former results from other sources of sound, such as moving vegetation, wind, sounds of other individuals, or from anthropogenic sources. Signal degradation are qualitative and quantitative changes of the signal itself resulting from interaction of the sound with the environment. This leads to an overall attenuation, frequency-dependent attenuation, reverberation, and to amplitude fluctuations (Wiley and Richards, 1978). As a result, birds using long-range signals always have to cope with sound degradation, which is inevitable and often at the same time with very noisy conditions. Degraded signals also may indicate that the signaler is very distant and possibly less relevant in terms of responding, specifically so in territorial signals (Naguib and Wiley, 2001). Thus, while degradation may provide important information about the signaler, noise is independent of the signal and as such does not provide information that is of similar utility to a receiver as is degradation of a signal. Noisy conditions are prominent for instance in urban habitats, near torrents, or at peaks in signaling by other individuals such as during the dawn chorus. Coping with degraded signals in noise thus may lead to specific adaptations where thresholds to respond to a signal may become wider than the actual acoustic space used by the signal. The latter has been demonstrated recently in distantly related tropical species, the plain-winged antshrike (*Thamnophilus schistaceus*) and the wing-barred piprites (*Piprites chloris*) (Luther and Wiley, 2009). Both species have distinct songs, but as receivers show strong response to songs intermediate between the species but did not respond to the song of the other species, respectively. Luther and Wiley conclude from these findings, that the two species share a continuous perceptual space despite a disjunct use in acoustic signal space. This is a plausible adaptation in response to signals in noisy habitats as signals will be substantially more variable in structure at the point of reception than at the point of production. Such more general problems a receiver faces when being confronted with a signal that is degraded or is partly masked by noise are well covered by signal detection theory, whose implications for animal communication are reviewed elsewhere (Wiley, 1983, 1994, 2006). The principles of signal detection theory do not only apply to the detection of a signal but also to detection and recognition of any signal component. Thus, a receiver needs to decide whether a signal or its component is present or not, resulting in four different scenarios that need to be considered in understanding the evolution of receiver responses: correct detection, missed detection, correct rejection, and false alarm. None of the outcomes can be optimized independently so that any decision threshold inherently has a certain level of uncertainty. The problem of detection and recognition inevitably increases with increasing levels of noise and signal degradation. As a consequence, receiver decisions under such conditions will always have an increased level of uncertainty regarding the presence and accuracy of information that is available for decision making.

A. Receiver Adaptations to Signal Degradation

There are different solutions to deal with uncertainties regarding information content of a signal, as we have discussed earlier. Receiver adaptations to increase the certainty and accuracy of information gathering can be on a physiological and also higher processing level as well as on a behavioral level. Receiver adaptations to degraded signals fall into at least three categories: (1) behavioral adaptations such as a reduced responsiveness to degraded signals or active movements to locations with increased signal perception, (2) use of sound degradation as a cue to assess the distance to the signaler, and (3) sensory and higher processing adaptations to "filter" degradation. The first two points are treated in the following subsections and point (3) in section B, along with adaptations to noise.

1. Behavioral Adaptations

One "response" to degraded signals that needs to be considered is a lack of response or a reduced response intensity. A difficulty in determining a possibly adaptive value of reduced responsiveness to degraded signals is that a reduced responsiveness can have at least two very different causes (Naguib and Wiley, 2001). It could result from a receiver having decided that the signal is so degraded that it is not salient, for instance, because it comes from far away. A receiver also may respond weakly or not at all because it misses the signal or because the signal lacks certain features that are required for a receiver to detect and recognize relevant information. In the latter case, the signal might be salient so that any reduced response may not be optimal. A reduced responsiveness to degraded signals, in this sense, differs from that to signals embedded in noise as degradation itself can provide salient information about the signaler (see Section IIIA2) whereas noise does not contain such information. A reduced responsiveness to degraded signals will be adaptive for some signals in some contexts. In territorial signals, such as bird song, an immediate response is usually required only when the song indicates a close rival that may pose a threat to the bird's own territory. In such cases, song degradation could be used as a distance cue, permitting an adaptive reduced response. In other cases, however, the signal may be important even after having traveled a long distance (Naguib et al., 2002) or when it is degraded over a short distance. Females seeking a mate may benefit by extracting relevant information from male song from a distance without having to approach all potential mates. Here, selection may well favor adaptations to detect and recognize information even when signals are degraded such as by applying a response threshold accepting a wider range of signal parameters (Luther and Wiley, 2009). How animals respond to a signal eventually depends on the nature of information that it needs in order to optimize a response. Not all information in a signal may be relevant in all contexts, so that lacking some information that degrades more than other information may not pose a problem (Mathevon et al., 2008; Naguib et al., 2008).

A behavioral adaptation to reception of degraded signals is to delay an immediate response but instead first move to positions of better sound reception. Holland et al. (2001a) and Mathevon and Aubin (1997) showed, for instance, that wrens (*Troglodytes troglodytes*) move upward in a tree in response to playback of degraded songs. Such upward movements could result in improved sound reception and may allow a bird to assess whether the lack of certain signal features is the outcome of degradation or due to the sender. Sound transmission experiments with different loudspeaker and microphone heights indeed support this notion by showing that signal degradation is not just a function of distance and habitat but also of the relative height of a sender and a receiver. Interestingly, the effect of perch height turned out to be more prominent for high microphone positions than for high loudspeaker positions (Dabelsteen et al., 1993; Holland et al., 1998; Mathevon et al., 1996; Nemeth et al., 2001). These findings suggest that birds perhaps sing from high perches not necessarily only to increase their signal range but also or even more so to increase their ability to detect and recognize responses from conspecifics (Holland et al., 1998; Mathevon et al., 1996) although singing height and perch height might have other causes as well (Nemeth et al., 2001).

In general, movements that result in better signal reception can also be linked to the time of day and occur over larger areas. Female nightingales have been shown to sample singing males particularly at night when mainly unmated males are singing and when noise levels and atmospheric turbulence is low (Roth et al., 2009). Roth et al. (2009) translocated females from a distant population into their study population and followed them over 48 h using radio-telemetry. Females moved larger distances almost exclusively at night when acoustic conditions are considerably better than during the day. This is also the time when mainly unmated males sing, showing that singing behavior and receiver spatial movements are well adapted to each other. Regardless of which specific factors have led to the evolution of these behaviors, the effect is that females benefit from good acoustic conditions to assess differences between songs of potential males. A similar sort of behavioral adaptation by receivers is to be responsive to signals mainly at those times when the signal is expected to occur, such as during species-specific peaks in signaling at certain times of the day. In tropical bird species which have different peaks in singing time during the day, responses to signalers were strongest at those times at which individuals of that species usually sing themselves (Luther, 2008). In this case, timing of signals and receiver responsiveness appear to be well adapted to each other in a way that avoids interferences with signals of other species.

2. Distance Assessment

The most intensely studied effect of signal degradation on receiver performance in the field is the relation between signal degradation and distance. This has been reviewed in more detail elsewhere (Naguib and Wiley, 2001). Distance assessment is based on cues that change with some predictability with distance. Auditory distance assessment is of particular importance in territorial signals such as bird song, as it allows investing time and energy in responding to rivals only when they are close enough to pose a threat (Morton, 1982). As signals increasingly degrade and attenuate with increasing propagation distance, any such cue, or a combination of them, could be used to assess the distance of the sound source. These cues include relative and absolute song amplitude (Naguib, 1997a; Nelson, 2002), reverberation (Naguib, 1995, 1997b), and high-frequency attenuation (Naguib, 1995, 1997b); or other correlated features such as within element changes in amplitude patterns. (Dabelsteen et al., 1993; Holland et al., 2001b; Mathevon, 1998). Studies investigating the use of song degradation as cue to assess distance have commonly compared responses to playback of songs degraded in various natural or artificial ways to responses to undegraded songs (Fotheringham and Ratcliffe, 1995; Fotheringham et al., 1997; McGregor and Falls, 1984; McGregor and Krebs, 1984; McGregor et al., 1983; Richards, 1981; Shy and Morton, 1986). A resulting lower intensity of responses to degraded songs compared to undegraded songs has commonly been interpreted as evidence for distance assessment as under natural conditions more degraded songs will have traveled over a longer distance and thus are less salient for an immediate response. A lack of specific features due to degradation, however, would also result in reduced responsiveness so that response strength *per se* may be caused by factors other than distance assessment. More direct evidence for use of sound degradation as a distance cue comes from playbacks terminating before the bird could approach the loudspeaker. Playbacks using only a single song (Naguib, 1995, 1996, 1997b; Naguib et al., 2000) or that stop as soon as the bird is approaching (Nelson, 2000, 2002; Nelson and Stoddard, 1998; Wiley and Godard, 1996) have systematically yielded more discrete responses as birds could not localize the loudspeaker while approaching. In these cases, birds often flew well beyond the loudspeaker only in response to degraded songs, providing direct evidence for use of song degradation as a distance cue.

Using sound degradation to assess distance requires two processes, each of which has its own uncertainties (Naguib, 1998). In a first step, a receiver needs to determine the degree of degradation and in a second step it needs to map the level of degradation to a probable propagation distance. Both processes require some specific knowledge. Information about the structure of the signal at the source may be required to determine its degradation, and information on the acoustic properties of the transmission channel is required to link a level of degradation to a given distance. The information that is required to determine degradation of the signal will depend on the nature of the signal and the kind of degradation as well as the variation in parameters that are affected by degradation. There has been some discussion about the kind of information that is needed about the signal (Morton, 1998; Naguib, 1998; Wiley, 1998) but field (Naguib, 1997b) and laboratory studies (Phillmore et al., 2003) have shown that prior knowledge of the specific signal is not required to determine that it is degraded. The knowledge that songs do not contain reverberated features at the source would be sufficient to determine levels of reverberation. However, determination of frequency-dependent attenuation may be more accurate when the exact source characteristics are known (Naguib, 1998). The uncertainties in linking degradation to a distance, in any case, will constrain very accurate distance assessment. Signal degradation increases with distance but can substantially vary for any given distance (Brown and Handford, 1996, 2000; Dabelsteen et al., 1993; Mathevon, 1998; Naguib, 2003; Piercy et al., 1977; Richards and Wiley, 1980) and with seasonal changes in vegetation density (Naguib, 2003). Despite these uncertainties in the ability to adjust the mapping of degradation to propagation distance, there are ways to improve this assessment. Use of multiple cues, as known for humans and for visual communication (Davies and Green, 1993; Mershon and King, 1975; Naguib and Wiley, 2001) as well as the directionality of the signal may allow birds to be quite accurate in their assessment (Naguib et al., 2000; Nelson, 2000). Noise, however, will constrain the determination of degraded signal features as we will discuss in Section C.

B. RECEIVER ADAPTATIONS TO SIGNALS IN NOISE

Communication in noise has been particularly well studied in anurans and in birds. Both systems are remarkably similar to the way humans communicate under noisy conditions (Bee and Micheyl, 2008; Dooling, 1982; Klump, 1996). From a receiver's perspective, dealing with noise differs from dealing with degraded signals, as the later may lack certain information. In a signal embedded in noise, the information is there but masked. Thus, the task is to extract the signal parameters and separate them from the noise. As discussed in the previous sections, adaptations could be behavioral or peripheral and cognitive. Behavioral adaptations are similar to those in response to signal degradation and involve movements to positions of higher signal-to-noise ratios. Increasing perching height, for instance, results in lower signal degradation as discussed earlier, and in a better signal-to-noise ratio (Dabelsteen et al., 1993; but see Nemeth et al., 2001). However, there is rather little a receiver can do to reduce noise levels so that most research, namely psychoacoustic studies, focused on peripheral and cognitive adaptations to detect and recognize signals in noisy environments. These are reviewed elsewhere in great detail (Bee and Micheyl, 2008; Dooling, 2004; Klump, 1996), so that we will only summarize some key issues here.

Environmental noise can be highly variable in its frequency structure and temporal dynamic so that recognizing its nature is crucial to understanding how it may affect receiver performance. Noise overlapping in frequency with the signal can significantly reduce a receiver's performance, whereas noise that does not overlap with the frequency of the signal may have very little effect on receiver performance. Nightingales, for instance, have been shown to respond differently to playback of noise, depending on the noise-frequency spectrum. They responded with increasing sound amplitude only in response to playback of broadband noise or noise restricted to their own songs' frequency range (1–8 kHz) but not when the white noise had a notch in that range of 1–8 kHz. Subjects even sang louder when the noise was specified to their own songs' frequency range than when it was broadband. This indicates that responses to noise are very specific to those conditions in which the noise will indeed mask the song. Therefore, broadband measurements of the sound pressure level of noise provides only very limited insights, as long as no information on the spectral, spectrotemporal, and spatial characteristics of the noise in relation to the signal is at hand. Moreover, noise is commonly correlated across different frequency bands and the presence of signals in some frequency bands will affect that correlation. Use of this noise correlation to detect the presence of a signal is termed as comodulation masking release and leads to an improved signal detection (Bee, 2008; Bee and Micheyl, 2008).

A well-known perceptual adaptation to signal detection in noise is the so-called cocktail party effect, which refers to the human ability to detect significant signal features at very low (or negative) signal-to-noise ratios, such as at a party or in a bar (Bee and Micheyl, 2008; Bronkhorst, 2000). There are a series of processes that facilitate signal reception under noisy conditions. These are combined in auditory scene analyses which involve processes such as auditory object formation and auditory stream analysis.

These result in sequential or simultaneous integration of sounds. Sounds that have the same spatial origin, for instance, may be separated perceptually from sounds from other sources. Moreover, sound elements with specific temporal or spectral relations may be grouped into one sound. Specialized neurons and brain regions guide this process as their response to conspecific sound is not affected by background noise of up to a signal-to-noise ratio of -9 dB. This was shown, for instance, in zebra finches using ZENK gene expression and magnetic resonance imaging techniques (Boumans et al., 2008; Vignal et al., 2004). Similar findings on signal detection in negative signal-to-noise ratios have been found in penguins (Aubin and Jouventin, 1998). Such detection is facilitated if the signal-to-noise ratio is positive in the frequency band of interest even though the signal-to-noise ratio over all bands might be negative. This is specifically important as the ear is frequency sensitive and analyzes the spectrum within specific bands at a given instant in time. In a further series of experiments, Aubin and coworkers showed that penguins are well adapted to respond appropriately to calls, even when they are strongly degraded or embedded in noise or when they can only hear part of the call (Aubin and Jouventin, 1998; Aubin et al., 2000; Lengagne et al., 1999a,b,c, 2000). Not detecting the calls from a hungry chick by the parent returning from a foraging trip (or the call from a parent by the hungry chick) will be costly. Evolution has solved this problem by selecting for remarkable auditory abilities in penguins.

Signal detection in noise will further hinge on a receiver's familiarity with a signal. If a receiver has close range experience with a signal, the receiver will have prior information on its structural and temporal components. As a consequence, it may well predict some signal components based on the reception of other components. Unless the precise details of a signal are essential for decision making, receivers may perform well in their decision on whether or not and how to respond to a signal. Generating auditory objects is such an example which refers to a receiver's ability to create a complete auditory "object" even though only some components can be received. Such adaptations are well known in visual communication where incomplete signals are perceived as known signals in which missing components are "automatically" added by the processing system. Thus, receivers may be able to make an estimate of structural signal components that are embedded in noise of fully degraded or attenuated signals by the mere presence of other signal components. Moreover, there is good experimental evidence for auditory stream analysis (filtering of auditory objects from general background noise) and categorical perception in birds. Often, such assumptions on signal structure may well be sufficient for a receiver.

In summary, there are a number of peripheral and central processes that allow receivers to filter out signals from background noise (Bee and Micheyl, 2008; Dooling, 1982; Klump, 1996). Further research on this topic will be needed to obtain a better understanding of how these processes are actually integrated in decision making under natural conditions.

C. IMPLICATION OF NOISE ON DISTANCE ASSESSMENT

As we have seen in the previous sections, both the environmental degradation of signals during transmission and the noise level at the position of the receiver have implications for the information that can be extracted from a signal. In this section, we want to emphasize the effects of signal degradation and masking noise on auditory distance assessment, as noise strongly affects a receiver's ability to extract distance cues from a signal. This combined view will contribute to a deeper understanding of the effects of habitat acoustics on the evolution of bird song.

Use of cues for distance assessment requires that the signal-to-noise ratio is high enough to perceive and recognize subtle low-amplitude features. Detection of low-amplitude high frequencies, amplitude modulations, and the strength and length of a reverberated tail are all important for an accurate distance assessment (Holland et al., 2001b; Naguib, 2003). When noise levels are high, however, it may be difficult to detect such details. A receiver may then be in conflict over deciding whether a lack in signal features is due to a distant signaler, masking noise, or both. Even though a receiver may use information from the overall amplitude to assess distance, such a process will inevitably result in a less accurate distance assessment than one based on more reliable cues or a more complete set of cues. Thus, receivers will have to be more attentive to a signal, use repeated cues, or change the listening post to obtain additional information. Increased attention to signals that may be less relevant when distant, however, will constrain attentiveness to other relevant signals, such as signals or cues from other competitors, potential mates, or to predators. A lack of an ability to extract accurate distance information under noisy conditions can have implications for territory defense and spatial behavior. Males may have to spend more time in moving around their territory to ascertain that singing rivals are not claiming parts of it. Such effects may be particularly relevant when noisy habitats are low quality and therefore need to be larger to provide all necessary resources. Moreover, a shift of songs to higher frequencies in habitats with high levels of low-frequency noise may affect distance assessment in two ways. First, high frequencies do not travel as far as low frequencies. Thus, an upshift in frequency may result in better detectability at short ranges but also leads to a reduced signal range.

This has implications for songs aimed to repel others at larger distances, such as at a distant territory boundary. Such lowered effectiveness of signals may affect territory sizes and time budgets. Second, distance assessment is relevant in larger signaling associations such as in communication networks where relative and absolute distances of different signalers have to be monitored (McGregor and Dabelsteen, 1996; Todt and Naguib, 2000). Noise affects communication in such networks not only because it masks information encoded in songs by the sender but also the information needed for effective distance assessment. Future research must address this link between distance and cues and noise and provide more specific insights into receiver performance in relation to its acoustic environment and in relation to the spatial arrangement of receivers.

IV. CONCLUSION

Any signal must obviously get from the sender to the receiver if information is to be transmitted. In the case of bird song, the acoustic properties of the habitat may hinder this being achieved. However, birds as senders and receivers have evolved numerous adaptations to overcome the problem of getting the message across. In this chapter, we explore habitat-dependent patterns of sound transmission, the effects of noise, signal perception, and signal interpretation. In particular, we summarize and discuss key problems of communication in noise and under conditions resulting in increased signal attenuation and degradation. Our current knowledge suggests that the acoustic properties of the environment affect both the structure and performance of acoustic signals. Therefore, we emphasize the role of environmental acoustics for the evolution of bird song. However, song traits may vary in their ability to respond to selection, and it appears that the actual optimal song structure for signal transmission is the result of the interplay between the acoustic properties of the habitat, ambient noise profiles, and physical and phylogenetic constraints of the singer. At the same time, vocal production learning enables many birds to adapt their songs more quickly to the acoustic properties of their habitats compared to insects, anurans, and also most mammals. Birds as receivers also have evolved specific behavioral, peripheral, and central processing adaptations to cope with unfavorable acoustic conditions. The cocktail party effect is one such example. Adaptations by animals as senders and receivers are not independent and there are good examples that receiver adaptations are well tuned to signaler behavior and signaling strategies. We argue that along with other possible selective forces, such as sexual selection, one needs to consider the combination of environmental constraints on signal transmission, noise levels, and the use of signal degradation as a distance cue to gain a more thorough understanding of the astounding variety of avian song and the many different ways in which birds use it.

Acknowledgments

We thank Nicolas Mathevon and Vincent Janik for their helpful comments on the manuscript. Karl-Heinz Frommolt of the Tierstimmenarchiv Berlin kindly provided recordings of whistling thrushes. HB was supported by an Emmy Noether Fellowship granted by the German Research Foundation (award Br 2309/6-1).

References

Amrhein, V., Kunc, H.P., Naguib, M., 2004. Non-territorial nightingales prospect territories during the dawn chorus. Proc. R. Soc. Lond. B 271, S167–S169.

Arch, V.S., Narins, P.M., 2008. 'Silent' signals: selective forces acting on ultrasonic communication systems in terrestrial vertebrates. Anim. Behav. 76, 1423–1428.

Aubin, T., Jouventin, P., 1998. Cocktail-party effect in king penguin colonies. Proc. R. Soc. Lond. B 265, 1665–1673.

Aubin, T., Jouventin, P., 2002. How to vocally identify kin in a crowd: the penguin model. Adv. Study Behav. 31, 243–277.

Aubin, T., Jouventin, P., Hildebrand, C., 2000. Penguins use the two-voice system to recognize each other. Proc. R. Soc. Lond. B 267, 1081–1087.

Barker, N. K. S., Dabelsteen, T., Mennill, D. J. (in press). Degradation of male and female rufous-and-white wren songs in a tropical forest: effects of sex, perch height, and habitat. Behaviour.

Beckers, G.J.L., Suthers, R.A., ten Cate, C., 2003. Mechanisms of frequency and amplitude modulation in ring dove song. J. Exp. Biol. 206, 1833–1843.

Bee, M.A., 2008. Finding a mate at a cocktail party: spatial release from masking improves acoustic mate recognition in grey treefrogs. Anim. Behav. 75, 1781–1791.

Bee, M.A., Micheyl, C., 2008. The cocktail party problem: what is it? How can it be solved? And why should animal behaviorists study it? J. Comp. Psychol. 122, 235–251.

Bermúdez-Cuamatzin, E., Ríos-Chelén, A.A., Gil, D., Macías Garcia, C. (in press). Strategies of song adaptation to urban noise in the house finch: syllable pitch plasticity or differential syllable use? Behaviour.

Blumenrath, S.H., Dabelsteen, T., 2004. Degradation of great tit (*Parus major*) song before and after foliation: implications for vocal communication in a deciduous forest. Behaviour 141, 935–958.

Boncoraglio, G., Saino, N., 2007. Habitat structure and the evolution of bird song: a meta-analysis of the evidence for the acoustic adaptation hypothesis. Funct. Ecol. 21, 134–142.

Boumans, T., Vignal, C., Smolders, A., Sijbers, J., Verhoye, M., Van Audekerke, J., et al., 2008. Functional magnetic resonance imaging in zebra finch discerns the neural substrate involved in segregation of conspecific song from background noise. J. Neurophysiol. 99, 931–938.

Bradbury, J.W., Vehrencamp, S.L., 1998. Principles of animal communication. Sinauer Associates, Sunderland, MA.

Breitwisch, R., Whitesides, G.H., 1987. Directionality of singing and non-singing behaviour of mated and unmated northern mockingbirds, *Mimus polyglottos*. Anim. Behav. 35, 331–339.

Brenowitz, E.A., 1982. The active space of red-winged blackbird song. J. comp. Physiol. 147, 511–522.

Bronkhorst, A.W., 2000. The cocktail party phenomenon: a review of research on speech intelligibility in multiple-talker conditions. Acustica 86, 117–128.

Brown, T.J., Handford, P., 1996. Acoustic signal amplitude patterns: a computer simulation investigation of the acoustic adaptation hypothesis. Condor 98, 608–623.

Brown, T.J., Handford, P., 2000. Sound design for vocalizations: quality in the woods, consistency in the fields. Condor 102, 81–92.

Brown, T.J., Handford, P., 2003. Why birds sing at dawn: the role of consistent sound transmission. Ibis 145, 120–129.

Brumm, H., 2006a. Signalling through acoustic windows: nightingales avoid interspecific competition by short-term adjustment of song timing. J. Comp. Physiol. A 192, 1279–1285.

Brumm, H., 2006b. Animal communication: city birds have changed their tune. Curr. Biol. 16, R1003–R1004.

Brumm, H., Slabbekoorn, H., 2005. Acoustic communication in noise. Adv. Study Behav. 35, 151–209.

Brumm, H., Slater, P.J.B., 2006a. Ambient noise, motor fatigue and serial redundancy in chaffinch song. Behav. Ecol. Sociobiol. 60, 475–481.

Brumm, H., Slater, P.J.B, 2006b. Animals can vary signal amplitude with receiver distance: evidence from zebra finch song. Anim. Behav. 72, 699–705.

Brumm, H., Todt, D., 2002. Noise-dependent song amplitude regulation in a territorial songbird. Anim. Behav. 63, 891–897.

Brumm, H., Todt, D., 2003. Facing the rival: directional singing behaviour in nightingales. Behaviour 140, 43–53.

Brumm, H., Voss, K., Köllmer, I., Todt, D., 2004. Acoustic communication in noise: regulation of call characteristics in a New World monkey. J. Exp. Biol. 207, 443–448.

Brumm, H., Schmidt, R., Schrader, L. (in press). Noise-dependent vocal plasticity in domestic fowl. Anim. Behav.

Catchpole, C.K., Slater, P.J.B., 2008. Bird song. Biological Themes and Variations, 2nd edn. Cambridge University Press, Cambridge.

Clement, P., Hathway, R., 2000. Thrushes. A & C Black, London.

Cody, M.L., Brown, J.H., 1969. Song asynchrony in neighbouring bird species. Nature 222, 778–780.

Cuthill, I.C., Macdonald, W.A., 1990. Experimental manipulation of the dawn and dusk chorus in the blackbird *Turdus merula*. Behav. Ecol. Sociobiol. 26, 209–216.

Cynx, J., Lewis, R., Tavel, B., Tse, H., 1998. Amplitude regulation of vocalizations in noise by a songbird, *Taeniopygia guttata*. Anim. Behav. 56, 107–113.

Dabelsteen, T., Mathevon, N., 2002. Why do songbirds sing intensively at dawn? A test of the acoustic transmission hypothesis. Acta Ethol. 4, 65–72.

Dabelsteen, T., Larsen, O.N., Pedersen, S.B., 1993. Habitat-induced degradation of sound signals—quantifying the effects of communication sounds and bird location on blur ratio, excess attenuation, and signal-to-noise ratio in blackbird song. J. Acoust. Soc. Am. 93, 2206–2220.

Date, E.M., Lemon, R.E., 1993. Sound transmission: a basis for dialects in birdsong? Behaviour 124, 291–312.

Davies, M.N.O., Green, P.R, 1993. Multiple sources of depth information: an ecological approach. In: Davies, M.N.O., Green, P.R. (Eds.), Perception and Motor Control in Birds. Springer Verlag, Berlin, pp. 393–456.

Delacour, J., 1942. The whistling trushes (genus *Myiophoneus*). Auk 59, 246–264.

Dooling, R.J., 1982. Auditory perception in birds. In: Kroodsma, D.E., Miller, E.H. (Eds.), Acoustic Communication in Birds, Vol. 1. Academic Press, New York, pp. 95–129.

Dooling, R., 2004. Audition: can birds hear everything they sing. In: Marler, P., Slabbekoorn, H. (Eds.), Nature's Music: The Science of Birdsong. Academic Press, San Diego, pp. 206–225.

Doutrelant, C., Lambrechts, M.M., 2001. Macrogeographic variation in song a test of competition and habitat effects in blue tits. Ethology 107, 533–544.

Dubois, A., Martens, J., 1984. A case of possible vocal convergence between frogs and a bird in Himalayan torrents. J. Ornithol. 125, 455–463.

Endler, J.A., 1993. Some general comments on the evolution and design of animal communication systems. Philos. Trans. R. Soc. Lond. B 340, 215–225.

Feng, A.S., Narins, P.M., 2008. Ultrasonic communication in concave-eared torrent frogs (*Amolops tormotus*). J. Comp. Physiol. A 194, 159–167.

Feng, A.S., Narins, P.M., Xu, C.H., Lin, W.Y., Yu, Z.L., Qiu, Q., Xu, Z.M., Shen, J.X., 2006. Ultrasonic communication in frogs. Nature 440, 333–336.

Fernández-Juricic, E., Poston, R., Collibus, K.D., Morgan, T., Bastain, B., Martin, C., et al., 2005. Microhabitat selection and singing behavior patterns of male house finches (*Carpodacus mexicanus*) in urban parks in a heavily urbanized landscape in the western U.S. Urban Habitats 3, 49–69.

Ficken, R.W., Popp, J.W., Matthiae, P.E., 1985. Avoidance of acoustic interference by Ovenbirds. Wilson Bull. 97, 569–571.

Fotheringham, R.J., Ratcliffe, L., 1995. Song degradation and estimation of acoustic distance in black-capped chickadees (*Parus atricapillus*). Can. J. Zool. 73, 858–868.

Fotheringham, J.R., Martin, P.R., Ratcliffe, L., 1997. Song transmission and auditory perception of distance in wood warblers (Parulinae). Anim. Behav. 53, 1271–1285.

Fuller, R.A., Warren, P.H., Gaston, K.J., 2007. Daytime noise predicts nocturnal singing in urban robins. Biol. Lett. 3, 368–370.

Gochfeld, M., 1978. Intraspecific social stimulation and temporal displacement of songs of the lesser skylark, *Alauda gulgula*. Z. Tierpsychol. 48, 337–344.

Handford, P., 1981. Vegetational correlates of variation in the song of *Zonotrichia capensis*. Behav. Ecol. Sociobiol. 8, 203–206.

Handford, P., 2004. Song dialects, habitats, and genetics: the rofous-collared sparrow. In: Marler, P., Slabbekoorn, H. (Eds.), Nature's Music: The Science of Birdsong. Academic Press, San Diego, p. 201.

Handford, P., Lougheed, S.C., 1991. Variation in duration and frequency characters in the song of the rufous-collared sparrow, *Zonotrichia capensis*, with respect to habitat, trill dialects and body size. Condor 93, 644–658.

Henwood, K., Fabrick, A., 1979. A quantitative analysis of the dawn chorus: temporal selection for communicatory optimisation. Am. Nat. 114, 260–274.

Holland, J., Dabelsteen, T., Pedersen, S.B., Larsen, O.N., 1998. Degradation of wren *Troglodytes troglodytes* song: implications for information transfer and ranging. J. Acoust. Soc. Am. 103, 2154–2166.

Holland, J., Dabelsteen, T., Bjørn, C.P., Pedersen, S.B., 2001a. The location of ranging cues in wren song: evidence from calibrated interactive playback experiments. Behaviour 138, 189–206.

Holland, J., Dabelsteen, T., Paris, A.L., Pedersen, S.B., 2001b. Potential ranging cues contained within the energetic pauses of transmitted wren song. Bioacoustics 12, 3–20.

Hunter, M.L., 1989. Himalayan birds face uphill while singing. Auk 106, 728–729.

Hunter, M.L., Krebs, J.R., 1979. Geographical variation in the song of the great tit (*Parus major*) in relation to ecological factors. J. Anim. Ecol. 48, 759–785.

Janik, V., 2009. Acoustic communication in delphinids. Adv. Study Behav. 40, 123–158.

Janik, V.M., Slater, P.J.B., 2000. The different roles of social learning in vocal communication. Anim. Behav. 60, 1–11.

Jilka, A., Leisler, B., 1974. Die Einpassung dreier Rohrsängerarten (*Acrocephalus schoenobaenus. A. scirpaceus, A. arundinaceus*) in ihre Lebensräume in bezug aud das Frequenzspektrum ihrer Reviergesänge. J. Ornithol. 115, 192–212.

Katti, M., Warren, P.S., 2004. Tits, noise and urban bioacoustics. Trends Ecol. Evol. 19, 109–110.

Kime, N.M., Turner, W.R., Ryan, M.J., 2000. The transmission of advertisement calls in Central American frogs. Behav. Ecol. 11, 71–83.

Klump, G., 1996. Bird communication in the noisy world. In: Kroodsma, D.E., Miller, E.H. (Eds.), Ecology and Evolution of Acoustic Communication in Birds. Cornell University Press, Ithaca, NY, pp. 321–338.

Kobayashi, K., Okanoya, K., 2003. Context-dependent song amplitude control in Bengalese finches. Neuro Rep. 14, 521–524.

Krams, I., 2001. Perch selection by singing chaffinches: a better view of surroundings and the risk of predation. Behav. Ecol. 12, 295–300.

Krause, B.L., 1992. The habitat niche hypothesis: a hidden symphonie of animal sounds. Lit. Rev. 36, 40–45.

Kroon, F.J., Westcott, D.A., 2006. Song variation and habitat structure in the Golden Bowerbird. Emu 106, 263–272.

Larsen, O.N., Dabelsteen, T., 1990. Directionality of blackbird vocalization. Implications for vocal communication and its further study. Ornis Scand. 21, 37–45.

Lengagne, T., Aubin, T., Jouventin, P., Lauga, J., 1999a. Acoustic communication in a king penguin colony: importance of bird location within the colony and of the body position of the listener. Polar Biol. 21, 262–268.

Lengagne, T., Aubin, T., Lauga, J., Jouventin, P., 1999b. How do king penguins (*Aptenodytes patagonicus*) apply the mathematical theory of information to communicate in windy conditions? Proc. R. Soc. Lond. B 26, 1623–1628.

Lengagne, T., Jouventin, P., Aubin, T., 1999c. Finding one's mate in a king penguin colony: efficiency of acoustic communication. Behaviour 136, 833–846.

Lengagne, T., Aubin, T., Jouventin, P., Lauga, J., 2000. Perceptual salience of individually distinctive features in the calls of adult king penguins. J. Acoust. Soc. Am. 107, 508–516.

Luther, D.A., 2008. Signaller: receiver coordination and the timing of communication in Amazonian birds. Biol. Lett. 4, 651–654.

Luther, D.A., Wiley, R.H., 2009. Production and perception of communicatory signals in a noisy environment. Biol. Lett. 5, 183–187.

Mace, R., 1987. The dawn chorus in the great tit *Parus major* is directly related to female fertility. Nature 330, 745–746.

Marten, K., Marler, P., 1977. Sound transmission and its significance for animal vocalizations. I. Temperate habitats. Behav. Ecol. Sociobiol. 2, 271–290.

Martens, J., Geduldig, G., 1990. Acoustic adaptations of birds living close to Himalayan torrents. Proc. Int. 100 Meet. Deutsch Ornithol. Ges, pp. 123–131. Bonn.

Mathevon, N., 1998. Degraded temporal sound features as a function of distance and potential as cues for ranging in birds. Bioacoustics 9, 17–33.

Mathevon, N., Aubin, T., 1997. Reaction to conspecific degraded song by the wren *Troglodytes troglodytes*: territorial response and choice of song post. Behav. Proc. 39, 77–84.

Mathevon, N., Aubin, T., Dabelsteen, T., 1996. Song degradation during propagation: importance of song post for the wren *Troglodytes troglodytes*. Ethology 102, 397–412.

Mathevon, N., Aubin, T., Vielliard, J., da Silva, M.L., Sebe, F., 2008. Singing in the rain forest: how a tropical bird song transfers information. PLoS ONE 3(2), e1580.

McGregor, P.K., Falls, J.B., 1984. The response of western meadowlarks (*Sturnella neglecta*) to the playback of degraded and undegraded songs. Can. J. Zool. 62, 2125–2128.

McGregor, P.K., Krebs, J.R., 1984. Sound degradation as a distance cue in great tit (*Parus major*) song. Behav. Ecol. Sociobiol. 16, 49–56.

McGregor, P.K., Krebs, J.R., Ratcliffe, L.M., 1983. The reaction of great tits (*Parus major*) to playback of degraded and undegraded songs: the effect of familiarity with the stimulus song type. Auk 100, 898–906.

McGregor, P.K., Dabelsteen, T., 1996. Communication networks. In: Kroodsma, D.E., Miller, E.H. (Eds.), Ecology and Evolution of Acoustic Communication in Birds, University Press, Cornell, pp. 409–425.

Mershon, D.H., King, L.E., 1975. Intensity and reverberation as factors in the auditory perception of egocentric distance. Percept. Psychophys. 18, 409–415.

Michael, D.D., Siegel, G.M., Pick, H.L., 1995. Effects of distance on vocal intensity. J. Speech Hear Res. 38, 1176–1183.

Møller, A.P., 1986. On song post selection and the timing of song in the corn bunting (*Miliaria calandra*). Ökol. Vögel 8, 57–66.

Morton, E.S., 1975. Ecological sources of selection on avian sounds. Am. Nat. 109, 17–34.

Morton, E.S., 1982. Grading, discreteness, redundancy, and motivation-structural rules. In: Kroodsma, D.E., Miller, E.H. (Eds.), Acoustic Communication in Birds, Vol. 1. Academic Press, New York, pp. 183–212.

Morton, E.S., 1998. Degradation and signal ranging in birds: memory matters. Behav. Ecol. Sociobiol. 42, 135–137.

Naguib, M., 1995. Auditory distance assessment of singing conspecifics in Carolina wrens: the role of reverberation and frequency-dependent attenuation. Anim. Behav. 50, 1297–1307.

Naguib, M., 1996. Ranging by song in Carolina wrens *Thryothorus ludovicianus*: effects of environmental acoustics and strength of song degradation. Behaviour 133, 541–559.

Naguib, M., 1997a. Use of song amplitude for ranging in Carolina wrens, *Thryothorus ludovicianus*. Ethology 103, 723–731.

Naguib, M., 1997b. Ranging of songs in Carolina wrens: effects of familiarity with the song type on use of different cues. Behav. Ecol. Sociobiol. 40, 385–393, Err. in Behav. Ecol.Sociobiol. 341, 203.

Naguib, M., 1998. Perception of degradation in acoustic signals and its implications for ranging. Behav. Ecol. Sociobiol. 42, 139–142.

Naguib, M., 2003. Reverberation of rapid and slow trills: implications for signal adaptations to long range communication. J. Acoust. Soc. Am. 133, 1749–1756.

Naguib, M., Wiley, R.H., 2001. Estimating the distance to a source of sound: mechanisms and adaptations for long-range communication. Anim. Behav. 62, 825–837.

Naguib, M., Klump, G.M., Hillmann, E., Griessmann, B., Teige, T., 2000. Assessment of auditory distance in a territorial songbird: accurate feat or rule of thumb? Anim. Behav. 59, 715–721.

Naguib, M., Hammerschmidt, K., Wirth, J., 2001. Microgeographic variation, habitat effects and individual signature cues in calls of chiffchaffs (*Phylloscopus collybita canariensis*). Ethology 107, 341–355.

Naguib, M., Mundry, R., Hultsch, H., Todt, D., 2002. Responses to playback of whistle songs and normal songs in male nightingales: effects of song category, whistle pitch, and distance. Behav. Ecol. Sociobiol. 52, 216–223.

Naguib, M., Schmidt, R., Sprau, P., Roth, T., Floercke, C., Amrhein, V., 2008. The ecology of vocal signaling: male spacing and communication distance of different song traits in nightingales. Behav. Ecol. Sociobiol. 19, 1034–1040.

Narins, P.M., Feng, A.S., Lin, W.Y., Schnitzler, H.U., Denzinger, A., Suthers, R.A., et al., 2004. Old World frog and bird, vocalizations contain prominent ultrasonic harmonics. J. Acoust. Soc. Am. 115, 910–913.

Nelson, B.S., 2000. Avian dependence on sound pressure level as an auditory distance cue. Anim. Behav. 59, 57–67.

Nelson, B.S., 2002. Duplex auditory distance assessment in a small passerine bird (Pipilo erythrophthalmus). Behav. Ecol. Sociobiol. 53, 42–50.

Nelson, D.A., Marler, P., 1990. The perception of birdsong and an ecological concept of signal space. In: Stebbins, W.C., Berkley, M.A. (Eds.), Comparative Perception. Wiley, New York, pp. 443–477.

Nelson, B.S., Stoddard, P.K., 1998. Accuracy of auditory distance and azimuth perception by a passerine bird in natural habitat. Anim. Behav. 56, 467–477.

Nemeth, E., 2004. Measuring the sound pressure level of the song of the screaming piha Lipaugus vociferans: one of the loudest birds in the world? Bioacoustics 14, 225–228.

Nemeth, E., Brumm, H. (in press). Blackbirds sing higher pitched songs in cities: adaptation to habitat acoustics or side effect of urbanization? Anim. Behav.

Nemeth, E., Winkler, H., Dabelsteen, T., 2001. Differential degradation of antbird songs in a Neotropical rainforest: adaptation to perch height? J. Acoust. Soc. Am. 110, 3263–3274.

Nemeth, E., Dabelsteen, T., Pedersen, S.B., Winkler, H., 2006. Rainforests as concert halls for birds: are reverberations improving sound transmission of long song elements? J. Acoust. Soc. Am. 119, 620–626.

Nicholls, J.A., Goldizen, A.W., 2006. Habitat type and density influence vocal signal design in satin bowerbirds. J. Anim. Ecol. 75, 549–558.

Padgham, M., 2004. Reverberation and frequency attenuation in forests-implications for acoustic communication in animals. J. Acoust. Soc. Am. 115, 402–410.

Partecke, J., Van't Hof, T., Gwinner, E., 2004. Differences in the timing of reproduction between urban and forest European blackbirds (Turdus merula): result of phenotypic flexibility or genetic differences? Proc. R. Soc. Lond. B 271, 1995–2001.

Patricelli, G.L., Blickley, J.L., 2006. Avian communication in urban noise: causes and consequences of vocal adjustment. Auk 123, 639–649.

Patricelli, G.L., Dantzker, M.S., Bradbury, J.W., 2007. Differences in acoustic directionality among vocalizations of the male red-winged blackbird (Agelaius pheoniceus) are related to function in communication. Behav. Ecol. Sociobiol. 61, 1099–1110.

Phillmore, L.S., Sturdy, C.B., Weisman, R.G., 2003. Does reduced social contact affect discrimination of distance cues and individual vocalizations? Anim. Behav. 65, 911–922.

Piercy, J.E., Embelton, T.F.W., Sutherland, L.C., 1977. Review of noise propagation in the atmosphere. J. Acoust. Soc. Am. 61, 1403–1418.

Planqué, R., Slabbekoorn, H., 2008. Spectral overlap in songs and temporal avoidance in a Peruvian bird assemblage. Ethology 114, 262–271.

Potash, L.M., 1972. Noise-induced changes in calls of the Japanese quail. Psychon. Sci. 26, 252–254.

Richards, D.G., 1981. Estimation of distance of singing conspecifics by the Carolina wren. Auk 98, 127–133.

Richards, D.G., Wiley, R.H., 1980. Reverberations and amplitude fluctuations in the propagation of sound in a forest: implications for animal communications. Am. Nat. 115, 381–399.

Römer, H., Lewald, J., 1992. High-frequency sound transmission in natural habitats: implications for the evolution of insect acoustic communication. Behav. Ecol. Sociobiol. 29, 437–444.

Roth, T., Sprau, P., Schmidt, R., Naguib, M., Amrhein, V., 2009. Sex-specific timing of mate searching and territory prospecting in the nightingale: nocturnal life of females. Proc. R. Soc. Lond. B 276, 2045–2050.

Ryan, M.J., Brenowitz, E.A., 1985. The role of body size, phylogeny, and ambient noise in the evolution of bird song. Am. Nat. 126, 87–100.

Shannon, C.E., 1948. A mathematical theory of communication. Bell Syst. Tech. J. 27, 379–423.

Shannon, C.E., 1949. Communication in the presence of noise. Proc. Inst. Radio Eng. 37, 10–21.

Shen, J.X., Feng, A.S., Xu, Z.M., Yu, Z.L., Arch, V.S., Yu, X.J., et al., 2008. Ultrasonic frogs show hyperacute phonotaxis to female courtship calls. Nature 453, 914–U946.

Shy, E., Morton, E.S., 1986. The role of distance, familiarity, and time of day in Carolina wrens responses to conspecific songs. Behav. Ecol. Sociobiol. 19, 393–400.

Slabbekoorn, H., 2004. Singing in the wild: the ecology of birdsong. In: Marler, P., Slabbekoorn, H. (Eds.), Nature's Music: The Science of Birdsong. Elsevier Academic Press, San Diego, pp. 181–208.

Slabbekoorn, H., Boer-Visser, A.d., 2006. Cities change the songs of birds. Curr. Biol. 16, 2326–2331.

Slabbekoorn, H., Peet, M., 2003. Birds sing at a higher pitch in urban noise. Nature 424, 267.

Slabbekoorn, H., Ripmeester, E.A.P., 2007. Birdsong and anthropogenic noise: implications and applications for conservation. In: International Summit on Evolutionary Change in Human-Altered Environments. Blackwell Publishing, Los Angeles, CA, pp. 72–83.

Slabbekoorn, H., Smith, T.B., 2002. Habitat dependent song divergence in the little greenbul: an analysis of environmental selection pressures on acoustic signals. Evolution 56, 1849–1858.

Slabbekoorn, H., Ellers, J., Smith, T.B., 2002. Birdsong and sound transmission: the benefits of reverberations. Condor 104, 564–573.

Smith, D.G., Norman, D.O., 1979. "Leader-follower" singing in red-winged blackbirds (Agelaius phoeniceus). Condor 81, 83–84.

Stadler, H., 1926. Stimmenstudien. Ber. Verein Schles. Ornithol. 12, 22–94.

Todt, D., Naguib, M., 2000. Vocal interactions in birds: the use of song as a model in communication. Adv. Study Behav. 29, 247–296.

Traunmüller, H., Eriksson, A., 2000. Acoustic effects of variation in vocal effort by men, women, and children. J. Acoust. Soc. Am. 107, 3438–3451.

Vignal, C., Attia, J., Mathevon, N., Beauchaud, M., 2004. Background noise does not modify genic activation in the bird song-induced brain. Behav. Brain Res. 153, 241–248.

Wasserman, F.E., 1977. Intraspecific acoustical interference in the white-throated sparrow Zonotrichia albicollis. Anim. Behav. 25, 949–952.

Whitehead, J.M., 1987. Vocally mediated reciprocity between neighbouring groups of mantled howling monkeys, Alouatta palliata palliata. Anim. Behav. 35, 1615–1627.

Wilczynski, W., Ryan, M.J., Brenowitz, E.A., 1989. The display of the blue-black grassquit: the acoustic advantage of getting high. Ethology 80, 218–222.

Wiley, R.H., 1983. The evolution of communication: information and manipulation. In: Halliday, T.R., Slater, P.J.B. (Eds.), Animal Behaviour—Communication, Vol. 2. Blackwell Scientific Publications, Oxford, pp. 156–189.

Wiley, R.H., 1991. Associations of song properties with habitats for territorial oscine birds of eastern North America. Am. Nat. 138, 973–993.

Wiley, R.H., 1994. Errors, exaggeration and deception in animal communication. In: Real, L. (Ed.), Behavioral Mechanisms in Ecology. University of Chicago Press, Chicago, pp. 157–189.

Wiley, R.H., 1998. Ranging reconsidered. Behav. Ecol. Sociobiol. 42, 143–146.

Wiley, R.H., 2006. Signal detection and animal communication. Adv. Study Behav. 36, 217–247.

Wiley, R.H., Godard, R., 1996. Ranging of conspecific songs by Kentucky warblers and its implications for interactions of territorial males. Behaviour 133, 81–102.

Wiley, R.H., Richards, D.G., 1978. Physical constraints on acoustic communication in the atmosphere: implications for the evolution of animal vocalizations. Behav. Ecol. Sociobiol. 3, 69–94.

Wiley, R.H., Richards, D.G., 1982. Adaptations for acoustic communication in birds: sound transmission and signal detection. In: Kroodsma, D.E., Miller, E.H. (Eds.), Acoustic Communication in Birds, Vol. 2. Academic Press, New York, pp. 131–181.

Williams, J.M., Slater, P.J.B., 1993. Does chaffinch *Fringilla coelebs* song vary with the habitat in which it is sung? Ibis 135, 202–208.

Wollerman, L., 1999. Acoustic interference limits call detection in a Neotropical frog *Hyla ebraccata*. Anim. Behav. 57, 529–536.

Wood, W.E., Yezerinac, S.M., 2006. Song sparrow (*Melospiza melodia*) song varies with urban noise. Auk 123, 650–659.

The Evolution of Song in the *Phylloscopus* Leaf Warblers (Aves: Sylviidae): A Tale of Sexual Selection, Habitat Adaptation, and Morphological Constraints

Bettina Mahler* and Diego Gil[†]

*LABORATORIO DE ECOLOGÍA Y COMPORTAMIENTO ANIMAL, DEPARTAMENTO
DE ECOLOGÍA, GENÉTICA Y EVOLUCIÓN, FACULTAD DE CIENCIAS EXACTAS
Y NATURALES, UNIVERSIDAD DE BUENOS AIRES, 4 PISO, PAB. II,
CIUDAD UNIVERSITARIA, 1428 CAPITAL FEDERAL, ARGENTINA
[†]DEPARTAMENTO DE ECOLOGÍA EVOLUTIVA, MUSEO NACIONAL
DE CIENCIAS NATURALES (CSIC), JOSÉ GUTIÉRREZ ABASCAL 2,
E-28006 MADRID, SPAIN

*Un oiseau chante d'autant mieux qu'il chante dans son arbre généalogique**
Jean Cocteau (French poet and playwright, 1889–1963)

I. INTRODUCTION

Differences in song are often the most reliable criteria by which closely related bird species can be differentiated. For instance, only by carefully listening to the song of leaf warblers could the 18th century naturalist Gilbert White identify the chiffchaff, the willow and the wood warblers as different species (*Phylloscopus collybita, P. sybilatrix*, and *P. trochilus*) (White, 1789). Observations such as these have been interpreted as suggestive of speciation events being tightly linked to the evolution of bird song, a signal of great importance in sexual selection processes (Price, 2007).

*It is from its genealogical tree that the bird sings at its best

35

0065-3454/09 $35.00
DOI: 10.1016/S0065-3454(09)40002-0

Bird song presents some peculiarities that add an additional layer of complexity to the study of its evolution, by comparison with a standard morphological trait. In several avian groups, notably so in the oscine Passeriformes, songs are passed on down the generations by cultural transmission, often between neighbors (Lachlan and Slater, 2003; Nordby et al., 1999), or, more rarely, from father to son (Grant and Grant, 1996; Mann and Slater, 1995). This type of cultural evolution may, in principle, lead to a higher mutation rate than traits with a higher genetic component (Lynch and Baker, 1993; Slater et al., 1980). However, behavioral mechanisms may select for conformity and thus reduce mutation rates considerably (Baker and Gammon, 2008; Lachlan et al., 2004). In addition, not all aspects of song are culturally transmitted. Even in oscines, genetically transmitted sensory templates, singing styles and predispositions for certain sounds, filter and direct vocal learning to a large extent (Leitner and Catchpole, 2007; Mundinger, 1995).

Despite a remarkably high copying fidelity, colonization events by birds with poorly developed songs (Thielcke, 1983) and impoverished cultural transmission in small and fragmented populations (Laiolo and Tella, 2005) can lead to the establishment of diverging vocal traditions. Furthermore, mathematical models have shown that song learning can greatly facilitate the development of genetic isolation, thus fostering allopatric speciation rates (Lachlan and Servedio, 2004). Interestingly, a counterintuitive prediction of this model is that the probability of speciation is higher when the cultural mutation rate is low (Lachlan and Servedio, 2004).

Most comparative studies in a variety of avian groups, ranging from herons to several subfamilies of Passeriformes, have found that song encodes significant amounts of phylogenetic signal, and thus closely related species share certain features of the song due to common ancestry (Mann et al., 2009; McCracken and Sheldon, 1997; Päckert et al., 2003; Price and Lanyon, 2002; Seddon, 2005; ten Cate, 2004; van Buskirk, 1997). However, a general pattern that arises from these studies is that, despite phylogenetic similarity, song characteristics are not enough to reconstruct a reliable phylogeny, and that bird song is a labile trait. Several hypotheses, both adaptive and non-adaptive, have been proposed to account for this evolutionary lability of bird song. These are summarized in the following subsections.

A. MORPHOLOGICAL CONSTRAINTS

Song in birds is produced by a specialized organ, the syrinx, but is also shaped by other physical characteristics such as body size, or beak shape (Suthers, 2004). Since these traits can be subject to natural selection in relationship to food habits or other selective pressures, song characteristics may be hijacked by these particular selection regimes. For example, body size has been shown to be a limiting factor in the frequencies that can be produced. The negative relationship between body size and song frequency can be largely explained by large-bodied species not being able to produce high-pitched sounds (Ryan and Brenowitz, 1985; Tubaro and Mahler, 1998; Wallschläger, 1980). More specifically, selection for particular beak shapes due to trophic adaptation can cause correlated changes in song characteristics. For instance, selection for strong, deep beaks in Darwin finches (*Geospiza* spp.) has resulted in correlated changes in song: rapid trills of a wide frequency range are simply incompatible with deep beaks (Podos, 2001). Several recent studies suggest that this type of relationship between beak and song characteristics may be widespread and may explain a substantial part of variation in song between species (Badyaev et al., 2008; Ballentine, 2006; Palacios and Tubaro, 2000; Podos, 1997; Seddon, 2005).

B. FUNCTIONAL SELECTIVE PRESSURES

Experiments and observational evidence show that bird song has two basic functions: territorial defense and mate attraction (Catchpole and Slater, 2008; Eriksson and Wallin, 1986; Krebs et al., 1978; McDonald, 1989; Mountjoy and Lemon, 1991). Thus, it is to be expected that the evolution of several song characteristics may be related to variation in the strength of sexual selection (Catchpole, 1980; Kroodsma, 1977; Read and Weary, 1990, 1992). However, studies present conflicting evidence about the strength and the direction of this relationship (Garamszegi and Møller, 2004; Price and Lanyon, 2002; Shutler and Weatherhead, 1990). A possibility is that the different modes of sexual selection (male–male competition and female choice) may select for different song characteristics (Collins et al., 2009; Slater, 1981). Read and Weary (1992), in the largest comparative study so far, show that large repertoires are associated with a relatively long migration distance, which they considered to be a proxy of the strength of sexual selection. Similarly, in the different morphs of the ring species *Phylloscopus trochiloides*, evolutionary transitions toward higher latitudes correlate with increases in song complexity (Irwin, 2000; Irwin et al., 2001).

C. ADAPTATION TO ACOUSTIC PROPERTIES OF THE HABITAT

Habitats differ in their acoustic properties, thus filtering particular temporal and frequency characteristics of song (e.g., Martens, 1980; Morton, 1975; Ryan and Brenowitz, 1985; Wiley, 1991). Song is typically loud and directed at rather distant birds, and thus we expect selection for song characteristics that transmit well in the particular habitat where the bird lives (Brumm and Naguib, 2009). A recent meta-analysis does, indeed, show that the songs of species living in closed habitats have lower frequencies and narrower frequency ranges than those of species living in open habitats (Boncoraglio and Saino, 2007).

D. CHARACTER DISPLACEMENT

Although most species sing species-specific song patterns, differences between some species may sometimes be rather minor, given high phylogenetic loads in many song characters (e.g., Päckert et al., 2003; Seddon, 2005; ten Cate, 2004; van Buskirk, 1997). Thus, selection against heterospecific matings is expected to reinforce acoustic differences between species. Such a mechanism would lead to higher differences between species-specific songs in sympatric closely related species. For instance, a comparative study in the antbirds (Thamnophilidae, suboscine Passeriformes) showed evidence for character displacement of both temporal and pitch characteristics in sympatric species (Seddon, 2005).

The *Phylloscopus* warblers are a large genus of insectivorous warblers, encompassing 56 species, which inhabit forested areas mostly in Eurasia, as well as some regions in Africa (del Hoyo et al., 2006). Most species are migratory, and winter south of their breeding ranges either in India, Asia, or Africa. The highest local diversity is found in the Himalayas, an area which is considered the center of speciation for most *Phylloscopus* species (Price, 1991; Price et al., 1997). The relationship between distribution ranges and latitude follows Rappoport's rule (i.e., larger ranges in higher latitudes) and has been explained as a result of differential ability of taxa to colonize Northern habitats in the last 2 million years following glaciations (Price et al., 1997). Changes in species-specific midlatitudes show high evolutionary lability (Price et al., 1997), suggesting frequent North–South dispersal events that are at the base of several speciation events in this group (Irwin et al., 2005).

Phylloscopus males are highly vocal while defending territories (Martens, 1993), and sexual selection for particular song traits has been shown to be important in several species (Forstmeier et al., 2002; Gil et al., 2007; Radesäter et al., 1987). Thus, this genus seems to be a good model in which to study the evolution of song in a passerine group, and compare the different evolutionary forces that contribute to it. Previous studies have examined this problem in a limited number of species (Irwin, 2000, and also an unpublished MS by Liou, L. W., Tiainen, J., Higuchi, H., Richman, A. D., and Price, T. D.: "Song variation in the genus Phylloscopus"). In this paper, we study the evolution of song in a much larger sample of taxa (30 species). In the first part of this study, we will compare the evolutionary lability of temporal, pitch, and repertoire characteristics. This will indicate whether song characters are the valuable traits in this group for predicting phylogenetic relationships between taxa. In the second part of the study, we will test a series of hypotheses concerning morphological constraints, song function, adaptation to habitat sound transmission, and character displacement between sympatric species. Explicitly, we predict: (1) song frequency and temporal characteristics to be correlated with body size and beak shape; (2) repertoire size and song complexity to increase with the intensity of sexual selection across species; (3) song frequency and temporal characteristics to be associated with niche and habitat characteristics that determine sound transmission; and (4) increased divergence of song characteristics in closely related species sharing distribution ranges.

II. MATERIAL AND METHODS

A. TAXA SAMPLED

We analyzed song for all *Phylloscopus* species for which mitochondrial DNA sequence data were available, basically those covered by a phylogeny based on these molecular data (Price et al., 1997), and additional information obtained from Richman (1996), Olsson et al. (2005), and Bensch et al. (2006). We excluded the Caucasian chiffchaff (*Phylloscopus lorenzii*), since song recordings could not be obtained from this species. We included an additional species not considered in this phylogeny, the Canary Islands chiffchaff (*Phylloscopus canariensis*), which is a sister species of the common chiffchaff (Helbig et al., 1996). In total, 30 species of the genus *Phylloscopus* were considered (Fig. 1).

B. SONG DATA AND ANALYSIS

We studied vocalizations emitted in seemingly territorial contexts, which we will refer to as songs. For most species, we succeeded in obtaining recordings from three different individuals, except for Hume's, Tytler's, and Ijima's leaf warblers (*Phylloscopus humei, P. tytleri*, and *P. ijimae*) and Eastern Bonelli's Warbler (*Phylloscopus orientalis)* for which only one individual was obtained, and the pale-legged and ashy-throated warblers (*Phylloscopus tenellipes* and *P. maculipennis*) for which only two individuals were available. Given the very high repeatability of song characteristics within species (see the following section), we are confident that the small sample size that we obtained for some species is not a problem. For each individual, measurements of acoustic variables were taken on five successive songs, or on the number of songs contained in the recording when they were less than five, and mean values

FIG. 1. Phylogenetic tree of the *Phylloscopus* species used in this study. This tree is based on Price et al. (1997), with additional information taken from Richman (1996), Olsson et al. (2005), Bensch et al. (2006), and Helbig et al. (1996).

were calculated for each variable. In total, we analyzed recordings of 84 different birds belonging to 30 different species (Table I). Song recordings were obtained from several commercially available tapes and from sound libraries, mainly the National Sound Archive (London, UK) (Table I). Recordings for less common species were located by consulting Shaun Peters' web site catalog of recorded bird songs (http://aviandiscography.webs.com).

Recordings were digitized from CDs with Windows Media Player (Microsoft) and sonograms were created using Avisoft SASLab-Pro (www.avisoft-saslab.com) with the following parameters: FFT length 256; frame size 100%; Hamming window; frequency resolution 86 Hz; and temporal resolution 8 ms. Measurements of acoustic variables were performed on the sonograms. The smallest component of a leaf warbler's song is an element, defined as a continuous sound in time. Elements may be organized in syllables. We defined a syllable as a single element or a group of elements emitted consecutively forming a phrase. Introductory elements that are typical of some leaf warbler species were not considered in the analysis (Thielcke and Linsenmair, 1963). A group of elements emitted in the same successive order in different songs, forming a part or the whole song, was also considered a syllable. A phrase was defined as a repetition of one syllable two or more times.

Territorial song in the genus *Phylloscopus* varies markedly between species (Martens, 1980), and it is not straightforward to find a direct measure of complexity that could be applied to all species (see Fig. 2 for examples of songs). Additionally, previous studies in several species recommend a multivariate analysis of song (Gil and Slater, 2000b; Irwin, 2000). Thus, we established a comprehensive list of 29 song measurements, including temporal, structural, and frequency components of the songs which were taken on each song by BM. The precise definition of these measurements can be found in Table II.

All variables were highly repeatable among individuals of the same species (all $F_{25, 53} > 3.31$, $P < 0.001$), except for the pause between songs, which varied greatly among individuals and between different songs of the same individual ($F_{25, 52} = 1.19$, $P = 0.29$).

Inspection of the correlation matrix between all these variables led us to divide them in two categories: song complexity (temporal patterns and repertoire) and frequency characteristics, the former grouped since measures of repertoire size were highly correlated with many duration measurements. Thus, all measurements were categorized in two groups: song composition and frequency characteristics. Two different principal component analyses were performed upon each of these sets of variables.

The principal component analysis (PCA) on the song composition variables yielded up to five components of complexity. However, only the first component could be easily interpreted, and thus we restrict our analyses to

TABLE I

SPECIES CONSIDERED IN THE STUDY AND RECORDINGS' SOURCES

Species	Individuals	Sources
Phylloscopus affinis	3	(1, 2)
Phylloscopus bonelli	3	(3–5)
Phylloscopus borealis	3	(1, 4, 6)
Phylloscopus canariensis	3	(2, 7)
Phylloscopus chloronotus	3	(1, 8)
Phylloscopus collybita	3	(4, 5, 9)
Phylloscopus coronatus	4	(2, 4, 10)
Phylloscopus fuscatus	3	(2, 4, 11)
Phylloscopus griseolus	3	(1, 2, 11)
Phylloscopus humei	1	(11)
Phylloscopus ibericus	3	(5, 6, 9)
Phylloscopus ijimae	1	(10)
Phylloscopus inornatus	4	(2, 11)
Phylloscopus maculipennis	2	(2)
Phylloscopus magnirostris	3	(1, 8, 12)
Phylloscopus nitidus	3	(2, 11, 12)
Phylloscopus occipitalis	3	(1, 2)
Phylloscopus orientalis	1	(4)
Phylloscopus plumbeitarsus	3	(2, 11)
Phylloscopus proregulus	3	(2, 11)
Phylloscopus pulcher	3	(1, 2)
Phylloscopus reguloides	3	(1, 13)
Phylloscopus schwarzi	3	(2, 4, 11)
Phylloscopus sibilatrix	3	(6, 9)
Phylloscopus sindianus	3	(1, 2, 4)
Phylloscopus tenellipes	2	(1, 10)
Phylloscopus trochiloides	3	(1, 2, 14)
Phylloscopus trochilus	3	(2, 4, 15)
Phylloscopus tytleri	1	(1)
Phylloscopus viridanus	3	(6, 9, 11)

Sources

1. Farrow, D., 2002. 24 Phylloscopus Species. Privately published.

2. National Sound Archive. London, UK.

3. Roché, J.C., 1990. Tous les Oiseaux d'Europe. Sittelle, Mens.

4. Schulze, A., 2003. Die Vogelstimmen Europas, Nordafrikas und Vorderasiens. Ample, Germering.

5. Llimona, F., E. Matheu, J.C., 2000. Roché, Aves de nuestros bosques y montañas. Alosa, Barcelona.

6. Sample, G., 2003. Warbler Songs and Calls. HarperCollins, London.

7. Moreno, J.M., 2000. Cantos y Reclamos de las Aves de Canarias. Turquesa, Santa Cruz de Tenerife.

8. Connop, S., 1995. Birdsongs of the Himalayas. Cornell Laboratory of Ornithology, Ithaca.

9. Roché, J.C., J. Cheverau, 1999. Fauvettes aquatiques & Cie. Sittelle, Mens.

10. Ueda, H., 1998. 283 Wild Bird Songs of Japan. Yama-Key, Tokyo.

11. Mild, K., 1987. Soviet Bird Songs. Krister Mild Bioacoustics, Stockholm.

12. Warakagoda, D., 1998. The Bird Sounds of Sri Lanka. Part 2: Passerines. Library Nature Sounds, Sri Lanka.

13. Connop, S., 1993. Birdsongs of Nepal. Cornell Laboratory of Ornithology, Ithaca.

14. Scharringa, J., 2001. Birds of Tropical Asia. 2. Bird Songs International. BV, Westernieland.

15. Fonoteca Zoologica MNCN, Madrid.

it (Table III). This first component (hereafter "song complexity") can be described as a measure combining song repertoire size and complexity: birds with high scores in this component have large repertoires and sing long songs composed of many different syllables, which are also long and complex. The remainder of components does not have a straightforward biological interpretation. For instance, the second component is mostly loaded by switch rate, which is a measure of the turnover of new elements between consecutive songs, but also by measures of syllable length, reflecting thus some positive covariance between these measures. Only the first principal component will be used in the analysis.

The PCA of frequency measurements was simpler to interpret (Table III). The first principal component is loaded principally by maximum frequency and bandwidth (hereafter "pitch1"), whereas the second component is explained by minimum and emphasized frequencies (hereafter "pitch2").

C. Morphological Data

Measurements of skin specimens were taken at the Bird Section of the British Museum of Natural History (Tring, UK) by DG, following standard procedures (Svensson, 1984). We aimed at obtaining measurements of 10 individuals in total, 5 per sex, and this was achieved for most species (for sample sizes, see Appendix 1).

Wing and tail lengths were measured with a wing ruler to the nearest 0.1 mm. Tarsus length was taken with the aid of a pair of dividers onto the wing rule to the nearest 0.1 mm. Beak measurements were taken with a digital caliper (Mitutoyo, Japan) to the nearest 0.1 mm. Repeatability of measurements as determined by ANOVAs performed on 12 repeated measures was high for all measurements (all tests: $F_{11,12} > 6.5$; $P < 0.001$; intraclass coefficient of correlations >0.72). Descriptive data (means and S.D.) are presented in Appendix 1 for each species.

1. Body Size

We performed a PCA on the correlation matrix of log-transformed morphological characters, including wing, tail, tarsus, and beak lengths; beak width; and beak depth. The results follow closely those of Price (1991), who

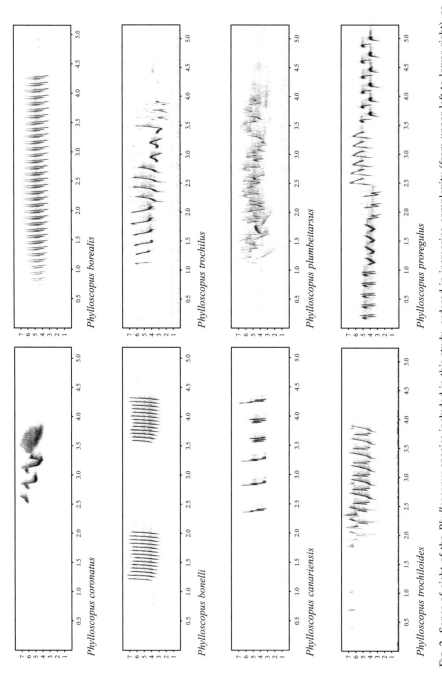

Phylloscopus coronatus

Phylloscopus borealis

Phylloscopus bonelli

Phylloscopus trochilus

Phylloscopus canariensis

Phylloscopus plumbeitarsus

Phylloscopus trochiloides

Phylloscopus proregulus

FIG. 2. Songs of eight of the *Phylloscopus* species included in this study, ordered in increasing complexity (from upper left to lower right), as defined by the song complexity measure used in this study (see text).

TABLE II

DEFINITIONS OF THE DIFFERENT SONG MEASUREMENTS, WHICH CAN BE CLASSIFIED IN THREE
TYPES: TEMPORAL (1–10), STRUCTURAL (11–21), AND FREQUENCY CHARACTERISTICS (22–29)

1	SONDUR	Song duration, measured from the beginning of the first to the end of the last element of the song
2	SONPAU	Pause between songs, measured from the end of the last element of one song to the beginning of the first element of the next consecutive song
3	SONPRO	Song proportion, calculated as the sum of the duration of the songs divided by the sum of the duration of the songs and the pauses between songs
4	DUSHOEL	Duration of the shortest element of the song
5	DULONEL	Duration of the longest element of the song
6	DUSHOSY	Duration of the shortest syllable of the song
7	DULONSY	Duration of the longest syllable of the song
8	SHOPAU	Shortest pause between elements of the song
9	LONPAU	Longest pause between elements of the song
10	SOUNPRO	Sound proportion, calculated as the sum of the duration of all the elements of one song divided by song duration
11	PRDIFSO	Number of different songs divided by the total number of analyzed songs
12	PRDIFSY	Number of different syllables present in all analyzed songs divided by the number of analyzed songs
13	PRDIFEL	Number of different elements present in all analyzed songs divided by the number of analyzed songs
14	REPBETSO	Repertoire between songs, measured as the number of shared elements by two consecutive songs divided by the total number of elements present in both songs (shared + different)
15	NPHRSO	Total number of phrases of one song
16	NDISYSO	Number of different syllables of one song
17	NTOSYSO	Total number of syllables of one song
18	NDIELSO	Number of different elements of one song
19	NTOELSO	Total number of elements of one song
20	SWITCH	Switch rate, measured as the transition to different syllables divided by the total number of pauses between syllables in one song (for the species in which the syllable composed the entire song, the switch ratio was calculated for the elements)
21	MODRAT	Modulation ratio, measured as the mean modulation of the elements of the song. The modulation was measured as the sum of the fragments of the element with ascending, descending, and constant frequencies
22	EMFREQ	Emphasized frequency, corresponding to the frequency with highest amplitude of the song
23	MAXFREQ	Maximum frequency
24	MINFREQ	Minimum frequency
25	ABSBNW	Bandwidth, measured as the difference between the maximum and minimum frequencies

(*Continued*)

TABLE II   (*Continued*)

26	MXBNWSO	Maximum bandwidth of one element of the song
27	MNBNWSO	Minimum bandwidth of one element of the song
28	MXBNWSY	Maximum bandwidth of one syllable of the song
29	MNBNWSY	Minimum bandwidth of one syllable of the song

TABLE III

SONG MEASUREMENTS AND THEIR CONTRIBUTION TO THE PRINCIPAL COMPONENT ANALYSES THAT
WERE CARRIED OUT

	Song organization PCA		Frequency PCA	
	PC1 (song complexity)	PC2	PC1 (pitch1)	PC2 (pitch2)
SONDUR	0.67	0.17	–	–
SONPAU	0.26	0.25	–	–
SONPRO	0.37	− 0.01	–	–
DUSHOEL	− 0.64	0.17	–	–
DULONEL	− 0.59	0.50	–	–
DUSHOSY	− 0.67	0.62	–	–
DULONSY	− 0.47	0.75	–	–
SHOPAU	0.11	− 0.01	–	–
LONPAU	0.48	0.39	–	–
SOUNPRO	− 0.65	0.04	–	–
PRDIFSO	0.65	− 0.01	–	–
PRDIFSY	0.81	0.36	–	–
PRDIFEL	0.72	0.50	–	–
REPBETSO	− 0.43	0.28	–	–
NPHRSO	0.42	− 0.48	–	–
NDISYSO	0.61	0.65	–	–
NTOSYSO	0.69	− 0.33	–	–
NDIELSO	0.80	− 0.27	–	–
NTOELSO	0.56	0.75	–	–
SWITCH	0.18	0.84	–	–
MODRAT	–	–	0.41	− 0.32
EMFREQ	–	–	0.25	0.90
MAXFREQ	–	–	0.77	0.56
MINFREQ	–	–	− 0.32	0.89
ABSBNW	–	–	0.93	− 0.14
MXBNWSO	–	–	0.87	− 0.17
MNBNWSO	–	–	0.24	0.09
MXBNWSY	–	–	0.94	− 0.11
MNBNWSY	–	–	0.70	0.19
Variance explained (%)	32.2	20.8	45.35	21.54

performed a similar analysis on a smaller data set of species from Kashmir. The first two principal components explained 85.6% of the total variance. The interpretation of the loadings (Table IV) is that PC1 measures common variance in body size (and hereafter we will refer to as "body size"). PC2 is a bipolar component, positively loaded by tarsus and tail length and negatively by beak length and width (hereafter "tarsus/beak ratio"). We interpret this component similarly to Price (1991), agreeing that it represents a ratio between beak and tarsus length (although the direction of this ratio was inverted in Price's study). PC3 explained very little variance and was difficult to interpret functionally, and is thus not further discussed.

We decided to use body size instead of body mass in our analysis, because the latter was not available for some of the species. However, there is a very strong relationship between our measure of body size and body mass as reported in another study (Price et al., 1997): $F_{1,26} = 111.5$, $P < 0.0001$; $R^2 = 0.81$; regression equation: body mass = 1.3 × body size + 8.14.

2. Beak Shape

Since we wished to specifically test the effect of beak shape on song structure, we performed an additional PCA including only the three beak measurements (length, width, and depth). The first two principal components explained 96% of the total variance. As expected, the first component was unidirectional, reflecting purely the size (Table IV). Since the scores of this component were highly correlated with body size ($r = 0.935$, $N = 30$, $P < 0.001$), it was not used further. On the contrary, PC2 provided us with a measure of beak shape unrelated to size, showing a ratio between beak width, length, and depth (hereafter "beak shape"). Although the percentage of variance explained by this component is low, it is functionally coherent and provides a useful size-free estimate of beak shape.

TABLE IV

Component Loadings of Log-Transformed Morphological Traits of the 30 *Phylloscopus* Species

	Morphology PCA			Beak PCA	
	PC1 (body size)	PC2 (tarsus/ beak ratio)	PC3	PC1	PC2 (beak shape)
Wing length	0.86	0.15	−0.38	−	−
Tail length	0.80	0.43	−0.28	−	−
Tarsus length	0.34	0.84	0.40	−	−
Beak length	0.92	−0.24	0.10	0.96	−0.14
Beak width	0.81	−0.49	0.21	0.94	0.34
Beak width	0.92	−0.15	0.15	0.96	−0.19
Variance explained (%)	64.8	20.7	7.8	90.8	5.67

D. PHYLOGENETIC SIGNAL OF SONG VARIABLES

We studied the degree to which song characters and morphological measures are influenced by species relatedness using the software PHYSIG (Blomberg et al., 2003). We studied the phylogenetic signal of the characters by means of the statistic K using the algorithms implemented in the package. We also estimated the amount of variation of the song characteristics among species using coefficients of variation (CV). The CVs for types of variables (temporal, structural, and frequency) were compared using one-way ANOVA and pairwise comparisons were performed using a *post hoc* Tukey test.

E. STRENGTH OF SEXUAL SELECTION

Species-specific differences in the strength of sexual selection correspond to the average level of male reproductive skew (Kokko et al., 2002). This skew has been typically taken as equivalent to the degree of polygyny, but the discovery of highly variable levels of extra-pair paternity in birds has reduced the value of this measure (Birkhead and Møller, 1998). Unfortunately, estimates of extra-pair paternity are lacking for most *Phylloscopus* species, so we decided to use other possible surrogates of strength of sexual selection. We selected two different measurements: the degree of sexual size dimorphism and the average latitude of the species.

Sexual dimorphism is one of the basic correlates of sexual selection, given the contribution of male–male competition to selection for large male body size (Trivers, 1972). Furthermore, sexual size dimorphism has been found to be related to more direct measures of sexual selection, such as polygynous and promiscuous mating systems, or testis size (Dunn et al., 2001). We estimated average sexual size dimorphism by calculating the difference between male and female size [log (mean male trait)−log (mean female trait)] for wing, tail, and tarsus length. These data were available for all species except Ijima's leaf warbler, for which only one individual per sex was available. Dimorphism scores calculated for each trait correlated positively among them, so we ran a PCA and extracted a first principal component in which all dimorphism scores contributed in the same direction (wing length: 0.76; tail length: 0.84; tarsus length: 0.62; variance explained: 55.7%). Scores for this PC1 will be referred to as the index of size dimorphism.

In the Northern Hemisphere, sexual selection has been shown to increase in intensity with increasing latitude, possibly because increases in latitude lead to shorter reproductive seasons and higher abundance of nutrients and breeding densities (Irwin, 2000). These regimes would favor male competition (Catchpole, 1980). Similarly, comparative analyses have shown that levels of extra-pair paternity increase with migration distance and synchronous breeding in birds, and these two factors are known to increase with latitude (Spottiswoode and Møller, 2004).

F. SOUND CHARACTERISTICS OF NICHE AND HABITAT

Martens suggested that the particularly high-pitched song of the large-billed leaf warbler (*Phylloscopus magnirostris*) was an adaptation to sound transmission in the noisy conditions of the Himalayan springs (Martens, 1980). However, this is a rather unique habitat, and the wider variation in habitat usage in the genus *Phylloscopus* could be explained along a continuum between the open and closed forest (Badyaev and Leaf, 1997). A recent meta-analysis has shown that the song characteristic that is mostly affected by habitat structure is emphasized frequency (Boncoraglio and Saino, 2007). To test the hypothesis of acoustic adaptation, we tried to find reliable descriptions of the openness of typical species-specific habitat (e.g., Baker, 1997), but these were difficult to systematize and quantify (but see Badyaev and Leaf, 1997). However, several field studies have found that habitat selection and feeding niche in the *Phylloscopus* are strongly related to morphological adaptations (Forstmeier et al., 2001; Gaston, 1974; Price, 1991). Although there are several differences between studies conducted in different geographical areas in their results on the relationship of morphology to habitat, several main patterns are shared by most studies. Large tarsi and small beaks in *Phylloscopus* species have been shown to relate to terrestrial habitats, with short tarsi and relatively large beaks selected in birds feeding in high canopies (Gaston, 1974; Price, 1991; Richman and Price, 1992). We thus decided to use the morphological PC2 (tarsus/beak ratio) as an ecomorphological characteristic correlated with habitat and niche choice.

G. CHARACTER DISPLACEMENT

A character reinforcement mechanism predicts that song should be more divergent between species in sympatry than in allopatry. We tested this prediction by comparing the differences in song variables between pairs of species differing in whether they were sympatric or not. For this, each pair of sister species was compared with the phylogenetically nearest species that is sympatric with one of them and allopatric with the other (Table V). This allowed us to control for differences related to divergence times. We did not include the pair composed by the Western-crowned and the Blyth's leaf warblers (*Phylloscopus occipitalis* and *P. reguloides)* because the nearest species on the tree fulfilling the requirement of sympatry was Hume's leaf warbler and this species is phylogenetically so distant that many factors other than sympatry might be responsible

TABLE V

NEAREST SPECIES ON THE TREE (FIRST COLUMN) BEING ALLOPATRIC WITH ONE (SECOND COLUMN)
AND SYMPATRIC WITH ANOTHER (THIRD COLUMN) SPECIES OF A PAIR OF SISTER SPECIES

	Allopatric	Sympatric
P. magnirostris	P. plumbeitarsus	P. trochiloides
P. borealis	P. magnirostris	P. tenellipes
P. plumbeitarsus	P. ijimae	P. coronatus
P. fuscatus	P. griseolus	P. affinis
P. affinis	P. canariensis	P. sindianus
P. ibericus	P. sibilatrix	P. bonelli
P. proregulus	P. humei	P. inornatus
P. pulcher	P. proregulus	P. chloronotus

for song differences. We considered a pair of species to be sympatric when they shared at least 20% of their distribution, otherwise they were considered allopatric.

H. STATISTICS AND DATA ANALYSIS

All morphological variables were log-transformed before use. Transformed variables were found to conform to normal distributions. Sound measurements were checked for normality and approached to normal distributions by transformations *ad hoc* (Sokal and Rohlf, 1995). We used parametric statistics throughout except for the test of sympatry–allopatry, where the small sample size made a sign test more appropriate (Siegel and Castellan, 1988). A priori hypotheses were tested using stepwise multiple regression procedures. Since species cannot be considered as the independent units in evolutionary terms, we used the method of independent contrasts to control for similarity due to common descent (Felsenstein, 1985). For this, we used the software CAIC, with the "crunch" algorithm and a phylogeny (Fig. 1) in which all branch lengths were considered of equal length (Purvis and Rambaut, 1995). Analyses of independent contrasts were conducted by multiple regressions through the origin (Felsenstein, 1985).

III. RESULTS

A. EVOLUTIONARY LABILITY OF SONG CHARACTERISTICS

Song characters were more labile than morphological traits (Mann-Whitney U-test: $Z = -2.45$, $P = 0.01$). The mean K value for song characters was 0.585 while for morphological characters it was 0.809. The K values closer to 1 indicate higher phylogenetic signal (Blomberg et al., 2003).

Although K values were lower for song characters, the majority of them showed significant phylogenetic signal when analyzed individually, as did all the principal components that we studied: song complexity, pitch1, and pitch2. When the variation of temporal, structural, and frequency variables were compared, a significant difference in variation was found between types of variables ($F_{2,\ 24} = 13.56$; $P < 0.001$). The *post hoc* Tukey test showed that the CV of frequency variables (mean CV = 27%) was significantly lower than the CV of temporal (mean CV = 81%) and structural variables (mean CV = 84%; $P < 0.001$ for both comparisons), which did not differ significantly from each other ($P > 0.9$). Thus, song frequency characters are more conserved between warbler species than temporal and structural ones.

B. MORPHOLOGICAL CONSTRAINTS

Our initial hypotheses predicted that frequency characteristics could be affected by both the bird's overall body size and also by beak shape. Thus, we conducted stepwise regressions including these two predictors in the initial model. In the final model for the species data of pitch1, only body size remained in the model, showing the expected negative relationship ($F_{1,\ 28} = 6.53$, $P = 0.016$; β (S.E.) $= -0.43$ (0.17); $R^2 = 0.16$; Fig. 3). The same relationship was found in the analysis of independent contrasts ($F_{1,\ 28} = 5.97$, $P = 0.021$; β (S.E.) $= -0.49$ (0.20); $R^2 = 0.14$; Fig. 3). The exclusion of beak shape in these analyses was not due to collinearity with body size (tolerance > 0.95, FIV < 1.10).

Similarly, in the analysis of pitch2, the final model also included body size, after dropping beak shape for lack of significance ($F_{1,\ 28} = 5.75$, $P = 0.02$; β (S.E.) $= -0.41$ (0.17); $R^2 = 0.14$). The analysis of independent contrasts confirmed this relationship ($F_{1,\ 28} = 4.47$, $P = 0.043$; β (S.E.) $= -0.47$ (0.26); $R^2 = 0.10$). Again, collinearity between independent variables was not a problem in the analyses (tolerance > 0.90, FIV < 1.10).

C. SEXUAL SELECTION

1. Size Dimorphism

In the species data set, we found a nonsignificant trend toward a positive relationship between sexual size dimorphism and song complexity ($F_{1,\ 27} = 3.10$, $P = 0.089$; β (S.E.) $= 0.32$ (0.18); $R^2 = 0.10$). In the regression of independent contrasts through the origin, this pattern disappeared entirely ($F_{1,\ 27} = 0.16$, $P = 0.68$; β (S.E.) $= 0.07$ (0.17); $R^2 = 0.03$).

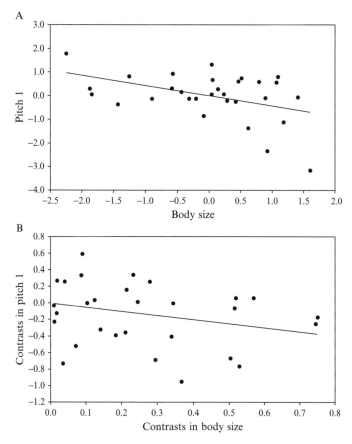

Fig. 3. Relationship between pitch1 and body size, as shown by linear regression using species data points (A) and linear regression through the origin using independent contrasts (B). See text for statistics.

2. Latitude

Midlatitude was positively, but not significantly related to song complexity in the species data set ($F_{1, 28} = 2.71$, $P = 0.11$; β (S.E.) = 0.030 (0.018); $R^2 = 0.05$; Fig. 4). However, the analysis of contrasts by means of linear regression through the origin showed a significant relationship in the same direction ($F_{1, 28} = 6.59$, $P = 0.016$; β (S.E.) = 0.032 (0.012); $R^2 = 0.16$; Fig. 4). Evolutionary transitions to higher latitudes have thus been followed by increases in song complexity. Body size was not significantly related to song complexity either in species data or contrasts, and was dropped from the models.

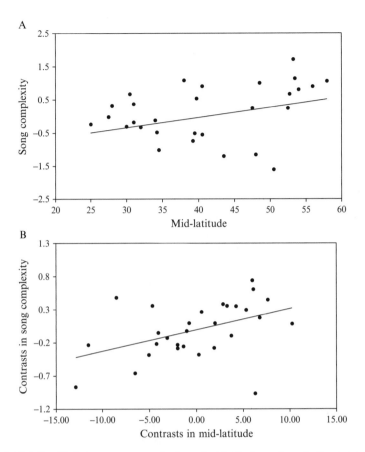

Fig. 4. Relationship between song complexity and midlatitude, as shown by linear regression using species data points (A) and linear regression through the origin using independent contrasts (B). See text for statistics.

D. HABITAT ACOUSTIC ADAPTATION

As predicted, the tarsus/beak ratio, an ecomorphological correlate of habitat use, was negatively related to pitch2 ($F_{1,\ 28} = 4.42$, $P = 0.045$; β (S.E.) $= -0.37$ (0.17); $R^2 = 0.10$; Fig. 5). However, the analysis of contrasts did not confirm this relationship ($F_{1,\ 28} = 0.21$, $P = 0.64$; β (S.E.) $= -0.09$ (0.20); $R^2 = 0.01$; Fig. 5).

We have previously shown (see Section III.B) that pitch2 is also affected by body size. Including the two predictors in a single model strengthens both relationships (overall model: $F_{1,\ 27} = 5.95$, $P = 0.007$, $R^2 = 0.25$; body size:

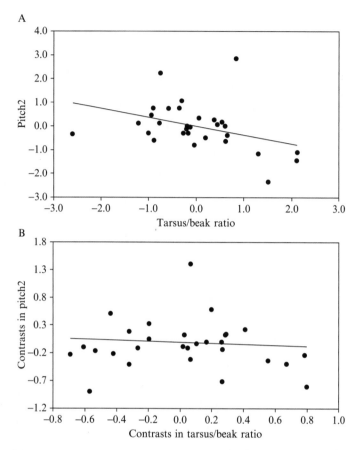

Fig. 5. Relationship between pitch2 and tarsus/beak ratio, as shown by linear regression using species data points (A) and linear regression through the origin using independent contrasts (B). See text for statistics.

β (S.E.) = -0.41 (0.16); tarsus/beak ratio: β (S.E.) = -0.37 (0.16)). When independent contrasts are analyzed, the effect of tarsus/beak ratio is dropped, and only body size remains in the model.

E. CHARACTER DISPLACEMENT

We did not find larger differences in frequency (pitch1: $N = 8$, $Z = 1.06$, $P = 0.28$; pitch2: $N = 8$, $Z = -0.35$, $P = 0.72$) or song complexity ($N = 8$, $Z = 0.35$, $P = 0.72$) between sympatric than between allopatric species.

IV. Discussion

Previous comparative analyses have shown that the evolution of bird song is driven by a series of different selective pressures, both adaptive and nonadaptive (Read and Weary, 1992). Bird song is a complex set of multiple characters, and each of them is expected to be influenced by different selective pressures (Gil and Gahr, 2002). Our analysis of the song of 30 species of *Phylloscopus* warblers confirms previous studies in other bird groups in showing that phylogenetic drive, acoustic adaptation to the habitat, sexual selection, and morphological constraints have all played a role in shaping different aspects of the song of these species as we hear them today. Let us consider each of these mechanisms in turn.

A. Speciation and Differentiation

Ecological divergence between species of this group is not large (Price et al., 2000), and the extremely high number of species seems to have evolved through multiple invasions and dispersal events, but with limited habitat and niche specialization (Price et al., 2000; Richman, 1996). Detailed molecular analysis of mitochondrial DNA and amplified fragment length polymorphism (AFLP) markers within the greenish warbler superspecies (*Phylloscopus trochiloides*) shows that the formation of genetically isolated species in this group can be best explained by gradual dispersion and divergence in song characteristics (Irwin et al., 2005; Irwin et al., 2001). These data show that increased selection for song complexity following dispersal toward more Northern latitudes has led to reproductive isolation and formation of new species.

We found substantial phylogenetic signal in song characteristics, with lower among-species variance for frequency traits than structural or temporal characteristics. A similar conclusion was reached in a previous study in *Phylloscopus*, using a smaller sample size (Liou, L.W., Tiainen, J., Higuchi, H., Richman, A.D., and Price, T.D., unpublished: "Song variation in the genus *Phylloscopus*"). Studies in other taxa also find significant phylogenetic signal in song variables, but studies differ in whether temporal or frequency characters are those which are better preserved.

For instance, in the herons, an evolutionarily very distant group, the largest phylogenetic information was contained in vocal traits that were not subjected to habitat adaptation processes (McCracken and Sheldon, 1997). However, since frequency components are highly dependent on morphology (see Section III), it is not surprising that these vocal characteristics are those that contain a higher phylogenetic signal. In the case of *Phylloscopus*, this pattern is expected because changes in body size have been shown to appear at the very start of the radiation, in the deepest part of the tree, with modifications of beak shape following shortly thereafter (Richman, 1996). A study on the song of *Regulus* warblers compared the phylogenetic signal of song characteristics that are present in birds that have been reared in acoustic isolation (Kaspar-Hauser birds) with that of signals that are due to learning (Päckert et al., 2003). Despite the rather arbitrary distinction (Kaspar-Hauser birds were not available for all species), the study suggests that higher phylogenetic signal is contained in unlearnt that in learned characters (Päckert et al., 2003). Similarly, in Paruline warblers, details of the fine note structure had a higher phylogenetic signal than song structure (van Buskirk, 1997).

In contrast, Price and Lanyon (2002) found that temporal components were more phylogenetically informative than frequency components in the Neotropical Oropendolas (suboscine Passerines). However, the authors selected characters that were judged to be phylogenetically informative a priori, and thus it is difficult to compare their results with studies in which no previous selection of variables is performed.

B. HABITAT ADAPTATION

In the absence of good quality habitat selection data, we used an ecomorphological correlate of habitat, the tarsus/beak ratio, as an index of habitat selection (Price, 1991; Richman and Price, 1992). Data from the Himalayan leaf warbler guild shows that increases in this ratio have coevolved with changes in the use of coniferous trees (Richman and Price, 1992): species with high tarsus/beak ratios are more prone to use short understory vegetation and deciduous trees, whereas species with low ratios will be more frequently found foraging in taller coniferous trees. Sound transmission characteristics are expected to differ dramatically between these habitats, favoring low frequencies in leafy, understory habitats (Badyaev and Leaf, 1997; Morton, 1975; Wiley, 1991).

As expected, we found that tarsus/beak ratio was negatively related to pitch2, indicating that species with relatively large tarsus and a small beak in relation to their size, and thus preferring understory habitats, have songs with comparatively lower emphasized and minimum frequencies (cf. Badyaev and Leaf, 1997). However, this relationship was not confirmed when correcting for common descent, suggesting that the above relationship could be driven by the bias of a subgroup of highly related species.

Similar relationships have been found for the New World Parulid warblers, where species living in deciduous forests had songs with lower frequencies than those using conifers (van Buskirk, 1997).

Interestingly, the beak/tarsus ratio was correlated with pitch2 and not with pitch1. This is in agreement with a recent meta-analysis in which the strongest effect of habitat on song was detected in the emphasized frequencies, much more strongly than in the maximum frequency (Boncoraglio and Saino, 2007). Despite maximum and minimum frequencies being strongly correlated, our principal component analyses separated the highest contribution of these two measurements in two distinct, uncorrelated components. The uncoupling of maximum frequency and bandwidth in pitch1 and minimum and emphasized frequency in pitch2 suggests that separate mechanisms are responsible for these two components. Indeed, physiological studies have shown that the left and right sides of the syrinx can contribute differently to song bandwidth, with each side specialized in a given frequency band (Suthers, 2004; Suthers et al., 1999). See the next section for additional evidence for dissociation between maximum and minimum frequencies.

The acoustic adaptation of song between different habitats has been shown to explain subspecific differences in song in *Melospiza melodia* (Patten et al., 2004), contributing to reproductive isolation in an area of sympatry. However, our results suggest that selection for songs with optimal sound transmission in populations expanding into new habitats has not considerably contributed to song differentiation and reproductive isolation.

C. MORPHOLOGICAL CORRELATES

We found a negative relationship between both components of frequency (pitch1 and pitch2) and body size. This pattern corroborates previous studies on a large diversity of avian species which report similarly negative relationships between body mass and song frequency, although the slope of this relationship depends on the avian group that is being considered (Ryan and Brenowitz, 1985; Tubaro and Mahler, 1998; Wallschläger, 1980). Examining the graph for pitch1 (Fig. 3), we can see that in the genus *Phylloscopus*, small-bodied species consistently lack low frequencies, suggesting that low frequencies are constrained when the body size is small. This is in contrast to the larger study of Ryan and Brenowitz (1985), in which the general pattern suggests that large species are limited in the production of high-pitched sounds.

Body size can be subject to directional sexual or natural selection (Endler, 1986; Trivers, 1972) and, thus, such selective regimes could force song characteristics to trail along because of correlated change (Price and Langen, 1992). A major divergence in body size has been found at the root of the phylogenetic tree of *Phylloscopus* (Richman, 1996), suggesting that divergence for this characteristic had a determinant role in the evolution of the song in this group very early in their evolutionary history. Our data, thus, suggest that a correlated change in song frequency must have taken place from the onset of the evolution of this group.

Another morphological correlate that was examined in relationship to song frequency characteristics was beak shape; however, we found no evidence for beak shape to limit overall frequency patterns in the leaf warblers. Podos (2001) has found that evolutionary transitions toward deeper beaks in *Geospiza* finches are negatively associated with a measure of vocal agility, namely the capacity to produce quick trills encompassing a wide frequency range. This suggests that selection on beak morphology as a response to seed availability may have driven vocal characteristics during evolution, probably reinforcing prezygotic isolation and speeding up speciation processes. Similar trills are typical of some *Phylloscopus* species (e.g., Bonelli's, Wood warbler, etc.; Martens, 1980), so we do not discard the idea that beak shape may limit some trill performance measurements in some species.

D. SEXUAL SELECTION

We used two surrogates of intensity of sexual selection: size dimorphism and midlatitude. Of these two, only the expected positive relationship between midlatitude and song complexity was confirmed when controlling for common descent. This relationship shows that transitions to Northern latitudes have coevolved with increases in song complexity, the same pattern that has been found for a set of different populations and species included in the greenish warbler superspecies (Irwin, 2000; Irwin et al., 2001).

Furthermore, a previous comparative analysis on 165 species of birds provides similar evidence in showing that song complexity is positively related to migratory behavior (Read and Weary, 1992), which is itself a very good proxy of midlatitude (Newton and Dale, 1996). The interpretation of this pattern is not straightforward, since an increase in midlatitude involves a large series of changes in life history traits, and it is difficult to single out the most likely causal factor. Catchpole (1980, 1982) has argued that high latitude, migratory species have less time than resident species to obtain a territory and mate, and thus are subjected to higher levels of sexual selection. In agreement with this, extra-pair paternity rates are positively related to synchronous breeding and migratory distance, two traits that increase with increasing latitude (Spottiswoode and Møller, 2004).

Our measure of song complexity, encompassing increases in song length, versatility, and repertoire size, would suggest that species living in more Northern latitudes have developed more complex song repertoires. Additionally, Slater (1981) has argued that the two modes of sexual selection, male–male competition and mate choice, select for different song characteristics, the former favoring shorter songs which are more quickly perceived and used in countersinging by males. Although a specific test of this hypothesis is still lacking, a recent study in a *Sylvia* warbler provides some evidence by comparing two populations differing in latitude and migratory behavior (Collins et al., 2009). To the extent that this song divergence due to the two modes of sexual selection is real, our results could be interpreted in the same sense, namely an effect of mate attraction rather than male–male competition on song complexity.

Do the two modes of sexual selection correlate with latitude, or is this true just for mate choice? It is difficult to answer this question in the absence of more direct data, but some evidence does show that these two pressures may not correlate with each other. For instance, populations of the greenish warbler living in Northern latitudes have much lower densities than those in the south (Irwin, 2000). Although density should be a close correlate of the strength of male–male competition, intersexual selection for signals that attract females may be stronger at lower densities (Irwin, 2000).

However, not all studies are unanimous in finding a relationship between sexual selection and song complexity. A study relating levels of extra-pair paternity to song repertoire size in a large sample of species found a lack of support for this hypothesis (Garamszegi and Møller, 2004). This lack of relationship is reminiscent of the low power of song repertoire size as a predictor of reproductive success in many field studies (Byers and Kroodsma, 2009). Although the positive relationship between repertoire size and pairing success is strong in some species (e.g., Buchanan and Catchpole, 1997), it is remarkably absent in many others (e.g., Byers and Kroodsma, 2009; Gil and Slater, 2000a; Gil et al., 2007), questioning the current adaptive value of a trait that may have been used by sexual selection in the past (for evidence of temporal heterogeneity in the value of repertoire size for sexual selection, see Forstmeier and Leisler, 2004).

E. CHARACTER DISPLACEMENT

We did not find evidence for a reinforcement of song differences (character displacement) across the genus. Differences in song were similar for allopatric and sympatric pairs of species. Although the sample size of this test was small, a similar lack of character displacement was found in the secondary contact zone of two morphs of the greenish warbler superspecies (Irwin, 2000). In their contact area in central Siberia, the difference between songs of the two morphs (*Phylloscopus plumbeitarsus* and *P. viridanus*) can be explained by the progressive change accumulated through evolutionary time along two South–North axes, and there seems to be no added differentiation that could be explained by character displacement.

In contrast, a study on antbird acoustics (Thamnophilidae, suboscine Passeriformes) found evidence for higher differences in temporal and pitch characteristics of songs between sympatric than allopatric species (Seddon, 2005). Although the evidence is too scant to venture an explanation, future studies should consider whether greater selection for character displacement could be explained by the absence of song learning in the suboscines.

F. GENERAL PATTERN OF SONG EVOLUTION

Bird song is a remarkably difficult phenomenon to capture in quantitative measurements (Kroodsma, 1977), and thus our analysis can only attempt to explain some general patterns. Large species-specific differences in song content and overall syllable composition are probably due to stochastic events linked to colonization processes. In 1983, Gerhardt Thielcke proposed that the evolution of song in the common chiffchaff superspecies was due to colonization events by birds that had not properly crystallized their song (Thielcke, 1983). He reached this conclusion after finding that the song of common chiffchaff males that had been hand-reared in acoustic isolation resembled that of the Iberian and Canary islands chiffchaffs (*Phylloscopus ibericus* and *P. canariensis*). He proposed that such a mechanism (*Lernentzug:* withdrawal of learning) could be at the base of song differentiation between subspecies and song evolution in islands.

We can assume that the high evolutionary lability of midlatitude distribution in the genus *Phylloscopus* (Price et al., 1997) is an indication of the high frequency of dispersal events along North–South axes, and this is expected to have led to frequent and progressive degrees of allopatry where speciation can occur (Irwin et al., 2001, 2005). *Phylloscopus* warblers need to learn their songs (Schubert, 1976; Thielcke, 1983), and thus haphazard dispersal of song variants plus song learning by males and females could lead to new populations having distinctive songs and being isolated from each other (Lachlan and Servedio, 2004).

Although we cannot answer the question of why a given species sings a given syllable repertoire, we can offer some explanation about species differences in more quantitative estimates of song (Fig. 6). Thus, our study suggests that song frequency characteristics have coevolved with likely adaptive changes in body size (Gaston, 1974). Differences in minimum and emphasized peak frequencies show a relationship with a morphological character related to microhabitat choice, but this relationship disappears when controlling for common descent, suggesting that song is not adapted to sound transmission characteristics of specific habitats.

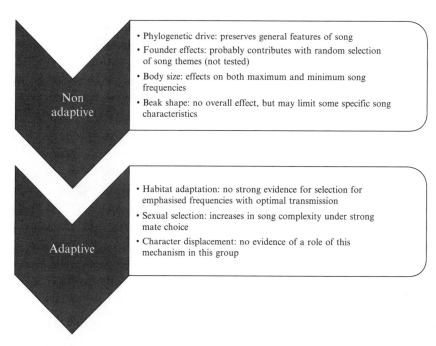

FIG. 6. List of different mechanisms that are likely to have influenced the evolution of song in the *Phylloscopus* warblers.

Song complexity, a wide-ranging measurement encompassing temporal and structural sound complexity estimates, is best explained by breeding latitude. We interpret this relationship as a correlate of increased sexual selection by mate choice toward more Northern latitudes. Thus, superimposed upon haphazard selection of themes, selective pressures for higher song elaboration in areas of high sexual selection, and correlative change in song brought about by natural selection of body size, would have lead to the diversity of songs that are found within the genus *Phylloscopus*.

Acknowledgments

We thank Trevor Price, who allowed us to examine an unpublished manuscript by Liu and coauthors, which tested some of the ideas of this study, and which was at the base of this research. Robert Prys-Jones and Katerina Cook at the bird collection of the British Museum kindly allowed access to the Tring bird skin collection, where the morphological data were taken. Richard Ranft provided recordings of some species from the British National Sound Archive. Rafael Márquez at the Fonoteca Zoologica of the Museo Nacional de Ciencias Naturales (Madrid, Spain) allowed access to commercial recordings held in the sound library. Peter Slater, Pablo Tubaro, Jose Luis Copete, and an anonymous referee provided valuable

MORPHOLOGICAL DATA OBTAINED FROM SKINS OF THE BRITISH MUSEUM OF NATURAL HISTORY

Species	Sample size		Wing length		Tail length		Tarsus length		Beak length		Beak width		Beak depth	
	Males	Females	Male	Female	Male	Female	Male	Female	Male	Female	Male	Female	Male	Female
Phylloscopus affinis	5	5	56.2 (1.8)	55.4 (4.8)	43.6 (4.4)	42.6 (3.6)	17.4 (0.9)	17.9 (0.8)	12.22 (0.17)	12.71 (0.3)	3.49 (0.33)	3.35 (0.23)	2.55 (0.11)	2.55 (0.2)
Phylloscopus bonelli	6	4	63 (0.9)	61.3 (1.3)	46.2 (2.4)	46.5 (1.8)	16.8 (1.1)	16.7 (0.7)	12.41 (0.76)	12.85 (0.26)	3.82 (0.2)	3.51 (0.05)	2.71 (0.13)	2.63 (0.23)
Phylloscopus borealis	5	5	65.6 (1.6)	64.8 (2.6)	46.4 (2.5)	44.4 (2.3)	18 (1.2)	18.2 (0.5)	14.24 (0.41)	12.83 (1.17)	4.21 (0.33)	4 (0.11)	3.06 (0.14)	3.25 (0.2)
Phylloscopus canariensis	5	5	51.6 (2.3)	49.8 (2.3)	46.4 (1.7)	43.8 (1.3)	17.3 (1.6)	17.8 (1.4)	12.8 (0.47)	12.7 (0.84)	3.63 (0.42)	3.74 (0.26)	2.72 (0.21)	2.89 (0.21)
Phylloscopus chloronotus	5	5	49.6 (3.8)	48.2 (2)	38.4 (2.9)	33.4 (2.2)	15.5 (1.2)	14.7 (1.1)	10.56 (0.58)	9.57 (0.66)	3.21 (0.14)	3.24 (0.26)	2.31 (0.19)	2.25 (0.17)
Phylloscopus collybita	5	5	59.4 (1.4)	55 (1.9)	47.2 (1.3)	43 (1.5)	17.2 (1.9)	16.8 (0.4)	11.73 (0.32)	11.63 (0.26)	3.34 (0.32)	3.42 (0.37)	2.57 (0.19)	2.53 (0.12)
Phylloscopus coronatus	5	5	62.4 (1.9)	60.6 (2)	46.8 (1.3)	45 (3)	15.7 (0.3)	16.2 (1.1)	13.89 (0.57)	13.49 (0.35)	3.88 (0.27)	4.42 (0.41)	3.32 (0.2)	3.15 (0.06)
Phylloscopus fuscatus	5	5	59.6 (4.3)	56.2 (2.8)	46.8 (3.6)	45.2 (2.9)	20.9 (2.4)	20.7 (1.4)	12.51 (0.51)	12.81 (0.93)	3.39 (0.34)	3.69 (0.32)	2.64 (0.18)	2.66 (0.11)
Phylloscopus griseolus	7	3	62.5 (2.2)	62 (3.7)	47.9 (3.3)	48 (4.4)	19.4 (0.9)	19.3 (0.7)	13.57 (0.98)	13.22 (1.01)	3.42 (0.31)	3.43 (0.11)	2.9 (0.25)	2.54 (0.32)
Phylloscopus humei	5	5	55.6 (2.2)	53.4 (3.4)	40.8 (3.2)	37.6 (3.3)	17.3 (0.5)	16.6 (0.7)	10.73 (0.43)	10.8 (0.83)	2.9 (0.27)	3.43 (0.36)	2.34 (0.09)	2.35 (0.21)
Phylloscopus ibericus	5	5	59.4 (2.2)	53.8 (2)	45.4 (1.2)	41.8 (1.5)	18 (0.9)	16.2 (1.2)	12.24 (0.85)	12.07 (0.61)	3.51 (0.28)	3.49 (0.35)	2.66 (0.19)	2.7 (0.09)
Phylloscopus ijimae	1		62.0 (n/a)	64.0 (n/a)	42.0 (n/a)	45.0 (n/a)	15.3 (n/a)	18.1 (n/a)	15.1 (n/a)	15.7 (n/a)	4.8 (n/a)	4.7 (n/a)	3.09 (n/a)	3.21 (n/a)
Phylloscopus inornatus	5	5	55.2 (1.1)	52.6 (3)	39 (1)	36.2 (2.8)	16.3 (0.4)	16.8 (1.1)	11.36 (0.39)	10.54 (0.21)	3.23 (0.17)	3.16 (0.37)	2.37 (0.23)	2.37 (0.12)
Phylloscopus maculipennis	5	5	48.6 (2.2)	47.4 (2.9)	33.2 (1.7)	32.2 (1.8)	17.6 (1.2)	16.3 (1)	10.14 (0.61)	10.06 (0.77)	3.11 (0.25)	3.28 (0.28)	2.26 (0.15)	2.32 (0.17)
Phylloscopus magnirostris	6	4	67.5 (1.7)	67.3 (2.7)	49.4 (0.9)	49.5 (1.3)	17.6 (0.8)	17.7 (1.2)	14.74 (0.92)	14.34 (0.53)	4.23 (0.35)	4.61 (0.28)	3.31 (0.32)	3.32 (0.3)
Phylloscopus nitidus	5	5	62.2 (1.1)	59 (1.9)	46.8 (1.3)	43.6 (1.6)	17.9 (1)	16.6 (0.5)	12.67 (0.92)	12.51 (0.65)	3.71 (0.37)	3.6 (0.39)	2.92 (0.43)	2.92 (0.11)
Phylloscopus occipitalis	5	5	65.2 (3.5)	62.4 (2.3)	46.8 (2.9)	43 (1)	16.9 (1.3)	17 (1.1)	14.01 (0.31)	13.07 (0.65)	4.26 (0.51)	3.91 (0.5)	3.06 (0.13)	3.03 (0.28)
Phylloscopus orientalis	5	5	66.6 (1.4)	63.6 (1.2)	47.4 (2)	44.6 (0.9)	17.4 (1)	16.7 (0.9)	12.6 (0.26)	12.47 (0.43)	3.63 (0.32)	3.65 (0.27)	2.73 (0.14)	2.75 (0.15)
Phylloscopus plumbeitarsus	5	5	58.4 (2.9)	55.2 (2.2)	44.2 (2)	40.8 (1.5)	17 (0.6)	15.9 (0.9)	12.55 (0.1)	12.81 (0.48)	3.66 (0.35)	4.16 (0.24)	2.86 (0.19)	2.93 (0.28)
Phylloscopus proregulus	5	5	52.6 (1.4)	48.2 (1.3)	37.8 (1.7)	34.6 (1.4)	15 (1.5)	15.7 (1)	10.38 (0.5)	9.99 (0.52)	3.11 (0.29)	2.88 (0.18)	2.31 (0.11)	2.27 (0.18)
Phylloscopus pulcher	5	5	56.2 (2.4)	54 (3.3)	40.2 (2.3)	39.2 (2.3)	16.7 (0.5)	17.4 (1.9)	12.16 (0.34)	12.08 (0.9)	3.64 (0.33)	3.69 (0.2)	2.56 (0.21)	2.56 (0.23)
Phylloscopus reguloides	5	5	58.8 (2.8)	56.8 (3.7)	43.2 (1.7)	41.6 (2.3)	16.4 (1)	16.2 (0.9)	12.38 (0.37)	11.95 (0.55)	4.02 (0.28)	4.31 (0.15)	2.79 (0.07)	2.86 (0.17)
Phylloscopus schwarzi	5	5	63.6 (2.6)	58.4 (4.1)	52 (2.4)	49 (5.4)	20.6 (1)	19.5 (1.1)	12.81 (0.74)	12.73 (0.48)	4.07 (0.25)	3.89 (0.17)	3.4 (0.17)	3.41 (0.19)
Phylloscopus sibilatrix	5	5	72.6 (3.4)	69.2 (1.8)	47.6 (2.3)	44 (1)	16.6 (1.1)	17 (0.5)	12.71 (1.4)	12.98 (0.4)	3.86 (0.38)	3.89 (0.22)	2.84 (0.1)	2.82 (0.14)
Phylloscopus sindianus	5	5	58 (2.6)	51.8 (1.3)	46.2 (2.3)	44.6 (0.6)	16.4 (1.1)	16.5 (0.5)	11.37 (0.32)	11.14 (0.78)	3.04 (0.13)	3.05 (0.26)	2.36 (0.19)	2.42 (0.19)
Phylloscopus tenellipes	6	4	61.4 (1.3)	57.5 (0.6)	44.2 (1.8)	41.5 (2.1)	17.2 (0.7)	17.6 (0.6)	13.66 (0.48)	13.6 (0.6)	4.28 (0.22)	4.14 (0.14)	3.25 (0.27)	3.17 (0.15)
Phylloscopus trochiloides	5	5	62.8 (2.3)	57.8 (2.8)	50.2 (3.2)	46.2 (1.3)	17.4 (1.4)	16.9 (1.1)	12.86 (0.29)	12.21 (0.52)	3.57 (0.26)	3.7 (0.24)	2.84 (0.25)	2.81 (0.17)
Phylloscopus trochilus	5	5	66.4 (1.2)	62.4 (3)	48.8 (2.2)	44.2 (3.7)	19.6 (0.8)	18.9 (0.4)	12.29 (0.31)	12.15 (0.95)	3.13 (0.16)	3.3 (0.06)	2.71 (0.23)	2.75 (0.18)
Phylloscopus tytleri	5	5	56.4 (1.2)	55.6 (2.3)	38.2 (2.1)	38.2 (2.3)	16.3 (1.3)	16.2 (1.1)	12.79 (0.37)	12.2 (0.81)	3.49 (0.23)	3.32 (0.25)	2.68 (0.17)	2.58 (0.14)
Phylloscopus viridanus	5	5	60 (2.5)	56.4 (1.6)	45.6 (1.6)	44 (0.8)	16.6 (1.1)	17.5 (1.7)	12.69 (0.52)	12.09 (0.39)	3.5 (0.51)	3.36 (0.22)	2.79 (0.19)	2.66 (0.16)

comments on an earlier version of the manuscript. BM was supported by Fundación Antorchas and a UNESCO-TWAS travel grant while in Madrid, and DG was recipient of a Ramon y Cajal fellowship from the Spanish Ministry of Science and Innovation while this research was conducted.

References

Badyaev, A.V., Leaf, E.S., 1997. Habitat associations of song characteristics in *Phylloscopus* and *Hippolais* warblers. Auk. 114, 40–46.

Badyaev, A.V., Young, R.L., Oh, K.P., Addison, C., 2008. Evolution on a local scale: developmental, functional, and genetic bases of divergence in bill form and associated changes in song structure between adjacent habitats. Evolution 62, 1951–1964.

Baker, K., 1997. Warblers of Europe, Asia and North Africa. Christopher Helm, London.

Baker, M.C., Gammon, D.E., 2008. Vocal memes in natural populations of chickadees: why do some memes persist and others go extinct? Anim. Behav. 75, 279–289.

Ballentine, B., 2006. Morphological adaptation influences the evolution of a mating signal. Evolution 60, 1936–1944.

Bensch, S., Irwin, D.E., Kvist, L., Akesson, S., 2006. Conflicting patterns of mitochondrial and nuclear DNA diversity in *Phylloscopus* warblers. Mol. Ecol. 15, 161–171.

Birkhead, T.R., Møller, A.P., 1998. Sperm competition and sexual selection. Academic Press, London.

Blomberg, S.P., Garland, T., Ives, A.R., 2003. Testing for phylogenetic signal in comparative data: behavioral traits are more labile. Evolution 57, 717–745.

Boncoraglio, G., Saino, N., 2007. Habitat structure and the evolution of bird song: a meta-analysis of the evidence for the acoustic adaptation hypothesis. Funct. Ecol. 21, 134–142.

Brumm, H., Naguib, M., 2009. Environmental acoustics and the evolution of bird song. Adv. Stud. Behav. 40, 1–33.

Buchanan, K.L., Catchpole, C.K., 1997. Female choice in the sedge warbler, *Acrocephalus schoenobaenus*: multiple cues from song and territory quality. Proc. R. Soc. B-Biol. Sci. 264, 521–526.

Byers, B.E., Kroodsma, D.E., 2009. Female mate choice and songbird song repertoires. Anim. Behav. 77, 13–22.

Catchpole, C.K., 1980. Sexual selection and the evolution of complex songs among European warblers of the genus *Acrocephalus*. Behaviour 74, 149–165.

Catchpole, C.K., 1982. The evolution of bird sounds in relation to mating and spacing behaviour. In: Kroodsma, D.E., Miller, E.H. (Eds.), Acoustic Communication in Birds. Vol. 1. Production, Perception and Design Features of Sounds. Academic Press, New York, NY, pp. 253–295.

Catchpole, C.K., Slater, P.J.B., 2008. Bird Song: Biological Themes and Variations. Cambridge University Press, Cambridge, UK.

Collins, S.A., de Kort, S.R., Perez-Tris, J., Telleria, J.L., 2009. Migration strategy and divergent sexual selection on bird song. Proc. R. Soc. B-Biol. Sci. 276, 585–590.

del Hoyo, J., Elliott, A., Christie, D.A., 2006. In: Handbook of the Birds of the World Vol. 11. Old World Flycatchers to Old World Warblers, Lynx Edicions, Barcelona.

Dunn, P.O., Whittingham, L.A., Pitcher, T.E., 2001. Mating systems, sperm competition, and the evolution of sexual dimorphism in birds. Evolution 55, 161–175.

Endler, J.A., 1986. Natural Selection in the Wild. Princeton University Press, Princeton, NJ.

Eriksson, D., Wallin, L., 1986. Male bird song attracts females: a field experiment. Behav. Ecol. Sociobiol. 19, 297–299.

Felsenstein, J., 1985. Phylogenies and the comparative method. Am. Nat. 125, 1–15.

Forstmeier, W., Leisler, B., 2004. Repertoire size, sexual selection, and offspring viability in the great reed warbler: changing patterns in space and time. Behav. Ecol. 15, 555–563.

Forstmeier, W., Bourski, O.V., Leisler, B., 2001. Habitat choice in *Phylloscopus* warblers: the role of morphology, phylogeny and competition. Oecologia 128, 566–576.

Forstmeier, W., Kempenaers, B., Meyer, A., Leisler, B., 2002. A novel song parameter correlates with extra-pair paternity and reflects male longevity. Proc. R. Soc. B-Biol. Sci. 269, 1479–1485.

Garamszegi, L.Z., Møller, A.P., 2004. Extrapair paternity and the evolution of bird song. Behav. Ecol. 15, 508–519.

Gaston, A.J., 1974. Adaptation in the genus *Phylloscopus*. Ibis 116, 432–450.

Gil, D., Gahr, M., 2002. The honesty of bird song: multiple constraints for multiple traits. Trends Ecol. Evol. 17, 133–141.

Gil, D., Slater, P.J.B., 2000a. Multiple song repertoire characteristics in the willow warbler (*Phylloscopus trochilus*): correlations with female choice and offspring viability. Behav. Ecol. Sociobiol. 47, 319–326.

Gil, D., Slater, P.J.B., 2000b. Song organisation and singing patterns of the willow warbler *Phylloscopus trochilus*. Behaviour 137, 759–782.

Gil, D., Graves, J.A., Slater, P.J.B., 2007. Extra-pair paternity and song characteristics in the willow warbler *Phylloscopus trochilus*. J. Avian Biol. 38, 291–297.

Grant, B.R., Grant, P.R., 1996. Cultural inheritance of song and its role in the evolution of Darwin's finches. Evolution 50, 2471–2487.

Helbig, A.J., Martens, J., Seibold, I., Henning, F., Schottler, B., Wink, M., 1996. Phylogeny and species limits in the Palaearctic chiffchaff *Phylloscopus collybita* complex: mitochondrial genetic differentiation and bioacoustic evidence. Ibis 138, 650–666.

Irwin, D.E., 2000. Song variation in an avian ring species. Evolution 54, 998–1010.

Irwin, D.E., Bensch, S., Price, T.D., 2001. Speciation in a ring. Nature 409, 333–337.

Irwin, D.E., Bensch, S., Irwin, J.H., Price, T.D., 2005. Speciation by distance in a ring species. Science 307, 414–416.

Kokko, H., Brooks, R., McNamara, J.M., Houston, A.I., 2002. The sexual selection continuum. Proc. R. Soc. B-Biol. Sci. 269, 1331–1340.

Krebs, J.R., Ashcroft, R., Webber, M., 1978. Song repertoires and territory defence in the Great Tit. Nature 271, 539–542.

Kroodsma, D.E., 1977. Correlates of song organization among North-American wrens. Am. Nat. 111, 995–1008.

Lachlan, R.F., Servedio, M.R., 2004. Song learning accelerates allopatric speciation. Evolution 58, 2049–2063.

Lachlan, R.F., Slater, P.J.B., 2003. Song learning by chaffinches: how accurate, and from where? Anim. Behav. 65, 957–969.

Lachlan, R.F., Janik, V.M., Slater, J.B., 2004. The evolution of conformity-enforcing behaviour in cultural communication systems. Anim. Behav. 68, 561–570.

Laiolo, P., Tella, J.L., 2005. Habitat fragmentation affects culture transmission: patterns of song matching in Dupont's Lark. J. Appl. Ecol. 42, 1183–1193.

Leitner, S., Catchpole, C.K., 2007. Song and brain development in canaries raised under different conditions of acoustic and social isolation over two years. Dev. Neurobiol. 67, 1478–1487.

Lynch, A., Baker, A.J., 1993. A population memetics approach to cultural evolution in chaffinch song: meme diversity within populations. Am. Nat. 141, 597–620.

Mann, N.I., Slater, P.J.B., 1995. Song tutor choice by zebra finches in aviaries. Anim. Behav. 49, 811–820.

Mann, N.I., Dingess, K.A., Barker, F.K., Graves, J.A., Slater, P.J.B., 2009. A comparative study of song form and duetting in neotropical *Thryothorus* wrens. Behaviour 146, 1–43.

Martens, J., 1980. Lautäußerungen, verwandtschaftliche Beziehungen und Verbreitungs-geschichte asiatischer Laubsänger (Phylloscopus). Z. Tierpsychol. 22 (Suppl.), 71.

Martens, J., 1993. Lautäußerungen von Singvögel und die Entstehung neuer Arten. Forschungsmagazin der Johannes Gutenberg-Universität Mainz 9, 34–44.

McCracken, K.G., Sheldon, F.H., 1997. Avian vocalizations and phylogenetic signal. Proc. Natl. Acad. Sci. USA 94, 3833–3836.

McDonald, M.V., 1989. Function of song in Scott's seaside sparrow *Ammodramus maritimus peninsulae*. Anim. Behav. 38, 468–485.

Morton, E.S., 1975. Ecological sources of selection on avian sounds. Am. Nat. 109, 17–34.

Mountjoy, D.J., Lemon, R.E., 1991. Song as an attractant for male and female European starlings, and the influence of song complexity on their response. Behav. Ecol. Sociobiol. 28, 97–100.

Mundinger, P.C., 1995. Behaviour-genetic analysis of canary song: inter-strain differences in sensory learning, and epigenetic rules. Anim. Behav. 50, 1491–1511.

Newton, I., Dale, L., 1996. Relationship between migration and latitude among west European birds. J. Anim. Ecol. 65, 137–146.

Nordby, J.C., Campbell, S.E., Beecher, M.D., 1999. Ecological correlates of song learning in song sparrows. Behav. Ecol. 10, 287–297.

Olsson, U., Alström, P., Ericson, P.G.P., Sundberg, P., 2005. Non-monophyletic taxa and cryptic species: evidence from a molecular phylogeny of leaf-warblers (*Phylloscopus*, Aves). Mol. Phylogenet. Evol. 36, 261–276.

Päckert, M., Martens, J., Kosuch, J., Nazarenko, A.A., Veith, M., 2003. Phylogenetic signal in the song of crests and kinglets (Aves: *Regulus*). Evolution 57, 616–629.

Palacios, M.G., Tubaro, P.L., 2000. Does beak size affect acoustic frequencies in wood-creepers? Condor 102, 552–560.

Patten, M.A., Rotenberry, J.T., Zuk, M., 2004. Habitat selection, acoustic adaptation, and the evolution of reproductive isolation. Evolution 58, 2144–2155.

Podos, J., 1997. A performance constraint on the evolution of trilled vocalizations in a songbird family (Passeriformes: Emberizidae). Evolution 51, 537–551.

Podos, J., 2001. Correlated evolution of morphology and vocal signal structure in Darwin's finches. Nature 409, 185–188.

Price, T., 1991. Morphology and ecology of breeding warblers along an altitudinal gradient in Kashmir. Indian J. Anim. Ecol. 60, 643–664.

Price, T.D., 2007. Speciation in Birds. Roberts & Co., Greenwood Village.

Price, T., Langen, T., 1992. Evolution of correlated characters. Trends Ecol. Evol. 7, 307–310.

Price, J.J., Lanyon, S.M., 2002. Reconstructing the evolution of complex bird song in the oropendolas. Evolution 56, 1514–1529.

Price, T.D., Helbig, A.J., Richman, A.D., 1997. Evolution of breeding distributions in the old world leaf warblers (genus *Phylloscopus*). Evolution 51, 552–561.

Price, T., Lovette, I.J., Bermingham, E., Gibbs, H.L., Richman, A.D., 2000. The imprint of history on communities of North American and Asian warblers. Am. Nat. 156, 354–367.

Purvis, A., Rambaut, A., 1995. Comparative analysis by independent contrasts (CAIC): an Apple-Macintosh application for analyzing comparative data. Comput. Appl. Biosci. 11, 247–251.

Radesäter, T., Jakobsson, S., Andbjer, N., Bylin, A., Nyström, K., 1987. Song rate and pair formation in the willow warbler *Phylloscopus trochilus*. Anim. Behav. 35, 1645–1651.

Read, A.F., Weary, D.M., 1990. Sexual selection and the evolution of bird song: a test of the Hamilton-Zuk hypothesis. Behav. Ecol. Sociobiol. 26, 47–56.

Read, A.F., Weary, D.M., 1992. The evolution of bird song: comparative analyses. Philos. Trans. R. Soc. B 338, 165–187.

Richman, A.D., 1996. Ecological diversification and community structure in the old world leaf warblers (genus *Phylloscopus*): a phylogenetic perspective. Evolution 50, 2461–2470.

Richman, A.D., Price, T., 1992. Evolution of ecological differences in the Old World leaf warblers. Nature 355, 817–821.

Ryan, M.J., Brenowitz, E.A., 1985. The role of body size, phylogeny, and ambient noise in the evolution of bird song. Am. Nat. 126, 87–100.

Schubert, M., 1976. Das akustische Repertoire des Fitislaubsängers (*Phylloscopus t. trochilus*) und seine erblichen und durch Lernen erwobenen Bestandteile. Beitr. Vogelk. 22, 167–200.

Seddon, N., 2005. Ecological adaptation and species recognition drives vocal evolution in Neotropical suboscine birds. Evolution 59, 200–215.

Shutler, D., Weatherhead, P.J., 1990. Targets of sexual selection: song and plumage of wood warblers. Evolution 44, 1967–1977.

Siegel, S., Castellan, N.J., 1988. Nonparametric Statistics. McGraw Hill, New York, NY.

Slater, P.J.B., 1981. Chaffinch song repertoires: observations, experiments and a discussion of their significance. Z. Tierpsychol. 56, 1–24.

Slater, P.J.B., Ince, S.A., Colgan, P.W., 1980. Chaffinch song types: their frequencies in the population and distribution between repertoires of different individuals. Behaviour 75, 207–218.

Sokal, R.R., Rohlf, F.J., 1995. Biometry. Freeman, New York, NY.

Spottiswoode, C., Møller, A.P., 2004. Extrapair paternity, migration, and breeding synchrony in birds. Behav. Ecol. 15, 41–57.

Suthers, R.A., 2004. How birds sing and why it matters. In: Marler, P., Slabbekoorn, H. (Eds.), Nature's Music: The Science of Birdsong. Elsevier, San Diego, pp. 272–295.

Suthers, R., Goller, F., Pytte, C., 1999. The neuromuscular control of birdsong. Philos. Trans. R. Soc. B 29, 927–939.

Svensson, L., 1984. Identification Guide to European Passerines. Published by the author, Stockholm.

ten Cate, C., 2004. Birdsong and evolution. In: Marler, P., Slabbekoorn, H. (Eds.), Nature's Music: The Science of Birdsong. Elsevier, San Diego, pp. 296–317.

Thielcke, G., 1983. Entstanden Dialekte des Zilpzalps *Phylloscopus collybita* durch Lernentzug? J. Ornithol. 124, 333–368.

Thielcke, G., Linsenmair, K.E., 1963. Zur geographischen Variation des Gesanges des Zilpzalps, *Phylloscopus collybita*, in Mittel- und Südwesteuropa mit einem Vergleich des Gesanges des Fitis, *Phylloscopus trochilus*. J. Ornithol. 104, 372–402.

Trivers, R.L., 1972. Parental investment and sexual selection. In: Campbell, B. (Ed.), Sexual Selection and the Descent of Man. Aldine Publishing Company, Chicago, pp. 136–179.

Tubaro, P.L., Mahler, B., 1998. Acoustic frequencies and body mass in new world doves. Condor 100, 54–61.

van Buskirk, J., 1997. Independent evolution of song structure and note structure in American wood warblers. Proc. R. Soc. B-Biol. Sci. 264, 755–761.

Wallschläger, D., 1980. Correlation of song frequency and body weight in passerine birds. Experientia 36, 412.

White, G., 1789. The Natural History and Antiquities of Selborne. Bensley, London.

Wiley, R.H., 1991. Associations of song properties with habitats for territorial oscine birds of Eastern North America. Am. Nat. 138, 973–993.

A Review of Vocal Duetting in Birds

Michelle L. Hall

BEHAVIORAL ECOLOGY OF SEXUAL SIGNALS GROUP, MAX PLANCK INSTITUTE
FOR ORNITHOLOGY, VOGELWARTE RADOLFZELL, D-78315, GERMANY

I. Introduction

There have been over one hundred years of research on duetting, most focusing on the form and function of duetting, and less is known about other aspects of this unusual communication strategy (Farabaugh, 1982; Hall, 2004; Langmore, 1998; Thorpe, 1972; von Helversen, 1980). The accurately timed duets of Australian magpie-larks (*Grallina cyanoleuca*) were first described in the *Agricultural Gazette of New South Wales* more than a century before experimental demonstration of the value of precise duet timing in creating threatening territorial displays by signaling the stability of partnerships to territorial rivals (Fig. 1, Cobb, 1897; Hall and Magrath, 2007). In that time, studies focusing on the form of duets have revealed considerable diversity among species, not only in the temporal precision with which partners coordinate their songs to form duets, but also in the consistency with which they associate particular song types in duets, and many other aspects of duet structure (Logue, 2006; Mann et al., 2009; Thorpe, 1963). An increasing focus on the individual behavioral patterns that underlie this variety in duet structure, and how these differ between species and between the sexes, is informing understanding of duet function (Grafe et al., 2004; Logue et al., 2008; Wright and Dahlin, 2007). Most detailed studies on duet function reveal multiple functions of duetting within a species in different contexts (Grafe and Bitz, 2004b; Logue, 2007b; Marshall-Ball et al., 2006; Mennill and Vehrencamp, 2008; Sonnenschein and Reyer, 1983). However, while much is known about duet structure and function, its ontogeny, hormonal basis, and underlying neural structures remain poorly understood.

Duets comprise a vocalization initiated by one individual and answered by its partner such that their vocalizations overlap or alternate (see Glossary in Box 1). Distinguishing between pair-level aspects of duetting

67

0065-3454/09 $35.00
DOI: 10.1016/S0065-3454(09)40003-2

THE COMMON MUD-LARK OR PEE-WEE.

NATURAL SIZE.

(Also called Magpie Lark.)

FIG. 1. Long-standing and broad-ranging interest in duetting species is evidenced by this illustration of a pair of nesting Australian magpie-larks that appeared in the Agricultural Gazette of New South Wales in 1897 (original copy owned by the National Library of Australia). The illustration accompanied a detailed description of the accurately timed duets produced by magpie-larks, given in the context of descriptions of some snail-eating birds in an article on an agricultural pest, a sheep-fluke hosted by a snail (Cobb, 1897).

BOX 1

GLOSSARY

Song	
Call	Short, simple vocalization, usually in particular contexts such as alarm, flight, begging
Song	Vocalization advertising for mates and territory ownership, usually longer and more complex than calls
Phrase	Unit within a song, may be an element (uninterrupted trace on a sonogram) or a syllable (set of elements occurring together in a particular pattern)
Song initiating	Singing (nonduetting species), or producing the first phrase of a duet (duetting species)
Phrase type	Version of a phrase—the set of phrase types produced by one individual comprise its phrase type repertoire
Song type	Version of a song—the set of song types produced by one individual comprise its song type repertoire
Duetting	
Duet	Coordinated singing by two individuals so that their phrases alternate or overlap
Duet type	Particular combination of the phrase types or song types of two individuals – the set of duet types produced by a pair comprise their duet type repertoire
Song answering	Initiating a song in response to another individual to form a duet – the individual-level behavior resulting in duets
Reaction time	Time interval between the start of an individual's song/phrase and the start/end of its partner's preceding song/phrase
Answering rule	Consistent answering of a phrase type or song type in the partner's repertoire with a particular phrase type or song type from own repertoire—the individual-level behavior resulting in duet types

and the underlying individual behaviors, as well as distinguishing between those individual-level behaviors that occur in response to a partner and those that occur independently, is essential to understanding how and why duetting occurs. Songs that initiate duets are independent of the partner, but song answering represents a response to the partner that is coordinated to varying degrees with respect to timing and song type (Todt and Naguib, 2000). The timing and types of phrases within duets may likewise be independent of the partner (following an autonomous tempo and pattern), or adjusted to suit the timing and sequence of phrase types used by the partner (von Helversen, 1980). Thus, though duet initiators begin singing independently of their partner, they may respond to their partner over the course of the duet by modifying the timing or types of phrases they use (Whitford, 1996). The ontogeny of those behaviors that are independent of the partner, such as calls, songs, phrases, syntax, singing styles, etc., is likely to be similar to their ontogeny in nonduetting species. However, behaviors that occur in response to a partner, such as song answering, consistent reaction times, and consistent answering rules, are likely to have ontogenetic pathways unique to duetting species, and perhaps differing between the sexes. Likewise, the neural and hormonal bases of duetting can be separated into those components that are shared with nonduetting species, and those that underlie responsive behaviors distinct to duetting species. Understanding how the two individuals contributing to the duet differ in the extent to which they modify their singing pattern in response to their partner, and how that is affected by context, is necessary to understand the function of duetting, and the evolution of the individual behaviors that underlie duets.

Vocal interactions between duetting partners have many parallels with vocal interactions between countersinging male songbirds (Todt and Naguib, 2000). Both are interactive processes that involve time- and pattern-specific relationships among the exchanged signals (Todt and Naguib, 2000). Since song is a broadcast signal, males overlap or match the song types of conspecifics to direct aggressive signals at particular rivals (Vehrencamp et al., 2007). Conspecifics in the wider communication network may pay attention to the temporal and song type aspects of these vocal interactions to obtain information about status relationships between countersinging rivals (Logue and Forstmeier, 2008; Mennill et al., 2002; Naguib and Todt, 1997; Naguib et al., 1999). In general, the vocal interactions between duetting partners occur on a much faster timescale, and responding to a partner in duet requires that an individual is attentive, not only to when its partner begins singing, but also, for certain styles of duetting, to the timing and phrase types of its partner throughout the duet. Duets that involve individuals reacting to their partner in just fractions of a second demonstrate how attentive they are to when and what their partner is singing (von Helversen, 1980), with this information available, not only to the partner, but also to other conspecifics in the communication network.

Avian duetting has some similarities with duetting in other taxa. Insect duets are also characterized by extremely short latencies between calls with, for example, latencies of just 25 ms between the end of the male call and the start of the female call in phaneropterid bushcrickets (*Ancistrura nigrovittata*) (Dobler et al., 1994). However, while avian duets may be initiated by males or females, insect duets are usually formed by females replying to male calls with species-specific latencies that allow males and females to find one another for mating (Bailey, 2003). In an unusual case of duetting among anurans, female South African clawed frogs (*Xenopus laevis*) advertise their fertility with a rapping call to which males respond with an answering call and approach for mating (Tobias et al., 1998). Duetting birds share more ecological characteristics with duetting primates, which form long-term socially monogamous partnerships and defend territories (Mitani, 1987). Gibbon duets comprise long bouts of sex-specific phrases, and their coordination into duets takes time to develop in newly formed pairs (Geissmann, 2002; Maples et al., 1989), sharing with some avian duets a greater complexity in structure.

II. DUET STRUCTURE

Understanding duet structure is a fundamental first step, not only for defining duetting, but also for understanding many other aspects of this unusual communication strategy including its function. There is considerable variation both within and between species in how often individuals coordinate their songs with those of their partner to form duets, how precisely they do so, and in the types and sequences of vocalizations that they use in their duets. In eastern whipbirds (*Psophodes olivaceus*), males sing simple songs to which their partner sometimes rapidly replies with a different song (Fig. 2A, Rogers, 2005). Male–male pairs of lekking manakins (*Chiroxiphia* spp.) sing the same song virtually in unison as they display to attract females (Fig. 2B, Trainer et al., 2002; Duval, 2007b). In pheasant coucals (*Centropus phasianinus*), partners often sing simultaneously so that male and female songs overlap in time, though not in pitch, to form duets (Fig. 2C, Maurer et al., 2008). Australian magpie-larks also overlap their songs to form duets, but coordinate phrases within the duet so that male and female phrases alternate without overlap (Fig. 2D, Hall, 2006). In plain wrens (*Thryothorus modestus zeledoni*), males sing a series of introductory phrases, with a reply from their partner causing progression to a series of male and female phrases alternating in duet (Fig. 2E, Mann et al., 2003). Yellow-naped amazon (*Amazona auropalliata*) duets begin with male and female contact calls, and then progress through antiphonally given sex-specific calls (Fig. 2F, Wright and Dahlin, 2007). In white-crested laughing thrushes (*Garrulax leucolophus*), males and females each contribute multiple phrase types from their individual repertoire to each duet (Fig. 2G, Vencl and Soucek, 1976). In many species, solo songs are essentially unanswered duets, either because individual contributions to duets are similar to their solo songs (Fig. 2C and Dd), or because duets have introductory components that are also sung solo (Fig. 2E and F), so both duets and solo songs need to be examined to understand when and why partners coordinate their songs. Species where this is not the case, and partners never sing alone (Klenova et al., 2008), or use different repertoires for

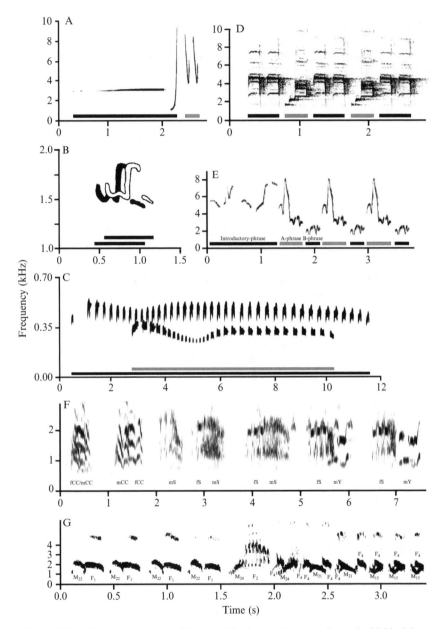

FIG. 2. Diversity in duet structure. Male contributions to duets are denoted with black bars, and female contributions with gray bars in (A)–(E). In (F) and (G), the letters M and F denote male and female phrases respectively, with different phrase types distinguished. (A) Eastern whipbird duet showing the male whistle and whipcrack that initiate duets, followed by the

solo and duet singing (Voigt et al., 2006), suggest either an extraordinary level of attentiveness to the initiator by the responding partner, or that initiators only begin singing when their partner is nearby and attentive.

A. COORDINATION OF TIMING

Duets are characterized by the temporal coordination of vocalizations between partners, so any attempts to explain the function and evolutionary significance of duetting depend on understanding which pair member is responsible for this coordination, its nature, how it is achieved, and what the consequences of such coordination are. Responding with rapid and consistent reaction times requires that individuals are very attentive to their partner's songs (Smith, 1994). In some species, individuals initiate their song in response to a song of their partner, but there is no further coordination, either because the song comprises a single phrase as in Eastern whipbirds (Fig. 2A, Rogers, 2005), or because the timing of subsequent phrases depends only on the timing of the singer's initial phrase and not on subsequent phrases of the partner as in, for example, pheasant coucals (Fig. 2C, Maurer et al., 2008), some barbets (Payne and Skinner, 1970), and rufous-and-white wrens (*Thryothorus rufalbus*) (Mennill and Vehrencamp, 2005). However, many duetting species have an additional level of temporal coordination, with partners coordinating the timing of phrases within their songs throughout the duet as in magpie-larks (Fig. 2D, Hall, 2006), plain

---

answering song of the female (taken from Fig. 1 in Rogers, 2005, with permission from http://www.publish.csiro.au/nid/91/issue/1013.htm). (B) Long-tailed manakin duet showing the overlapping "toledo" songs of the two males, the initiator shown in black and the answering song in white (taken from Fig. 1 in Trainer et al., 2002, with permission from Oxford University Press). (C) Pheasant coucal "scale call" duet showing the lower pitched call of the larger female (taken from Fig. 3A in Maurer et al., 2008, with permission from http://www.publish.csiro.au/nid/91/issue/4189.htm). (D) Australian magpie-lark duet with nonoverlapping male and female phrases that alternate repeatedly through the duet (taken from Fig. 1C in Hall, 2006, with permission from Brill). (E) Plain wren duet initiated by a distinct repertoire of male introductory phrases before progressing into the antiphonal cycling of female and male duet phrases (taken from Fig. 1 in Mann et al., 2003, with permission from the Cooper Ornithological Society). (F) Yellow-naped amazon duet starting with contact calls (CC) by both sexes and progressing through sex-specific scree (S) and yoohoo (Y) calls given antiphonally by males and females, showing shorter male reaction times (taken from Fig. 1 in Wright and Dahlin, 2007, with permission from Brill). (G) White-crested laughing thrush duet showing the sequence of different male (M) and female (F) phrase types used over the course of the duet (taken from Fig. 2 in Vencl and Soucek, 1976, with permission from Brill).

wrens (Fig. 2E, Mann et al., 2003), and black-bellied wrens (*Thryothorus fasciatoventris*) (Logue et al., 2008). The temporal structure of duets can therefore be examined quantitatively at two levels.

1. Song Answering

Temporal coordination of songs is the defining feature of duets (Farabaugh, 1982), but quantitative measurements have rarely been used to show how species that duet differ from those that do not, and how duets differ from solo songs within duetting species. Usually the distinction between duetting and nonduetting species is clear, because in many nonduetting species the female does not sing. However, when both sexes sing, their songs may occasionally overlap by chance. Unfortunately, studies on nonduetting species where both sexes sing typically describe male and female singing behavior independently and do not quantify the temporal relationship between partners' songs (Brunton and Li, 2006; Price et al., 2008). Greig and Pruett-Jones (2008) note simultaneous singing by two birds in response to an intruder's song in splendid fairy-wrens (*Malurus splendens melanotus*), but argue it is accidental rather than duetting though they did not demonstrate this quantitatively. Cooney and Cockburn (1995) quantified coordination between songs in superb fairy-wrens (*Malurus cyaneus*), reporting that females sang 60% of their songs in conjunction with other group members, initiating the interaction in 32% of those cases, but they did not consider superb fairy-wrens duetters. Clearly, in species where both sexes sing, it is necessary to formally quantify the relative timing of partners' songs to determine whether song overlap occurs more often than expected by chance.

Quantifying temporal aspects of vocal interactions, such as song overlap and reaction times, makes it possible to formally demonstrate nonrandom song overlap and close temporal coordination of songs, and distinguish between duetting and nonduetting species, and between duetting and solo singing. A simple way of assessing whether song overlap is more frequent than expected by chance is to compare the percentage of an individual's songs initiated while its partner is singing with the percentage of time that its partner spends singing, a method that has been used to show that male birds avoid singing during the songs of other birds (Ficken et al., 1974). For example, if a bird sings 10 songs in an hour, initiating 7 of these while its partner is silent and 3 while its partner is singing, then 30% of its songs overlap those of its partner. If its partner also sings 10 songs an hour, each 6 s long, and is thus spending 60 s singing in each hour, or 1.7% of its time singing, then song overlap is clearly nonrandom. However, if its partner sings 100 songs per hour, each 12 s long, and is thus singing 33% of the time, then song overlap occurs no more often than expected by chance. Nonrandom song overlap suggests that birds might be duetting, but could also arise if two individuals respond independently to the same external stimulus.

Quantifying fine-scale temporal coordination of songs by measuring reaction times (Thorpe, 1963), including all songs sung and not only "duets," avoids the potential confound of external stimuli, and provides stronger evidence of duetting by testing whether an individual sings in response to its partner. A histogram showing the distribution of intervals between the start time of an individual's songs and either the start or end of its partner's previous song will show a clear peak if it is singing nonrandomly with respect to its partner. For example, a histogram showing the distributions of reaction times of male and female Cocos flycatchers shows that females respond to male songs at a shorter and more consistent time interval than males respond to females (Fig. 3, Kroodsma et al., 1987). This example only shows duets, but including solo songs as well would allow quantitative distinguishing of duets and solos. Variability in reaction

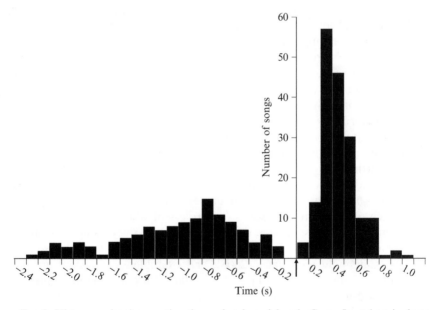

Fig. 3. Histogram showing reaction times of male and female Cocos flycatchers in duets (taken from Fig. 4 in Kroodsma et al., 1987, with permission from the Cooper Ornithological Society). The female usually initiates vocal interactions, the male contributes his song as hers fades, and then the female rapidly sings a second song. Time zero (marked by the arrow) is the time the terminal trill of the male song began, thus the first peak illustrates reaction times of the male responding to the first female song, and the second peak, reaction times of the female responding to the male song.

times (coefficient of variation of reaction times, $CV = 100 \times SD/mean$) can be used to distinguish duets from nonduets much as it is used to quantify precision within duets (Farabaugh, 1982; Levin, 1996a; Thorpe, 1963). Calculating reaction times from the end time of the initiating song to the start time of the answering song also quantifies song overlap (values less than zero), but coefficients of variation become meaningless when mean reaction times are close to zero. So for certain styles of duetting, reaction times are best calculated from start time to start time. Movements of the body, tail, and wings that can accompany vocal contributions to duets could also serve as visual stimuli to which partners respond (Todt and Fiebelkorn, 1980). Variation in reaction times has also been used to examine temporal aspects of vocal interactions between countersinging male birds. The distributions of time intervals between the start of a male nightingale's (*Luscinia megarhynchos*) songs and the start or end of the preceding song by a neighboring male reveal individual differences in singing strategies, with some males singing autonomously while others time their songs to overlap or alternate with the songs of nearby males (Hultsch and Todt, 1982). This approach could be extended to quantify temporal aspects of the multilevel vocal interactions occurring between counterduetting pairs by testing the relative importance in predicting the start time of an individual's song of (1) the time since it last sang, (2) the time since a territorial opponent last sang, and (3) the time since its partner last sang. Such an analysis would reveal similarities and differences between duetting and the song overlapping that characterizes countersinging interactions between some male birds (Todt and Naguib, 2000).

Vocal strategies often differ between the sexes and, in most duetting species, the majority of duets are formed by females answering the songs of their partners (Fig. 4). The number of duets and solo songs produced by the male and female in a pair is a consequence of their individual singing strategies—how often each of them answers their partner's songs, and how often each of them initiates songs (regardless of whether these songs are solos songs or duets, since that depends on their partner's singing strategy rather than their own). Females are less vocal than males in most bird species (Catchpole and Slater, 2008), and examples to the contrary are relatively infrequent (Brunton and Li, 2006; Illes and Yunes-Jimenez, 2009; Kroodsma et al., 1987; Price et al., 2008). However, females are often primarily responsible for duetting, since males initiate a majority of duets in most duetting species (Table I). Usually males also do some answering, but song answering is exclusively a female behavior in species like mohos (*Hypergerus atriceps*), white-bellied antbirds (*Myrmeciza longipes*), eastern whipbirds, Steere's liocichlas (*Liocichla steerii*), and warbling

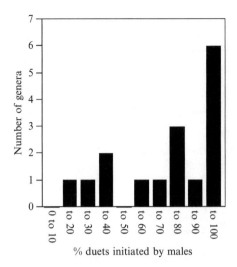

FIG. 4. Variation among genera in the percentage of duets formed by females answering their partner's songs. Histogram showing the distribution of percentages of duets initiated by males in 17 genera (32 species). On average, 71% of duets are initiated by males (based on 17 genera; 72% based on 32 species), and males initiate more than 50% of duets in 76% of genera and 84% of species (see Table I for species details).

antbirds (*Hypocnemis cantator*), where all duets are formed by females responding to the songs of their partners (Fedy and Stutchbury, 2005; Mays et al., 2006; Rogers, 2005; Seddon and Tobias, 2006; Slater et al., 2002). The percentage of duets initiated by one sex or the other is not a good measure of the propensity of the opposite sex to duet, as it does not consider the unanswered (solo) songs of either sex, and probably just reflects sex differences in song initiation rates. Instead, an individual's propensity to duet can be quantified both in relation to its partner's song initiations and in relation to its own song initiations (Farabaugh, 1982):

i. The percentage of its partner's songs that it answers to form duets (e.g., female responsiveness = 100 × male-initiated duets/(male solos + male-initiated duets).

ii. The percentage of its own songs sung as song answers (e.g., female songs sung as answers = 100 × male-initiated duets/(female solos + female-initiated duets + male-initiated duets).

For example, in white-bellied antbirds, males initiate 100% of all duets, females join 27% of male songs to form duets, and sing 56% of their songs as answers (Fedy and Stutchbury, 2005). Thus male and female vocal

TABLE I
PERCENTAGE OF DUETS INITIATED BY MALES

| Common name | Scientific name | Duets initiated by males (%) | | Source |
		Species[a]	Genus[b]	
Black swan	*Cygnus atratus*	75	75	Kraaijeveld and Mulder (2002)
Red-crowned crane	*Grus japonensis*	36	36	Klenova et al. (2008)
Cocos Flycatcher	*Nesotriccus ridgwayi*	14	14	Kroodsma et al. (1987)
Warbling antbird	*Hypocnemis cantator*	100	100	Seddon and Tobias (2006)
White-bellied antbird	*Myrmeciza longipes*	100	100	Fedy and Stutchbury (2005)
Purple-crowned fairy-wren	*Malurus coronatus*	76	76	Hall and Peters (2008)
White-browed robin-chat	*Cossypha heuglini*	95	95	Todt et al. (1981)
Eastern whipbird	*Psophodes olivaceus*	100	100	Rogers (2005)
Australian magpie-lark	*Grallina cyanoleuca*	58	58	Hall (2006)
Tropical boubou	*Laniarius aethiopicus*	89	85	Grafe et al. (2004)
Yellow-crowned gonolek	*L. barbarus*	77		Slater et al. (2002)
Slate-colored Boubou	*L. funebris*	89		Sonnenschein and Reyer (1983)
Rufous-and-white wren	*Thryophilus rufalbus*	73	73	Topp and Mennill, (2008); Mann et al. (2009)
Black-throated wren	*Pheugopedius atrogularis*	75	67	Mann et al. (2009)
Coraya wren	*P. coraya*	70		Mann et al. (2009)
Plain-tailed wren	*P. euophrys*	22		Mann et al. (2009)
Black-bellied wren	*P. fasciatoventris*	78		Mann et al. (2009)
Happy wren	*P. felix*	60		Brown and Lemon, (1979); Mann et al. (2009)
Spot-breasted wren	*P. maculiplectus*	84		Mann et al. (2009)
Whiskered wren	*P. mystacalis*	74		Mann et al. (2009)
Rufous-breasted wren	*P. rutilis*	74		Mann et al. (2009)
Speckle-breasted wren	*P. sclateri*	66		Mann et al. (2009)

(Continued)

TABLE I (*Continued*)

Common name	Scientific name	Duets initiated by males (%)		Source
		Species[a]	Genus[b]	
Plain wren	*Cantorchilus modestus*	93		Mann et al. (2003, 2009); Gill et al. (2005); Cuthbert and Mennill (2007)
Buff-breasted wren	*C. leucotis galbraithii*	75	74	Gill et al. (2005); Mann et al. (2009)
Bay wren	*C. nigricapillus*	55		Levin (1996b); Mann et al. (2009)
Riverside wren	*C. semibadius*	67		Mann et al. (2009)
Superciliated wren	*C. superciliaris*	72		Mann et al. (2009)
Stripe-breasted wren	*C. thoracicus*	82		Mann et al. (2009)
Moho	*Hypergerus atriceps*	100	100	Slater et al. (2002)
Steere's liocichla	*Liocichla steerii*	100	100	Mays et al. (2006)
Red-shouldered blackbird	*Agelaius assimilis*	38	38	Whittingham et al. (1997)
Stripe-headed sparrow	*Aimophila r. ruficauda*	24	24	Illes and Yunes-Jimenez (2009)

[a]Where multiple estimates were available, prenesting or preplayback periods and averaged values from more than one study are used.

[b]Averaged values for all species in the genus (*Thryothorus* wrens are split into the genera proposed by Mann et al., 2006).

strategies in this species are very different, as males are more vocal than females but do not answer, while females are responsible for all duets, but initiate songs independently nearly as often as they answer their partners.

Though it is the answering individual that is responsible for forming duets, the initiator's participation can be evidenced by how long it continues singing after its partner joins in. Magpie-larks, especially females, sing longer songs when their partner joins in to form a duet (Hall, 2006). In contrast, male warbling antbirds cut their songs short when the female responds to them in duet, and slate-colored boubous (*Laniarius funebris*) also continue singing for longer when their partner does not join in, suggesting that the initiator does not benefit from singing with its partner and potential conflict between the sexes (Seddon and Tobias, 2006; Sonnenschein and Reyer, 1983). Alternatively, if the initiator sings to solicit a response so that it can locate and approach its mate (Logue, 2007b; Mennill and Vehrencamp, 2008), it may cut its songs short to listen to and locate its mate. In a number of species, it is usually the male that sings the last note (Brown and Lemon, 1979; Mann et al., 2003; Wright and Dahlin, 2007), suggesting again that the female is largely responsible for producing duets if she stops singing first, leaving the male to continue singing solo.

2. Fine-Scale Temporal Coordination

Although temporal coordination merely involves overlapping songs in some species, there are many species in which partners coordinate phrases within the duet in a variety of ways. One of the simplest and most stereo-typed are the antiphonal duetters, where each pair member repeats a phrase so that they alternate again and again within the duet, often with little or no overlap (examples in Fig. 2D and E). Duets and choruses of white-browed sparrow weavers (*Plocepasser mahali*) involve both alternat-ing and unison phrases within a duet coordinated with a high degree of temporal precision (Voigt et al., 2006). Different rhythmic interactions between partners have been identified in white-browed robin-chats (*Cossy-pha heuglini*) and South American horneros (*Furnarius rufus*) with females answering, or shifting the tempo of their own calling, in response to shifts in the tempo of male calls (Amador et al., 2005; Laje and Mindlin, 2003; Todt et al., 1981). The form and precision of temporal coordination in the complex syncopated duets and choruses of kookaburras (*Dacelo* spp.) has not yet been quantified (Baker, 2004; Reyer and Schmidl, 1988), but further investigation of these and other species is likely to reveal additional com-plicated forms of temporal coordination between partners.

Coordinating a series of alternating phrases within a duet requires a higher level of sustained attention to the partner than just overlapping songs, and probably requires adjustments by both the initiator and responder. In black-bellied wrens, the start time of each individual's phrase in the duet is strongly predicted by the timing of their partner's previous phrase (reaction time) and, to a lesser extent, by the timing of their own previous phrase (tempo) (Logue et al., 2008). The start time of female phrases are better predicted by the end time of the previous male phrase, and the start time of male phrases are better predicted by the start time of the previous female phrase (Logue et al., 2008). Magpie-larks also duet antiphonally (Fig. 2D) and partners match the tempos at which they sing their alternating phrases, but they sing different duet types at different tempos (Hall, 2006). Tempos also vary with distance between partners, being slower when partners are further apart, also consistent with the idea that they respond to one another phrase by phrase throughout the duet with the delay imposed by the slow speed of sound (Hall, 2006). It is likely that high levels of attention are required from both partners in most antiphonally duetting species that produce a long series of coordinated phrases. It seems that in this type of duet, long duets may only be beneficial if they are highly coordinated, since both black-bellied wrens and white-browed robin-chats cut poorly coordinated duets short (Logue et al., 2008; Todt et al., 1981).

Whether or not phrases within a duet alternate with or without overlap may give insight into duet function because of the potential for overlapping signals to mask one another, though caution is needed in determining whether phrase overlap in duets masks or enhances the signal. Male songbirds generally perceive song overlappers as threatening (Naguib and Todt, 1997), and respond aversively when their songs are overlapped by rivals (Hall et al., 2006; Hultsch and Todt, 1982). Nonduetting birds modify their song timing or structure to avoid signal masking, not only by conspecifics (Naguib, 1999), but also by other birds (Brumm, 2006; Ficken et al., 1974), or urban noise (Slabbekoorn and den Boer-Visser, 2006). Masking-avoidance is thus a widespread phenomenon among birds, and may be a mechanism used by duetting species to achieve temporal precision in antiphonal duets (Brumm and Slater, 2007). Phrase-overlap within duets may indicate an attempt by one individual to mask the signal of its partner, as suggested for male overlap of female phrases in yellow-naped amazons (Fig. 2F, Wright and Dahlin, 2007), and female overlap of male song in warbling antbirds (Seddon and Tobias, 2006). However, signal overlap does not automatically imply masking or jamming—for a human analogy, consider a singer whose performance is amplified or enhanced by the simultaneous performance of an accompanying orchestra, but masked or jammed by loud music from a nearby radio. Objective determination of whether overlapping phrases in duets enhance or mask one another is challenging, but the behavior of senders and receivers may provide clues. For example, male warbling antbirds modify their song timing when their partners answer them in duet, apparently to avoid being overlapped (Tobias and Seddon, 2009). In contrast, the overlapping songs of long-tailed manakins (Fig. 2B) are most effective at attracting females when the songs are sung at closely matching frequencies (increasing overlap), and these "high quality" duets take years of practice to achieve (Trainer and McDonald, 1995; Trainer et al., 2002), suggesting that overlap leads to signal enhancement in this case.

B. COORDINATION OF SONG TYPES

1. Answering Rules

In many duetting species, when individuals reply to their partner's song in duet, they are attentive to and answering, not only the timing, but also the song type of their partner (Todt and Naguib, 2000). Though duetting partners could combine their individual repertoires to produce a much larger repertoire of duet types, in all duetting species studied so far, pairs consistently produce fewer duet types than they have the potential to produce (reviewed in Logue, 2006). This nonrandom association of individual song types into duets could arise in a number of ways, not all of which require attentiveness to the partner (from Logue, 2006): (1) both individuals could select a song type based on the same external cue (e.g., if certain song types are given in particular contexts, Sonnenschein and Reyer, 1983; Grafe and Bitz, 2004a), (2) partners could cycle through their repertoires in phase with one another, (3) an individual could select its song type based on a visual signal from its partner, or (4) an individual could select its song type based on the preceding song type of its partner. In the last case, an individual answering its partner in a duet replies to each song in its partner's repertoire with a specific song type from its own repertoire, "fitting" the song type of its partner (Rogers et al., 2006), or following a "code" or "set of rules" (Logue, 2006). Similarly to song timing, an individual's choice of song type may be predicted to different degrees by its own previous song type (own repertoire cycling), the preceding song type of its partner (answering rules), and the preceding song type of a rival (song matching), as seems to be the case in slate-colored boubous (Wickler, 1972). Distinguishing between the alternatives requires a combination of experimental and statistical approaches to determine the stimulus and to compare observed and expected patterns of association given the repertoire and delivery patterns of interacting individuals.

Playback experiments show that it is the duet partner's song type, rather than any other cue, that predicts the answering type, and thus that answering rules followed by individuals (especially females) constitute the individual-level behavior underlying the nonrandom association of song types in duets. The existence of, and sex differences in, answering rules have been demonstrated with an experimental approach in black-bellied wrens, where individuals were induced to "duet" with playback of their mates' songs, demonstrating that stimulus type predicted answering types, with partners using the reciprocal of one another's answering rules, and stimulus type a stronger predictor of female than male answering types (Logue, 2006, 2007a). In eastern whipbirds and tropical boubous (*Laniarius aethiopicus*), females sometimes respond to solo playback of males other than their partner by answering these songs in duet, selecting their song types to create the standard duet types shared in the population (Grafe and Bitz, 2004b; Rogers et al., 2006). In slate-colored boubous, females may be particularly responsible for the fact that certain combinations are more common than others (Seibt and Wickler, 2000). The answering rules that females follow are individually distinctive and stable over time in black-bellied wrens (Logue, 2006), but answering rules appear to be shared between individuals in eastern whipbirds and tropical boubous because there is high sharing of both individual and pair repertoires within populations (Grafe et al., 2004; Rogers et al., 2006). Most of these are species where males initiate most duets, and work on species where the sexes initiate duets at similar frequencies is necessary to examine sex differences in adherence to answering rules more fully.

Individuals in duetting species often repeat the same song type multiple times before switching to another, perhaps facilitating adherence to answering rules. The duetting happy wren (*Thryothorus felix*) sings with eventual variety, while the nonduetting sinaloa wren (*Thryothorus sinaloa*) sings with immediate variety, leading to the suggestion that repeat-mode singing may facilitate duetting (Brown and Lemon, 1979). Repeat-mode singing appears to be the norm in duetting species (Grafe et al., 2004; Hall, 2006; Logue, 2006; Mann et al., 2003; Mennill and Vehrencamp, 2005; Rogers, 2005). Comparing duetting and solo singing within species, white-browed robin-chats sing more repetitively during duetting than solo singing (Todt et al., 1981), though happy wren males switch song types at a higher rate when they duet, than when they sing alone (Brown and Lemon, 1979). If repeat-mode singing makes it easier to adhere to answering rules, then unanswered songs or unusual duet types should be more likely after a partner switches song type. In a captive pair of slate-colored boubous, when the male or female ended a run of one duet type by switching to a different element type, the partner would often (about one-third of switches) remain silent, but if it responded to form a duet, most were consistent with the normal association, with females especially following male switches so that a male switch led to a female switch, and thus a switch in duet type (Seibt and Wickler, 2000). However, plain wren females are more, rather than less, likely to answer their partner following a switch in phrase type, and switches by one individual usually elicit switches from their partner—females switched phrase types on 88% of occasions after their partner switched phrase types, while 86% of female phrase switches elicited a phrase switch by their partner (Mann et al., 2003). This nonindependence of the timing of partner switches suggests that individuals use answering rules to select a song type for answering their partner in duet.

2. Fine-Scale Coordination of Phrase Types

Some duets contain switches of phrase or element types within the duet, with switches of one individual triggering switches by its partner, suggesting that answering rules, like temporal coordination, could also operate on a fine scale, with these rapid reactions again likely to require high levels of attentiveness (von Helversen, 1980). In some species, switches between multiple phrase types within the duet do not appear to occur in answer to changes in the partner's phrase type. In the duets and choruses of black-breasted wood-quail (*Odontophorus leucolaemus*), paired syllables repeated by one contributor ("whoop chia") are interlaced with one syllable repeated by the other contributor (kiow) to form the duet (whoop kiow chia kiow whoop kiow chia kiow) (Hale, 2006). In the duets and choruses of plain-tailed wrens (*Thryothorus euophrys*), both contributions comprise paired phrases that are interlaced and alternated with a high degree of temporal precision (Mann et al., 2005, 2009). Yellow-naped amazon duets begin with an exchange of contact calls, and then progress to antiphonally given sex-specific calls, with males and females equally likely to initiate the progression, the female repeating her one call type (scree), while the male repeats one call type (scree) before switching to a second (yoohoo) not associated with any type switch by the female (Fig. 2F, Wright and Dahlin, 2007). However, in other species, at least some switches occur in answer to a partner's switch. White-crested laughing thrushes (*Garrulax leucolophus*) progress through an even more complex sequence of antiphonally given phrases that depends both on the endogenous patterns of each individual (males and females progress through their most common phrases, F1 to F2 to F3 to F4 and M22 to M23 to M24, repeating each a variable number of times, occasionally missing one, and giving rarer phrases at the end of the duet), and on answering rules (or exogenous patterns, e.g., the male switch from M22 triggers the female switch from F1 to F2) (Fig. 2G, Vencl and Soucek, 1976). In African drongos (*Dicrurus adsimilis*) and white-browed sparrow weavers, individuals also have large repertoires and each switches syllable types multiple times within each duet, with the syllable type depending both on their own previous syllable and their partners' previous syllable (Voigt et al., 2006; von Helversen and Wickler, 1971). Male white-browed sparrow weavers appear to make the task even more complex by switching syllable types within songs more often when they are duetting than when they are singing alone (Voigt et al., 2006). The sexes were not identified in African drongos, but it seemed that one bird dominated the duet with its own syllable sequence (von Helversen and Wickler, 1971). This suggests that the sexes could differ in whether their phrase types were more strongly predicted by their own or their partner's phrases, with one sex perhaps cycling through its own repertoire independently while the other adhered to answering rules.

III. Development of Duets

A. Duet Ontogeny

Since duetting birds include both passerine and nonpasserine species, and both songs and calls are incorporated into duets (Farabaugh, 1982; Thorpe, 1972); the ontogeny of duetting is likely to involve complex interactions between nature and nurture. Two hand-reared slate-colored boubous both developed poor individual vocal repertoires and the pair never developed a typical precise duet, though one bird did seem stimulated to call on hearing its partner's calls (Wickler and Sonnenschein, 1989). This observation suggests that duetting might require learning, but poorly developed individual repertoires were a confounding factor. Anecdotal observations of young birds in the wild joining in when their parents duet suggest juveniles may learn song answering by imitating their parents prior to pairing (personal observations on magpie-larks, also in Logue, 2006). However, virtually nothing is known about the ontogeny of duetting. It is unclear whether the two key individual behaviors underlying duetting, the timing of song answering, and the rules used for selecting answering types, are learned. If they are learned, it is not known whether learning occurs before or after pair formation or whether it is ongoing. It is also unknown who the tutors are and whether there are sex differences in the process of learning to answer a partner in duet. In this section, therefore, I review studies on the ontogeny of song (rather than duetting) in duetting birds, and studies that have inferred sex differences in song learning processes based on dialects and song sharing in duetting birds.

Research on vocal development in birds in general has focused on the ontogeny of learned song in male songbirds, and little is known about vocal development in many nonpasserines, in female birds, or in species that duet (Riebel, 2003). Oscine passerines (songbirds) learn their songs from conspecifics, memorizing and practicing them during a sensitive phase of development, and will not develop normal songs without auditory feedback (Catchpole and Slater, 2008). This vocal learning ability is shared with humans and has been a focus of research, with models of the vocal learning process in songbirds based largely on male song in a half-dozen species (Hultch and Todt, 2004). Among nonpasserines, vocal learning is also common among parrots (a sister taxon to passerine birds, Hackett et al., 2008), many of which duet (Farabaugh, 1982). Some other species among suboscines and nonpasserines are thought to have vocal learning abilities because of geographic variation (dialects), including blue-throated hummingbirds (*Lampornis clemenciae*) where females sing complex songs that often overlap male songs (Ficken et al., 2000; Gaunt et al., 1994).

Otherwise, most nonpasserines are thought to develop normal vocalizations regardless of their auditory experience as juveniles (vocalizations are "innate") though vocal development is unstudied in most bird families (Kroodsma, 2004; Nottebohm, 1972).

Though nothing is known about the ontogeny of song answering, there have been a few studies investigating basic song learning patterns in passerine duetting birds. Work on captive African forest weavers (*Ploceus bicolor*), where individuals are long-lived (10 years or more) and partners sing the same song in synchrony, showed that each individual sings only one song type that is learned from conspecifics within its first two years of life (Seibt et al., 2002). Contact with conspecifics is necessary to develop species-specific song, and changes in social context result in changes in song form within the first two years but not thereafter. Recordings from free-living birds over 21 years in the same area demonstrated site-specific dialects that remained constant over long time periods. A study on captive slate-colored boubous showed that song developed over the first 6–8 months and was fixed thereafter (Wickler and Sonnenschein, 1989). Young reared in the absence of conspecifics developed imprecise versions of the species-specific vocalizations, and those reared with conspecifics copied their song types, usually learning from same-sex conspecifics. Bay wrens (*Thryothorus nigricapillus*) sing antiphonal duets, and tape and live tutoring showed sex-specific imitation of model songs by males and females (Levin et al., 1996). Passerine duetters thus appear to go through a similar song learning process to other passerine birds.

Studies on dialects and song sharing have been used to make inferences about sex differences in song learning processes in duetting birds, with song sharing providing better evidence, as dialects can arise without learning if dispersal is limited. Australian magpies (*Gymnorhina tibicen*), group-living Australo-Papuan songbirds in which females and males sing duets and choruses for territorial defense, have contributed to a broader understanding of vocal learning and how it is influenced by complex social relationships (Brown and Farabaugh, 1991, 1997). Individuals can imitate human whistles, and patterns of syllable sharing in wild birds suggest that individuals are more likely to learn their syllables from same-sex than opposite-sex birds, more likely to learn from kin than non-kin group members, and less likely to learn from birds outside their social group (Brown and Farabaugh, 1991, 1997). Slate-colored boubous are also more likely to learn from same-sex song tutors, and this sex specificity in song types combined with regional song dialects results in "gender dialects" (Wickler, 1972; Wickler and Sonnenschein, 1989). Yellow-naped amazons similarly have regional dialects in their contact calls and antiphonal duets that include sex-specific components (Wright and Dorin, 2001), suggesting sex-specific learning preferences.

In contrast, magpie-larks share three-quarters of their repertoire with their partner, and both sexes share a similar proportion of their repertoire with other same-sex individuals (Hall, 2006), suggesting similar vocal learning patterns between the sexes. Rufous-and-white wren breeding partners share only a third of their repertoire with their partner, and males share significantly more of their repertoire with other males than females share with other females, but repertoire sharing declined with distance between territories among both males and females, suggesting that both sexes learn their songs locally (Mennill and Vehrencamp, 2005). Sex-differences in song learning are likely in eastern whipbirds, where male songs are remarkably consistent throughout the geographic range of the species, whereas females have marked regional dialects with females sharing song types within an area and showing far more variation in song types than males across the species range (Mennill and Rogers, 2006). A detailed study on sharing and similarity of phrases between sexes and populations in plain wrens suggests that both sexes learn their songs by direct imitation after dispersal, with females learning from fewer tutors than males (Marshall-Ball and Slater, 2008).

B. Duetting After a Change of Partner

Divorce, or death of a partner, may necessitate developing duets with a new mate, and it seems temporal precision in duets with new partners is achieved fairly rapidly in most species. In magpie-larks, highly coordinated duets are more common among established pairs than among new pairs in their first few weeks together, suggesting that some learning is necessary to coordinate songs with a new partner (Hall and Magrath, 2007). Bay wrens experiencing a change in mates sang duets with slightly more variable reaction times with the new partner than with the old partner in all four cases, though the difference was only statistically significant in one (Levin, 1996a). Studies on canary-winged parakeets (*Brotogeris v. versicolurus*) and plain wrens found no evidence that the duets of new pairs lacked temporal precision, suggesting that no learning is necessary (Arrowood, 1988; Marshall-Ball et al., 2006). It seems that if adjustments to a new partner do occur, changes are likely to be subtle and rapid, so testing whether individuals have to learn precise timing when duetting with a new partner requires assessment of a fairly large number of pairs over relatively fine time scales following pair formation. Furthermore, control for context may be necessary if aggressive interactions influence duet coordination (Todt et al., 1981) and new pairs have more territorial interactions with neighbors than established pairs. Longitudinal assessment of new pairs is necessary to distinguish between new pairs improving over time, and selective attrition of new pairs that perform poorly coordinated duets.

Coordination of song types may be learned with a change of partners, though it seems that answering rules, the individual-level behavior structuring duet-types, may not change. Plain wren pairs that have been together for at least two years are significantly more consistent in the way they match phrase types to form duets than pairs in their first year together (Marshall-Ball et al., 2006). However, it is unclear whether the increase in consistency is a consequence of individual-level behaviors of males or females or both. Female black-bellied wrens have individually distinctive rules that they use to answer their partners' phrases which remain stable over time, but it is unclear whether this "code" is modified after a change in mate, though a degree of flexibility in answering rules could alleviate the need for learning a new set of rules when re-pairing (Logue, 2006). Males use answering rules that are the reciprocal of their partner's answering rules (forming the same couplets), and would therefore also be affected by re-pairing (Logue, 2007a). Two male bay wrens whose partners were experimentally removed generally used the same song phrases to respond to phrases that their new partner shared with their removed partner (Levin, 1996a), suggesting that a set of phrase associations learned during development may not be modified when partners change. Likewise, captive slate-colored boubous did not modify their individual vocal repertoires when new pairs were formed artificially, using their pre-existing individual repertoires to form duets, but shifting the relative frequencies with which different song types were used (Wickler and Sonnenschein, 1989). African forest weavers sing the same song type in unison, but captive individuals more than 2 years old did not modify their song types even if their partner changed—the fitness consequences for wild birds of singing mismatched songs are unknown (Seibt et al., 2002). Further work is needed to determine whether or not individuals modify the rules they use to link song types in duets after a change in partner.

IV. Neural Basis of Duetting

The vocal learning ability that songbirds share with humans has made them a powerful model system for understanding the neural basis of behavior, and work on duetting species has been important in exploring the evolution of sex differences in the brain. Sexual dimorphism in vertebrate brains was first demonstrated by Nottebohm and Arnold (1976), who showed that differences in the singing behavior of male and female zebra finches (*Taeniopygia guttata*) and canaries (*Serinus canarius*) were correlated with marked size differences in the vocal control areas of the brain. Brenowitz and Arnold (1986) went on to examine sexual dimorphism in the brain structure of closely related duetters, showing that the similar song repertoire sizes of male bay wrens and rufous-and-white wrens were associated with similarly sized song control regions, while female rufous-and-white wrens, with song repertoires half the size of female bay wrens, had significantly smaller song control regions. In Carolina wrens (*Thryothorus ludovicianus*), the large song repertoires of males are associated with large song control regions while nonsinging females do not have detectable song control regions (Nealen and Perkel, 2000). Phylogenetically controlled comparative analyses including duetting species show that sex differences in both song output and complexity are statistically correlated with the extent of sexual dimorphism in brain morphology (MacDougall-Shackleton and Ball, 1999). The considerable variation among species in sexual dimorphism highlight the importance of investigating female as well as male song for a full understanding of the evolution of song systems (Riebel et al., 2005).

Studies on the neuroethology of duetting species have focused on structures underlying the output and complexity of learned song, but the neural basis of song answering is unknown. The rapid vocal response of individuals to their partners in duets was the focus of several early papers on duetting investigating avian auditory reaction times (Grimes, 1965; Power, 1966; Thorpe, 1963). The neural basis of complex rhythms in duets has been modeled for horneros (*Furnarius rufus*) (Amador et al., 2005). The production of highly coordinated antiphonal duets in many duetting species involves fine-scale adjustments of the elements they contribute to the duet with the elements of their partner through the course of the duet as well as matching of particular combinations of element types (see Section II). Since these adjustments require integration of vocal production and perception on a scale of milliseconds, such species should have highly developed pathways linking the auditory and vocal pathways, and serve as an ideal model system for investigating these connections. Such a model system would have application to the slower temporal interactions between countersinging male songbirds that may overlap or match the songs of their opponents (Vehrencamp et al., 2007), as well as to duetting species among nonpasserine birds and in other taxa.

V. HORMONAL BASIS OF DUETTING

A. TERRITORIAL DEFENSE

Testosterone appears to mediate territorial song in female as well as male birds and may also stimulate duetting, though the relationship between testosterone and song is poorly understood even in nonduetting species, and only one study has looked at the relationship between testosterone and duetting. In male songbirds in the north-temperate zone, increasing photoperiod in spring causes testicular growth and secretion of testosterone, which leads to seasonal increases in song production as males compete to establish territories and attract females (Catchpole and Slater, 2008). However, high song rates can occur in the absence of elevated testosterone. Territorial song in male European robins (*Erithacus rubecula*) is associated with elevated testosterone levels in spring but not in winter, while females have elevated testosterone in winter when they defend territories with song (Schwabl, 1992). Tropical species typically have low testosterone levels (Goymann et al., 2004; Garamszegi et al., 2008), and studies on a tropical duetter, the buff-breasted wren (*Thryothorus leucotis*), have shown that song and other aggressive responses to experimental intrusion are associated with elevated testosterone in females in the pre-breeding period but not during breeding, and not in males in either period (Gill et al., 2007, 2008). These studies assessed male and female song independently, and did not test whether there were hormonal changes associated specifically with duetting in buff-breasted wrens. Schwabl and Sonnenschein (1992) found that in captive slate-colored boubous, male song rates were not correlated with their testosterone levels, but female answering of male territorial songs (M4) in duet correlated with their own testosterone levels, suggesting that song answering could have a similar hormonal basis to singing independently of a partner. However, further work is needed to determine the hormonal mechanisms driving territorial duetting behavior.

B. REPRODUCTION

Both male and female vocalizations are important in triggering the chain of neuroendocinological events leading to reproduction, and such social cues may be particularly important when breeding within a population is asynchronous. Male song affects female reproductive physiology, with exposure to male song alone sufficient to stimulate ovarian development and nest-building (Catchpole and Slater, 2008). Male song can effect very rapid changes in females, with exposure to male song triggering release of luteinizing hormone in less than an hour in female white-crowned sparrows (*Zonotrichia albicollis*) (Maney et al., 2007). Female vocalizations can also be important in affecting their own reproductive neuroendocrinology, as shown by work on the ring dove (*Streptopelia risoria*) (Cheng, 1992; Cheng et al., 1998). Male ring doves initiate courtship with cooing, to which their partner responds with her own nest cooing, laying her eggs 5–7 days later. Preventing females from cooing blocks their ovarian growth, and female nest coos trigger neuronal responses from specialized cells in the hypothalamus that cause increases in luteinizing hormone concentrations within an hour. Social cues that allow such rapid stimulation of reproductive hormones may be important in ensuring synchrony in the reproductive states of breeding partners where nesting within a population is not highly synchronous (Moore et al., 2005).

The close coordination of male and female vocalizations in duetting species suggests that duetting could be a potent social cue for synchronizing the reproductive physiology of breeding partners, but only a single study has examined the relationship between duetting and hormones through the breeding cycle. Dilger (1953) suggested a role for duetting in achieving reproductive synchrony between partners, and studies on many duetting species have shown peaks in duetting during prebreeding, nest-building, and renesting periods (Hall, 2006; Merkle, 2006; Sonnenschein and Reyer, 1983; Topp and Mennill, 2008). No nesting occurred in white-browed robin-chats prevented from duetting by experimentally modifying male song (sectioning the hypoglossus) or deafening the female (Todt and Hultsch, 1982). Schwabl and Sonnenschein (1992) studied duetting and hormones in relation to breeding stage in slate-colored boubous, where pairs laid up to four clutches over a 5 month breeding season. Song output was greater by males than females, and males initiated 68.4% of duets. Females responded to male song by duetting most during prebreeding and courtship, and least during incubation and nestling feeding. The rate at which males sang their most common song type (M1, suggested to function in attracting and guarding mates) tended to correlate positively with their mate's estradiol level, but female song answering was unrelated to their own levels of luteinizing hormone or estradiol (though female duetting responses to male territorial songs (M4) correlated with their testosterone levels, above). These results suggest that, like other songbirds, male song stimulates hormones that trigger nesting in females, but female duetting responses correlate more with aggression-linked than reproduction-linked hormones. With rapid advances in understanding the neuroendocrinological mechanisms underlying the independent effects of male and female song on reproductive physiology, duetting birds provide a good model system for exploring how social interactions between partners impact on both the activation and synchronizing of their reproductive systems.

VI. Ecology and Life History

Broadscale comparative studies of correlates of duetting have identified several ecological and life history characteristics shared by duetting species. Long-term monogamy and year-round territoriality are the two key characteristics most consistently identified as being associated with duetting (Benedict, 2008a; Farabaugh, 1982; Malacarne et al., 1991; Payne, 1971). However, there are few studies on color-marked duetting species that have quantified divorce rates and mortality rates, so quantitative information on pair bond duration is lacking. Thorpe (1972) also suggested that duetting was characteristic of birds occupying densely vegetated habitat, a proposal rejected by most other studies (Kunkel, 1974; Malacarne et al., 1991; Payne, 1971; Short and Horne, 1983). There is no consensus on whether duetting is associated with plumage monomorphism (Malacarne et al., 1991; Thorpe, 1972) or not (Benedict, 2008a; Farabaugh, 1982). Duetting is thought to be more common among tropical species (Kunkel, 1974; Thorpe, 1972), an association supported by Farabaugh's (1982) comparison of Panamanian and North American species. Phylogenetically controlled analysis is necessary to test whether duetting is more common in the tropics, and whether the association relates to life history traits that are common among duetting species as well as in the tropics (Payne, 1971). Recent work on the evolution of female song in New World blackbirds (Icterids) used a phylogenetic approach to show that female song in species breeding in the tropics was lost repeatedly with multiple evolutionary transitions from tropical to temperate breeding ranges, and that female song is associated with a suite of life-history traits associated with living in the tropics, occurring in species that are nonmigratory, monogamous, and with dispersed nest sites (Price et al., 2009; Price, 2009).

Most comparative studies examining ecological and life history correlates of duetting lack adequate control for evolutionary history and possible confounding factors. Early studies involved large numbers of duetting species, but no quantitative comparisons with nonduetting species or control for shared ancestry (Kunkel, 1974; Payne, 1971; Thorpe, 1972). Farabaugh's (1982) quantitative comparisons of all Panamanian and North American breeding species compared duetters with nonduetters and controlled for some confounding factors, but did not take phylogeny into account. Benedict's (2008a) analysis of North American passerines grouped duetting species into clades, but did not control for evolutionary history among nonduetters. Malacarne et al. (1991) examined western palearctic nonpasserines, controlling for phylogeny by comparing all duetting species with nonduetters sampled from all taxa in the group, and conducting analyses at the level of the genus as well as the species.

Since duetting is strongly dependent on evolutionary history and duetting genera may be disproportionately speciose (see Section VII.B), it is particularly important that comparative studies take phylogeny into account.

A. A SOUTHERN PHENOMENON?

The frequency of female song and duetting among tropical and south-temperate birds is likely to relate to ecological and life history differences that distinguish them from their north-temperate counterparts (Morton, 1996; Slater and Mann, 2004). Annual periodicity in most tropical climates is defined by rainfall, with annual cycles of plants and animals linked to changes between wet and dry seasons. Breeding seasons are typically longer and less synchronous than in the high latitudes of the northern hemisphere where annual variation in daylength is marked and breeding seasons are short and synchronous (Kunkel, 1974). The southern hemisphere has much less landmass at high latitudes than the northern hemisphere, and south-temperate birds share life history characteristics with tropical birds such as small clutch sizes, many nesting attempts, slow development with extended parental care, and high adult survival compared to their north-temperate counterparts (Martin, 1996; Peach et al., 2001; Russell et al., 2004). Northern breeders are more likely to migrate than southern breeders, and high testosterone levels among males breeding at high latitudes associated with strong male-male competition during annual re-establishment of territories are related to short breeding seasons and synchronous nesting (Garamszegi et al., 2008; Goymann et al., 2004).

A nonmigratory lifestyle may be a particularly important correlate of duetting, allowing year-round residence on territories and persistent pair-bonds. Year-round territoriality has long been thought to be a reason female song and duetting are more common in southern than northern temperate areas (Cobb, 1897; Robinson, 1949), and may reflect similar sex roles (Slater and Mann, 2004). Year-round territoriality combined with high annual survival may contribute to the persistence of the pair bond because partnerships do not have to re-form each year. Migrating individuals have to search for their partner every year after migration, and divorce rates increase as mortality rates increase (Jeschke and Kokko, 2008), making long-term partnerships less likely. Long-term partnerships could also be maintained if they confer fitness benefits or because of constraints on acquiring a new partner or territory where habitat is saturated and occupied year-round (Russell and Rowley, 1996). An exception to year-round territorial defense are the duetting parrots, geese, and swans, which do maintain long-term pair bonds, and appear to use duetting for joint resource defense (Arrowood, 1988; Kraaijeveld and Mulder, 2002; Wright and Dahlin, 2007). Anseriformes, in particular, have exceptionally low divorce rates (mean 9.9%) among birds, associated with low mortality and continuous partnerships (Jeschke and Kokko, 2008). To determine the importance of a nonmigratory lifestyle, long-term pair bonds, and year-round territoriality as key ecological and life history factors predicting duetting will require phylogenetically controlled comparative analyses that examine relationships between duetting, pair bond duration, and terri-toriality, while controlling for other factors such as adult survival, breeding season length, nesting synchrony, and latitude.

VII. EVOLUTION

A. PHYLOGENETIC DIVERSITY OF DUETTING SPECIES

Duetting has evolved independently in many different taxonomic groups. There are over 360 duetting species in 18 passerine and 32 nonpasserine families worldwide listed in reviews (Benedict, 2008a; Diamond, 1972; Farabaugh, 1982; Harris and Franklin, 2000; Immelmann, 1961; Kunkel, 1974; Malacarne et al., 1991; Short and Horne, 1983; Thorpe, 1972). In addition to the species listed in these reviews, there are published accounts of duetting in at least another 60 species, including some that represent new families such as southern ground hornbills (*Bucorvus lead-beateri*, family Bucorvidae) (Seibt and Wickler, 1977), kokakos (*Callaeas cinerea wilsoni*, Family Callaeatidae) (Molles et al., 2006), subdesert mesites (*Monias benschi*, Family Mesitornithidae) (Seddon, 2002), western and rufous bristlebirds (*Dasyornis longirostris* and *D. broadbenti*, Family Pardalotidae) (Chapman, 1999; Smith, 1987), and gray-crowned babblers (*Pomatostomus temporalis*, Family Pomatostomidae) (King, 1980). Duet-ting species thus represent approximately 4.3% of species and 40% of families of birds (following the classification of Sibley and Ahlquist, 1990). Furthermore, there are other species with little or no published information on their vocalizations that sometimes duet, for example buff-sided robins (*Poecilodryas cerviniventris*, Family Petroicidae) (personal observation). Further investigation among little-known species will no doubt reveal more duetters and more independent origins of duetting. Studies on duetting species in nonduetting clades, and on species in duetting clades with duetting styles that differ from their close relatives are likely to be most informative for identifying factors selecting for duetting and for increased complexity in duets.

B.   ANCESTRY AS A PREDICTOR OF DUETTING

Evolutionary history appears to be a strong predictor of whether or not species duet in a nonpasserine group known for their duetting, the barbets. There are duetting species in barbet families in the New World (Ramphastidae), Asia (Megalaimidae), and Africa (Lybiidae) (Dilger, 1953; Farabaugh, 1982; Kunkel, 1974; Thorpe, 1972), but information on duetting and phylogenetic history have not yet been integrated. In Figure 5, I combine information on duetting with Moyle's (2004) phylogenetic analysis of relationships among barbets to informally explore the evolution of duetting in this family. Among Asian barbets, the great barbet (*Megalaima virens*) and the crimson-breasted, or coppersmith, barbet (*M. haemacephala*) duet (Dilger, 1953), with crimson-breasted barbets ancestral in Megalaimidae (Moyle, 2004). Among New World barbets, toucan barbets (*Semnornis ramphastinus*) also duet (Dilger, 1953), but whether or not they are ancestral in Ramphastidae is unresolved (Moyle, 2004). *Trachyphonus* is the basal taxon in African barbets (Moyle, 2004) and has universal duetting (Short and Horne, 1983). If duetting is ancestral in African barbets, then it has been lost in two lineages, the tinkerbarbets (*Pogoniulus*) and another lineage comprising *Gymnobucco, Buccanodon,* and *Stactolaema*, with the exception of *S. olivacea* which duets occasionally (Short and Horne, 1983), and is not closely related to nonduetting *Stactolaema* (Moyle, 2004). In a third lineage comprising *Lybius* and *Tricholaema*, duetting has been retained in *Lybius* with nearly all of the 12 species duetting, but lost in those *Tricholaema* not closely related to *Lybius*. While the one duetting *Stactolaema* and two duetting *Tricholaema* are exceptions in their nonduetting genera (Short and Horne, 1983), there is a phylogenetic basis for these differences in the paraphyly of the two groups (Moyle, 2004). The single real exception appears to be the nonduetting *L. melanopterus* in the otherwise duetting *Lybius*, inviting examination of ecological and life history differences that might explain the loss of duetting in this species. Evolutionary history thus explains the presence or absence of duetting in African barbets almost perfectly.

A comprehensive study combining molecular and bioacoustic analysis of neotropical *Thryothorus* wrens provides compelling evidence that duet structure is strongly dependent on evolutionary history in this group (Mann et al., 2006, 2009). Assessment of fine-scale phylogenetic relationships in the group showed four clades, sufficiently distinct to propose division of the *Thryothorus* wrens into four genera (Mann et al., 2006). Singing styles and duet structure differ between these groups, but are similar within each, indicating that ancestry is a strong predictor of singing styles (Mann et al., 2009). In the *Thryothorus* and *Thryophilus* groups, duetting is rare and

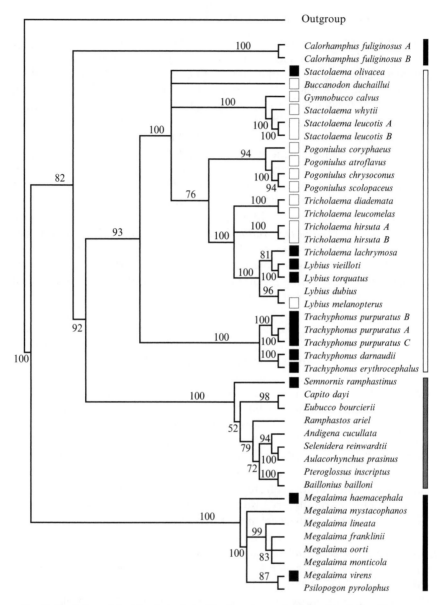

FIG. 5. Evolution of duetting in barbets. The tree shows phylogenetic relationships among barbets and toucans, including at least one representative of all genera in Ramphastidae (9 genera, 55 species, black vertical line on the right), Megalaimidae (3 genera, 26 species, gray line), and Lybiidae (7 genera, 42 species, white line), with numbers at each node showing the percentage of bootstrap replicates in which that node was recovered (taken from Fig. 3 in Moyle, 2004, with permission from Elsevier). Black boxes indicate duetting species and white boxes nonduetting species (from Dilger, 1953; Short and Horne, 1983).

simple, while in the *Pheugopedius* and *Cantorchilus* groups all species sing complex antiphonal duets. However, the analysis also highlighted a few species, like *rufalbus, euophrys*, and *genibarbis*, with singing styles atypical of their group that may provide insights into ecological factors influencing the evolution of complex duetting behavior (Mann et al., 2009).

Song form in African malaconotid bush-shrikes also appears to be dependent on ancestry to some extent, but further work is needed. Wickler and Seibt (1982) compared duetting of a few species in the group and suggested that duet complexity evolved by a process of song splitting, while Harris and Franklin (2000) mapped general communication charac-teristics of most species, but a lack of phylogenetic information hampered conclusions regarding the evolution of duetting. Molecular phylogenies now available for the bush-shrikes (Fuchs et al., 2004; Nguembock et al., 2008) indicate that some of the vocal similarities identified by Harris and Franklin (2000) are a consequence of common ancestry, but others are not. For example, vocal similarities between *L. barbarus* and *erythrogaster*, and *atroflavus* and *mufumbiri*, reflect sister species relationships between the two species pairs, but *atrococcineus* shares vocal characteristics with *bar-barus* and *erythrogaster* although it is not closely related, but ancestral in the *Laniarius* group. Likewise, vocal characteristics shared by *L. leucor-hynchus, fuelleborni, and poensis* reflect the sister species relationship between the latter two species, but *L. leucorhynchus* is ancestral in the *Laniarius* group. Genetic relationships in *Chlorophoneus*, however, predict the vocal characteristics identified by Harris and Franklin (2000), with the closely related *C. sulfureopectus, bocagei* and *nigrifrons* sharing vocal char-acteristics with one another, but not with *C. dohertyi*, which is more closely related to *Telophorus zeylonus* with which it shares vocal characteristics. Further work on duetting styles and duetting complexity in this group in relation to phylogenetic relationships among species is necessary to understand the evolution of duetting in malaconotid bush-shrikes.

Patterns of sympatry and species diversity in relation to duetting suggest the possibility that duetting is involved in speciation. Vocal complexity is correlated with species richness in antbirds (Thamnophilidae), suggesting that acoustic signals can be important drivers of speciation (Seddon et al., 2008). Diamond and Terborgh (1968) first suggested that duetting might serve as an isolating mechanism based on observations on cuckoo-shrikes in Papua New Guinea, where the duetting black-bellied cuckoo-shrike (*Coracina montana*) has an altitudinal range just above the closely related gray-headed cuckoo-shrike (*C. schisticeps*) whose songs are similar but lack the female duetting element. A similar example from the neotropics involves the duetting gray-breasted wood-wren (*Henicorhina leucophrys*) which has an altitudinal range just above its nonduetting sister species, the white-breasted wood-wren (*H. leucosticta*) (Stiles and Skutch, 1989). Song divergence in two duetting subspecies of the gray-breasted wood-wren appear to be driven by ecological differences (Dingle et al., 2008). Habitat is also likely to influence vocalizations in African barbets, as duetting species rarely inhabit forests (Short and Horne, 1983). African barbet taxa with similar duets tend to occur allopatrically while sympatric congeners have very different duets, and duetting genera tend to have more species and subspecies than nonduetting genera (Short and Horne, 1983). A similar association of duetting with high species diversity occurs in neotropical wrens, where new genera proposed for *Thryothorus* that have no or simple duets (*Thryothorus* and *Thryophilus*) comprise one to three species while proposed genera with complex duetting (*Pheugopedius* and *Cantorchilus*) contain almost a dozen species each (Mann et al., 2009). Likewise, in bush-shrikes the genus *Laniarius* has the most widespread and complex duetting behavior and is also the largest among the core malaconotids, with nearly twenty species and many subspecies (Nguembock et al., 2008). These patterns are suggestive of a relationship between duetting, habitat, and speciation that invites further investigation.

Duetting and female song are likely to have independent evolutionary origins. In many songbirds, females both sing and coordinate their songs with those of their partner to form duets (Langmore, 1998). Despite the relative rarity of female song among north-temperate species (Slater and Mann, 2004), the likely Australasian origin of passerines (Barker et al., 2004) and the prevalence of female song among Australian birds (Robinson, 1949), suggest that female song could be the ancestral state in oscine passerines (Garamszegi et al., 2007; Riebel et al., 2005). However, female song is not necessary for duetting, as duets can be comprised of calls as well as songs (Harris and Franklin, 2000), and duetting is common in many nonpasserine as well as passerine bird families (Farabaugh, 1982). It is therefore possible that duetting in birds could have first evolved prior to, and independently of, female song.

VIII. FUNCTION

Hypotheses for the functional significance of avian duetting have to explain why an individual coordinates the timing and type of its songs with those of its partner instead of singing independently. Depending on the structure of the duet, such coordination can require a high level of attentiveness to a mate (Smith, 1994). Therefore, regardless of the primary function of the duet, the degree of coordination an individual achieves when duetting with its partner will reveal, both to its partner and other listeners, how attentive to its partner the individual is. It is possible that interspecific comparison would reveal a correlation between the precision of temporal coordination in duets and the strictness of answering rules linking song types for two reasons. First, the signal of attentiveness provided by the temporal precision of a duetted response may be amplified by the nonrandom association of song types, if the intended receiver is aware of the rules linking song types. Second, responding with a predictable song type may facilitate the achievement of temporal precision (Mann et al., 2003). If the latter is the case then, within pairs, duets that are consistent with answering rules should have higher temporal precision than those that are not. However, relationships between these two aspects of coordination in duetting are yet to be investigated.

Hypotheses for the function of duetting have often been dichotomized into those where duetting is a consequence of cooperation between the sexes versus those where duetting results from sexual conflict (Hall, 2004). Duets were initially regarded as pair displays for cooperative functions such as pair bond maintenance, joint territorial defense, and achieving reproductive synchrony (Armstrong, 1947). Subsequently, it was suggested that duetting might result from conflict between the sexes if an individual answered its partner's song in duet to thwart its attempts to attract birds of the opposite sex (the mate-guarding hypothesis, Sonnenschein and Reyer, 1983; Levin, 1996b). However, recent studies on a number of species are again concluding that duets are largely cooperative displays, where either the male, or the female, or both sexes, coordinate their songs with those of their partner to achieve an outcome beneficial to both individuals (Hall and Magrath, 2007; Logue et al., 2008; Mann et al., 2003; Mennill and Vehrencamp, 2008). "Cooperative," in this sense, acknowledges the separate interests of the individuals coordinating their songs into a duet, with the implication that the cooperative display will break down if the interests of both individuals are not met. Early formulations of hypotheses for cooperative functions of duetting often did not make consideration of individual interests explicit, but it is evident from Armstrong's (1947) observations on behaviors such as duetting that he was aware of the tension implicit in cooperative endeavors between two individuals:

As every close observer knows, birds as well as men have their individual idiosyncrasies, dependent on various factors, temperamental and physiological. Conjugal accord is a matter of mutual accommodation and adjustment as with human beings. The ideal of, "Two minds with but a single thought, Two hearts that beat as one," is not easy of attainment, but the way to it is made smoother when the two individuals concerned, human or avian, unite frequently and enthusiastically in common endeavors and mutual rites.

Though Armstrong's (1947) language seems old fashioned and anthropo-morphic by today's standards, and is very different from the language used by modern-day evolutionary biologists, it seems that he too saw that coop-erative endeavors could be fraught with conflict and that duetting might serve as a display facilitating and promoting cooperation (or resolving conflict) between the sexes.

A. JOINT RESOURCE DEFENSE

Joint resource defense is believed to be the primary function of duetting in many species (Logue, 2005; Todt and Naguib, 2000; Wickler, 1980). Like male territorial song, duets are usually loud and easy to locate, performed from prominent places close to territory boundaries, and used in counter-singing interactions with neighbors and in response to intrusion (Wickler, 1976). Also, like male songbirds, duetting species are able to distinguish duets of neighbors from those of strangers, responding less aggressively to the duets of familiar pairs (Grafe and Bitz, 2004b; Hall, 2000; Wiley and Wiley, 1977). However, to show that duetting itself has a territorial func-tion, it is necessary to demonstrate that features distinct to duetting, partic-ularly the temporal coordination of songs, play a role in territorial defense over and above that achieved by the solo songs of males and females.

Duets appear to be more threatening territorial signals than solo songs in some species, but not in others. Playback experiments broadcasting duets and solo songs to territorial birds have shown that duets elicit more aggressive responses than solo songs in some species (Hall, 2000; Illes and Yunes-Jimenez, 2009; Molles and Waas, 2006), similar levels of aggression in others (Appleby et al., 1999; Bradley and Mennill, 2009; Fedy and Stutchbury, 2005; Grafe and Bitz, 2004b), and less aggression than same-sex solo songs in some cases (Rogers et al., 2007; Seddon and Tobias, 2006). If duets are more threatening, this may be because they signal the presence of two birds acting in concert rather than one, as vocal choruses can indicate group size to allow assessment of relative threat (Hale, 2006; Seddon and Tobias, 2003). Consis-tent with this, kokako responded more quickly to songs produced from two sound sources than from one (Molles and Waas, 2006). Also, duets are much more threatening to unpaired than paired plain wrens (Marshall-Ball et al., 2006). From a sender's perspective, duetting seems to be used as a more threatening signal than solo singing, as duet playback is more likely to elicit a duetting response than solo playback in tropical boubous (Grafe and Bitz, 2004b), and individuals are more likely to respond to their partners in duet when faced with territorial threats (Hall, 2000; Hall and Peters, 2008; Logue and Gammon, 2004; Mennill and Vehrencamp, 2008; Rogers et al., 2004). Experiments comparing responses to duet and solo playback typically broadcast either male *or* female solo songs—no study has yet compared responses to male *and* female solo songs with responses to duets to determine whether the coordination of male and female solo songs into duets itself adds to the territorial threat by signaling their cooperation in a defensive coalition.

However, temporal coordination *within* duets does add to the threat level of the territorial signal in some species. Experimental manipulation of temporal precision in magpie-lark duets revealed that highly coordinated duets elicited more vocalizations from males than uncoordinated duets, suggesting that precisely coordinated duets represent a greater threat (Hall and Magrath, 2007). Since established partners are more likely to produce highly coordinated duets than new pairs, this component of the territorial signal appears to indicate the stability of the defending partnership to rivals (Hall and Magrath, 2007). However, the speed of duets (reaction times) and duet precision (variability of reaction times) also varies within pairs on a finer scale, probably depending on factors like distance between partners, their skill, motivation, and context (Hall and Magrath, 2007; Logue et al., 2008; Marshall-Ball et al., 2006; Thorpe, 1963; Todt et al., 1981). Temporal coordination of white-browed robin-chat duets was reduced during agonistic interactions, with highly coordinated longer duets typically given after partners had already performed some duets (Todt et al., 1981), suggesting that highly coordinated duets are difficult to produce in a highly aroused state. In plain wrens, both males and females sang with shorter reaction times (to produce faster duets) in response to playback of slow short duets versus fast long duets (Marshall-Ball et al., 2006). These intriguing results suggest that an individual's reaction times in duets are affected by a complex array of factors that are still poorly understood.

Individuals may face trade-offs when they coordinate phrase types with their partner in duets given in territorial contexts, with choices of phrase types potentially depending on whether answering rules are shared in the population or not. In many nonduetting songbirds, countersinging males match the song type of rivals (Logue and Forstmeier, 2008; Vehrencamp, 2000). However, in most duetting species, an individual's song type is strongly dependent on the song type its partner sings (see Section II.B), suggesting the potential for trade-offs between following answering rules and matching rivals when replying to a partner while duetting in territorial contexts, especially in species where duet types are pair specific. In plain wrens, individuals share on average 52% of their phrase type repertoires with other individuals, but pairs share less than 20% of their duet type repertoire with other pairs (Marshall-Ball and Slater, 2008). Males and females both match the phrase types of simulated same-sex intruders more often than expected by chance, but pairs do not match duet-types of simulated pairs more often than expected by chance (Marshall-Ball and Slater, 2004). The relative importance of the partner and the same-sex rival as predictors of phrase type choice were not directly assessed in this study, but high song switching rates driven by both pair members allowed both sexes to independently phrase-match playback without matching duet types (Marshall-Ball and Slater, 2004), suggesting that individuals switching to phrase-match same-sex playback were accommodated by their duetting partner switching with them according to an answering rule rather than also phrase-matching playback. In eastern whipbirds, giving an appropriate song type in response to their partner always takes priority over matching the song type of a simulated intruder (Rogers et al., 2006). In whipbirds, duet types are shared throughout the population (Rogers, 2005). Adherence to response type rules in forming duets would thus be meaningful to both the partner and territorial rivals in eastern whipbirds, but to the partner only in plain wrens (unless the rivals were familiar established neighbors, perhaps).

Close proximity between duetting partners adds a visual dimension, sometimes enhanced with visual displays, to the coordination of timing and song types in joint territorial displays. In many duetting species, partners perch side by side as they duet (Kunkel, 1974), and individuals are more likely to reply to their partner the closer they are to them (Hall and Magrath, 2000; Logue and Gammon, 2004). Close proximity between partners is important during territorial defense as well as advertisement, with partners typically responding together to simulated threats (Grafe and Bitz, 2004b; Hall and Peters, 2008; Mennill, 2006; Rogers et al., 2004). Close proximity has been shown experimentally to increase the perceived threat level of joint territorial displays in white-browed robin-chats (Hultsch and Todt, 1984). Duets are accompanied by synchronized wing movements in some species (Tingay, 1974; Todt and Fiebelkorn, 1980; Todt et al., 1981; Zimmer et al., 2001), while triumph ceremonies given in aggressive contexts by geese and swans involve vocal and visual components (Kraaijeveld and Mulder, 2002; Whitford, 1996). These visual components could direct attention to the vocal signal or reduce the likelihood of habituation (Todt and Fiebelkorn, 1980). It has also been suggested that visual displays and close proximity between partners could improve the precision of temporal coordination (Mann et al., 2003).

1. Sex-Specific Defense: Territory or Mate?

Aggressive responses to same-sex intruders could represent either territorial defense or mate guarding, but in view of the ecology of many duetting species are more likely to represent both. Long-lived, year-round residents often inhabit stable neighborhoods with limited opportunities for acquiring a new territory or mate (Russell and Rowley, 1996). This is likely to be the case for many duetting species that defend territories year round and have long-term partnerships (see Section VI), so that excluding a same-sex intruder from the territory effectively achieves defense of a valuable territory and partnership simultaneously. Information about the ecology of duetting species is necessary to determine whether territories or mates are more limiting, and whether same-sex defense is therefore likely to be related more to one or the other.

The sex-specific responses to intrusion found in some duetting species are even more marked among nonduetting species. In general, male birds are more aggressive to male intruders and females are more aggressive to female intruders, but this sex-bias in defense is significantly lower in duetting species compared to nonduetting species, consistent with the idea that duetting partners cooperate in territorial defense to exclude all intruders (Fig. 6, Logue, 2005). Sex-specific defense may result from independent pursuit of conflicting male and female interests regarding male and female intruders, or common benefit to division of labor, for example, if size

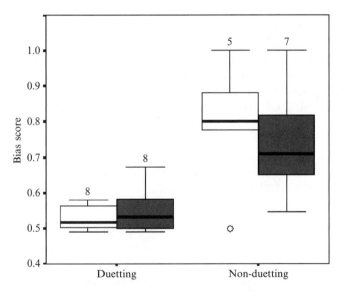

Fig. 6. Sex specificity in response to intrusion in duetting and nonduetting species (taken from Fig. 1 in Logue, 2005, with permission from the author). Box plots showing sex bias in male (white boxes) and female (shaded boxes) responses to playback and decoy experiments (numbers above boxes indicate sample sizes). Bias scores greater than 0.5 indicate that nonvocal responses to simulated intrusion were biased toward intruders of the same sex, while bias scores less than 0.5 indicate bias toward intruders of the opposite sex.

dimorphism makes sex-specific defense more efficient (Marshall-Ball et al., 2006). A nonduetting species unusual for its lack of sex specificity in defense is the rufous-collared sparrow (*Zonotrichia capensis*), a species with eco-logical similarities to some duetting species (resident year round in the tropics) where males are more active than females in defense, but both sexes defend against intruders of either sex (Busch et al., 2004). As sex specificity of defense is assessed in more duetters, it should be possible to examine variation within duetting species to determine whether the sex bias in defense is reduced more in species with complex duets that require coordination throughout the duet by both partners compared to species with simpler duets that involve less coordination or coordination by only one sex.

Assessing sex specificity of defense experimentally using solo song play-back poses challenges of design and interpretation. Most experimenters create male and female solo song stimuli by presenting the same number of male and female songs at the same rate. However, where the natural rate of solo singing by males and females is very different, these may not represent equivalent stimuli. For example, in species where female solo songs are much rarer than male solo songs, the female solo playback will represent a much more intense stimulus than the male solo playback and hence be likely to elicit an elevated aggressive response. One alternative is to present male and female solo songs at different rates, reflecting natural sex differ-ences in song rates (Fedy and Stutchbury, 2005). Experiments using model or decoy intruders instead of song playback may provide more comparable stimuli representing unpaired male and female intruders (Farabaugh et al., 1992; Gill et al., 2007, 2008; Hau et al., 2004). Another method of examining sex specificity of defense is to use stereo duet playback (Logue and Gammon, 2004; Mennill, 2006; Molles and Waas, 2006; Rogers et al., 2004), with separate speakers playing male and female components of the duet placed sufficiently far apart to identify which is approached more closely by each member of the defending pair.

B. MATE GUARDING (PARTNERSHIP OR PAIR BOND)

A comprehensive study integrating knowledge of ecology and life history with bioacoustic analysis and playback experiments has demonstrated that duetting in eastern whipbirds is a result of female mate guarding behavior (Rogers, 2005; Rogers and Mulder, 2004; Rogers et al., 2006, 2007). Eastern whipbirds are insectivorous passerines endemic to Australia in the family Corvidae (Cinclosomatinae, Sibley and Ahlquist, 1990), and both they and their sister species, the western whipbird, duet (Smith, 1991; Watson, 1969). Male eastern whipbirds are more vocal than females (over 60% of songs are male solo songs) and initiate all duets, and thus duetting in this species results exclusively from female song answering behavior (Rogers, 2005). Monogamous pairs defend territories year round, and partnerships are long term as a result of high adult annual survival (90–100%) and low divorce rates (0–5%) (Rogers and Mulder, 2004). Males invest heavily in parental care, and production of two surviving offspring depends on investment by both parents because of strict brood division during postfledging care (Rogers and Mulder, 2004). Sex ratios of nestlings and unpaired, nonterritorial adults are strongly female biased, suggesting intense intrasexual competition among females for mates and the male care necessary for successful reproduction (Rogers and Mulder, 2004). Consistent with this, females respond more aggressively to playback of female solo songs and duets than to male solo songs, sing solo songs only in response to playback of female solos and duets, and are more likely to duet with their partner in response to playback of female than male solos (Rogers et al., 2007). Females do not coordinate their approach to playback with their partners, but their vocal duetting response is tightly coordinated with that of their partner temporally (female songs typically follow male songs in duets with an average delay of only 230 ms, Rogers, 2005) as well as in song type, with females using a song type that fits their partner's song type in preference to matching the song type of the female rival (Rogers et al., 2006). Because female answering rules do not differ between individuals, but are consistent throughout the population (Rogers, 2005), this signal that the female is being attentive to the song type choices of her partner is meaningful not only within the pair, but also to other conspecifics. Females thus appear to duet to defend their own position within the partnership, with these partner-directed signals (extremely close coordination with the partner with respect to both timing and song type) serving for intrapair communication to indicate their attentiveness and commitment to their male, and for extrapair communication to signal their male's paired status to rival females (Rogers et al., 2007). Females occasionally duet with males other than their partner, with the significance of these nonpartner directed signals currently unclear (Rogers et al., 2007).

Playback experiments in bay wrens showed that female song attracts males, suggesting that males could benefit by answering their partner's songs to repel rivals by advertising her mated status (Levin, 1996b). Although her work is often cited as evidence for mate guarding, Levin (1996b) argued rather that "although the results of this study provide strong evidence of the necessary preconditions for the evolution of duetting as acoustic mate guarding, they cannot be used to directly evaluate the role of male song in this context." Levin (1996a) considered virtually all duets as initiated by females and thus a consequence of male song answering, but over 50% of duets were preceded by male vocalizations (calls, Levin, 1996a), and Mann et al. (2003; 2009) argue that these "introductory phrases" are integral to this style of duetting (see Fig. 2E), implying that male and female bay wrens are equally likely to initiate duets and thus that both sexes, rather than males only, are responsible for the song answering that creates duets. Further work is therefore needed to determine whether duetting has a mate-guarding function in bay wrens.

Several other species may use duetting for mate-guarding, though there is often insufficient information on life history and ecology to explain why mate-guarding is necessary. Subdesert mesites are group-living birds endemic to Madagascar, in the family Mesitornithidae, that defend year-round territories with joint vocal displays (Seddon, 2002). Male solos are the least common vocalization, and females initiate more than 75% of duets and are more likely than males to terminate duets, indicating that male behavior is primarily responsible for duets in this species, and male notes also follow female notes more closely than vice versa (Seddon, 2002; Seddon et al., 2002). A male-biased sex ratio in the population, stronger response by groups to playback of male solos and duets than to playback of female solos, suggest competition among males for mates (Seddon et al., 2002). Male tropical boubous answer a higher proportion of their partner's songs during playback of male solos than of male-initiated duets, suggesting that unpaired male intruders represent more of a threat than paired intruders, and that males use song answering to guard the partnership (Grafe and Bitz, 2004b). Interestingly, like eastern whipbirds, females occasionally duet with males other than their partner, whereupon her partner joins in, apparently to try to block his rival's signal (Grafe and Bitz, 2004b). The most common song type in the repertoire of male slate-colored boubous (M1) is thought to have a mate-guarding function because it is the song type most likely to elicit an answer from their partner, and is most likely to be used for answering female song initiations (which are rare compared to the male), and males also use this song type in response to playback of male solos (rather than matching rival song types as they do when counter-duetting with neighboring pairs) (Sonnenschein and Reyer, 1983). However, the underlying assumption that males and females initiate songs to attract birds of the opposite sex has not been demonstrated. In warbling antbirds, female solo songs are rare, males initiate all duets, and males cut their songs short when the female answers, so that duetting results only from female behavior in this species (Seddon and Tobias, 2006). Females respond more aggressively to playback of female solos than playback of duets or male solos: they almost never sing in response to playback of male solos, and reply to their partner in duet more often and more quickly during playback of female solos than duets (Seddon and Tobias, 2006). Males seem to try to avoid being overlapped by their partner's songs by cutting their own songs short and commencing a new song more quickly (Tobias and Seddon, 2009). Little is known about the ecology of warbling antbirds, and it is unclear why females use song answering to guard males, as they do not appear to use song initiating for intrasexual competition.

1. Conflict or Cooperation?

The costs and benefits of using duetting for mate guarding are poorly understood, but there is currently no evidence to support the idea that it is a consequence of sexual conflict. Mate guarding involves sexual conflict if the duet initiator is initiating songs to attract a new partner, and if it does not benefit from being guarded. Few studies have tested directly whether duet initiators use song initiation to attract a new partner. Removal experiments in bay wrens showed that, while unpaired males sang at high rates, females did not increase their song rates when they were unpaired, suggesting that females use song for intrasexual aggression in territorial contexts rather than for mate attraction (Levin, 1996a), with the implication that male song answering to form duets is unlikely to indicate sexual conflict. Likewise, females northern cardinals do not increase their song rates for mate attraction when their mates are removed (McElroy and Ritchison, 1996), suggesting that the simple duets formed when males answer rare female songs (Ritchison, 1986) probably do not involve sexual conflict. Some nonduetters have been shown to benefit from being guarded by a reduction in harassment (Low, 2008). Another potential benefit of being guarded, for birds with long-term pair bonds, is avoiding a loss of fitness associated with mate exchange (Black, 2001). In dusky antbirds, however, reproductive success is so low that moving to a higher quality territory may contribute more to lifetime fitness than remaining with a familiar mate (Morton et al., 2000; Morton and Stutchbury, 2000). Demonstrating sexual conflict is likely to be challenging, requiring information on individual quality of pair mates (if only individuals with low-quality partners benefit from re-pairing), as well as opportunities for re-mating.

Divorce is rare in some duetters, but this may not be the case for all duetting species. Mate-guarding in eastern whipbirds is associated with extremely low divorce rates (Rogers and Mulder, 2004), suggesting that males do not use song to attract new females, and thus that female song answering is driven more by intrasexual competition than intrapair conflict. Annual divorce rates are also very low in magpie-larks and black swans (*Cygnus atratus*) (Hall, 1999; Kraaijeveld and Mulder, 2002). However, vacancies created experimentally by removals led dusky antbirds (*Cercomacra tyrannina*) to switch territories and abandon mates, suggesting high divorce rates if opportunities arise, though natural divorce rates were not reported (Morton et al., 2000). Likewise partnerships did not seem to be long term in bay wrens (Levin, 1996a), though partnerships ending in divorce and death were not distinguished, and mortality rates and divorce rates have not been quantified for bay wrens and most other duetters. Comparative analysis has shown that low divorce rates are associated with traits often associated with duetting such as low adult mortality and continuous partnerships (Jeschke and Kokko, 2008).

If duetting species derive fitness benefits from maintaining long-term partnerships, using duetting for mate guarding (guarding the partnership) is likely to be mutually beneficial. Individuals could use duetting to maintain the pair bond by signaling commitment to their partner, as high rates of song answering, short and consistent reaction times, and adherence to answering rules all require partner-directed attention (Wickler, 1980). Furthermore, by being extremely responsive to their partner in duets, individuals may also warn off rivals throughout their communication network by signaling that their partner is mated and unavailable (Smith, 1994). If duetting does function for cooperative mate guarding, then partnerships that are not mutually beneficial are likely to be characterized by a reduction in some or all of the individual-level aspects of duetting behavior that require partner-directed attention.

Lekking *Chiroxiphia* manakins derive fitness benefits from maintaining long-term male–male partnerships, and pairs of males produce duets as part of their cooperative courtship displays (Snow, 1977). Long-tailed manakin (*C. linearis*) duets improve over a number of years, and better frequency matching between partners attracts more females (Trainer and McDonald, 1995; Trainer et al., 2002). Alpha male manakins benefit from these long-term alliances by gaining mating access to females, while it has been shown in lance-tailed manakins (*C. lanceolata*) that beta males receive delayed benefits from their participation in cooperative alliances, by increasing their probability of achieving alpha status (Duval, 2007a). Individual males may participate in more than one alliance, apparently related to changing opportunities for acquisition of partners and territories (DuVal, 2007). It would be interesting to know whether individual duetting behavior differs between alliances and whether differences in duetting performance relate to differences in the success or persistence of the alliances. The high degree of temporal coordination in the duets of *Chiroxiphia* manakins (Fig. 2B; Duval, 2007b; Snow, 1977; Trainer and McDonald, 1995), and the fact that coordination between partners (frequency matching) is learned over extended periods of time and important for achieving fitness benefits, suggests that, despite its unusual social context, duetting between male–male pairs of manakins has much in common with duetting of breeding partners in many songbirds.

C. MATE GUARDING (PATERNITY)

There is little empirical evidence to support the paternity-guarding hypothesis that males join fertile female songs to form duets to repel rival males, or that such duets indicate conflict between the sexes because fertile females sing to attract extrapair males. Duetting rates in many species peak at the start of the breeding season, broadly consistent with this hypothesis (Hall, 2006; Harcus, 1977; Sonnenschein and Reyer, 1983; Topp and Mennill, 2008), but the few studies that have looked in detail at sex differences in singing behavior in relation to female fertility do not support it. When females are fertile, males respond to fewer, rather than more, of their partner's songs by duetting in magpie-larks, buff-breasted wrens, and purple-crowned fairy-wrens (*Malurus coronatus*) (Gill et al., 2005; Hall and Magrath, 2000; Hall and Peters, 2009). Rates of extrapair paternity are very low in these species (Gill et al., 2005; Hall and Magrath, 2000; Hall and Peters, 2009), and the hypothesis has not been tested in a duetter with higher rates of extrapair paternity such as the California towhee (*Pipilo crissalis*) (Benedict, 2008b). However, male rufous-and-white wrens do respond to more of their partner's songs when females are fertile, consistent with paternity guarding, but duets appear not to be a consequence of sexual conflict over paternity as most duets are initiated by males in this species, and females initiate even fewer songs when they are fertile, apparently not attempting to attract extrapair males by singing (Topp and Mennill, 2008).

An obvious cost to using duetting as a paternity guard is that males replying to the song of their fertile female advertise to eavesdropping rivals how far they are from their partner. A study on an unusual orthopteran highlights this cost (Donelson and van Staaden, 2005). Male bladder grasshoppers (*Bullacris membracioides*) have inflated abdomens that allow them to produce calls detectable at distances of up to 2 km. Receptive females are stationary, but respond to males in duet, allowing males to locate and approach them in a series of duets. An alternative male morph lacks the bladder necessary for long-range communication, but achieves mating with females by exploiting the mate location system of duetting pairs, using female duetting responses to bladdered males to locate them for matings (Donelson and van Staaden, 2005). Similar exploitation by eavesdropping males may have led to initiating males producing additional calls to mask female responses in *Caedicia*, an Australian genus of duetting phaneropterine bushcrickets (Hammond and Bailey, 2003). Duetting birds may avoid exploitation by eavesdroppers by being less likely to reply to their partner in duet when they are far from them (Hall and Magrath, 2000; Logue, 2007b), and by approaching a distant partner that replies to their song in duet (Logue, 2007b; Mennill and Vehrencamp, 2008). However, the decline in vocal responsiveness with distance is true of both males and females, in both fertile and nonfertile periods in magpie-larks (Hall and Magrath, 2000), and approach responses in the wrens are true not only of males, but of females also, suggesting they are for other reasons than guarding paternity (see Sections VII.A and VII.B), though the role of duetting in maintaining contact between partners during the fertile period has not yet been examined.

D. RECOGNITION AND CONTACT

Birds sometimes duet cooperatively to reveal their identity and location to their partner, facilitating maintenance of contact in dense habitat. Duetting may be more effective than contact calls if a rapid reply with a predictable song type facilitates identifying and locating a mate when attention is limited or the environment is noisy (Lamprecht et al., 1985; Logue, 2006; Thorpe and North, 1966). Observations that duetting by widely separated partners is followed by them moving closer together provide anecdotal support for the hypothesis (Benedict, 2009; Brown and Lemon, 1979), with additional indirect support from Steere's liocichla (*Liocichla steerii*), where females living in denser habitat respond to a higher percentage of their partner's songs in duet (Mays et al., 2006). Direct evidence comes from two studies using innovative approaches to quantify spatial relationships between duetting birds. The first study radio-tracked black-bellied wrens to show that male or female songs given when partners were more than 10 m apart were more likely to be followed by approach if the partner replied in duet than if the partner did not sing (Logue, 2007b). Interestingly, these approaches were more likely to be by the initiating bird than by the responding bird, suggesting that the initiator may be soliciting information about its partner's location when it sings, and that duetting in this context therefore represents a cooperative response by the partner that reveals its location. The second study used an array of microphones to triangulate the positions of rufous-and-white wrens when they sang, and showed that partners were significantly more likely to approach one another than to move apart over the course of a bout of duetting (Mennill and Vehrencamp, 2008). Males and females covered similar distances in their approaches, but the bird that sang first moved further than the bird that duetted in reply suggesting that, as in black-bellied wrens, the answering bird is cooperatively revealing its location to allow its partner to approach it.

Though contact maintenance is not usually a primary function of duetting, quantifying spatial interactions between partners may reveal this secondary function in more duetting species. Since simple contact calls would suffice to maintain contact between partners, it seems unlikely that this function would select for the evolution of complex duets, particularly since partners perch close together when they duet in many duetting species (Wickler, 1980). However, even though black-bellied wrens and rufous-and-white wrens were more likely to duet when partners were closer together, duets by distant partners were nevertheless associated with approach (Logue, 2007b; Mennill and Vehrencamp, 2008). Studies on other species that usually duet when partners are close together should quantify movements associated with the subset of songs given when birds are far apart to determine whether duetting functions in contact maintenance in this context.

E. Ensuring Reproductive Synchrony

Dilger (1953) suggested that duetting could help partners achieve reproductive synchrony after observing crimson-breasted barbets duetting together after courtship feeding. Kunkel (1974) suggested that prolonged and asynchronous breeding seasons in tropical areas favor long-term pair bonds and behavioral mechanisms such as duetting for synchronizing the reproductive states of partners. Since then, studies on several duetting species have shown that duetting rates peak during prebreeding or nest-building, and when pairs renest after nest failure (Hall, 2006; Sonnenschein and Reyer, 1983; Topp and Mennill, 2008), much as male song rates do in nonduetting species. Since both male and female vocalizations can stimulate ovarian development and nest building (Catchpole and Slater, 2008; Cheng, 1992; Cheng et al., 1998), and behavioral cues may be important for synchronizing breeding partners where nesting within a population is not highly synchronous (Moore et al., 2005), it seems likely that duetting could be important in activating and synchronizing male and female reproductive systems. Consistent with this, no nesting activity occurred in two pairs of white-browed robin-chats that were experimentally prevented from duetting (Todt and Hultsch, 1982). Only one study has investigated the relationship between duetting and reproductive hormones during the breeding cycle, and female song answering was correlated with testosterone rather than reproductive hormones (Schwabl and Sonnenschein, 1992), so it is currently unclear whether duetting plays a role in activating and synchronizing male and female reproductive states. Studies that quantify changes in duetting behavior on a fine scale to determine whether the answering rates of one or both sexes peak before or after the commencement of nest building, and whether pairs that duet more in the prebreeding period commence laying sooner than pairs that duet less would be useful for testing this hypothesis.

IX. Conclusions

Duets that comprise loosely overlapping songs formed as a result of one bird initiating its song soon after its partner are likely to differ functionally from duets comprising a long series of coordinated phrases where both partners make very rapid adjustments to the timing and type of their vocalizations in response to those of their partner over the course of the duet. The latter form of duetting is more likely to require cooperation from both partners, and thus serve functions that are mutually beneficial to both sexes. Furthermore, the partner-directed effort required in these duets means that even if the joint display is directed at others (primary function is inter-pair), the individual behaviors will signal motivation or commitment to the partner (intrapair communication occurs, Smith, 1994; Wickler, 1980). It is not surprising therefore, that duets are multifunctional in many species, though the effect of duetting behavior on aspects of fitness such as territory tenure and the duration or productivity of partnerships is yet to be assessed.

Many studies on duetting have focused on the form and function of duetting, but more work is needed on its ontogeny and causes. Studies on song ontogeny in duetting birds have investigated the development of song more than the development of duetting, and hence the ontogeny of duetting is poorly understood, particularly in wild birds (Seibt et al., 2002; Wickler and Sonnenschein, 1989). Studies on the neural basis of song in duetting species have investigated sex differences in neural structures underlying song type complexity (Brenowitz and Arnold, 1986), but the neural pathways involved in precise temporal coordination of songs into duets and linking particular song types on very rapid time scales have not been examined. Likewise, the hormonal basis of song, but not duetting, has been examined in endocrinological studies on duetting birds.

Despite being a relatively rare phenomenon, avian duetting is taxonomically widespread, with many independent evolutionary origins indicating strong selective pressure favoring coordination of vocalizations into duets. Ancestry appears to be a strong predictor of both the presence and form of duetting, but ecological and life history traits are also likely to be important. Many of the life history traits believed to be associated with duetting are also characteristic of tropical and south temperate birds, and there is a need for quantitative analyses controlling for the confound of latitude as well as phylogeny. Examining variation in ecological and life history traits within and between families, and relating these traits to variation in the individual-level behaviors underlying different duetting styles, will help shed light on differences between species and between the sexes in the intensity and nature of the selective pressures driving the evolution of duetting.

Acknowledgments

Many thanks to Peter Slater for his enthusiasm and encouragement of research in avian duetting. Thanks also to David Logue, Peter Slater, and Naomi Langmore for discussion and comments that significantly improved this chapter. I was supported during the writing of this review by the Max Planck Society "Sonderprogramm zur Förderung hervorragender Wissenschaftlerinnen."

References

Amador, A., Trevisan, M.A., Mindlin, G.B., 2005. Simple neural substrate predicts complex rhythmic structure in duetting birds. Phys. Rev. E 72, 031905.

Appleby, B.M., Yamaguchi, N., Johnson, P.J., MacDonald, D.W., 1999. Sex specific territorial responses in tawny owls *Strix aluco*. Ibis 141, 91–99.

Armstrong, E.A., 1947. Bird Display and Behaviour. Lindsay & Drummond Ltd., London.

Arrowood, P.C., 1988. Duetting, pair bonding and agonistic display in parakeet pairs. Behaviour 106, 129–157.

Bailey, W.J., 2003. Insect duets: underlying mechanisms and their evolution. Physiol. Entomol. 28, 157–174.

Baker, M.C., 2004. The chorus song of cooperatively breeding laughing kookaburras (Coraciiformes, Halcyonidae: Dacelo novaeguineae): characterization and comparison among groups. Ethology 110, 21–35.

Barker, F.K., Cibois, A., Schikler, P., Feinstein, J., acraft, J., 2004. Phylogeny and diversification of the largest avian radiation. Proc. Natl. Acad. Sci. USA 101, 11040–11045.

Benedict, L., 2008a. Occurrence and life history correlates of vocal duetting in North American passerines. J. Avian. Biol. 39, 57–65.

Benedict, L., 2008b. Unusually high levels of extrapair paternity in a duetting songbird with long-term pair bonds. Behav. Ecol. Sociobiol. 62, 983–988.

Benedict, L., 2009. Context, structural variability and distinctiveness of California towhee (*Pipilo crissalis*) vocal duets. Ethology 115, 77–86.

Black, J.M., 2001. Fitness consequences of long-term pair bonds in barnacle geese: monogamy in the extreme. Behav. Ecol. 12, 640–645.

Bradley, D.W., Mennill, D.J., 2009. Strong ungraded responses to playback of solos, duets and choruses in a cooperatively breeding Neotropical songbird. Anim. Behav. 77, 1321–1327.

Brenowitz, E.A., Arnold, A.P., 1986. Interspecific comparisons of the size of neural song control regions and song complexity in duetting birds: evolutionary implications. J. Neurosci. 6, 2875–2879.

Brown, E.D., Farabaugh, S.M., 1991. Song sharing in a group-living songbird, the Australian magpie, *Gymnorhina tibicen*. 3. Sex specificity and individual specificity of vocal parts in communal chorus and duet songs. Behaviour 118, 244–274.

Brown, E.D., Farabaugh, S.M., 1997. What birds with complex social relationships can tell us about vocal learning: vocal sharing in avian groups. In: Snowdon, C.T., Hausberger, M. (Eds.), Social Influences on Vocal Development. Cambridge University Press, Cambridge, pp. 98–127.

Brown, R.N., Lemon, R.E., 1979. Structure and evolution of song form in the wrens *Thryothorus sinaloa* and *T. Felix*. Behav. Ecol. Sociobiol. 5, 111–131.

Brumm, H., 2006. Signalling through acoustic windows: nightingales avoid interspecific competition by short-term adjustment of song timing. J. Comp. Physiol. A 192, 1279–1285.

Brumm, H., Slater, P., 2007. Animal communication: timing counts. Curr. Biol. 17, R521–R523.

Brunton, D.H., Li, X.L., 2006. The song structure and seasonal patterns of vocal behavior of male and female bellbirds (*Anthornis melanura*). J. Ethol. 24, 17–25.

Busch, D.S., Wingfield, J.C., Moore, I.T., 2004. Territorial aggression of a tropical passerine, *Zonotrichia capensis*, in response to a variety of conspecific intruders. Behaviour 141, 1173–1188.

Catchpole, C.K., Slater, P.J.B., 2008. Bird Song: Biological Themes and Variations. Cambridge University Press, Cambridge.

Chapman, G., 1999. Bristlebirds: see how they run. Wingspan 8–15 March.

Cheng, M.F., 1992. For whom does the female dove coo—a case for the role of vocal self-stimulation. Anim. Behav. 43, 1035–1044.

Cheng, M.F., Peng, J.P., Johnson, P., 1998. Hypothalamic neurons preferentially respond to female nest coo stimulation: demonstration of direct acoustic stimulation of luteinizing hormone release. J. Neurosci. 18, 5477–5489.

Cobb, N.A., 1897. The sheep-fluke. Agric. Gaz. NSW 8, 470–480.

Cooney, R., Cockburn, A., 1995. Territorial defence is the major function of female song in the superb fairy-wren, *Malurus cyaneus*. Anim. Behav. 49, 1635–1647.

Cuthbert, J.L., Mennill, D.J., 2007. The duetting behavior of Pacific Coast plain wrens. Condor 109, 686–692.

Diamond, J.M., 1972. Further examples of dual singing by southwest Pacific birds. Auk 89, 180–183.

Diamond, J.M., Terborgh, J.W., 1968. Dual singing by New Guinea birds. Auk 85, 62–82.

Dilger, W.C., 1953. Duetting in the crimson-breasted barbet. Condor 55, 220–221.

Dingle, C., Halfwerk, W., Slabbekoorn, H., 2008. Habitat-dependent song divergence at subspecies level in the grey-breasted wood-wren. J. Evol. Biol. 21, 1079–1089.

Dobler, S., Heller, K.G., von Helversen, O., 1994. Song pattern recognition and an auditory time window in the female bushcricket *Ancistrura nigrovittata* (Orthoptera: Phaneropteridae). J. Comp. Physiol. A 175, 67–74.

Donelson, N.C., van Staaden, M.J., 2005. Alternate tactics in male bladder grasshoppers *Bullacris membracioides* (Orthoptera: Pneumoridae). Behaviour 142, 761–778.

DuVal, E.H., 2007. Social organization and variation in cooperative alliances among male lance-tailed manakins. Anim. Behav. 73, 391–401.

Duval, E.H., 2007a. Adaptive advantages of cooperative courtship for subordinate male lance-tailed manakins. Am. Nat. 169, 423–432.

Duval, E.H., 2007b. Cooperative display and lekking behavior of the Lance-tailed Manakin (*Chiroxiphia lanceolata*). Auk 124, 1168–1185.

Farabaugh, S.M., 1982. The ecological and social significance of duetting. In: Kroodsma, D.E., Miller, E.H. (Eds.), Acoustic Communication in Birds. Academic Press, New York, pp. 85–124.

Farabaugh, S.M., Brown, E.D., Hughes, J.M., 1992. Cooperative territorial defense in the Australian magpie, *Gymnorhina tibicen* (Passeriformes, Cracticidae), a group-living songbird. Ethology 92, 283–292.

Fedy, B.C., Stutchbury, B.J.M., 2005. Territory defence in tropical birds: are females as aggressive as males? Behav. Ecol. Sociobiol. 58, 414–422.

Ficken, R.W., Ficken, M.S., Hailman, J.P., 1974. Temporal pattern shifts to avoid acoustic interference in singing birds. Science 183, 762–763.

Ficken, M.S., Rusch, K.M., Taylor, S.J., Powers, D.R., 2000. Blue-throated hummingbird song: a pinnacle of nonoscine vocalizations. Auk 117, 120–128.

Fuchs, J., Bowie, R.C.K., Fjeldsa, J., Pasquet, E., 2004. Phylogenetic relationships of the African bush-shrikes and helmet-shrikes (Passeriformes: Malaconotidae). Mol. Phylogenet. Evol. 33, 428–439.

Garamszegi, L.Z., Pavlova, D.Z., Eens, M., Moller, A.P., 2007. The evolution of song in female birds in Europe. Behav. Ecol. 18, 86–96.

Garamszegi, L.Z., Hirschenhauser, K., Bokony, V., Eens, M., Hurtrez-Bousses, S., Moller, A.P., et al., 2008. Latitudinal distribution, migration, and testosterone levels in birds. Am. Nat. 172, 533–546.

Gaunt, S.L.L., Baptista, L.F., Sanchez, J.E., Hernandez, D., 1994. Song learning as evidenced from song sharing in two hummingbird species (*Colibri coruscans and C. Thalassinus*). Auk 111, 87–103.

Geissmann, T., 2002. Duet-splitting and the evolution of gibbon songs. Biol. Rev. 77, 57–76.

Gill, S.A., Vonhof, M.J., Stutchbury, B.J.M., Morton, E.S., Quinn, J.S., 2005. No evidence for acoustic mate-guarding in duetting buff-breasted wrens (*Thryothorus leucotis*). Behav. Ecol. Sociobiol. 57, 557–565.

Gill, S.A., Alfson, E.D., Hau, M., 2007. Context matters: female aggression and testosterone in a year-round territorial neotropical songbird (*Thryothorus leucotis*). Proc. R. Soc. Lond. B 274, 2187–2194.

Gill, S.A., Costa, L.M., Hau, M., 2008. Males of a single-brooded tropical bird species do not show increases in testosterone during social challenges. Horm. Behav. 54, 115–124.

Goymann, W., Moore, I.T., Scheuerlein, A., Hirschenhauser, K., Grafen, A., Wingfield, J.C., 2004. Testosterone in tropical birds: effects of environmental and social factors. Am. Nat. 164, 327–334.

Grafe, T.U., Bitz, J.H., 2004a. An acoustic postconflict display in the duetting tropical boubou (*Laniarius aethiopicus*): a signal of victory? BMC Ecol. 4, 1.

Grafe, T.U., Bitz, J.H., 2004b. Functions of duetting in the tropical boubou, *Laniarius aethiopicus*: territorial defence and mutual mate guarding. Anim. Behav. 68, 193–201.

Grafe, T.U., Bitz, J.H., Wink, M., 2004. Song repertoire and duetting behaviour of the tropical boubou, *Laniarius aethiopicus*. Anim. Behav. 68, 181–191.

Greig, E., Pruett-Jones, S., 2008. Splendid songs: the vocal behaviour of Splendid Fairy-wrens (*Malurus splendens melanotus*). Emu 108, 103–114.

Grimes, L., 1965. Antiphonal singing in *Laniarius barbarus* and the auditory reaction time. Ibis 107, 101–104.

Hackett, S.J., Kimball, R.T., Reddy, S., Bowie, R.C.K., Braun, E.L., Braun, M.J., et al., 2008. A phylogenomic study of birds reveals their evolutionary history. Science 320, 1763–1768.

Hale, A.M., 2006. The structure, context and functions of group singing in black-breasted wood-quail (*Odontophorus leucolaemus*). Behaviour 143, 511–533.

Hall, M.L., 1999. The importance of pair duration and biparental care to reproductive success in the monogamous Australian magpie-lark. Aust. J. Zool. 47, 439–454.

Hall, M.L., 2000. The function of duetting in magpie-larks: conflict, cooperation, or commitment? Anim. Behav. 60, 667–677.

Hall, M.L., 2004. A review of hypotheses for the functions of avian duetting. Behav. Ecol. Sociobiol. 55, 415–430.

Hall, M.L., 2006. Convergent vocal strategies of males and females are consistent with a cooperative function of duetting in Australian magpie-larks. Behaviour 143, 425–449.

Hall, M.L., Magrath, R.D., 2000. Duetting and mate-guarding in Australian magpie-larks (*Grallina cyanoleuca*). Behav. Ecol. Sociobiol. 47, 180–187.

Hall, M.L., Magrath, R.D., 2007. Temporal coordination signals coalition quality. Curr. Biol. 17, R406–R407.

Hall, M.L., Peters, A., 2008. Coordination between the sexes for territorial defence in a duetting fairy-wren. Anim. Behav. 76, 65–73.

Hall, M.L., Peters, A., 2009. Do male paternity guards ensure female fidelity in a duetting fairy-wren? Behav. Ecol. 20, 222–228.

Hall, M.L., Illes, A., Vehrencamp, S.L., 2006. Overlapping signals in banded wrens: long-term effects of prior experience on males and females. Behav. Ecol. 17, 260–269.

Hammond, T.J., Bailey, W.J., 2003. Eavesdropping and defensive auditory masking in an Australian Bushcricket, *Caedicia* (Phaneropterinae: Tettigoniidae: Orthoptera). Behaviour 140, 79–95.

Harcus, J.L., 1977. The functions of vocal duetting in some African birds. Z. Tierpsychol. 43, 23–45.

Harris, T., Franklin, K., 2000. Shrikes and Bush-Shrikes. A & C Black, London.

Hau, M., Stoddard, S.T., Soma, K.K., 2004. Territorial aggression and hormones during the non-breeding season in a tropical bird. Horm. Behav. 45, 40–49.

Hultsch, H., Todt, D., 1982. Temporal performance roles during vocal interactions in nightingales (*Luscinia megarhynchos B*). Behav. Ecol. Sociobiol. 11, 253–260.

Hultsch, H., Todt, D., 1984. Spatial proximity between allies: a territorial signal tested in the monogamous duet singer *Cossypha heuglini*. Behaviour 91, 286–293.

Hultch, H., Todt, D., 2004. Learning to sing. In: Slabbekoorn, H. (Ed.), Nature's Music: The Science of Birdsong. Elsevier Academic Press, Oxford, pp. 80–107.

Illes, A.E., Yunes-Jimenez, L., 2009. A female bird out-sings male conspecifics during simulated territorial intrusions. Proc. R. Soc. Lond. B 276, 981–986.

Immelmann, K., 1961. Beitrage zur biologie u. Ethologie australischer honigfresser (Meliphagidae). J. Ornithol. 102, 164–207.

Jeschke, J.M., Kokko, H., 2008. Mortality and other determinants of bird divorce rate. Behav. Ecol. Sociobiol. 63, 1–9.

King, B.R., 1980. Social organisation and behaviour of the grey-crowned babbler *Pomatostomus temporalis*. Emu 80, 59.

Klenova, A.V., Volodin, I.A., Volodina, E.V., 2008. Duet structure provides information about pair identity in the red-crowned crane (*Grus japonensis*). J. Ethol. 26, 317–325.

Kraaijeveld, K., Mulder, R.A., 2002. The function of triumph ceremonies in the black swan. Behaviour 139, 45–54.

Kroodsma, D.E., 2004. The diversity and plasticity of birdsong. In: Marler, P., Slabbekoorn, H. (Eds.), Nature's Music: The Science of Birdsong. Elsevier Academic Press, Oxford, pp. 108–131.

Kroodsma, D.E., Ingalls, V.A., Sherry, T.W., Werner, T.K., 1987. Songs of the Cocos flycatcher: vocal behaviour of a suboscine on an isolated oceanic island. Condor 89, 75–84.

Kunkel, P., 1974. Mating systems of tropical birds: the effects of weakness or absence of external reproduction-timing factors with special reference to prolonged pair bonds. Z. Tierpsychol. 34, 265–307.

Laje, R., Mindlin, G.B., 2003. Highly structured duets in the song of the South American Hornero. Phys. Rev. Lett. 91, 258104.

Lamprecht, J., Kaiser, A., Peters, A., Kirchgessner, C., 1985. Distance call duets in bar-headed geese (*Anser indicus*): co-operation through visual relief of the partner? Z. Tierpsychol. 70, 211–218.

Langmore, N.E., 1998. Functions of duet and solo songs of female birds. Trends Ecol. Evol. 13, 136–140.

Levin, R.N., 1996a. Song behaviour and reproductive strategies in a duetting wren, *Thryothorus nigricapillus*: I. Removal experiments. Anim. Behav. 52, 1093–1106.

Levin, R.N., 1996b. Song behaviour and reproductive strategies in a duetting wren, *Thryothorus nigricapillus*: II. Playback experiments. Anim. Behav. 52, 1107–1117.

Levin, R.N., Paris, T.I., Bester, J.K., 1996. Social versus innate influences on the development of sex-specific song in a tropical duetting wren. Am. Zool. 36, 92A.

Logue, D.M., 2005. Cooperative defence in duet singing birds. Cogn. Brain Behav. 9, 497–510.

Logue, D.M., 2006. The duet code of the female black-bellied wren. Condor 108, 326–335.

Logue, D.M., 2007a. How do they duet? Sexually dimorphic behavioural mechanisms structure duet songs in the black-bellied wren. Anim. Behav. 73, 105–113.

Logue, D.M., 2007b. Duetting in space: a radio-telemetry study of the black-bellied wren. Proc. R. Soc. Lond. B 274, 3005–3010.

Logue, D.M., Forstmeier, W., 2008. Constrained performance in a communication network: implications for the function of song-type matching and for the evolution of multiple ornaments. Am. Nat. 172, 34–41.

Logue, D.M., Gammon, D.E., 2004. Duet song and sex roles during territory defence in a tropical bird, the black-bellied wren, *Thryothorus fasciatoventris*. Anim. Behav. 68, 721–731.

Logue, D.M., Chalmers, C., Gowland, A.H., 2008. The behavioural mechanisms underlying temporal coordination in black-bellied wren duets. Anim. Behav. 75, 1803–1808.

Low, M., 2008. Laying gaps in the New Zealand Stitchbird are correlated with female harassment by extra-pair males. Emu 108, 28–34.

MacDougall-Shackleton, S.A., Ball, G.F., 1999. Comparative studies of sex differences in the song-control system of songbirds. Trends Neurosci. 22, 432–436.

Malacarne, G., Cucco, M., Camanni, S., 1991. Coordinated visual displays and vocal duetting in different ecological situations among Western Palearctic non-passerine birds. Ethol. Ecol. Evol. 3, 207–219.

Maney, D.L., Goode, C.T., Lake, J.I., Lange, H.S., O'Brien, S., 2007. Rapid neuroendocrine responses to auditory courtship signals. Endocrinology 148, 5614–5623.

Mann, N.I., Marshall-Ball, L., Slater, P.J.B., 2003. The complex song duet of the plain wren. Condor 105, 672–682.

Mann, N.I., Dingess, K.A., Slater, P.J.B., 2005. Antiphonal four-part synchronized chorusing in a neotropical wren. Biol. Lett. 2, 1–4.

Mann, N.I., Barker, F.K., Graves, J.A., Dingess-Mann, K.A., Slater, P.J.B., 2006. Molecular data delineate four genera of *"Thryothorus"* wrens. Mol. Phylogenet. Evol. 40, 750–759.

Mann, N.I., Dingess, K.A., Barker, F.K., Graves, G.R., Slater, P.J.B., 2009. A comparative study of song form and duetting in neotropical *Thryothorus* wrens. Behaviour 146, 1–43.

Maples, E.G., Haraway, M.M., Hutto, C.W., 1989. Development of coordinated singing in a newly formed siamang pair (*Hylobates syndactylus*). Zoo Biol. 8, 367–378.

Marshall-Ball, L., Slater, P.J.B., 2004. Duet singing and repertoire use in threat signalling of individuals and pairs. Proc. R. Soc. Lond. B 271, S440–S443.

Marshall-Ball, L., Slater, P.J.B., 2008. Repertoire sharing by the individual and the pair: insights into duet function and development in the plain wren *Thryothorus modestus*. J. Avian. Biol. 39, 293–299.

Marshall-Ball, L., Mann, N., Slater, P.J.B., 2006. Multiple functions to duet singing: hidden conflicts and apparent cooperation. Anim. Behav. 71, 823–831.

Martin, T.E., 1996. Life history evolution in tropical and south temperate birds—what do we really know? J. Avian. Biol. 27, 263–272.

Maurer, G., Smith, C., Susser, M., Magrath, R.D., 2008. Solo and duet calling in the pheasant coucal: sex and individual call differences in a nesting cuckoo with reversed size dimorphism. Aust. J. Zool. 56, 143–149.

Mays, H.L., Yao, C.T., Yuan, H.W., 2006. Antiphonal duetting in Steere's liocichla (*Liocichla steerii*): male song individuality and correlation between habitat and duetting behavior. Ecol. Res. 21, 311–314.

McElroy, D.B., Ritchison, G., 1996. Effect of mate removal on singing behavior and movement patterns of female northern cardinals. Wilson Bull. 108, 550–555.

Mennill, D.J., 2006. Aggressive responses of male and female rufous-and-white wrens to stereo duet playback. Anim. Behav. 71, 219–226.

Mennill, D.J., Rogers, A.C., 2006. Whip it good! Geographic consistency in male songs and variability in female songs of the duetting eastern whipbird *Psophodes olivaceus*. J. Avian. Biol. 37, 93–100.

Mennill, D.J., Vehrencamp, S.L., 2005. Sex differences in singing and duetting behavior of neotropical rufous-and-white wrens (*Thryothorus rufalbus*). Auk 122, 175–186.

Mennill, D.J., Vehrencamp, S.L., 2008. Context-dependent functions of avian duets revealed by microphone-array recordings and multispeaker playback. Curr. Biol. 18, 1314–1319.

Mennill, D.J., Ratcliffe, L.M., Boag, P.T., 2002. Female eavesdropping on male song contests in songbirds. Science 296, 873–873.

Merkle, T.F.C., 2006. Territoriality, breeding biology and vocalisations of the crimson-breasted shrike. Ostrich 77, 136–141.

Mitani, J.C., 1987. Territoriality and monogamy among agile gibbons (*Hylobates agilis*). Behav. Ecol. Sociobiol. 20, 265–269.

Molles, L.E., Waas, J.R., 2006. Are two heads better than one? Responses of the duetting kokako to one- and two-speaker playback. Anim. Behav. 72, 131–138.

Molles, L.E., Hudson, J.D., Waas, J.R., 2006. The mechanics of duetting in a New Zealand endemic, the kokako (*Callaeas cinerea wilsoni*): song at a snail's pace. Ethology 112, 424–436.

Moore, I.T., Bonier, F., Wingfield, J.C., 2005. Reproductive asynchrony and population divergence between two tropical bird populations. Behav. Ecol. 16, 755–762.

Morton, E.S., 1996. A comparison of vocal behavior among tropical and temperate passerine birds. In: Kroodsma, D.E., Miller, E.H. (Eds.), Ecology and Evolution of Acoustic Communication in Birds. Cornell University Press, Ithaca, pp. 258–268.

Morton, E.S., Stutchbury, B.J.M., 2000. Demography and reproductive success in the dusky antbird, a sedentary tropical passerine. J. Field Ornithol. 71, 493–500.

Morton, E.S., Derrickson, K.C., Stutchbury, B.J.M., 2000. Territory switching behavior in a sedentary tropical passerine, the dusky antbird (*Cercomacra tyrannina*). Behav. Ecol. 11, 648–653.

Moyle, R.G., 2004. Phylogenetics of barbets (Aves: Piciformes) based on nuclear and mito-chondrial DNA sequence data. Mol. Phylogenet. Evol. 30, 187–200.

Naguib, M., 1999. Effects of song overlapping and alternating on nocturnally singing night-ingales. Anim. Behav. 58, 1061–1067.

Naguib, M., Todt, D., 1997. Effects of dyadic vocal interactions on other conspecific receivers in nightingales. Anim. Behav. 54, 1535–1543.

Naguib, M., Fichtel, C., Todt, D., 1999. Nightingales respond more strongly to vocal leaders of simulated dyadic interactions. Proc. R. Soc. Lond. Ser. B Biol. Sci. 266, 537–542.

Nealen, P.M., Perkel, D.J., 2000. Sexual dimorphism in the song system of the Carolina wren *Thryothorus ludovicianus*. J. Comp. Neurol. 418, 346–360.

Nguembock, B., Fjeldsa, J., Couioux, A., Pasquet, E., 2008. Phylogeny of *Laniarius*: molecular data reveal *L. liberatus* synonymous with *L. erlangeri* and "plumage coloration" as unreliable morphological characters for defining species and species groups. Mol. Phylogenet. Evol. 48, 396–407.

Nottebohm, F., 1972. The origins of vocal learning. Am. Nat. 106, 116–140.

Nottebohm, F., Arnold, A.P., 1976. Sexual dimorphism in vocal control areas of songbird brain. Science 194, 211–213.

Payne, R.B., 1971. Duetting and chorus singing in African birds. Ostrich (Suppl. 9), 125–146.

Payne, R.B., Skinner, N.J., 1970. Temporal patterns of duetting in African barbets. Ibis 112, 173–183.

Peach, W.J., Hanmer, D.B., Oatley, T.B., 2001. Do southern African songbirds live longer than their European counterparts? Oikos 93, 235–249.

Power, D.M., 1966. Antiphonal duetting and evidence for auditory reaction time in the orange-chinned parakeet. Auk 83, 314–319.

Price, J.J., 2009. Evolution and life history correlates of female song in the New World blackbirds. Behav. Ecol. doi: 10.1093/beheco/arp085.

Price, J.J., Yunes-Jimenez, L., Osorio-Beristain, M., Omland, K.E., Murphy, T.G., 2008. Sex-role reversal in song? Females sing more frequently than males in the streak-backed oriole. Condor 110, 387–392.

Price, J.J., Lanyon, S.M., Omland, K.E., 2009. Losses of female song with changes from tropical to temperate breeding in the New World blackbirds. Proc. Roy. Soc. Lond. B 276, 1971–1980.

Reyer, H.U., Schmidl, D., 1988. Helpers have little to laugh about: group structure and vocalisation in the laughing kookaburra Dacelo novaeguineae. Emu 88, 150–160.

Riebel, K., 2003. The "mute" sex revisited: vocal production and perception learning in female songbirds. Adv. Study Behav. 33, 49–86.

Riebel, K., Hall, M.L., Langmore, N.E., 2005. Female songbirds still struggling to be heard. Trends Ecol. Evol. 20, 419–420.

Ritchison, G., 1986. The singing behaviour of female northern cardinals. Condor 88, 156–159.

Robinson, A., 1949. The biological significance of bird song in Australia. Emu 48, 291–315.

Rogers, A.C., 2005. Male and female song structure and singing behaviour in the duetting eastern whipbird, Psophodes olivaceus. Aust. J. Zool. 53, 157–166.

Rogers, A.C., Mulder, R.A., 2004. Breeding ecology and social behaviour of an antiphonal duetter, the eastern whipbird (Psophodes olivaceus). Aust. J. Zool. 52, 417–435.

Rogers, A.C., Ferguson, J.E., Harrington, H.M., McDowell, S., Miller, A., Panagos, J., 2004. Use of stereo duet playback to investigate traditional duet playback methods and mechanisms of cooperative territorial defence in magpie-larks. Behaviour 141, 741–753.

Rogers, A.C., Mulder, R.A., Langmore, N.E., 2006. Duet duels: sex differences in song matching in duetting eastern whipbirds. Anim. Behav. 72, 53–61.

Rogers, A.C., Langmore, N.E., Mulder, R.A., 2007. Function of pair duets in the eastern whipbird: cooperative defense or sexual conflict? Behav. Ecol. 18, 182–188.

Russell, E., Rowley, I., 1996. Partnerships in promiscuous splendid fairy-wrens. In: Black, J.M. (Ed.), Partnerships in Birds: The Study of Monogamy. Oxford University Press, Oxford, pp. 162–173.

Russell, E.M., Yom-Tov, Y., Geffen, E., 2004. Extended parental care and delayed dispersal: northern, tropical, and southern passerines compared. Behav. Ecol. 15, 831–838.

Schwabl, H., 1992. Winter and breeding territorial behavior and levels of reproductive hormones of migratory European robins. Orn. Scand. 23, 271–276.

Schwabl, H., Sonnenschein, E., 1992. Antiphonal duetting and sex hormones in the tropical bush shrike Laniarius funebris. Horm. Behav. 26, 295–307.

Seddon, N., 2002. The structure, context and possible functions of solos, duets and choruses in the subdesert mesite (Monias benschi). Behaviour 139, 645–676.

Seddon, N., Tobias, J.A., 2003. Communal singing in the cooperatively breeding subdesert mesite Monias benschi: evidence of numerical assessment? J. Avian. Biol. 34, 72–80.

Seddon, N., Tobias, J.A., 2006. Duets defend mates in a suboscine passerine, the warbling antbird (Hypocnemis cantator). Behav. Ecol. 17, 73–83.

Seddon, N., Butchart, S.H.M., Odling-Smee, L., 2002. Duetting in the subdesert mesite Monias benschi: evidence for acoustic mate defence? Behav. Ecol. Sociobiol. 52, 7–16.

Seddon, N., Merrill, R.M., Tobias, J.A., 2008. Sexually selected traits predict patterns of species richness in a diverse clade of suboscine birds. Am. Nat. 171, 620–631.

Seibt, U., Wickler, W., 1977. Ein stimmfuhlungs-duett beim hornraben, *Bucorvus leadbeateri* (Vigors). J. Orn. 118, 195–198.

Seibt, U., Wickler, W., 2000. "Sympathetic song": the silent and the overt vocal repertoire, exemplified with a dueting pair of the African slate-coloured boubou, *Laniarius funebris*. Ethology 106, 795–809.

Seibt, U., Wickler, W., Kleindienst, H.U., Sonnenschein, E., 2002. Structure, geography and origin of dialects in the traditive song of the forest weaver *Ploceus bicolor sclateri* in Natal, S. Africa. Behaviour 139, 1237–1265.

Short, L.L., Horne, J.F.M., 1983. A review of duetting, sociality and speciation in some African barbets (Capitonidae). Condor 85, 323–332.

Sibley, C.G., Ahlquist, J.E., 1990. Phylogeny and Classification of Birds: A Study in Molecular Evolution. Yale University Press, London.

Slabbekoorn, H., den Boer-Visser, A., 2006. Cities change the songs of birds. Curr. Biol. 16, 2326–2331.

Slater, P.J.B., Mann, N.I., 2004. Why do the females of many bird species sing in the tropics? J. Avian. Biol. 35, 289–294.

Slater, P.J.B., Gil, D., Barlow, C.R., Graves, J.A., 2002. Male-led duets in the moho, *Hypergerus atriceps*, and yellow-crowned gonolek, *Laniarius barbarus*. Ostrich 73, 49–51.

Smith, G.T., 1987. Observations on the biology of the western bristlebird *Dasyornis longirostris*. Emu 87, 111–118.

Smith, G.T., 1991. Ecology of the western whipbird *Psophodes nigrogularis* in Western Australia. Emu 91, 145–157.

Smith, W.J., 1994. Animal duets: forcing a mate to be attentive. J. Theor. Biol. 166, 221–223.

Snow, D.W., 1977. Duetting and other synchronised displays of the blue-backed manakins, *Chiroxiphia* spp. In: Stonehouse, B., Perrins, C.M. (Eds.), Evolutionary Ecology. Macmillan, London, pp. 239–251.

Sonnenschein, E., Reyer, H.U., 1983. Mate-guarding and other functions of antiphonal duets in the slate-coloured boubou (*Laniarius funebris*). Z. Tierpsychol. 63, 112–140.

Stiles, F.G., Skutch, A.F., 1989. A Guide to the Birds of Costa Rica. Cornell University Press, Ithaca, NY.

Thorpe, W.H., 1963. Antiphonal singing in birds as evidence for avian auditory reaction time. Nature 197, 774–776.

Thorpe, W.H., 1972. Duetting and antiphonal song in birds: its extent and significance. Behaviour (Suppl. 18), 1–197.

Thorpe, W.H., North, M.E.W., 1966. Vocal imitation in the tropical bou-bou shrike *Laniarius aethopicus major* as a means of establishing and maintaining social bonds. Ibis 108, 432–435.

Tingay, S.R., 1974. Antiphonal song in the magpie-lark. Emu 74, 11–17.

Tobias, J.A., Seddon, N., 2009. Signal jamming mediates sexual conflict in a duetting bird. Curr. Biol. 19, 577–582.

Tobias, M.L., Viswanathan, S.S., Kelley, D.B., 1998. Rapping, a female receptive call, initiates male-female duets in the South African clawed frog. Proc. Natl. Acad. Sci. USA 95, 1870–1875.

Todt, D., Fiebelkorn, A., 1980. Display, timing and function of wing movements accompanying antiphonal duets of *Cichladusa guttata*. Behaviour 72, 82–106.

Todt, D., Hultsch, H., 1982. Impairment of vocal signal exchange in the monogamous duet-singer *Cossypha heuglini* (Turdidae): effects on pair bond maintenance. Z. Tierpsychol. 60, 265–274.

Todt, D., Naguib, M., 2000. Vocal interactions in birds: the use of song as a model in communication. Adv. Study Behav. 29, 247–296.

Todt, D., Hultch, H., Duvall, F.P., 1981. Behavioural significance and social function of vocal and non-vocal displays in the monogamous duet-singer *Cossypha heuglini* H. Zool. Beitr. 27, 421–448.

Topp, S.M., Mennill, D.J., 2008. Seasonal variation in the duetting behaviour of rufous-and-white wrens (*Thryothorus rufalbus*). Behav. Ecol. Sociobiol. 62, 1107–1117.

Trainer, J.M., McDonald, D.B., 1995. Singing performance, frequency matching and courtship success of long-tailed manakins (*Chiroxiphia linearis*). Behav. Ecol. Sociobiol. 37, 249–254.

Trainer, J.M., McDonald, D.B., Learn, W.A., 2002. The development of coordinated singing in cooperatively displaying long-tailed manakins. Behav. Ecol. 13, 65–69.

Vehrencamp, S.L., 2000. Handicap, index, and conventional signal elements of bird song. In: Espmark, Y.O., Amundsen, T., Rosenqvist, G. (Eds.), Animal Signals: Signalling and Signal Design in Animal Communication. Tapir Academic Press, Trondheim, pp. 277–300.

Vehrencamp, S.L., Hall, M.L., Bohman, E.R., Depeine, C.D., Dalziell, A.H., 2007. Song matching, overlapping, and switching in the banded wren: the sender's perspective. Behav. Ecol. 18, 849–859.

Vencl, F., Soucek, B., 1976. Structure and control of duet singing in white-crested laughing thrush, (*Garrulax leucolophus*). Behaviour 57, 206–226.

Voigt, C., Leitner, S., Gahr, M., 2006. Repertoire and structure of duet and solo songs in cooperatively breeding white-browed sparrow weavers. Behaviour 143, 159–182.

von Helversen, D., 1980. Structure and function of antiphonal duets. Acta XVIII Int. Orn. Congr. Berlin 17, 682–688.

von Helversen, D., Wickler, W., 1971. Uber den duettgesang des afrikanischen drongo *Dicrurus adsimilis* Bechstein. Z. Tierpsychol. 29, 301–321.

Watson, M., 1969. Significance of antiphonal song in the Eastern whipbird, *Psophodes olivaceus*. Behaviour 35, 157–178.

Whitford, P.C., 1996. Temporal alternation and coordination of calls by paired Canada geese in duetted calling of aggression, territorial and triumph behavior. Passenger Pigeon 58, 249–258.

Whittingham, L.A., Kirkconnell, A., Ratcliffe, L.M., 1997. The context and function of duet and solo songs in the red-shouldered blackbird. Wilson Bull. 109, 279–289.

Wickler, W., 1972. Aufbau und paarspezifitat des gesangsduetters von *Laniarius funebris* (Aves, Passeriformes, Laniidae). Z. Tierpsychol. 30, 464–476.

Wickler, W., 1976. Duetting songs in birds: biological significance of stationary and non-stationary processes. J. Theor. Biol. 61, 493–497.

Wickler, W., 1980. Vocal duetting and the pair bond. I. Coyness and partner commitment. A hypothesis. Z. Tierpsychol. 52, 201–209.

Wickler, W., Seibt, U., 1982. Song splitting in the evolution of duetting. Z. Tierpsychol. 59, 127–140.

Wickler, W., Sonnenschein, E., 1989. Ontogeny of song in captive duet-singing slate coloured boubous (*Laniarius funebris*). A study in birdsong epigenesis. Behaviour 111, 220–233.

Wiley, R.H., Wiley, M.S., 1977. Recognition of neighbours' duets by stripe-backed wrens *Campylorhynchus nuchalis*. Behaviour 62, 10–34.

Wright, T.F., Dahlin, C.R., 2007. Pair duets in the yellow-naped amazon (*Amazona auropalliata*): phonology and syntax. Behaviour 144, 207–228.

Wright, T.F., Dorin, M., 2001. Pair duets in the yellow-naped amazon (Psittaciformes: *Amazona auropalliata*): responses to playbacks of different dialects. Ethology 107, 111–124.

Zimmer, K.J., Whittaker, A., Oren, D.C., 2001. A cryptic new species of flycatcher (Tyrannidae: Suiriri) from the cerrado region of central South America. Auk 118, 56–78.

Acoustic Communication in Delphinids

VINCENT M. JANIK

SEA MAMMAL RESEARCH UNIT, SCOTTISH OCEANS INSTITUTE, SCHOOL OF BIOLOGY,
UNIVERSITY OF ST ANDREWS, FIFE KY16 8LB, UNITED KINGDOM

I. INTRODUCTION

Communication is a crucial part of all social behavior. The interaction of mechanisms and functions in communication systems have most successfully been addressed in insects, anurans, and birds, giving insights into the evolutionary pathways leading to current phenotypes. The choice of animal in such studies is usually motivated by accessibility and suitability for observation and experimentation. Another aim is to choose an organism that is sufficiently complex to address interesting evolutionary questions, but also sufficiently simple to allow for a clear identification of the variables involved. Using all of these criteria, bird song became one of the most influential model systems in the study of animal communication (Catchpole and Slater, 1995).

A parallel development in the study of communication was a focus on our closest ancestors, the nonhuman primates, because of interest in the evolution of human language. However, biologists have argued that even here bird song is a better model system (e.g., Doupe and Kuhl, 1999), given that one of the most important skills for language acquisition, vocal production learning, is common in birds, but apparently absent in nonhuman primates (Janik and Slater, 1997).

The focus on very few taxa as model systems can sharpen our view for key elements in the evolution of communication. However, we also risk seeing specific features of communication as unique to single species while they, in fact, are more common than we expect. Several other taxa have been identified as interesting for the study of complexity in animal communication and its evolution. Among these are bats, elephants, pinnipeds, and cetaceans. All show vocal learning and at least some species of each group have complex social systems where sophisticated communication mechanisms can be expected (Janik and Slater, 1997).

123

0065-3454/09 $35.00
DOI: 10.1016/S0065-3454(09)40004-4

The wide phylogenetic diversity of these groups provides an interesting perspective on what conditions may be necessary for the evolution of complex communication and social behavior.

A group of particular interest in such comparisons is the delphinids, a family of approximately 35 species within the order of cetaceans. Phylogenetically, cetaceans are most closely related to the artiodactyls; their closest living terrestrial relative is the hippopotamus (Ursing and Arnason, 1998). Thus, they are far removed from the other mammalian taxa that show vocal learning. They are also of particular interest as a comparative group due to their exclusively aquatic life style. While their environment and anatomy is very different from that of terrestrial animals, there are surprising parallels in the social behavior of cetaceans and some terrestrial mammals. Delphinids are among the most social of cetaceans and display a variety of social structures. These range from aggregations of more than a thousand individuals to complex fission–fusion societies and closed matrilineal groups (Connor et al., 1998). Most of these structures can also be found in primates and birds. A similar resemblance can be found in the variety of foraging behaviors deployed by delphinids, birds, and primates. Some species are food specialists that show a high degree of coordination in their behavior to capture prey, while others are generalists and display an impressive variety of foraging strategies and inventiveness (Wells et al., 1999). Thus, we can find similarities in behavioral strategies even though the implementation of such strategies requires very different solutions from those applied in terrestrial environments.

The specific constraints on orientation, social interactions, and group cohesion imposed by the aquatic environment have been a driving force behind the evolution of delphinid acoustic systems (Janik, 1999a). Delphinids have a greatly reduced sense of olfaction and only limited visibility in their environment. Thus, the acoustic channel is the primary one available for social interactions and the only one that allows interaction over distances greater than a few body lengths. Even in less social delphinid species, contact between a mother and a calf has to be maintained while the calf depends on the mother. A dolphin's anatomy does not allow it to hold on to its offspring, and the need to surface for breathing does not allow the construction of a den to leave infants behind while foraging. Thus, mothers and infants need an efficient mechanism to stay together. Dolphins have evolved two different solutions to this problem. For short-range detection of up to a few hundred meters, they can use their sophisticated echolocation system (Au, 1993). In echolocation, the animal produces sounds to explore its environment, listening to the echoes returning from any targets that are present. For short- as well as long-range interactions, dolphins use communication sounds. Here the animals encode information in their signals that can be decoded by a receiver. For an interaction, the animal relies on a reaction from a conspecific and not on echoes of its own signals. Thus, echolocation and communication are two different uses of acoustic signals. These systems are particularly important for species that live offshore, where there are no landmarks for orientation. Such challenges imposed by the marine environment are the most likely explanation for the evolution of the advanced, acoustic capabilities in delphinids, such as their acoustic production and perception skills as well as vocal learning and invention (Janik and Slater, 2000).

In this review, I will focus on the communication system of delphinids. There are two reasons why our knowledge of delphinid communication systems lags behind that of primates and birds. Firstly, cetaceans are diffi-cult to observe in the wild since they spend most of their time underwater. Most studies concentrate on behavior that is visible at the surface, which represents only a very small percentage of the animals' lives. It is important not to extrapolate from surface observations to underwater behavior, unless it has been shown that such an extrapolation is valid. Secondly, the animals are adapted to produce sounds underwater. Their sound produc-tion apparatus is located in the nasal passages and produces acoustic signals that propagate through the tissue of the animal (Dormer, 1979). These signals then travel through an acoustic lens in the forehead straight into the aquatic environment. Thus, the animals do not open their mouths or show any other visible signs that they have produced a sound. Even in captive conditions, it is difficult to determine which animal is the sender and which one the receiver of a sound. When observing cetaceans, research-ers often assume that the animal under observation is the sound producer. However, it has been shown that such an assumption can lead to serious errors in the interpretation of acoustic data (Quick and Janik, 2008). To solve this problem, scientists increasingly use acoustic recording tags attached to animals (e.g., Madsen et al., 2005) or passive acoustic localiza-tion methods to identify callers (e.g., Janik et al., 2000; Quick et al., 2008). These methods have expanded our view on delphinid communication and allowed us to collect detailed data on their communication behavior.

II. Types of Vocalizations

Traditionally, delphinid signals have been described as belonging to one of three categories: whistles, burst-pulsed sounds, and clicks. Richardson et al. (1995) reviewed acoustic parameters of these signal types in different species. Whistles are tonal signals with fundamental frequencies lying in the bandwidth between 800 Hz (Schultz and Corkeron, 1994) and 28.5 kHz

(May-Collado and Wartzok, 2008) and durations between 100 ms and just over 4 s (Buckstaff, 2004). Clicks are relatively broadband, short signals that often reach far into the ultrasonic range. The highest frequency components of clicks found in dolphins lay beyond 200 kHz for the white-beaked dolphin (*Lagenorhynchus albirostris*) (Mitson and Morris, 1988, Rasmussen and Miller, 2004), and clicks extending beyond 100 kHz are common in all species (Richardson et al., 1995). Clicks appear to be most commonly used for echolocation, but also play a role in communication. Burst-pulsed signals consist of rapid click trains. Bray calls (Janik, 2000a) and what has been called moans or rasps (Caldwell and Caldwell, 1967) fall into this category. In fact, the term burst-pulsed sound has often been used as a descriptor for all sounds that are not whistles or clicks. While tonal whistles and single clicks stand out from other sounds that delphinids make, there are problems with this classification. The lower frequency sounds of killer whales (*Orcinus orca*), for example, are often described as burst-pulsed sounds consisting of separate clicks, but many of these calls include harmonics. Similarly, while whistles are relatively tonal signals, there can be side bands or a rasping quality that are caused by rapid amplitude modulation. This is particularly obvious in Atlantic spotted dolphins (*Stenella frontalis*), where 41% of whistles have this feature, while it is less common in other species such as the spinner dolphin (*Stenella longirostris*), where it occurs in only 2% of whistles (Lammers et al., 2003). Dolphins can produce burst-pulsed sounds and whistles simultaneously, so it is generally accepted that there are two sites of sound production that can be controlled independently (Dormer, 1979). These are suspected to be two identical sound producing structures (consisting of fatty dorsal bursae within a pair of phonic lips), one in the left and one in the right nasal passage (Cranford, 2000). While these sites may produce different kinds of sounds, Murray et al. (1998) argued that there is a continuum in the acoustic parameters of whistles and burst-pulsed sounds in false killer whales (*Pseudorca crassidens*). Thus, these signals may not be as different as we assume. A better understanding of sound production mechanisms and sound categorization by delphinids is required before we can arrive at a more conclusive terminology. Here, I will follow the established terminology, keeping in mind its caveats.

Whistles generally have varying numbers of harmonics. Usually only the first three are clearly detectable, but many studies on whistles were bandwidth limited and could not investigate upper harmonics. Using broadband equipment, Lammers et al. (2003) found that typically only one to three harmonics could be found in the whistles of Atlantic spotted dolphins and spinner dolphins; however, the maximum number of harmonics for Atlantic spotted dolphins was 11 and for spinner dolphins it was 7. While the fundamental frequency of whistles is relatively omnidirectional, high-frequency components such as higher order harmonics are more directional (Lammers and Au, 2003). Killer whales produce an independent high-frequency component that is superimposed on some of their burst-pulsed calls. This component is much more directional than the low-frequency part of the call and harmonically unrelated to it (Miller, 2002). It is possible that receivers can use the frequency spectrum of a received call to extract information on the orientation of a caller. However, so far there is no experimental or observational evidence for this idea.

The complexity of the frequency modulations dolphins use in their acoustic signals can vary between populations and between species. In bottlenose dolphins (*Tursiops truncatus*), varying degrees of complexity have been described for separate populations (May-Collado and Wartzok, 2008; Morisaka et al., 2005b; Wang et al., 1995b). Some dolphin species appear to have simpler whistles than others. Tucuxis (*Sotalia fluviatilis*), for example, appear to use whistles with complex modulation patterns much less frequently (Azevedo and Van Sluys, 2005; Monteiro-Filho and Monteiro, 2001) than bottlenose dolphins (Janik and Slater, 1998; Janik et al., 1994) or spinner dolphins (Bazúa-Durán and Au, 2002). However, interspecies comparisons are difficult as long as the definitions of whistles and burst-pulsed sounds are somewhat diffuse. Tucuxis have a complex repertoire of other calls (Monteiro-Filho and Monteiro, 2001), so that a broader comparison of complexity might not show any differences between species. In all cases where differences in complexity are identified, it is unclear whether they reflect the complexity of information that is transmitted or relate to environmental factors, such as background noise, which might necessitate greater variability to ensure even basic information transmission.

Early studies of bottlenose dolphin vocalizations tried to describe the repertoire for the whole species (Dreher and Evans, 1964; Evans and Dreher, 1962; Lilly and Miller, 1961a). In 1965, Caldwell and Caldwell (1965) discovered that apart from shared whistle types, every individual bottlenose dolphin also had its own individually distinctive signature whistle, which is produced primarily when individuals are isolated from conspecifics (Caldwell and Caldwell, 1965; Janik and Slater, 1998). Evidence for signature whistles also exists for common dolphins (*Delphinus delphis*) (Caldwell and Caldwell, 1968), Atlantic spotted dolphins (Caldwell et al., 1973b), Pacific white-sided dolphins (*Lagenorhynchus obliquidens*) (Caldwell and Caldwell, 1971), and Pacific humpback dolphins (*Sousa chinensis*) (Van Parijs and Corkeron, 2001b). Unlike identification calls in other animals, where identity information is provided in general voice features that affect all calls, signature whistles are individually distinctive frequency modulation patterns (Janik, 2006) that appear to be acquired by copying and then modifying sounds in the animals' environment (Tyack and

Sayigh, 1997). Thus, an animal can only be recognized by its signature whistle if conspecifics had the opportunity to learn the whistle's distinctive modulation pattern. Caldwell et al. (1990) described signature whistles for more than 100 individuals. McCowan and Reiss (2001) challenged this finding based on not being able to find signature whistles in a comparatively small sample of bottlenose dolphins of their own. However, a more detailed description of signature whistles (Sayigh et al., 2007) and a study reporting reactions to computer-generated signature whistles (Janik et al., 2006) seem to have convinced McCowan and Reiss of the existence of signature whistles (Marino et al., 2007). Janik et al. (2006) demonstrated that dolphins can extract identity information from computer-generated replicas of signature whistles that had all general voice features removed. Thus, bottlenose dolphins can identify individuals based solely on the frequency modulation pattern that is created by each individual for its signature whistle.

While signature whistles can dominate the recordings of isolated individuals, they are rare if animals swim in tight groups (Janik and Slater, 1998). In the wild in Sarasota Bay, Florida, 38–70% of all recorded whistles from bottlenose dolphins are signature whistles (Buckstaff 2004; Cook et al., 2004; Watwood et al., 2005). The rest are nonsignature whistles, which do not have individually distinctive frequency modulation patterns (Watwood et al., 2005).

Caldwell et al. (1990) distinguished between whistles and loops of whistles in their description of signature whistles. Loops of signature whistles are repeated modulation patterns that are connected or separated by a highly stereotyped interloop interval. This interval is on average 100 ms long, with a standard deviation of only 10–60 ms, depending on the animal under investigation (Esch et al., in press). Interwhistle intervals tend to be much longer and much more variable, justifying the treatment of several disconnected loops as one vocal unit. In some cases, the introductory and the final loop can be different from the middle loops in a whistle. While whistles with loop structure are common in bottlenose dolphins, it is unclear whether they occur in other species.

While whistles are a dominant type of vocalization in many species, others use them to a lesser extent. For example, killer whales primarily use discrete burst-pulsed sounds for long-distance interactions (Ford, 1989), while bottlenose dolphins use whistles in the same context (Smolker et al., 1993). The dolphins of the genus *Cephalorhynchus* (Richardson et al., 1995) and possibly other species that have been studied in less detail, such as the Peale's dolphin (*Lagenorhynchus australis*) (Schevill and Watkins, 1971), do not produce whistles at all; they use clicks for echolocation as well as communication. Dawson and Thorpe (1990) found nine different types of clicks in the vocal behavior of Hector's dolphins (*Cephalorhynchus hectori*), some of which are likely to be communication sounds (Dawson, 1991). This makes the study of their communication challenging since it is difficult to assess when a click is used in communication and when in echolocation. Most likely, there will be cases where the same click serves both purposes, which is not a problem that is exclusive to nonwhistling species. Clicks may be used in communication much more widely than we realize. Similarly, it is not always clear how to distinguish between click trains used for echolocation and burst-pulsed calls. However, there are some very distinct burst-pulsed sounds that are clearly different from echolocation click trains. Examples are the discrete burst-pulsed calls of killer whales (Ford 1989) and bottlenose dolphin bray calls (dos Santos et al., 1995; Janik, 2000a). Lammers et al. (2004) suggested that click trains of spinner dolphins with an average interclick interval (ICI) of less than 10 ms are communication signals. They found that the distribution of ICI's in click trains was bimodal, with peaks separated by a gap at 10 ms. Typical echolocation click trains had average ICIs of more than 10 ms.

A recent finding is the occurrence of stereotypic sequences of burst-pulsed sounds produced by northern right whale dolphins (*Lissodelphis borealis*) (Rankin et al., 2007). There is little evidence for syntactical rules in delphinid vocalizations, even though they have been found to comprehend relatively complex syntax in artificial sign systems (Herman et al., 1984). In delphinids, signals of the same type often occur in sequences (e.g., Ford, 1989). Studies on groups of killer whales have also shown that there are some preferred transitions between specific calls (Ford, 1989; Riesch *et al.*, 2008), although it is unclear whether such transitions are produced by a single individual or represent interactions between animals. Further studies on northern right whale dolphins are needed to explore the significance of the more complex patterns found in this species.

III.   PERCEPTION OF COMMUNICATION SIGNALS

Communication signals have to be produced in a frequency band that is audible to a conspecific. The hearing range of delphinids ranges from around 50 Hz to more than 150 kHz, with some variation between species (reviewed in Richardson et al., 1995). Thus, their hearing abilities match the production side closely and also allow for the perception of many harmonics of the tonal communication sounds. Furthermore, the frequency discrimination abilities of delphinids are exceptional; they can discriminate tonal sounds that differ by only 0.2–0.8% of the base frequency of the tone (Thompson and Herman, 1975).

Very few studies have addressed the question of how dolphins perceive and classify different types of communication signals. Since signature whistles are primarily defined through their frequency modulation pattern, it is of great interest to investigate whether dolphins can be trained to attend to this feature and how they treat variations in other parameters if the frequency modulation pattern is kept constant. Ralston and Herman (1995) addressed this question by training a bottlenose dolphin to respond to a specific modulation pattern. They showed that while the dolphin initially paid attention to frequency parameters, the animal could be trained to recognize different modulation patterns regardless of the frequency band in which they were presented. Early studies showed that bottlenose dolphins could distinguish different whistle types even if they were produced by other dolphin species (Caldwell et al., 1971, 1972, 1973a). Caldwell et al. (1972) also reported that a dolphin could distinguish between signature whistles of conspecifics after only hearing a small fraction of the whistle. However, they did not provide sufficient information to assess whether this result can be generalized or whether it represented the performance to a trained task specific to the whistles used in the experiment. Harley (2008) trained a bottlenose dolphin successfully to discriminate between signature whistles of six conspecifics. The animal was able to associate each whistle with a different lever in its pool and to place novel exemplars of a known signature whistle into the correct category. However, contrary to what Caldwell et al. (1972) found, the dolphin did not class abbreviated parts of a signature whistle with the original whistle.

All of these studies concentrated on the fundamental frequency of signature whistles, which is where identity information is encoded (Janik et al., 2006). However, harmonics are common in dolphin whistles and they may carry additional information (Lammers et al., 2003). Yuen et al. (2007) investigated whether a false killer whale can discriminate between a 5 kHz pure tone and a 5 kHz tone that had various numbers of harmonics added. They found that the animal's performance improved with each harmonic that was added, demonstrating that delphinids can distinguish between whistles with and without harmonics. Further studies are needed to determine what information might be encoded in harmonics.

Dolphins clearly do perceive features that are shared between communication signals while they also notice differences in those parameters where differences can be found. Given our limited knowledge of the perceptional issues surrounding communication signals, further studies are needed on which acoustic parameters are most important to dolphins for whistle categorization.

IV. Communication Ranges and Strategies

Source levels of delphinid vocalizations can vary considerably between contexts and locations. Echolocation clicks can have peak-to-peak source levels as low as 150 dB re 1 μPa (Evans, 1973) and as high as 230 dB re 1 μPa (Au et al., 1974). These are suitable for target detection over more than 100 m, but it is unclear what the detection range of any communicative content might be. Whistles of captive bottlenose dolphins have been reported to range from 110 to 140 dB re 1 μPa (Tyack, 1985). These were measured with tags that did not allow measurement beyond 140 dB, so this cannot be taken as the maximum source level of whistles from captive dolphins. Measurements of delphinid sounds in the wild concentrated on the loudest signals, since only then is there a sufficient signal-to-noise (S/N) ratio to determine received levels. Whistles of wild bottlenose dolphins in Scotland had a maximum source level of 169 dB re 1 μPa, while the average for whistles with a sufficient S/N ratio was 158 dB re 1 μPa (Janik, 2000b). Killer whales produce sounds at similar levels, ranging from 131 to 168 dB re 1 μPa, and with average values of 140 dB re 1 μPa for whistles and 153 dB re 1 μPa for stereotyped burst-pulsed sounds (Miller, 2006). Spinner dolphins have been reported to produce their whistles at lower source levels of only 109–125 dB re 1 μPa (Watkins and Schevill, 1974). However, these animals were recorded while resting while the studies on bottlenose dolphins and killer whales concentrated on foraging and socializing animals; source levels may vary in relation to context.

The transmission range over which a signal can be detected by a conspecific is often referred to as the active space of a call. Detection ranges have been calculated for bottlenose dolphins and killer whales. In a 10 m deep homogeneous habitat, bottlenose dolphins should be able to detect conspecific whistle sounds below 12 kHz at 10–20 km, depending on sea state (Janik, 2000b). This corresponds closely to the distance over which delphinid sounds have been detected in acoustic surveys offshore (Oswald et al., 2003). Higher frequencies attenuate more quickly; whistle sounds of 12 kHz are detectable at up to only 4 km (Janik, 2000b). Quintana-Rizzo et al. (2006) conducted a more detailed study by measuring sound transmission loss in a habitat where mother–calf separations were observed. They documented that the active space of whistles depends on the bottom substrate and water depth. The active space can be less than 200 m for a whistle of 7–13 kHz and 155 dB re 1 μPa source level in a shallow sea grass area of only 1.6 m depth. However, the same whistle could be heard by other dolphins over up to 6 km in an area with a sandy bottom and 3.5 m depth. Using transmission loss measurements (rather than basing loss on a model as done by Janik, 2000b), Quintana-Rizzo et al. (2006) also showed that the active space can be much larger for high-frequency components than esti-mated by a model (more than 20 km in a channel of 3.5 m depth for whistles of 13–19 kHz and 165 dB re 1 μPa source level). In killer whales, the estimated active space of long-range burst-pulsed calls is 10–16 km, while all other killer whale calls have an active space of 5–9 km (Miller, 2006). This was calculated for call components below 20 kHz, assuming a homog-enous habitat of 100 m depth.

In the study by Quintana-Rizzo et al. (2006), separation distances of mothers and calves did not exceed the active space of their whistles, so they could maintain acoustic contact throughout the separation. However, large transmission ranges of sounds are not always an advantage since they also increase the chance of detection by predators (Janik, 2005) or prey (Deecke et al., 2002). Furthermore, the very efficient propagation of sounds in the marine environment poses a challenge for receivers since it increases the background noise they have to cope with. Individual whistle rates have been found to increase as group size increases for small groups of bottle-nose dolphins (Cook et al., 2004; Jones and Sayigh, 2002) and Indo-Pacific humpback dolphins (Van Parijs et al., 2002). However, a more varied picture emerges when looking at larger groups. It seems that in groups of more than 5–10 bottlenose dolphins, individual whistle rates either do not change or start to decrease with increasing group sizes (Jones and Sayigh, 2002; Quick and Janik, 2008). The number of clicks per dolphin tends to decrease with group size even for smaller groups (Jones and Sayigh, 2002). In spinner dolphins, only one individual of a subgroup of a large aggrega-tion tends to produce whistles at a time, while quiet, short-range burst-pulses are produced simultaneously by several animals (Lammers et al., 2006). The most likely explanation for these findings is that in most cases dolphins restrict their acoustic signaling to the necessary minimum when noise levels start to impair information transmission. The exception to this pattern can be found when ambient noise is suddenly increased while animals are dispersed, such as when boats pass dolphin groups. Almost all reports show that if delphinids continue calling in this situation, they tend to increase the redundancy in their calls, presumably to increase the probabil-ity that their calls are detected by conspecifics. Bottlenose dolphins tend to increase their vocal rates when they first hear an approaching boat (Buckstaff, 2004), which may allow the group to get an update on where individuals are or to initiate reunions of dispersed animals. This is sup-ported by the finding that travelling groups of dolphins in which animals are close together do not seem to increase their whistle rates in the presence of boats (Lemon et al., 2006). Pacific humpback dolphins tend to increase their whistle rate after a boat has passed, suggesting a different strategy of coping with boat presence (Van Parijs and Corkeron, 2001a). Foote et al. (2004)

noted a longer term change in the calls of killer whales off Vancouver Island. They reported that an increase in overall call duration correlated with a considerable increase in boat traffic in the area. Pilot whale reactions have been studied in response to low-frequency sounds. Bowles et al. (1994) reported that in the Pacific there were no calls of long-finned pilot whales (*Globicepaha melas*) during the playback of a loud humming signal with a center frequency of 57 kHz, but that the whales could be heard before and after sound exposure in the same area. Rendell and Gordon (1999) found that individuals of the same species in the Mediterranean Sea increased their calling rates during and after exposure to military sonar sounds. Morisaka et al. (2005a) reported a correlation between ambient noise levels and whistle structure for three populations of Indo-Pacific bottlenose dolphins. Populations that lived in areas with high ambient noise levels had whistles with lower frequencies and less frequency modulation than whistles of animals living in quieter conditions.

For echolocation signals, it has been reported that bottlenose dolphins increase the source level and shift the peak frequency of their clicks in response to masking noise in their preferred frequency band (Au, 1993). These two parameters are most likely linked to each other; it appears that individuals are able to produce high-frequency clicks at high- and low-source levels, but low-frequency clicks only at relatively low-source levels (Au et al., 1985). This finding may also be relevant for clicks used in communicative interactions.

V. GEOGRAPHIC VARIATION AND DIALECTS

Intraspecific geographic variation has been found in many animal signals, ranging from insects to mammals. Negative data on such variation are difficult to interpret since each study only looks at a limited set of acoustic parameters. If no geographic variation is found, it is uncertain whether variation could be present in other signal features. Dialects differ from geographic variation in that groups showing different dialects are sympatric (Conner, 1982). Dialects require an isolation mechanism, which can be a social or genetic barrier to cross-breeding or to selecting a model for call learning. Dialects can be difficult to distinguish from simple group differences caused by genetics, such as when animals associate in matrilineal groups, and from geographic variation, if call differences correlate with geographic distance when animals are distributed continuously throughout an area.

Geographic variation can be caused by genetic, environmental, or cultural differences (Janik and Slater, 2000). Genetic factors can influence signal structure directly by encoding different call types or indirectly by leading to differences in morphology that affect call production. Such morphological differences could be found in the actual structure of the vocal apparatus, or simply in overall body size, which can affect the minimum frequency of calls. Geographic differences could also be due to energetics, caused either by genetic variation or by differences in the nutritional state of animals at different sites. Thus, animals that have less energy to spend may not produce energetically expensive call types as often, or they may call more quietly or at lower rates. Call rates can also be affected by different time budgets; animals that spend most of their time foraging will spend less time socializing, which may result in different call rates between sites. Similarly, morphological differences that affect vocalizations can also be caused by environmental factors, if different nutritional conditions affect the development of a population. Different acoustic transmission characteristics or differences in ambient noise levels may also influence animals to modify call structure or choice of call types. Finally, culture may cause geographic differences (Janik and Slater, 1997, 2000). If vocal development is influenced by vocal learning, isolation can lead to drift that is introduced either by learning errors or by differences in social pressures, for example the preferential copying of vocalizations from specific individuals, such as dominant animals, that show individual differences between sites.

Geographic variation in delphinid vocal behavior can be found in all species that have been investigated. Most commonly, studies investigated whistles without discriminating between different whistle types. Thus, they report on parameters of all whistle types combined. Some of the most commonly investigated parameters are start frequency, end frequency, minimum frequency, maximum frequency, frequency range, number of inflections in the frequency modulation pattern of the whistle, and duration. Some studies use additional variables such as number of harmonics, the overall modulation pattern of the whistle, and whistle rate. Bottlenose dolphins (Baron et al., 2008; Jones and Sayigh, 2002, Morisaka et al., 2005b; Wang et al., 1995b), Atlantic spotted dolphins (Baron et al., 2008), false killer whales, Risso's dolphins (*Grampus griseus*), and short-finned (*Globicephala macrorhynchus*) and long-finned pilot whales (Rendell et al., 1999) have been found to show intraspecific variation in selected acoustic parameters when compared between two different sites. When variation is studied in more than two sites, one of three patterns can emerge. In some species, variation appears to be continuous along their distribution. Bottlenose dolphins display a gradual change in acoustic parameters of their whistles along the coast of the Gulf of Mexico (Wang et al., 1995b). Another pattern is that of a discontinuity along an apparently continuous geographic distribution of dolphins. Rossi-Santos and Podos (2006) reported such a discontinuity for tucuxi on either side of the easternmost tip of South America, with higher start and minimum frequencies of whistles to the north, but no variation between northern sites or southern sites. A site near the divide showed intermediate values for start and minimum frequency. Finally, variation may not relate to geographic distance at all. In spinner dolphins, whistles from some sites in the Atlantic and the Pacific were more similar to each other than to their respective neighboring sites (Camargo et al., 2006). Similarly, May-Collado and Wartzok (2008) compared bottlenose dolphin whistles from different studies collected along the East coast of the USA, in the Gulf of Mexico, in the Caribbean, in the South of Brazil, and on the coast of the mainland of Portugal, and did not find a correlation between geographic distance and whistle parameters at a macrogeographic scale. However, they did find great similarities for two sites only 35 km apart, which were not used by the same individuals.

For killer whales, most information concentrates on the sharing of call types rather than general parameters. Killer whales show variation in acoustic signals between as well as within populations. Fish-eating killer whales in the Northeast Pacific have an unusual social structure, in that males and females stay in their natal group throughout their lives (Bigg et al., 1990). Mating occurs between groups when they meet. Killer whales that live in separate areas, such as the northern and southern communities around Vancouver Island, do not share pulsed call types (Ford, 1991). Within populations of fish-eating killer whales, there are separate acoustic clans that interact with each other but show no pulsed call type sharing (Ford, 1991). Genetic data for two clans in Southern Alaska show that matrilines within clans are more closely related than are matrilines in different clans (Yurk et al., 2002). Matrilines within clans also all share at least one pulsed call type, and those that associate closely share several (Ford, 1991). Ford and Fisher (1983), who discovered this pattern, called these differences dialects, which is a somewhat different use of the term than described earlier. Interestingly, this pattern can only be found in the discrete burst-pulsed sounds; different clans and even nonoverlapping populations seem to share the same whistle types (Riesch et al., 2006).

VI. VOCAL DEVELOPMENT AND VOCAL LEARNING

Learning can influence vocal development in different ways (Janik and Slater, 1997, 2000). In contextual learning, animals learn an association between an existing signal and its context. This context can be a specific behavioral context or a temporal position in a sequence of signals (Janik and Slater, 2000). If applied to sound production, this requires control over the delivery of signals that are already in the repertoire, so that they can be produced in novel contexts. Production learning is defined as instances when the vocalizations themselves are modified in form as a result of experience with those of other individuals. Vocal production learning is relatively rare and has only been identified in some bird and mammal species.

Bottlenose dolphins have been reported to spontaneously copy sounds they hear in their environment (Caldwell and Caldwell, 1972; Reiss and McCowan, 1993), including the whistles of conspecifics (Janik, 2000c; Tyack, 1986). Although these occurrences have been interpreted as evidence for vocal learning, it is unclear whether the animals used contextual learning, simply selecting signals that were already in their repertoire, or whether the use of production learning was required for copying. Much better evidence comes from experimental studies. Bottlenose dolphins have been trained to copy the number and duration of model sounds (Lilly, 1965) as well as the exact frequency modulation of arbitrary tonal signals (Richards et al., 1984; Sigurdson, 1993). These experimental studies used adult animals, indicating that the ability to copy such sounds is present throughout the animals' lives. In the Richards *et al.* (1984) study, the animal improved the accuracy of its copies over time, demonstrating the role of practice during learning.

The role of learning in the development of signature whistles in bottlenose dolphins is of particular interest, since signature whistles are individually distinctive. Caldwell and Caldwell (1979) investigated the development of captive bottlenose dolphin signature whistles and found that infants tended to develop a stereotyped signature whistle sometime in their first 2 years of life. They also reported that infant whistles have less frequency modulation and shorter durations than adult whistles. Multiple loops were only found in signature whistles of older animals. Miksis et al. (2002) reported that bottlenose dolphins born in captivity tended to have signature whistles with little frequency modulation. The authors interpreted this as evidence for the influence of vocal learning, since these signature whistles resembled the whistle signal given by trainers during training and feeding of the animals. Captive bottlenose dolphins tend to develop signature whistles that are unlike those of their parents (Tyack and Sayigh, 1997). However, there is also some evidence that captive mothers change their whistling pattern after the birth of the calf, possibly to provide a learning opportunity for the new infant (Fripp and Tyack, 2008).

In wild infant bottlenose dolphins in Sarasota, Florida, signature whistles of many male calves tended to resemble those of their mothers, while those of females did not (Sayigh et al., 1995). Females tend to associate more with their mothers later in life than do males, so that differing from one's mother might be more important to females than to males, to avoid unambiguous identification. In one case in which the signature whistle was similar to that of the mother, the calf spent most of its time alone with its mother. In this case the signature whistle of the calf was recognizable within the first 2 months, while several calves that developed signature whistles different to that of the mother took longer to develop their own whistle (Tyack and Sayigh, 1997). In the same population of dolphins, Fripp et al. (2005) compared the signature whistles of bottlenose dolphin calves to those that the calves were likely to have heard during development, based on association data between individuals. They found that the signature whistles of most calves were similar to those of infrequent associates, and were dissimilar to both close associates and to animals from another population. These data suggest that calves use whistles of other animals as templates and change them to produce their own unique signal.

Once a signature whistle is established, females seem to keep it for their entire lives (Sayigh et al., 1990, 2007). Males sometimes change their signature whistle when they form an alliance with other males. Alliance partners spend almost all their time together and collaborate in herding females (Connor et al., 1992). In such alliances, signature whistles of all members become more alike over time (Smolker and Pepper, 1999; Watwood et al., 2004).

McCowan and Reiss (1995b) investigated the whistle repertoire of eight captive infants over their first year of life while they were swimming in their group, a context in which signature whistle should be rare. They reported that most whistle types were unique to individuals, but that most whistles emitted belonged to shared whistle types. They also suggested that the complexity of infant whistles reached that of adults after only 4 months and that several whistle types emerged and disappeared again within the first year. McCowan and Reiss (1995b) used bubble streams emitted by dolphins as an indicator of which animal produced a whistle. Fripp (2005) demonstrated that this method was problematic, in that certain whistle types are more likely to be produced with bubble streams than others. Thus, the study by McCowan and Reiss (1995b) is difficult to interpret, since emerging and disappearing whistle types could reflect a change in whether they were produced with bubble streams or not. Future studies on developmental changes in bubble stream production during vocalizations will help to clarify this point.

In killer whales, evidence for vocal production learning comes from observations in the wild. Deecke et al. (2000) studied changes in two call types of two related killer whale matrilines over a period of 13 years. The structure of one call type underwent the same subtle changes in both groups, while the other did not change. This suggests that call morphology is not linked to one common factor such as maturational changes, but that there are different degrees of stability. This finding can be seen as evidence for production learning maintaining the similarity in one call type but not in another. Foote et al. (2006) reported apparent copying of sea lion barking sounds by killer whales in the wild. They recorded such sounds in the absence of sea lions and in sequence with typical killer whale calls. Furthermore, two studies described anecdotally that killer whales copied sounds of conspecifics (Bain, 1986; Ford, 1991). Bowles et al. (1988) studied the vocal development of one female calf held with its mother and two other killer whales. In the first 8 months the infant calls were too variable to recognize any stereotyped signals. After the first year, the infant's repertoire resembled that of her mother, but she did not seem to use the signals of other pool members or of her father, who was kept in a separate pool. The sample for this study was largely collected by observing bubble stream production that occurred during vocalizations. It thus suffers from the same problems as the McCowan and Reiss (1995b) study on bottlenose dolphins, since bubble streams do not provide an unbiased sample of an animal's repertoire (Fripp, 2005). However, it does appear that killer whales use their vocal learning skills to learn shared calls from their matriline. In wild killer whales, more matriline specific calls were heard after the birth of a calf, possibly giving the calf an opportunity to learn calls that are most important for group cohesion (Weiß et al., 2006).

Studies on learning or development of clicks are rare. Anecdotal reports suggest that bottlenose dolphin calves use echolocation clicks right after birth (Caldwell and Caldwell, 1977). In a female killer whale, clicks were not present at 12–15 days after birth, but were found in a second recording period after 8 months (Bowles et al., 1988). At that time, there was no apparent difference in structure between calf and adult clicks. Moore and Pawloski (1990) trained a bottlenose dolphin to change the amplitude and shift the peak frequency of its echolocation clicks. While click amplitude and peak frequency appeared to be positively correlated with each other, the animal also showed some evidence for conditional control over the frequency spectrum of its clicks independent of amplitude.

VII. FUNCTIONS OF DELPHINID COMMUNICATION SIGNALS

Identifying the function of vocalizations in cetaceans requires detailed study of individual vocal behavior and the responses of conspecifics. This kind of detail is often difficult to come by. Early studies with captive dolphins used acoustic links between separated individuals, and showed that animals would use them to exchange signals (Burdin et al., 1975; Lang and Smith, 1965; Lilly and Miller, 1961b). Dreher (1966) showed that dolphins reacted to the playback of different whistle types with varying strengths of reaction. These descriptive studies were unable to elucidate if any information was encoded in these signals. In the wild, most studies try to relate surface behavior to signaling events. However, definitions of behavioral contexts and caller identification in delphinids can be vague, making the interpretation of some studies difficult (e.g., Herzing, 1997). It is important to be aware of such limitations and to examine results carefully. Caller identification is crucial to drawing conclusions on call function. This usually requires the use of passive acoustic localization techniques (Janik et al., 2000; Quick et al., 2008) or the investigation of isolated animals. Perhaps not surprisingly, social calls such as whistles have often been found to be most common when dolphins were seen socializing, and general vocal activity is often lower when animals are traveling or milling than when they are socializing or foraging (Cook et al., 2004; Jones and Sayigh, 2002; Quick and Janik, 2008). Studies using sophisticated observations of delphinid behavior have helped to elucidate the functional aspects of some delphinid calls in greater detail, as described in more detail in the following sections.

A. SPECIES RECOGNITION

Species recognition is one of the most fundamental functions of animal communication signals. It is to be expected that species information is encoded in every animal signal, although it can be difficult to identify the specific parameters that animals are using. Unfortunately, there are no experimental data for species recognition in delphinids. Caldwell et al. (1971, 1973a) found that a bottlenose dolphin was able to discriminate between whistles of different individuals of two species, common dolphins and spotted dolphins. However, these studies were designed to test the ability of an animal to discriminate between signature whistles of different individuals, and did not address whether the dolphin could discriminate among whistles of different species.

Several studies have approached the problem from a different angle, by comparing signal parameters of different species. The main parameters used in such comparisons usually include measurements of the fundamental frequency including start, end, minimum, and maximum frequencies, duration, and number of inflection points in the frequency modulation pattern. Species clearly show significant differences in these parameters, with animals from the same genus being most difficult to distinguish (Oswald et al., 2003; Rendell et al., 1999; Steiner, 1981; Wang et al., 1995a). However, while there is a pattern that larger species tend to produce lower frequencies (Matthews et al., 1999; May-Collado et al., 2007b), discriminations between species based on acoustic parameters have had only limited success. The success rate depended greatly on how many and which species were included in the sample. Oswald et al. (2003), for example, found that 51.4% of whistles could be classified correctly in a sample that included nine different delphinid species, whereas the expected percentage at chance level would have been 11%. Thus, basic acoustic parameters can help to identify species, but do not provide unequivocal classification. It is likely that the animals themselves are much better at identifying at least their own species, and that we simply have not found the parameter combination(s) necessary for species identification. Furthermore, almost all studies on species identification have concentrated on delphinid whistles. It is possible that species identity is encoded in click sounds as has been found for beaked whales (Gillespie et al., 2009). While these sounds do not travel as far as whistles, it would be interesting to investigate their contribution to species recognition in delphinids.

B.   Group and Individual Recognition

The way in which cetaceans use identification signals are related to the requirements of their social systems. The dynamic fission–fusion systems found in many delphinids require a reliable system for individual recognition, while species that live in close family groups, such as some killer whales, need to ensure the recognition of close kin. Caldwell and Caldwell (1965, 1968) were the first to suggest that signature whistles were used for individual recognition. Several observations support this hypothesis. Signature whistles are used when animals are in isolation but rarely when they swim in close contact (Janik and Slater, 1998). In wild animals, Smolker et al. (1993) reported that signature whistles were heard shortly before mothers and calves in Shark Bay, Australia, reunite after long-distance separations. In playback experiments, individuals respond more strongly to signature whistles of close relatives than to unrelated associates (Sayigh et al., 1999). Janik et al. (2006) showed that individual identity information is encoded in the distinctive frequency modulation pattern that each individual invents early in life. Thus, general voice features that affect all vocal signals are not required to maintain individual identification in a social group as long as signature whistles are used. Boughman and Moss (2003) pointed out that this kind of learned recognition signal shows the greatest inter-individual variability of all recognition signals in the animal kingdom.

Studies by McCowan and Reiss (1995a, 2001) could not find signature whistles. They used bubble streams as the indicator of who produced a call in their study, a method that biases the sample toward upsweep whistles (Fripp, 2005). The most common whistle types found in McCowan and Reiss' studies were therefore, not surprisingly, upsweep whistles.

Furthermore, Janik (1999b) showed that the methods used by McCowan and Reiss were unable to detect signature whistles, even in a sample biased toward upsweep whistles.

In killer whales, differences in shared call types between different matrilines are much larger than individual differences within matrilines (Miller and Bain, 2000; Nousek et al., 2006). Matrilines that share at least some of their call types are classed as belonging to one vocal clan (Ford, 1991). Young killer whales appear to learn the existing calls from their matriline and do not invent new signals. This lack of invention is demonstrated in the remarkable stability of the repertoires over time (Ford, 1991). Resident killer whales in the northeastern Pacific live in maternal groups containing males and females; new groups form only when such family groups split. The pattern of dialects in discrete calls reflects these association patterns. If new calls appear they evolve through drift when learning occurs (Deecke et al., 2000). However, Yurk et al. (2002) pointed out that the emergence of new calls is too rare to assume that there is no direct selection pressure on maintaining a distinct repertoire for a matriline. Several authors suggested that repertoires are used for kin recognition (Ford, 1991; Hoelzel and Osborne, 1986; Miller and Bain, 2000; Yurk et al., 2002). Matriline specific calls are heard more often when killer whales interact with whales from other matrilines or vocal clans (Ford, 1989; Weiß et al., 2007). In a family-based social structure that does not have the frequent group changes typical of fission–fusion societies, vocal distinctiveness appears to be most important at the group level to avoid inbreeding and maintain group cohesion. Furthermore, there also is a distinct advantage to using a repertoire rather than individually specific calls when choosing a mate. Since call sharing relates to association patterns within acoustic clans, which in turn reflect the degree of relatedness, the amount of overlap in the repertoire between two individuals should give information about their degree of relatedness. Individual identity information seems to be encoded in general voice features of killer whales (Nousek et al., 2006). Such differences in subtle signal parameters are comparable to those found in all other mammalian species, and do not require vocal learning for their emergence.

Since vocal learning is present in delphinids throughout their lifetime, they are also able to copy the calls of other individuals in social situations. Tyack (1986, 1991) observed copying of signature whistles in two captive bottlenose dolphins. Copying is often observed as vocal matching, in which animals respond to a signal of a conspecific with one of the same type within a short time window. Matching has been described for bottlenose dolphins in captivity (Janik and Slater, 1998; Tyack, 1986, 1991) and in the wild (Janik, 2000c). The exact function of signature whistle copying or matching has not been demonstrated experimentally, but it has been suggested to serve as a mechanism for initiating or maintaining contact with a specific individual. In Sarasota Bay, Florida, bottlenose dolphins have also been found to produce whistles that closely resemble signature whistles of absent conspecifics (Watwood et al., 2005), which could constitute a case of referential signaling with learned signals; this clearly deserves further study. Matching appears to have several functions, since it has also been observed in interactions between more than two bottlenose dolphins (Janik, 2000c). In addition, matching of burst-pulsed calls has been observed in killer whales (Miller et al., 2004), which do not have individual signature call types. There is an extensive literature on the functions of matching in bird song (Catchpole and Slater, 1995), where it appears to be used in addressing and as a sign of aggression. The role of aggression in whistle copying in delphinids has yet to be investigated.

C. OTHER SOCIAL CONTEXTS

While we have relatively good data on the role of delphinid signals in individual and group recognition, there is much less information on their other roles in social interactions. No data exist for context specificity of whistle contours. Janik et al. (1994) showed that signature whistles can carry additional context-specific information beyond identity, without changing the overall frequency modulation pattern of the whistle. Nine out of 14 signal parameters of the signature whistles of a trained captive dolphin differed according to whether it was undisturbed or engaged in a training task. The individual also increased the frequency bandwidth of its signature whistle when it was rewarded for a correctly performed visual discrimination task. In contrast, only one of four parameters measured on upsweeps, the second most common whistle type in these contexts, differed between the undisturbed and training conditions. Caldwell et al. (1990) showed that signature whistle rate was positively correlated with the state of arousal in bottlenose dolphins. Esch et al. (2009) confirmed this finding relating increased whistle rates to stress in bottlenose dolphins. Earlier studies suggesting the existence of an alarm call that was shared between individuals (Lilly, 1963) could not be confirmed. It appears that bottlenose dolphins in distress produce their individually distinctive signature whistle encoding their level of distress in whistle rate and in altered acoustic parameters while keeping the overall frequency modulation pattern of the signature whistle constant.

Several studies have demonstrated a link between burst-pulsed sounds and aggression in bottlenose dolphins. Caldwell and Caldwell (1967) described several aggressive interactions that were accompanied by burst-pulsed sounds, and Overstrom (1983) described a sequence of escalation in aggressive interactions between bottlenose dolphins in which burst-pulsed sounds were used extensively. Connor and Smolker (1996) demonstrated that male bottlenose dolphins in Western Australia produced loud, low-frequency pop sounds when herding females and also when in aggressive interactions with other alliances. Females tended to turn toward the male after a pop, presumably to prevent further aggression. However, females were also observed to occasionally react aggressively after hearing a pop sound. Nowacek (2005) showed that in Florida, pops were also common while bottlenose dolphins foraged near the edge of sea grass flats and over sand, possibly to keep competitors away or to startle hiding fish.

Lammers et al. (2006) showed that in spinner dolphins, burst-pulsed sounds are usually exchanged between animals that are relatively close together, suggesting a role in contexts other than group cohesion and recognition. Interestingly, in killer whales, the opposite pattern appears to occur, in which burst pulsed sounds are used for long-distance communication and whistles are used in close contact interactions (Ford, 1989; Thomsen et al., 2002). Ford (1989) has identified several shared, discrete burst-pulsed call types in killer whales that are mainly used when different matrilines or vocal clans encounter each other. These appear to be more stable than other call types that are subject to change over time (Deecke et al., 2000).

Bastian (1967) used an experimental approach to investigate information transmission in bottlenose dolphins. He trained two animals to perform an identical task (pressing one of two levers), but only one animal was given a visual cue indicating the correct choice in each trial. The two animals swam in the same pool with a barrier that did not allow them to see each other, although acoustic signals could be exchanged. In the test phase of his experiment, rewards were only given when both animals responded correctly. The animals were successful in performing under these conditions, which led Bastian to conclude that the animals must have exchanged acoustic signals indicating the correct response. He analyzed the signals and showed that mainly burst-pulsed sounds were exchanged, although he did not analyze echolocation patterns. Since echolocation clicks are highly directional, it is likely that the acoustic signals received on the other side of the pool differed when the animal approached different levers. Thus, it is not clear whether the listener only learned to distinguish between these different sound patterns, or whether the dolphins intentionally encoded information about the choice in their signals.

D. FOOD-RELATED CALLS

Vocalizing during foraging can have many advantages. It may serve to attract conspecifics to a food source, maintain contact with other group members, manipulate prey behavior, or coordinate foraging between individuals of the same group (Janik, 2000a).

If conspecifics are attracted by food-related vocalizations, the main challenge is to understand how such calls benefit the caller. In most animals, the
crucial factor appears to be the amount and divisibility of the food. Animals
sharing information on food may benefit by reciprocal altruism or increased
social status in their group (Searcy and Nowicki, 2005). If group members
are closely related, then vocalizing may also increase their inclusive fitness.
A more direct benefit can lie in increased protection while foraging due to
increased vigilance levels of a group, direct defense of a sharable food
resource, or the dilution effect against predators.

Evidence for specific food calls in delphinids is relatively sparse. While
many delphinids show an impressive diversity of foraging strategies, their
prey is also very mobile and less diverse than that used by most food callers.
Individual animals may specialize in selected foraging strategies (Ford
et al., 1998; Mann and Sargeant, 2003; Nowacek, 2002), but there is little
evidence for food preferences from choice experiments other than trying to
maximize prey size (Dill et al., 2003). This suggests that information on the
type of food encountered could be of little significance to a receiver.
However, information on quantity might be of interest.

Generally, rates of non-echolocation signals often increase during foraging. Single bottlenose dolphins in Sarasota Bay, Florida, tend to have higher
whistle rates when foraging alone than when foraging in groups (Nowacek,
2005). Thus, whistles may serve to maintain contact with or attract other
group members. If this was the case, one might expect individuals to use
signature whistles in this context. This is a prediction that should be easy to
test given our extensive knowledge on signature whistles in this population.
Killer whales that specialize in foraging on marine mammals increase their
overall call rates after a kill, although there are no specific call types that are
used in this context (Deecke et al., 2005). These marine mammal hunters
tend to be very quiet during the hunt, since most marine mammals have
good hearing in the frequency range of killer whale calls (Barrett-Lennard
et al., 1996). Thus, the increase in call rate after a kill may simply indicate
the end of a period in which detection needed to be avoided (Deecke et al.,
2005). Using active sonar as an observation tool, Benoit-Bird and Au (2009)
found that burst-pulsed sounds increased before spinner dolphins engaged
in coordinated behavior during foraging. Further studies are needed here to
determine the exact function of these calls.

Two studies on food-related calls stand out, in that they report high
context specificity for the calls that are involved. Using passive acoustic
localization, Janik (2000a) documented food-related calls in bottlenose
dolphins in Scotland. These so-called bray calls are primarily produced
when dolphins forage on large prey items such as salmonids, and they
attract other dolphins to the call location. The rapid surface movements

of many dolphins rushing toward the same location are very noticeable when bray calls are heard. Similar calls have also been described from Portugal (dos Santos et al., 1995). Icelandic killer whales also produce a very context-specific, food-related call right before they try to debilitate herring with tail slaps (Simon et al., 2006). Norris and Møhl (1983) hypothesized that dolphins may use sounds to stun prey, in which case any attraction of conspecifics would be a by-product of call production. While the original idea that sound could be used to stun prey has not received much support, delphinids may use sounds to manipulate prey behavior. Bottlenose dolphin bray calls are burst-pulsed calls with most of their energy below 2 kHz (Janik, 2000a). If these calls had evolved to attract conpecifics, their peak frequency should be considerably higher to meet the most sensitive range in the auditory threshold of bottlenose dolphins. Salmonids, on the other hand, only perceive sounds at lower frequencies (Hawkins and Johnstone, 1978), and this suggests that bray calls evolved to manipulate prey behavior rather than to attract other dolphins (Janik, 2000a). Wild salmon appears to mainly swim near the surface (Yano et al., 1984). However, unlike clicks which are most common near the surface, bray calls are mainly produced at depths of more than 20 m (Hastie et al., 2006). Bray calls may lead salmon to evacuate their swim bladder and drop to the sea floor, a typical antipredator response in fish. Dolphins calling underneath salmon may increase their foraging success by eliciting such a response. Similarly, the peak frequency of food-related calls in Icelandic killer whales is at around 700 Hz (Simon et al., 2006), a band in which killer whales do not hear well. Killer whales may manipulate herring behavior by producing sounds that elicit strong vibrations in the swim bladder of the herring, since the resonance frequency of the swim bladder is close to the peak frequency of the killer whale food call. Interestingly, the structure of these calls is similar to that of calls produced by humpback whales (*Megaptera novaeangliae*) before they set bubble nets around herring (Cerchio and Dahlheim, 2001).

While the possibility of prey manipulation with sound is intriguing, it is important to note that so far there has been no experimental confirmation that these sounds do indeed alter prey behavior. Thus, attraction of conspecifics is still a viable alternative hypothesis for the evolution of food calls. Associated animals are often related to each other and food calling may increase the inclusive fitness of the caller. Alternatively, the presence of more conspecifcs may increase the foraging success of the caller. This can occur when mobile prey can be herded more effectively by larger groups as reported for cliff swallows feeding on mosquitoes (Brown et al., 1991). Further studies are needed to decide what the most dominant functional advantage of these calls is.

VIII. EVOLUTIONARY ASPECTS

The distribution of whistles among delphinids is somewhat unusual, in that some species do not produce whistles while others use them extensively. Nonwhistling species tend to have smaller body sizes, and appear to have simpler social structures, tending to occur in smaller groups than whistling delphinids. Based on these findings, Herman and Tavolga (1980) suggested that whistles evolved in relation to large group sizes. Podos et al. (2002) suggested that whistles are a unique derived feature within the delphinids, with secondary loss of whistles in the genus *Cephalorynchus*. Morisaka and Connor (2007) proposed that whistles are a derived feature within the odontocetes, with secondary losses in several taxa. They argue that most odontocetes that do not whistle produce high-pitched, narrow-band echolocation clicks, which lie beyond the hearing range of killer whales. Thus, killer whale predation pressure may have led to this secondary whistle loss, since whistles are easily detectable by killer whales. May-Collado et al. (2007a) analyzed whistle presence and structure in all odontocetes and reported a correlation between group size and whistle complexity as indicated by the number of inflection points in the frequency modulation pattern of the whistle. Their analysis also suggested that whistles of species with large group sizes have higher minimum frequencies and shorter durations than those of species with small group sizes. These authors also pointed out that the current terminology makes it difficult to decide when whistles evolved, since scientists disagree on what constitutes a whistle.

IX. COGNITION

Comparisons of great apes and delphinids show that these taxa rival each other in the complexity of their cognitive skills (Janik, in press). Furthermore, just like in great apes, many complex cognitive skills of delphinids can be found in a single species, the bottlenose dolphin (Herman, 2006). Some of these skills are directly relevant for communication, such as the understanding of complex syntax (Herman et al., 1984) or the referential pointing gesture (Herman et al., 1999). Acoustic communication skills seem even further advanced in delphinids since they are capable of vocal production learning, while nonhuman primates have limited abilities in this domain (Janik and Slater, 1997). In experimental work, delphinids have been found to use learned acoustic signals to label objects in a referential way (Richards et al., 1984), to copy contextual use of vocal behavior patterns without any apparent reward (Reiss and McCowan, 1993), and to share attention through eavesdropping on conspecific echolocation sounds and the returning echoes (Xitco and Roitblat, 1996). Finally, there are numerous reports of cooperation in delphinids in the wild (e.g., Gazda et al., 2005; Hoelzel, 1991; Hoese, 1971). Many of these skills are reminiscent of those championed as uniquely human by primatologists (Tomasello et al., 2005). It is intriguing to ask how far such parallels go, given that dolphins have evolved in such a different environment from the great apes.

X. FUTURE DIRECTIONS

The acoustic communication system in several delphinids is clearly very complex. While there are many impressive studies on this subject, a variety of questions remain. One of these is the role of burst-pulsed sounds in dolphin communication. The variability of burst-pulsed sounds and also of non-signature whistles is staggering, which is certainly one of the reasons why many scientists have concentrated on stereotyped signals such as signature whistles in bottlenose dolphins or discrete calls in killer whales. However, non-signature whistles and variable burst-pulsed calls make up a considerable proportion of sounds heard from these animals and we know little about their function. This clearly deserves further study. Closely linked to this is the question of how dolphins categorize such variable signals. Context specificity can be used to confirm signal categories as biologically relevant to the animals (Janik, 1999b). However, most signals are used in a variety of contexts.

One of the main gaps in the study of dolphin cognition in connection with communication skills is the scarcity of data on a theory of mind, particularly whether dolphins understand intentions, knowledge and beliefs of conspecifics. Many recent accounts of the evolution of complex cognition suggest that the presence of different cognitive modules may lead to the rise of novel skills that are a by-product of combining existing ones. The presence of a theory of mind would suggest that such integration might occur, while without it each skill could be seen as a separate adaptation to a specific problem that does not stand out from those of other mammals. While dolphins are capable of motor imitation (Herman, 1980, 2002), a skill that has been seen as indicative of a theory of mind, no study has been successful in repeating more direct experiments in this area carried out on primates and humans (but see Tschudin, 2006 for a first attempt). Given that delphinids have such complex cognition, further studies are mandatory to explore the observed similarities between delphinids and the great apes in greater detail.

Finally, there are conservation issues that need addressing. The levels of masking noise through shipping and other anthropogenic activities are increasing in the marine environment. The more dramatic effects are when animals strand (Balcomb and Claridge, 2001) or change their distribution patterns in relation to noise (Allen and Read, 2000; Morton and Symonds, 2002). However, the potential for anthropogenic noise sources to disrupt communication (Erbe, 2002), as well as to cause progressive hearing damage (Mooney et al., 2009) are real concerns. Such effects would not result in immediately obvious changes, but can potentially have population-level impacts over longer periods. Masking through ship noise can be considerable. Using a modeling approach, Erbe (2002) showed that killer whale calls can be masked over large distances by small boat activity. Long-term changes in killer whale call durations in relation to an increase in boat traffic (Foote et al., 2004) are an indicator that noise poses a real threat to communication systems.

Delphinid communication is an interesting study subject, due to its great complexity and the adaptation to the marine environment. However, both of these factors make the study of delphinid communication challenging. There are many species for which data on acoustic signals are almost absent. Many inventive approaches have been developed, which have been crucial to some of the results presented here. Future studies need to continue to find innovative study designs and methods that allow collecting data on these interesting animals without compromising the validity of their conclusions. If we succeed in this challenge, we will be rewarded with further insights into one of the most complex acoustic communication systems in the animal kingdom.

Acknowledgments

I am very grateful to Volker Deecke, Marc Naguib, Laela Sayigh, and Klaus Zuberbühler for their comments on earlier drafts of this chapter. The chapter was written with the support of a Royal Society University Research Fellowship.

References

Allen, M.C., Read, A.J., 2000. Habitat selection of foraging bottlenose dolphins in relation to boat density near Clearwater, Florida. Mar. Mamm. Sci. 16, 815–824.

Au, W.W.L., 1993. The Sonar of Dolphins. Springer-Verlag, New York.

Au, W.W.L., Floyd, R.W., Penner, R.H., Murchison, A.E., 1974. Measurement of echolocation signals of the Atlantic bottlenose dolphin, *Tursiops truncatus* Montagu, in open waters. J. Acoust. Soc. Am. 56, 1280–1290.

Au, W.W.L., Carder, D.A., Penner, R.H., Scronce, B.L., 1985. Demonstration of adaptation in beluga whale echolocation signals. J. Acoust. Soc. Am. 77, 726–730.

Azevedo, A.F., Van Sluys, M., 2005. Whistles of tucuxi dolphins (*Sotalia fluviatilis*) in Brazil: comparisons among populations. J. Acoust. Soc. Am. 117, 1456–1464.

Bain, D.E., 1986. Acoustic behavior of *Orcinus*: sequences, periodicity, behavioral correlates and an automated technique for call classification. In: Kirkevold, B.C., Lockard, J.S. (Eds.), Behavioral Biology of Killer Whales. Alan R. Liss, New York, pp. 335–371.

Balcomb, K.C., Claridge, D.E., 2001. A mass stranding of cetaceans caused by naval sonar in the Bahamas. Bahamas J. Sci. 8, 2–12.

Baron, S.C., Martinez, A., Garrison, L.P., Keith, E.O., 2008. Differences in acoustic signals from delphinids in the western North Atlantic and northern Gulf of Mexico. Mar. Mamm. Sci. 24, 42–56.

Barrett-Lennard, L.G., Ford, J.K.B., Heise, K.A., 1996. The mixed blessing of echolocation: differences in sonar use by fish-eating and mammal-eating killer whales. Anim. Behav. 51, 553–565.

Bastian, J., 1967. The transmission of arbitrary environmental information between bottlenose dolphins. In: Busnel, R.G. (Ed.), Animal Sonar Systems—Biology and Bionics. Laboratoire de Physiologie Acoustique, Jouy-en-Josas, pp. 803–873.

Bazúa-Durán, C., Au, W.W.L., 2002. The whistles of Hawaiian spinner dolphins. J. Acoust. Soc. Am. 112, 3064–3072.

Benoit-Bird, K.J., Au, W.W.L., 2009. Phonation behavior of cooperatively foraging spinner dolphins. J. Acoust. Soc. Am. 125, 539–546.

Bigg, M.A., Olesiuk, P.F., Ellis, G.M., Ford, J.K.B., Balcomb, K.C., 1990. Social organization and genealogy of resident killer whales (*Orcinus orca*) in the coastal waters of British Columbia and Washington State. Rep. Int. Whal. Comm. Spec. Issue 12, 383–405.

Boughman, J.W., Moss, C.F., 2003. Social sounds: vocal learning and development of mammal and bird calls. In: Simmons, A.M., Popper, A.N., Fay, R.R. (Eds.), Acoustic Communication. Springer-Verlag, New York, pp. 138–224.

Bowles, A.E., Young, W.G., Asper, E.D., 1988. Ontogeny of stereotyped calling of a killer whale calf, *Orcinus orca*, during her first year. Rit Fisk. 11, 251–275.

Bowles, A.E., Smultea, M., Würsig, B., DeMaster, D.P., Palka, D., 1994. Relative abundance and behavior of marine mammals exposed to transmissions from the Heard Island Feasibility Test. J. Acoust. Soc. Am. 96, 2469–2482.

Brown, C.R., Brown, M., Shaffer, M.L., 1991. Food-sharing signals among socially foraging cliff swallows. Anim. Behav. 42, 551–564.

Buckstaff, K.C., 2004. Effects of watercraft noise on the acoustic behavior of bottlenose dolphins, *Tursiops truncatus*, in Sarasota Bay, Florida. Mar. Mamm. Sci. 20, 709–725.

Burdin, V.I., Reznik, A.M., Skornyakov, V.M., Chupakov, A.G., 1975. Communication signals of the Black Sea bottlenose dolphin. Sov. Phys. Acoust. 20, 314–318.

Caldwell, M.C., Caldwell, D.K., 1965. Individualized whistle contours in bottlenose dolphins (*Tursiops truncatus*). Nature 207, 434–435.

Caldwell, M.C., Caldwell, D.K., 1967. Intraspecific transfer of information via the pulsed sound in captive odontocete cetaceans. In: Bullock, R.G. (Ed.), Animal Sonar Systems—Biology and Bionics. Laboratoire Physiologie Acoustique, Jouy-en-Josas, pp. 879–936.

Caldwell, M.C., Caldwell, D.K., 1968. Vocalization of naive captive dolphins in small groups. Science 159, 1121–1123.

Caldwell, M.C., Caldwell, D.K., 1971. Statistical evidence for individual signature whistles in Pacific whitesided dolphins, *Lagenorhynchus obliquidens*. Cetology 3, 1–9.

Caldwell, M.C., Caldwell, D.K., 1972. Vocal mimicry in the whistle mode by an Atlantic bottlenosed dolphin. Cetology 9, 1–8.

Caldwell, D.K., Caldwell, M.C., 1977. Cetaceans. In: Sebeok, T.A. (Ed.), How Animals Communicate. Indiana University Press, Bloomington, pp. 794–808.

Caldwell, M.C., Caldwell, D.K., 1979. The whistle of the Atlantic bottlenosed dolphin (*Tursiops truncatus*)—ontogeny. In: Winn, H.E., Olla, B.L. (Eds.), Behavior of Marine Animals: Current Perspectives in Research. Vol. 3. Cetaceans. Plenum Press, New York, pp. 369–401.

Caldwell, M.C., Caldwell, D.K., Hall, N.R., 1973a. Ability of an Atlantic bottlenosed dolphin (*Tursiops truncatus*) to discriminate between, and potentially identify to individual, the whistles of another species, the common dolphin (*Delphinus delphis*). Cetology 14, 1–7.

Caldwell, M.C., Hall, N.R., Caldwell, D.K., 1971. Ability of an Atlantic bottlenosed dolphin to discriminate, and potentially identify to individual, the whistles of another species, the spotted dolphin. Cetology 6, 1–6.

Caldwell, M.C., Hall, N.R., Caldwell, D.K., 1972. Ability of an Atlantic bottlenosed dolphin to discriminate between, and respond differentially to, whistles of eight conspecifics. In: Laboratory, B.S. (Ed.), Proceedings of the Eight Annual Conference on Biological Sonar and Diving Mammals. Marine Mammal Study Center, Fremont, pp. 57–65.

Caldwell, M.C., Caldwell, D.K., Miller, J.F., 1973b. Statistical evidence for individual signature whistles in the spotted dolphin, *Stenella plagiodon*. Cetology 16, 1–21.

Caldwell, M.C., Caldwell, D.K., Tyack, P.L., 1990. Review of the signature-whistle-hypothesis for the Atlantic bottlenose dolphin. In: Leatherwood, S., Reeves, R.R. (Eds.), The Bottlenose Dolphin. Academic Press, San Diego, CA, pp. 199–234.

Camargo, F.S., Rollo, M.M., Giampaoli, V., Bellini, C., 2006. Whistle variability in South Atlantic spinner dolphins from the Fernando de Noronha Archipelago off Brazil. J. Acoust. Soc. Am. 120, 4071–4079.

Catchpole, C.K., Slater, P.J.B., 1995. Bird Song: Biological Themes and Variations. Cambridge University Press, Cambridge.

Cerchio, S., Dahlheim, M., 2001. Variation in feeding vocalizations of humpback whales *Megaptera novaeangliae* from southeast Alaska. Bioacoustics 11, 277–295.

Conner, D.A., 1982. Dialect versus geographic variation in mammalian vocalizations. Anim. Behav. 30, 297–298.

Connor, R.C., Smolker, R.A., 1996. "Pop" goes the dolphin: a vocalization male bottlenose dolphins produce during consortships. Behaviour 133, 643–662.

Connor, R.C., Smolker, R., Richards, A.F., 1992. Two levels of alliance formation among male bottlenose dolphins (*Tursiops* sp.). Proc. Natl. Acad. Sci. USA 89, 987–990.

Connor, R.C., Mann, J., Tyack, P.L., Whitehead, H., 1998. Social evolution in toothed whales. Trends Ecol. Evol. 13, 228–232.

Cook, M.L.H., Sayigh, L.S., Blum, J.E., Wells, R.S., 2004. Signature-whistle production in undisturbed free-ranging bottlenose dolphins (*Tursiops truncatus*). Proc. R. Soc. Lond. B 271, 1043–1049.

Cranford, T.W., 2000. In search of impulse sound sources in odontocetes. In: Au, W.W.L., Popper, A.N., Fay, R.R. (Eds.), Hearing by Whales and Dolphins. Springer, New York, pp. 109–155.

Dawson, S.M., 1991. Clicks and communication: the behavioural and social contexts of Hector's dolphin vocalizations. Ethology 88, 265–276.

Dawson, S.M., Thorpe, C.W., 1990. A quantitative analysis of the sounds of Hector's dolphin. Ethology 86, 131–145.

Deecke, V.B., Ford, J.K.B., Spong, P., 2000. Dialect change in resident killer whales: implications for vocal learning and cultural transmission. Anim. Behav. 60, 629–638.

Deecke, V.B., Slater, P.J.B., Ford, J.K.B., 2002. Selective habituation shapes acoustic predator recognition in harbour seals. Nature 420, 171–173.

Deecke, V.B., Ford, J.K.B., Slater, P.J.B., 2005. The vocal behaviour of mammal-eating killer whales: communicating with costly calls. Anim. Behav. 69, 395–405.

Dill, L.M., Dill, E.S., Charles, D., 2003. Feeding preferences of the Monkey Mia dolphins: results from a simultaneous choice protocol. Mar. Mamm. Sci. 19, 650–660.

Dormer, K.J., 1979. Mechanism of sound production and air recycling in delphinids: cineradiographic evidence. J. Acoust. Soc. Am. 65, 229–239.

dos Santos, M.E., Ferreira, A.J., Harzen, S., 1995. Rhythmic sound sequences by aroused bottlenose dolphins in the Sado estuary, Portugal. In: Kastelein, R.A., Thomas, J.A., Nachtigall, P.E. (Eds.), Sensory Systems of Aquatic Mammals. De Spil Publishers, Woerden, pp. 325–334.

Doupe, A.J., Kuhl, P.K., 1999. Birdsong and human speech: common themes and mechanisms. Annu. Rev. Neurosci. 22, 567–631.

Dreher, J.J., 1966. Cetacean communication: small-group experiment. In: Norris, K.S. (Ed.), Whales, Dolphins, and Porpoises. University of California Press, Berkeley, CA, pp. 529–541.

Dreher, J.J., Evans, W.E., 1964. Cetacean communication. In: Tavolga, W.N. (Ed.), Marine Bio-Acoustics. Pergamon Press, Oxford, pp. 373–393.

Erbe, C., 2002. Underwater noise of whale-watching boats and potential effects on killer whales (Orcinus orca), based on an acoustic impact model. Mar. Mamm. Sci. 18, 394–418.

Esch, H.C., Sayigh, L.S., Blum, J.E., Wells, R.S., 2009. Whistles as potential indicators of stress in bottlenose dolphins (Tursiops truncatus) J. Mamm. 90, 638–650.

Esch, H.C., Sayigh, L.S., Wells, R.S., (in press). Quantifying parameters of bottlenose dolphin signature whistles. Mar. Mamm. Sci.

Evans, W.E., 1973. Echolocation by marine delphinids and one species of fresh-water dolphin. J. Acoust. Soc. Am. 54, 191–199.

Evans, W.E., Dreher, J.J., 1962. Observations on scouting behavior and associated sound production by the Pacific bottlenosed porpoise (Tursiops gilli Dall). Bull. S. Calif. Acad. Sci. 61, 217–226.

Foote, A.D., Osborne, R.W., Hoelzel, A.R., 2004. Whale-call response to masking boat noise. Nature 428, 910.

Foote, A.D., Griffin, R.M., Howitt, D., Larsson, L., Miller, P.J.O., Hoelzel, A.R., 2006. Killer whales are capable of vocal learning. Biol. Lett. 2, 509–512.

Ford, J.K.B., 1989. Acoustic behaviour of resident killer whales (Orcinus orca) off Vancouver Island, British Columbia. Can. J. Zool. 67, 727–745.

Ford, J.K.B., 1991. Vocal traditions among resident killer whales (Orcinus orca) in coastal waters of British Columbia. Can. J. Zool. 69, 1454–1483.

Ford, J.K.B., Fisher, H.D., 1983. Group-specific dialects of killer whales (Orcinus orca) in British Columbia. In: Payne, R. (Ed.), Communication and Behavior of Whales. Westview Press, Boulder, CO, pp. 129–161.

Ford, J.K.B., Ellis, G.M., Barrett-Lennard, L.G., Morton, A.B., Palm, R.S., Balcomb, K.C., 1998. Dietary specialization in two sympatric populations of killer whales (Orcinus orca) in coastal British Columbia and adjacent waters. Can. J. Zool. 76, 1456–1471.

Fripp, D., 2005. Bubblestream whistles are not representative of a bottlenose dolphin's vocal repertoire. Mar. Mamm. Sci. 21, 29–44.

Fripp, D., Tyack, P., 2008. Postpartum whistle production in bottlenose dolphins. Mar. Mamm. Sci. 24, 479–502.

Fripp, D., Owen, C., Quintana-Rizzo, E., Shapiro, A., Buckstaff, K., Jankowski, K., et al., 2005. Bottlenose dolphin (Tursiops truncatus) calves appear to model their signature whistles on the signature whistles of community members. Anim. Cogn. 8, 17–26.

Gazda, S.K., Connor, R.C., Edgar, R.K., Cox, F., 2005. A division of labour with role specialization in group-hunting bottlenose dolphins (*Tursiops truncatus*) off Cedar Key, Florida.
Proc. R. Soc. Lond. B 272, 135–140.

Gillespie, D., Dunn, C., Gordon, J., Claridge, D., Embling, C., Boyd, I., 2009. Field recordings
of Gervais' beaked whales *Mesoplodon europaeus* from the Bahamas. J. Acoust. Soc. Am.
125, 3428–3433.

Harley, H.E., 2008. Whistle discrimination and categorization by the Atlantic bottlenose
dolphin (*Tursiops truncatus*): a review of the signature whistle framework and a perceptual
test. Behav. Processes 77, 243–268.

Hastie, G.D., Wilson, B., Thompson, P.M., 2006. Diving deep in a foraging hotspot: acoustic
insights into bottlenose dolphin dive depths and feeding behaviour. Mar. Biol. 148,
1181–1188.

Hawkins, A.D., Johnstone, A.D.F., 1978. The hearing of the Atlantic salmon, *Salmo salar*.
J. Fish Biol. 13, 655–674.

Herman, L.M., 1980. Cognitive characteristics of dolphins. In: Herman, L.M. (Ed.), Cetacean
Behavior: Mechanisms and Functions. John Wiley & Sons, New York, pp. 363–429.

Herman, L.M., 2002. Vocal, social, and self-imitation by bottlenosed dolphins.
In: Dautenhahn, K., Nehaniv, C.L. (Eds.), Imitation in Animals and Artifacts. MIT
Press, Cambridge, MA, pp. 63–108.

Herman, L.M., 2006. Intelligence and rational behaviour in the bottlenosed dolphin.
In: Hurley, S., Nudds, M. (Eds.), Rational Animals? Oxford University Press, Oxford,
pp. 439–467.

Herman, L.M., Tavolga, W.N., 1980. The communication systems of cetaceans. In: Herman, L.M.
(Ed.), Cetacean Behavior: Mechanisms and Functions. John Wiley & Sons, New York,
pp. 149–209.

Herman, L.M., Richards, D.G., Wolz, J.P., 1984. Comprehension of sentences by bottlenosed
dolphins. Cognition 16, 129–219.

Herman, L.M., Abichandani, S.L., Elhajj, A.N., Herman, E.Y.K., Sanchez, J.L., Pack, A.A.,
1999. Dolphins (*Tursiops truncatus*) comprehend the referential character of the human
pointing gesture. J. Comp. Psychol. 113, 347–364.

Herzing, D.L., 1997. Vocalizations and associated underwater behavior of free-ranging Atlantic spotted dolphins, *Stenella frontalis* and bottlenose dolphins, *Tursiops truncatus*. Aquat.
Mamm. 22, 61–79.

Hoelzel, A.R., 1991. Killer whale predation on marine mammals at Punta Norte, Argentina;
food sharing, provisioning and foraging strategy. Behav. Ecol. Sociobiol. 29, 197–204.

Hoelzel, A.R., Osborne, R.W., 1986. Killer whale call characteristics: implications for cooperative foraging strategies. In: Kirkevold, B.C., Lockard, J.S. (Eds.), Behavioral Biology of
Killer Whlaes. Alan R. Liss, New York, pp. 373–403.

Hoese, H.D., 1971. Dolphin feeding out of water in a salt marsh. J. Mamm. 52, 222–223.

Janik, V.M., 1999a. Origins and implications of vocal learning in bottlenose dolphins.
In: Box, H.O., Gibson, K.R. (Eds.), Mammalian Social Learning: Comparative and
Ecological Perspectives. Cambridge University Press, Cambridge, pp. 308–326.

Janik, V.M., 1999b. Pitfalls in the categorization of behaviour: a comparison of dolphin whistle
classification methods. Anim. Behav. 57, 133–143.

Janik, V.M., 2000a. Food-related bray calls in wild bottlenose dolphins (*Tursiops truncatus*).
Proc. R. Soc. Lond. B 267, 923–927.

Janik, V.M., 2000b. Source levels and the estimated active space of bottlenose dolphin (*Tursiops truncatus*) whistles in the Moray Firth, Scotland. J. Comp. Physiol. A 186, 673–680.

Janik, V.M., 2000c. Whistle matching in wild bottlenose dolphins (*Tursiops truncatus*). Science
289, 1355–1357.

Janik, V.M., 2005. Acoustic communication networks in marine mammals. In: McGregor, P.K. (Ed.), Animal Communication Networks. Cambridge University Press, Cambridge, pp. 390–415.

Janik, V.M., 2006. Communication in marine mammals. In: Brown, K. (Ed.), Encyclopedia of Language and Linguistics—2nd Edition. Elsevier, Oxford, pp. 646–654.

Janik, V.M., (in press). Vocal communication and cognition in cetaceans. In: Tallerman, M., Gibson, K.R. (Eds.), Oxford University Press Handbook of Language Evolution. Oxford University Press, Oxford.

Janik, V.M., Slater, P.J.B., 1997. Vocal learning in mammals. Adv. Study Behav. 26, 59–99.

Janik, V.M., Slater, P.J.B., 1998. Context-specific use suggests that bottlenose dolphin signature whistles are cohesion calls. Anim. Behav. 56, 829–838.

Janik, V.M., Slater, P.J.B., 2000. The different roles of social learning in vocal communication. Anim. Behav. 60, 1–11.

Janik, V.M., Dehnhardt, G., Todt, D., 1994. Signature whistle variations in a bottlenosed dolphin, *Tursiops truncatus*. Behav. Ecol. Sociobiol. 35, 243–248.

Janik, V.M., Van Parijs, S.M., Thompson, P.M., 2000. A two-dimensional acoustic localization system for marine mammals. Mar. Mamm. Sci. 16, 437–447.

Janik, V.M., Sayigh, L.S., Wells, R.S., 2006. Signature whistle contour shape conveys identity information to bottlenose dolphins. Proc. Natl. Acad. Sci. USA 103, 8293–8297.

Jones, G.J., Sayigh, L.S., 2002. Geographic variation in rates of vocal production of free-ranging bottlenose dolphins. Mar. Mamm. Sci. 18, 374–393.

Lammers, M.O., Au, W.W.L., 2003. Directionality in the whistles of Hawaiian spinner dolphins (*Stenella longirostris*): a signal feature to cue direction of movement? Mar. Mamm. Sci. 19, 249–264.

Lammers, M.O., Au, W.W.L., Herzing, D.L., 2003. The broadband social acoustic signaling behavior of spinner and spotted dolphins. J. Acoust. Soc. Am. 114, 1629–1639.

Lammers, M.O., Au, W.W.L., Aubauer, R., Nachtigall, P.E., 2004. A comparative analysis of the pulsed emissions of free-raging Hawaiian spinner dolphins (*Stenella longirostris*). In: Thomas, J.A., Moss, C.F., Vater, M. (Eds.), Echolocation in Bats and Dolphins. University of Chicago Press, Chicago, IL, pp. 414–419.

Lammers, M.O., Schotten, M., Au, W.W.L., 2006. The spatial context of free-ranging Hawaiian spinner dolphins (*Stenella longirostris*) producing acoustic signals. J. Acoust. Soc. Am. 119, 1244–1250.

Lang, T.G., Smith, H.A.P., 1965. Communication between dolphins in separate tanks by way of an electronic acoustic link. Science 150, 1839–1844.

Lemon, M., Lynch, T.P., Cato, D.H., Harcourt, R.G., 2006. Response of travelling bottlenose dolphins (*Tursiops aduncus*) to experimental approaches by a power boat in Jervis Bay, New South Wales, Australia. Biol. Conserv. 127, 363–372.

Lilly, J.C., 1963. Distress call of the bottlenosed dolphin: stimuli and evoked behavioral responses. Science 139, 116–118.

Lilly, J.C., 1965. Vocal mimicry in *Tursiops*: ability to match numbers and durations of human vocal bursts. Science 147, 300–301.

Lilly, J.C., Miller, A.M., 1961a. Sounds emitted by the bottlenose dolphin. Science 133, 1689–1693.

Lilly, J.C., Miller, A.M., 1961b. Vocal exchanges between dolphins. Science 134, 1873–1876.

Madsen, P.T., Johnson, M., Aguilar de Soto, N., Zimmer, W.M.X., Tyack, P., 2005. Biosonar performance of foraging beaked whales (*Mesoplodon densirostris*). J. Exp. Biol. 208, 181–194.

Mann, J., Sargeant, B., 2003. Like mother, like calf: the ontogeny of foraging traditions in wild Indian Ocean bottlenose dolphins (*Tursiops* sp.). In: Fragaszy, D.M., Perry, S. (Eds.), The Biology of Traditions: Models and Evidence. Cambridge University Press, Cambridge, pp. 236–266.

Marino, L., Connor, R.C., Fordyce, R.E., Herman, L.M., Hof, P.R., Lefebvre, L., et al., 2007. Cetaceans have complex brains for complex cognition. PLoS Biol. 5, e139.

Matthews, J.N., Rendell, L.E., Gordon, J.C.D., MacDonald, D.W., 1999. A review of frequency and time parameters of cetacean tonal calls. Bioacoustics 10, 47–71.

May-Collado, L.J., Wartzok, D., 2008. A comparison of bottlenose dolphin whistles in the Atlantic Ocean: factors promoting whistle variation. J. Mamm. 89, 1229–1240.

May-Collado, L.J., Agnarsson, I., Wartzok, D., 2007a. Phylogenetic review of tonal sound production in whales in relation to sociality. BMC Evol. Biol. 7, 136.

May-Collado, L.J., Agnarsson, I., Wartzok, D., 2007b. Reexamining the relationship between body size and tonal signals frequency in whales: a comparative approach using a novel phylogeny. Mar. Mamm. Sci. 23, 524–552.

McCowan, B., Reiss, D., 1995a. Quantitative comparison of whistle repertoires from captive adult bottlenose dolphins (Delphinidae, *Tursiops truncatus*): a re-evaluation of the signature whistle hypothesis. Ethology 100, 194–209.

McCowan, B., Reiss, D., 1995b. Whistle contour development in captive-born infant bottlenose dolphins (*Tursiops truncatus*): role of learning. J. Comp. Psychol. 109, 242–260.

McCowan, B., Reiss, D., 2001. The fallacy of 'signature whistles' in bottlenose dolphins: a comparative perspective of 'signature information' in animal vocalizations. Anim. Behav. 62, 1151–1162.

Miksis, J.L., Tyack, P.L., Buck, J.R., 2002. Captive dolphins, *Tursiops truncatus*, develop signature whistles that match acoustic features of human-made model sounds. J. Acoust. Soc. Am. 112, 728–739.

Miller, P.J.O., 2002. Mixed-directionality of killer whale stereotyped calls: a direction of movement cue? Behav. Ecol. Sociobiol. 52, 262–270.

Miller, P.J.O., 2006. Diversity in sound pressure levels and estimated active space of resident killer whale vocalizations. J. Comp. Physiol. A 192, 449–459.

Miller, P.J.O., Bain, D.E., 2000. Within-pod variation in the sound production of a pod of killer whales, *Orcinus orca*. Anim. Behav. 60, 617–628.

Miller, P.J.O., Shapiro, A.D., Tyack, P.L., Solow, A.R., 2004. Call-type matching in vocal exchanges of free-ranging resident killer whales, *Orcinus orca*. Anim. Behav. 67, 1099–1107.

Mitson, R.B., Morris, R.J., 1988. Evidence of high-frequency acoustic emissions from the white-beaked dolphin (*Lagenorhynchus albirostris*). J. Acoust. Soc. Am. 83, 825–826.

Monteiro-Filho, E.L.A., Monteiro, K.D.K.A., 2001. Low-frequency sounds emitted by *Sotalia fluviatilis guianensis* (Cetacea: Delphinidae) in an estuarine region in southeastern Brazil. Can. J. Zool. 79, 59–66.

Mooney, T.A., Nachtigall, P.E., Vlachos, S., 2009. Sonar induced temporary hearing loss in dolphins. Biol. Lett. 5, 565–567.

Moore, P.W.B., Pawloski, D.A., 1990. Investigations on the control of echolocation pulses in the dolphin (*Tursiops truncatus*). In: Thomas, J., Kastelein, R.A. (Eds.), Sensory Abilities of Cetaceans. Plenum Press, New York, pp. 305–316.

Morisaka, T., Connor, R.C., 2007. Predation by killer whales (*Orcinus orca*) and the evolution of whistle loss and narrow-band high frequency clicks in odontocetes. J. Evol. Biol. 20, 1439–1458.

Morisaka, T., Shinohara, M., Nakahara, F., Akamatsu, T., 2005a. Effects of ambient noise on the whistles of Indo-Pacific bottlenose dolphin populations. J. Mamm. 86, 541–546.

Morisaka, T., Shinohara, M., Nakahara, F., Akamatsu, T., 2005b. Geographic variations in the whistles among three Indo-Pacific botlenose dolphins *Tursiops aduncus* populations in Japan. Fish Sci. 71, 568–576.

Morton, A.B., Symonds, H.K., 2002. Displacement of *Orcinus orca* (L.) by high amplitude sound in British Columbia, Canada. ICES J. Mar. Sci. 59, 71–80.

Murray, S.O., Mercado, E., Roitblat, H.L., 1998. Characterizing the graded structure of false killer whale (*Pseudorca crassidens*) vocalizations. J. Acoust. Soc. Am. 104, 1679–1688.

Norris, K.S., Møhl, B., 1983. Can odontocetes debilitate prey with sound? Am. Nat. 122, 85–104.

Nousek, A.E., Slater, P.J.B., Wang, C., Miller, P.J.O., 2006. The influence of social affiliation on individual vocal signatures of northern resident killer whales (*Orcinus orca*). Biol. Lett. 2, 481–484.

Nowacek, D.P., 2002. Sequential foraging behaviour of bottlenose dolphins, *Tursiops truncatus*, in Sarasota Bay, FL. Behaviour 139, 1125–1145.

Nowacek, D.P., 2005. Acoustic ecology of foraging bottlenose dolphins (*Tursiops truncatus*), habitat-specific use of three sound types. Mar. Mamm. Sci. 21, 587–602.

Oswald, J.N., Barlow, J., Norris, T.F., 2003. Acoustic identification of nine delphinid species in the eastern tropical Pacific ocean. Mar. Mamm. Sci. 19, 20–37.

Overstrom, N.A., 1983. Association between burst-pulse sounds and aggressive behavior in captive Atlantic bottlenosed dolphins (*Tursiops truncatus*). Zoo Biol. 2, 93–103.

Podos, J., da Silva, V.M.F., Rossi-Santos, M.R., 2002. Vocalizations of Amazon river dolphins, *Inia geoffrensis*: insights into the evolutionary origin of delphinid whistles. Ethology 108, 601–612.

Quick, N.J., Janik, V.M., 2008. Whistle rates of wild bottlenose dolphins: influences of group size and behavior. J. Comp. Psychol. 122.

Quick, N.J., Rendell, L.E., Janik, V.M., 2008. A mobile acoustic localization system for the study of free-ranging dolphins during focal follows. Mar. Mamm. Sci. 24, 979–989.

Quintana-Rizzo, E., Mann, D.A., Wells, R.S., 2006. Estimated communication range of social sounds used by bottlenose dolphins (*Tursiops truncatus*). J. Acoust. Soc. Am. 120, 1671–1683.

Ralston, J.V., Herman, L.M., 1995. Perception and generalization of frequency contours by a bottlenose dolphin (*Tursiops truncatus*). J. Comp. Psychol. 109, 268–277.

Rankin, S., Oswald, J., Barlow, J., Lammers, M., 2007. Patterned burst-pulse vocalizations of the northern right whale dolphin, *Lissodelphis borealis*. J. Acoust. Soc. Am. 121, 1213–1218.

Rasmussen, M.H., Miller, L.A., 2004. Echolocation and social signals from white-beaked dolphins, *Lagenorhynchus albirostris*, recorded in Icelandic waters. In: Thomas, J.A., Moss, C.F., Vater, M. (Eds.), Echolocation in Bats and Dolphins. University of Chicago Press, Chicago, IL, pp. 50–53.

Reiss, D., McCowan, B., 1993. Spontaneous vocal mimicry and production by bottlenose dolphins (*Tursiops truncatus*): evidence for vocal learning. J. Comp. Psychol. 107, 301–312.

Rendell, L.E., Gordon, J.C.D., 1999. Vocal response of long-finned pilot whales (*Globicephala melas*) to military sonar in the Ligurian Sea. Mar. Mamm. Sci. 15, 198–204.

Rendell, L.E., Matthews, J.N., Gill, A., Gordon, J.C.D., MacDonald, D.W., 1999. Quantitative analysis of tonal calls from five odontocete species, examining interspecific and intraspecific variation. J. Zool. 249, 403–410.

Richards, D.G., Wolz, J.P., Herman, L.M., 1984. Vocal mimicry of computer-generated sounds and vocal labeling of objects by a bottlenosed dolphin, *Tursiops truncatus*. J. Comp. Psychol. 98, 10–28.

Richardson, W.J., Greene, C.R., Malme, C.I., Thomson, D.H., 1995. Marine Mammals and Noise. Academic Press, San Diego, CA.

Riesch, R., Ford, J.K.B., Thomsen, F., 2006. Stability and group specificity of stereotyped whistles in resident killer whales, *Orcinus orca*, off British Columbia. Anim. Behav. 71, 79–91.

Riesch, R., Ford, J.K.B., Thomsen, F., 2008. Whistle sequences in wild killer whales. J. Acoust. Soc. Am. 124, 1822–1829.

Rossi-Santos, M.R., Podos, J., 2006. Latitudinal variation in whistle structure of the estuarine dolphin *Sotalia guianensis*. Behaviour 143, 347–364.

Sayigh, L.S., Tyack, P.L., Wells, R.S., Scott, M.D., 1990. Signature whistles of free-ranging bottlenose dolphins, *Tursiops truncatus*: mother-offspring comparisons. Behav. Ecol. Sociobiol. 26, 247–260.

Sayigh, L.S., Tyack, P.L., Wells, R.S., Scott, M.D., Irvine, A.B., 1995. Sex differences in signature whistle production of free-ranging bottlenose dolphins, *Tursiops truncatus*. Behav. Ecol. Sociobiol. 36, 171–177.

Sayigh, L.S., Tyack, P.L., Wells, R.S., Solow, A.R., Scott, M.D., Irvine, A.B., 1999. Individual recognition in wild bottlenose dolphins: a field test using playback experiments. Anim. Behav. 57, 41–50.

Sayigh, L.S., Esch, H.C., Wells, R.S., Janik, V.M., 2007. Facts about signature whistles of bottlenose dolphins (*Tursiops truncatus*). Anim. Behav. 74, 1631–1642.

Schevill, W.E., Watkins, W.A., 1971. Pulsed sounds of the porpoise *Lagenorhynchus australis*. Breviora 366, 1–10.

Schultz, K.W., Corkeron, P.J., 1994. Interspecific differences in whistles produced by inshore dolphins in Moreton Bay, Queensland, Australia. Can. J. Zool. 72, 1061–1068.

Searcy, W.A., Nowicki, S., 2005. The Evolution of Animal Communciation: Reliability and Deception of in Signaling Systems. Princeton University Press, Princeton, NJ.

Sigurdson, J., 1993. Frequency-modulated whistles as a medium for communication with the bottlenose dolphin (*Tursiops truncatus*). In: Roitblat, H.L., Herman, L.M., Nachtigall, P.E. (Eds.), Language and Communication: Comparative Perspectives. Lawrence Erlbaum Associates, Hillsdale, NJ, pp. 153–173.

Simon, M., Ugarte, F., Wahlberg, M., Miller, L.A., 2006. Icelandic killer whales *Orcinus orca* use a pulsed call suitable for manipulating the schooling behaviour of herring *Clupea harengus*. Bioacoustics 16, 57–74.

Smolker, R., Pepper, J.W., 1999. Whistle convergence among allied male bottlenose dolphins (Delphinidae, *Tursiops* sp.). Ethology 105, 595–617.

Smolker, R.A., Mann, J., Smuts, B.B., 1993. Use of signature whistles during separations and reunions by wild bottlenose dolphin mothers and infants. Behav. Ecol. Sociobiol. 33, 393–402.

Steiner, W.W., 1981. Species-specific differences in pure tonal whistle vocalizations of five Western North Atlantic dolphin species. Behav. Ecol. Sociobiol. 9, 241–246.

Thompson, R.K.R., Herman, L.M., 1975. Underwater frequency discrimination in the bottle-nosed dolphin (1–140 khz) and the human (1–8 khz). J. Acoust. Soc. Am. 57, 943–948.

Thomsen, F., Franck, D., Ford, J.K.B., 2002. On the communicative significance of whistles in wild killer whales (*Orcinus orca*). Naturwissenschaften 89, 404–407.

Tomasello, M., Carpenter, M., Call, J., Behne, T., Moll, H., 2005. Understanding and sharing intentions: the origins of cultural cognition. Behav. Brain Sci. 28, 675.

Tschudin, A.J.P.C., 2006. Belief attribution tasks with dolphins: what social minds can reveal about animal rationality. In: Hurley, S., Nudds, M. (Eds.), Rational Animals? Oxford University Press, Oxford, pp. 413–436.

Tyack, P.L., 1985. An optical telemetry device to identify which dolphin produces a sound. J. Acoust. Soc. Am. 78, 1892–1895.

Tyack, P., 1986. Whistle repertoires of two bottlenosed dolphins, *Tursiops truncatus*: mimicry of signature whistles. Behav. Ecol. Sociobiol. 18, 251–257.

Tyack, P., 1991. Use of a telemetry device to identify which dolphin produces a sound. In: Pryor, K., Norris, K.S. (Eds.), Dolphin Societies: Discoveries and Puzzles. University of California Press, Berkeley, CA, pp. 319–344.

Tyack, P.L., Sayigh, L.S., 1997. Vocal learning in cetaceans. In: Snowdon, C.T., Hausberger, M. (Eds.), Social Influences on Vocal Development. Cambridge University Press, Cambridge, pp. 208–233.

Ursing, B.M., Arnason, U., 1998. Analyses of mitochondrial genomes strongly support a hippopotamus-whale clade. Proc. R. Soc. Lond. B 265, 2251–2255.

Van Parijs, S.M., Corkeron, P.J., 2001a. Boat traffic affects the acoustic behaviour of Pacific humpback dolphins, *Sousa chinensis*. J. Mar. Biol. Assoc. UK 81, 533–538.

Van Parijs, S.M., Corkeron, P.J., 2001b. Evidence for signature whistle production by a Pacific humpback dolphin, *Sousa chinensis*. Mar. Mamm. Sci. 17, 944–949.

Van Parijs, S.M., Smith, J., Corkeron, P.J., 2002. Using calls to estimate the abundance of inshore dolphins: a case study with Pacific humpback dolphins, *Sousa chinensis*. J. Appl. Ecol. 39, 853–864.

Wang, D., Würsig, B., Evans, W., 1995a. Comparisons of whistles among seven odontocete species. In: Kastelein, R.A., Thomas, J.A., Nachtigall, P.E. (Eds.), Sensory Systems of Aquatic Mammals. De Spil Publishers, Woerden, pp. 299–323.

Wang, D., Würsig, B., Evans, W.E., 1995b. Whistles of bottlenose dolphins: comparisons among populations. Aquat. Mamm. 21, 65–77.

Watkins, W.A., Schevill, W.E., 1974. Listening to Hawaiian spinner porpoises, *Stenella cf. longirostris*, with a three-dimensional hydrophone array. J. Mamm. 55, 319–328.

Watwood, S.L., Tyack, P.L., Wells, R.S., 2004. Whistle sharing in paired male bottlenose dolphins, *Tursiops truncatus*. Behav. Ecol. Sociobiol. 55, 531–543.

Watwood, S.L., Owen, E.C.G., Tyack, P.L., Wells, R.S., 2005. Signature whistle use by temporarily restrained and free-swimming bottlenose dolphins, *Tursiops truncatus*. Anim. Behav. 69, 1373–1386.

Weiß, B.M., Ladich, F., Spong, P., Symonds, H., 2006. Vocal behavior of resident killer whale matrilines with newborn calves: the role of family signatures. J. Acoust. Soc. Am. 119, 627–635.

Weiß, B.M., Symonds, H., Spong, P., Ladich, F., 2007. Intra- and intergroup vocal behavior in resident killer whales, *Orcinus orca*. J. Acoust. Soc. Am. 122, 3710–3716.

Wells, R., Boness, D.J., Rathbun, G.B., 1999. Behavior. In: Reynolds, J.E., Rommel, S.A. (Eds.), Biology of Marine Mammals. Smithsonian Institution Press, Washington, pp. 324–422.

Xitco, M.J., Roitblat, H.L., 1996. Object recognition through eavesdropping: passive echolocation in bottlenose dolphins. Anim. Learn. Behav. 24, 355–365.

Yano, K., Ichihara, T., Nakamura, A., Tanaka, S., 1984. Escape behavior of the chum salmon *Onchorhynchus keta* upon encountering Dall's porpoise *Phocoenoides dalli*. Bull. Jpn. Soc. Sci. Fish 50, 1273–1277.

Yuen, M.M.L., Nachtigall, P.E., Breese, M., Vlachos, S.A., 2007. The perception of complex tones by a false killer whale (*Pseudorca crassidens*). J. Acoust. Soc. Am. 121, 1768–1774.

Yurk, H., Barrett-Lennard, L., Ford, J.K.B., Matkin, C.O., 2002. Cultural transmission within maternal lineages: vocal clans in resident killer whales in southern Alaska. Anim. Behav. 63, 1103–1119.

Vocal Performance and Sensorimotor Learning in Songbirds

Jeffrey Podos, David C. Lahti and Dana L. Moseley

DEPARTMENT OF BIOLOGY AND GRADUATE PROGRAM IN ORGANISMIC &
EVOLUTIONARY BIOLOGY, UNIVERSITY OF MASSACHUSETTS, AMHERST,
MASSACHUSETTS 01003, USA

I. Introduction

Since the pioneering studies of William Thorpe and Peter Marler, song-birds and their songs have served continuously as an inspirational muse to behavioral biologists (Catchpole and Slater, 2008; Marler and Slabbekoorn, 2004; Marler, 1957; Thorpe, 1958a). This is due not only to songbirds' improbably rich diversity in song form and function, but also to the fascinating intricacy and complexity of the mechanisms that guide vocal production and development. Of particular interest in recent years has been the interplay between evolutionary and proximate realms. Representative questions raised in recent literature reviews well-illustrate this point: How is song diversity and function enriched by varying programs for song learning (Beecher and Brenowitz, 2005; Nelson et al., 1995)? How does variation in mechanisms underlying vocal learning and production contribute to vocal diversity and evolution (Jarvis, 2004; ten Cate, 2004)? How do mechanisms of song learning contribute to the reliability of information encoded in song (Buchanan, 2000; Nowicki et al., 1998)?

This chapter focuses on the interface of vocal performance and song development. Evidence is mounting that birds' vocal performance capacities can limit or bias aspects of the song phenotype (reviewed by Lambrechts, 1996; Podos and Nowicki, 2004; Suthers, 2004; Suthers and Goller, 1997). Less clear is the nature of the relationship between vocal performance and the processes that guide song development. As we review below, songs of many bird species develop through imitative learning, a two-step process in which young birds first memorize the structure of adult models (the "memorization" phase), and then match memorized models by

159

0065-3454/09 $35.00
DOI: 10.1016/S0065-3454(09)40005-6

comparing them to their own developing vocal output (the "sensorimotor" phase). Within the framework of imitative learning, where and how are limits or biases of vocal performance expressed? How might variation in vocal performance influence model imitation? And how might this relationship influence aspects of song function and evolution?

We begin with an overview of recent evidence that pertains to vocal performance and its influence on song production and evolution. Empirical evidence for vocal performance limits in numerous species is accumulating rapidly. We then provide a brief overview of the processes that guide song learning, and argue that a comprehensive understanding of vocal performance requires particular attention to sensorimotor learning. This is because vocal performance biases are most likely expressed as birds attempt to develop and crystallize copies of memorized models. We then consider the implications of the relationship between vocal performance and development for the "developmental stress" hypothesis, which posits that songs produced by adults provide reliable information about singers' developmental histories. Studies of the developmental stress hypothesis have focused so far on brain development and sensory learning; we suggest expanding the hypothesis to likewise consider vocal performance limitations as expressed and codified during sensorimotor learning. We conclude by describing additional avenues for study suggested by the connections drawn between vocal performance and sensorimotor learning.

II. Vocal Performance

A. Acoustic Signal Production and the Concept of Performance

As with all types of behavior, acoustic signals are circumscribed in their structure by mechanisms underlying their expression (reviewed by Bradbury and Vehrencamp, 1998). For instance, for vertebrates that produce sound via phonation (pneumatically induced source vibrations), small animals with small source structures tend to vocalize at high frequencies, because of the intrinsically high resonant frequencies of smaller masses (e.g., Gerhardt, 1994; Ryan and Brenowitz, 1985). Similarly, the acoustic frequencies and amplitudes of sounds produced by stridulation (striking of plectrum on file) are dictated largely by the size and arrangement of these structures, and by the neuromuscular mechanisms that control their movement. These and similar examples do not necessarily imply, however, that acoustic output is readily predicted by source anatomy and function. On the contrary, there is substantial room for variation in vocal output within any given mechanistic framework. To return to the example of phonation, within many animal taxa (e.g., anurans, birds, primates), individuals or species of similar body size vocalize at widely divergent frequencies, in a form of behavioral or evolutionary plasticity that overrides morphological similarities (e.g., Hauser, 1993). This is partly because many individuals or species do not vocalize at frequencies as low as their mechanisms might conceivably allow. Behavioral plasticity is also evident as animals adjust when and where they produce sound, modulating aspects of source–medium coupling and thus vocal output. Orthopterans that stridulate in chambers or burrows, for example, can amplify their calls through resonance matching, to levels beyond that which could be achieved in other acoustic environments (Bennett-Clark, 1987).

A concept with particular utility here is that of "performance," which addresses the dynamic nature of the relationship between behavioral mechanisms and behavioral output, and the fitness consequences of this relationship (e.g., Arnold, 1983; Irschick, 2003; Wainwright, 1994). Two recurring findings in studies of performance are that animals often perform the same behavior in different contexts with widely varying levels of performance, and that animals typically do not behave at performance maxima during day to day activities, instead reserving maximal performance for key fitness-defining contexts such as predator avoidance. These themes are well illustrated in the literature on locomotion in lizards (Garland and Losos, 1994; Irschick and Garland, 2001). Lizards can be induced to sprint in track tests or on treadmills, from which maximal sprint speeds can be inferred. Observational studies indicate that maximal sprint speeds are approached only rarely in nature, as lizards attempt to evade predators (Irschick, 2003). By contrast, locomotion speeds are much slower in typical contexts, for example, in *Anolis* typically approaching only 10–40% maximum speed (Irschick, 2003). Distinguishing typical versus maximal performance is important because it helps specify the loci on which selection may act. In the case of lizard locomotion, individuals within a given population overlap widely in typical locomotion speeds, but separate reliably in maximal sprint speeds. That is, while all lizards can move at slow speeds, only some can reach the highest speeds. A recent survey of this literature indicates that natural and sexual selection indeed often favor animals that express higher maximal performance capacities (Irschick et al., 2008).

While the concept of performance has been applied with rigor to the study of locomotion and feeding behavior, its utility has been considered only occasionally for behavioral communication displays such as bird songs. Here are five representative questions that can be asked about behavioral communication displays from a performance-based perspective: (1) To what extent do individuals modulate display performance across different contexts, for example, across a breeding season or to different audiences?; (2) Do signalers sometimes encounter performance limitations as they display, and if so when?; (3) How do individuals vary in maximal display performance?; (4) Are signal receivers particularly attentive to maximal display events, as opposed to typical display events?; and (5) How does variation in maximal display behavior bear upon sexual selection?

These questions seem particularly relevant to the study of avian vocal displays, given the intricate nature of the vocal production mechanism, the complex time-varying structure of many vocalizations, and the corresponding likelihood that performance limits shape aspects of the avian vocal phenotype (Podos and Nowicki, 2004). To elaborate, birds typically generate sounds at the syrinx, a bilateral sound source with partly independent contributions from the left and right sides (Greenewalt, 1968; Nottebohm, 1971; Nowicki and Capranica, 1986; Suthers, 1990). Syringeal tissues vibrate and produce sound when activated by respiratory airflow (Goller and Larsen, 1997), and patterns of breathing are finely coordinated with syringeal activity, such that vocalizations are typically uttered only as birds breathe out (Suthers, 2004). Vocal structure is also influenced by the trachea and associated structures (the "vocal tract"), which selectively filter harmonic overtones and thus enable the production of sounds with high pure-tonal quality (Nowicki, 1987; Nowicki and Marler, 1988). Birds actively modulate vocal tract configurations during song production, in a manner that tracks modulations at the syrinx (Beckers et al., 2003; Hoese et al., 2000; Riede et al., 2006; Westneat et al., 1993). Vocal tract modulations are presumed to enable birds to retain the vocal tract's resonance function across a range of vocal frequencies. The multiple motor systems of bird song production are coordinated by a complex hierarchical neural control system (Brainard and Doupe, 2002; Jarvis, 2004; Suthers, 2004). Overall, vocal production is a nearly "beak-to-foot effort" (Podos and Nowicki, 2004) that seems to present birds substantial production challenges for its successful execution.

Songs that feature rapid modulations in vocal frequencies, or rapid repetitions of notes, should be particularly susceptible to performance limitations. For example, consider song production in Northern cardinals (*Cardinalis cardinalis*), which Suthers (2004, p. 281) refers to as an "extraordinary feat of virtuosity." Cardinal songs typically consist of trilled sequences, with notes repeated numerous times per second, and each often spanning at least two octaves (Suthers, 2004). Measurements of respiratory pressure in the bronchi demonstrate that low frequency note components (below ~3.5 kHz) are produced by the left side of the syrinx, whereas higher frequencies are produced by the right side of the syrinx (Suthers and Goller, 1997). By coordinating the two sides of the syrinx, birds are able to span a range of vocal frequencies with a speed and degree of precision that presumably could not be achieved if sound production was limited to only a single vocal source. Moreover, note production involves a tight interplay of activation or closure of the two syrinx sides at the appropriate time, of precisely timed respiratory inspirations and expirations, and of precisely modulated vocal tract reconfigurations (Suthers, 2004). Similar patterns have been observed in a diversity of species, confirming the generality of these patterns (Suthers, 2004). Thus the seemingly simple structure of some songbird songs, and of their constituent notes, belies the daunting intricacy and complexity of the vocal performance that enables their production.

B.   INFERRING VOCAL PERFORMANCE LIMITS IN SONGBIRDS

How can we know if and when songbirds vocalize at their maximal performance abilities? If birds never push their vocal displays to maximal effort, then the discussion of variation in performance abilities would be largely moot. In general, the most direct way to infer performance limitations in animals is to motivate them with experimental tasks that push their performance envelopes. Motivating animals to perform maximally is fairly straightforward in studies of feeding or locomotion; for the former one merely needs a hungry animal, and for the latter one needs an animal that is under threat from a predator (e.g., in the guise of a scientist wielding a stick) or that is placed in an environment or situation that challenges typical locomotory performance (e.g., Chai and Dudley, 1995; Gillis et al., 2009; Jayne and Ellis, 1998). It is less straightforward to motivate songbirds to sing at high vocal performance. Birds almost never sing for their survival (but see Cresswell, 1994), which means that motivation typically cannot be induced by hunger or fear.

One method that has been used with success to infer vocal performance limitations has been to train young birds with song models that are rigged to challenge birds' vocal abilities. In a study of swamp sparrows (*Melospiza georgiana*), a species that typically produces simple trills, Podos (1996) trained hand-reared males with song models that contained species-typical notes arranged with artificially elevated trill rates. The reasoning behind this approach is that young birds are intrinsically motivated to reproduce model songs with accuracy, yet might encounter performance limitations in reproducing models that challenge their vocal production capacities. The experimental birds in this study proved able to memorize rapid trill models, but unable to reproduce the models at their elevated rates. Instead birds introduced copying inaccuracies in ways suggesting that they had indeed encountered performance constraints during development. Some models were reproduced at slower trill rates, others with notes omitted, and others with "broken" syntax, in which multisyllable segments were separated by brief pauses (Podos, 1996). The vocal structure of the models used in this study was thus beyond the realm of possibility, at least as specified by the current structure and function of the swamp sparrow vocal apparatus. A parallel demonstration was offered by Zollinger and Suthers (2004) for Northern mockingbirds (*Mimus polyglottis*), which are accomplished vocal mimics of other species. Mockingbirds were reared and exposed to song models from four species, including Wasserslager canaries (*Serinus canaries*), which sing trills that are both rapid and of extended duration. Two mockingbirds that attempted to copy canary trills proved unable to reproduce the "mini-breath" breathing patterns that allow canaries to produce rapid trills of extended duration. Rather, these birds reproduced canary models using "pulsatile" breathing patterns, which required occasional brief pauses between trill segments, thus resulting in broken syntax parallel to that observed in swamp sparrows.

A more common yet less direct approach for inferring vocal performance limits is through descriptive analyses of vocal variation, especially with reference to expectations about vocal performance boundaries. Perhaps the most traditional measure of vocal performance has been song output, that is, the number of vocalizations performed per unit time, or the duration of vocalizations relative to that of silent intervals between songs. Birds with greater levels of vocal proficiency presumably could produce relatively more vocal material per unit time. Indeed there is wide-ranging evidence that birds within given populations vary in their vocal output (e.g., Alatalo et al., 1990; Arvidsson and Neergaard, 1991; Hofstad et al., 2002; Kempenaers et al., 1997; Otter et al., 1997; Pinxten and Eens, 1998; Poesel et al., 2001). It has been difficult, however, to attribute such results with confidence to individual variation in performance abilities, for at least three reasons. First, available evidence indicates that the actual metabolic cost of song production is rather low (Oberweger and Goller, 2001). The absence of a clear energetic cost to song production raises the question of what other costs or constraints could render vocal output an honest signal of vocal performance (Searcy and Nowicki, 2005). Second, individual variation in vocal output might result instead as a correlated effect of food availability, such that birds with ready access to food are able to spend more time singing. This alternative hypothesis is supported by experimental studies in which birds provided with supplementary food sang more, presumably because of reduced time required for foraging (Lucas et al., 1999; Nystrom, 1997; Thomas, 1999). Third, birds which vocalize infrequently may do so not because of a physical inability to produce more, but because of an inability to withstand other kinds of costs associated with increased song output such as increased vulnerability or likelihood of retaliation from territorial neighbors (Vehrencamp, 2001).

Variation in vocal performance abilities may be easier to identify as it occurs with respect to vocal structural parameters, that is, the structure of specific songs, song sequences, or song components (Gil and Gahr, 2002; Podos et al., 2004a). We now review recent advances in the study of two classes of vocal parameters—consistency and trill structure—that link directly to expectations about vocal performance, and for which empirical evidence has been accumulating rapidly. We do not regard these categories as collectively exhaustive, as additional categories of performance constraints can be envisaged.

1. Consistency

Birds' performance abilities might be revealed in their ability to produce repetitive songs or song components with consistency, that is, with little variation across renditions. Variation in the consistency of note structure was illustrated in Lambrechts' (1997) study of great tits (*Parus major*), a species whose songs include trilled sequences of varying tempos. Lambrechts showed that note frequencies within slow trills tend to be highly consistent, but to vary substantially within trills of faster tempo. Birds repeating notes within fast trills presumably face greater difficulties maintaining note frequencies at constant levels. Similarly, Christie et al. (2004) documented, in black-capped chickadees (*Poecile atricapillus*), variation among birds in the consistency of note pitch ratios across song renditions. Some chickadees are able to maintain highly consistent ratios among "fee" and "bee" notes, even as the absolute frequencies of these notes vary, whereas other birds fail to maintain consistent note pitch ratios. In a recent study of chestnut-sided warblers (*Dendroica pensylvanica*), Byers (2007) documented individual variation in song consistency across a number of frequency and temporal song parameters, using coefficients of variation (CV). CVs were found to range from $\sim$3–10% on the stereotyped end of the spectrum to about $\sim$20–35% on the variable end of the spectrum. Other studies of song consistency have focused on the maintenance of consistent timing relationships among songs within bouts (Lambrechts and Dhondt, 1986; Poesel et al., 2001). In all of the above studies, variation in consistency is inferred to be a product of vocal performance, with only the highest quality singers able to perform with the highest levels of consistency.

2. Trill Structure

Many birds' songs include trilled sequences, in which notes or note groups (syllables) are repeated two or more times in sequence (e.g., Podos, 1997; Thorpe and Lade, 1961). Birds' vocal competency might be revealed in their ability to include trilled vocal sequences in their songs and repertoires, given the intricacy of the mechanisms involved in trill production (see above). In their studies of nightingales (*Luscinia megarhynchos*), Kunc et al. (2006) and Schmidt et al. (2006) found that males challenged with song playback tend to augment the proportion of songs they sing that contain broadband trills. Similarly, Trillo and Vehrencamp (2005) report that banded wrens (*Pheugopedius pleurostictus*) are more likely to produce trilled vocal sequences during intense male–male interactions, border disputes, and also during dawn song as compared to daytime song.

Internal trill characteristics might also be dictated by singers' vocal performance abilities. Trill rate, that is the number of syllables delivered within a trill per unit time, should be limited in part by birds' abilities to perform rapid modulations of the syrinx, respiratory, and vocal tract motor systems, as described above. For trills of slow to moderate tempo, birds normally take "mini-breaths" between every note and syllable. Use of mini-breaths maintains birds' respiratory tidal volume at fairly constant levels, thus enabling the production of trills of extended duration (Hartley and Suthers, 1989). To produce faster trills, however, birds typically shift to "pulsatile" respiration, in which respiratory tidal volume is depleted rapidly, thus limiting trill duration (Hartley and Suthers, 1989). Increasing trill rates may thus reduce maximal trill durations (Suthers, 2004).

Another widespread structural tradeoff that appears to define many trills is between trill rate and frequency bandwidth, that is, the range of frequencies a trill spans. This tradeoff was first described for 34 species of emberizid songbirds and has been attributed to a performance constraint on trill production (Podos, 1997; see also Podos and Nowicki, 2004). A brief explanation for this tradeoff is as follows: Increases in either trill rate or frequency bandwidth are expected to push a bird's performance envelope, because of required increases in the rapidity or scope of required syrinx, respiratory, and vocal tract reconfigurations. If a bird maximizes its trill rate, it necessarily limits the time span during which frequency modulations can be performed within given syllables, and thus necessarily sets limits on frequency bandwidth. Likewise, producing syllables that span broad frequency bandwidths requires corresponding long periods of time, thus limiting trill rate. In actuality, the tradeoff between the two parameters is not linear but triangular, because birds can produce trills that are both slow and narrowband, well below the hypothesized performance limit. An upper boundary regression of the triangular distribution defining the trill rate × frequency tradeoff has thus been used to infer maximal performance limits (Podos, 1997; see also Ballentine, 2006; Podos, 2001; Podos and Nowicki, 2004). Tradeoffs between trill rate and frequency bandwidth have since been described in greater detail for two of those emberizid species, swamp sparrows (Ballentine et al., 2004; Liu et al., 2008) and dark-eyed juncos (*Junco hyemalis*; Cardoso et al., 2007), as well as for a number of additional species or groups including yellow warblers (*Dendroica petechia*; Beebee, 2004, with trills described as "phrases"), oropendolas and caciques (Icteridae; Price and Lanyon, 2004), banded wrens (Illes et al., 2006), red-winged blackbirds (*Ageliaus phoeniceus*; Cramer and Price, 2007), and brown skuas (*Catharacta antarctica*; Janicke et al., 2008). The observed tradeoff in brown skuas may arise through a mechanism distinct from that in passerines, given that vocalizations in this species are not pure tonal, and that frequency bandwidth is adjusted not by modulation of fundamental frequencies but rather via enhancement or suppression of harmonic overtones (Cardoso, 2008; Janicke and Hahn, 2008).

Other structural relationships identified within trills illuminate additional possible loci of variation in vocal performance. Forstmeier et al. (2002) showed that in dusky warblers (*Phylloscopus fuscatus*), trills (or strophes) with rapid frequency modulations contain less signal energy, measured as relative amplitude, as compared to trills with more limited frequency modulations. Signaling advantages gained by enhanced frequency modulation might thus be offset by reductions in amplitude and thus overall signal efficacy. Brumm and Slater (2006) report that chaffinches (*Fringilla coelebs*) switch song types more frequently when singing songs with fast trills, perhaps as a result of motor fatigue (see also Lambrechts and Dhondt, 1988). Birds that can produce many consecutive iterations of a song type with fast trills may thus be able to distinguish themselves from other singers in a population.

Performance limitations likely shape trill structure in additional ways that have not yet been explored. To illustrate, consider two hypothetical trills, A and B (Fig. 1). Both trills contain syllables comprised of two notes, each a simple frequency sweep with identical frequency ranges. Moreover, syllables are produced with identical durations and tempos. In trill A, the two notes alternate in direction of frequency modulation, with the first note sweeping upward and the second note sweeping downward. By contrast, the two notes in trill B syllables are modulated in the same direction, both sweeping upward. A simple of analysis of trill rate, frequency bandwidth, or the relation between these two parameters would suggest identical performance levels for these trills. However, we would actually expect trill A to be easier to produce than trill B. In trill A, during the silent intervals between notes, the vocal apparatus (particularly the syrinx and vocal tract) would already be in an appropriate configuration for the production of the next note, because of the frequency match between the end of the prior note and the start of the next note. By contrast, trill B would require considerable syrinx and vocal tract reconfiguration during silent intervals, to account for the difference between the ending and starting frequency of sequential notes. Many similar scenarios can be envisioned, not only with respect to trills but also to other types of vocal parameters.

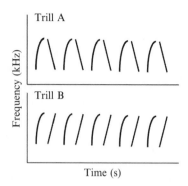

FIG. 1. Two hypothetical trills, equivalent in trill rate and frequency bandwidth, but which would still be expected to differ in performance requirements. See text for further explanation.

C. Does Performance Matter?

Inferring limits on vocal performance is a worthwhile task in its own right, because it allows us to document the ranges of song variants that may be expressed within a species or population (Podos, 1997; Podos et al., 2004a). Of perhaps greater interest is the possibility that signal receivers attend to performance variation among singers, and use this information to differentiate singers in terms of their quality. The question of whether vocal performance provides a reliable indicator of singer quality represents an area of significant recent activity (e.g., Gil and Gahr, 2002; Searcy and Nowicki, 2005).

With respect to variation in vocal output, high song rates have been linked to a range of factors associated with fitness such as territory quality, food availability, metabolic condition, and immunocompetence (reviewed by Podos et al., 2004a). However, while song rate variation is likely shaped in part by performance abilities, alternative hypotheses for observed variations in vocal output have been difficult to exclude (see above). More definitive conclusions have been emerging from studies focusing on song consistency and trill structure.

Available evidence indicates that birds that sing with high consistency fare better in attributes related to reproductive success (reviewed by Byers, 2007). Lambrechts and Dhondt's (1986) study of great tits revealed that males that deliver songs with more consistent timing, as measured by variation in internote intervals, tend to be socially dominant. Social dominance in black-capped chickadees is also revealed by consistency, not in the timing of delivery but in internote frequency ratios (Christie et al., 2004). In their study of blue tits (*Cyanistes caeruleus*), Poesel et al. (2001) found that males with consistent inter-song intervals tend to sire larger clutches. Similarly, Byers (2007) found that female chestnut-sided warblers tend to choose extra-pair mates who sing with high consistency in frequency and timing parameters. In this latter study, a comparison of singing by extra-pair mates and cuckolded social fathers revealed superior consistency among the extra-pair mates. Dusky warblers who sing with consistently high relative amplitudes across trill syllables ("peak performance") appear to enjoy enhanced longevity and greater success in achieving extra-pair paternity (Forstmeier et al., 2002). Finally, male brown skuas that produce vocalizations with higher peak performance, and also with relatively high trill rates and frequency bandwidths ("vocal deviation"), obtain disproportionately high reproductive success (Janicke et al., 2008). Descriptive studies such as these, which report correlations among song performance and measures of reproductive success, are invaluable yet face one major limitation: It is not known whether signal receivers respond directly to variation in vocal performance *per se* or to other indicators of male quality with which vocal performance might correlate. More comprehensive conclusions about the functional consequences of vocal performance variation thus require experimental studies, in which song performance variants are presented via playback in the absence of singing males (see Searcy and Andersson, 1986, p. 508, for a parallel argument). A number of recent studies have taken this approach:

Schmidt et al. (2008) tested whether the presence versus absence of trills may have functional consequences. Territorial male nightingales were presented simulated rivals from two playback speakers, the first speaker broadcasting songs that featured some rapid broadband trills, and the second speaker broadcasting nontrilled songs exclusively. Birds were found to respond much more strongly to the playback speaker broadcasting trills, thus suggesting that trills are regarded by rivals as particularly aggressive signals. However, these results contrast with those reported for blue tits by Doutrelant et al. (1999) and Poesel and Dabelsteen (2006), who found no response differences to playback of trilled versus nontrilled songs. It is not yet clear if and how the ability to deliver broadband trills varies among singers of differing quality.

With regard to variations in trill structure, female canaries and swamp sparrows were found to solicit copulations more frequently and more vigorously in response to playback of trills with comparatively or artificially high trill rates and frequency bandwidth (Ballentine et al., 2004; Draganoiu et al., 2002; Vallet and Kreutzer, 1995; Vallet et al., 1998). Territorial male red-winged blackbirds were also found to discriminate songs of high versus low trill rates and frequency bandwidth, although responses were stronger to low rather than high-performance songs (Cramer and Price, 2007). One possible explanation for the direction of this response is that territorial males found high-performance songs relatively intimidating (Collins, 2004; Cramer and Price, 2007; Searcy and Nowicki, 2000).

Other recent playback studies have focused on variation in either trill rate or frequency bandwidth alone. Illes et al. (2006) used a two-speaker design to assess whether male banded wrens discriminate playback trills that vary by trill rate, pairing slow trills against fast trills. Birds were found to approach faster trills first, suggesting that fast trills are perceived by territory owners as a more immediate threat. More telling were subsequent reactions; after initial approach, test subjects were generally repelled by the faster trills, and to a degree that corresponded to the overall performance levels of these songs relative to the song population. This finding was expanded upon in Schmidt et al.'s (2008) study of night-ingales, a species in which approximately half of all males remain unmated throughout a given breeding season. Males that remained unmated responded to song playback in a manner parallel to that described by Illes et al. (2006) for banded wrens; birds avoided playback trills to degrees corresponding to trill rates. However, males that eventually paired later in the season showed the opposite trend, responding more aggressively to playback trills with higher trill rates. Male responses to songs of varying performance levels may thus vary with signaling context and with attributes of signal receivers. de Kort et al. (2009) presented territorial banded wrens with playback songs from three categories; control, with experimentally increased frequency bandwidths, or with experimentally decreased frequency bandwidths. The strongest territorial responses were directed toward unmanipulated songs. Detailed analysis of response patterns suggests that low-bandwidth songs were perceived as comparatively nonthreatening, whereas high-bandwidth songs were perceived as unusually intimidating.

Emerging descriptive and experimental evidence thus indicates that vocal performance varies among individuals, and suggests that singers who maximize vocal performance gain advantages in song function and ultimately in reproductive success. For these reasons, the specific processes by which varying vocal performance shapes the vocal phenotype merit special attention. As we argue below, the impact of vocal performance on song structure in songbirds is likely realized most significantly during vocal development and especially during sensorimotor learning. Before addressing the specifics of this argument, we provide a general overview of the process of vocal imitation, with emphasis on sensorimotor learning.

III. SONG LEARNING IN SONGBIRDS

Along with a handful of other vertebrate groups, songbirds develop vocalizations through imitative learning ("production learning," Janik and Slater, 2000). Songbirds are especially renowned for the accuracy and precision with which song models can be memorized and reproduced. In this section, we offer a brief review of the processes that underlie imitative learning, first with regard to factors that govern the acquisition and memorization of song models, and second with regard to sensorimotor learning, in which song memories are transformed into vocal output (Marler, 1970). This review is based largely on research on sparrows and zebra finches (*Taeniopygia guttata*), for which the majority of data are available; additional research on song learning in other bird groups will undoubtedly reveal additional kinds of song learning and development programs.

A. SONG ACQUISITION

Song acquisition occurs as young birds listen to song models and commit them to memory. A major theme to emerge from over half a century of empirical studies is that song acquisition is often circumscribed by innate predispositions, such that only a subset of potentially available models is memorized. A first example of this concerns species that show innate predispositions in recognizing and memorizing song models of conspecifics versus heterospecifics (Braaten and Reynolds, 1999; Nelson, 2000a; Slater et al., 1988; Soha and Marler, 2001; Thorpe, 1958b). Remarkably, this preference can be based on the acoustic structure of models alone, in the absence of social tutors, as has been shown in song learning studies in which birds are presented song models over loudspeakers (Dooling and Searcy, 1980; Marler and Peters, 1977; Soha and Marler, 2000). Innate predispositions for learning conspecific songs have been mapped to particular regions of the avian forebrain, within which neurons respond more strongly to conspecific than to heterospecific song (e.g., Chew et al., 1995; Doupe, 1997; Janata and Margoliash, 1999). A second bias in song acquisition is that birds are often predisposed to learn songs mainly during a "sensitive period" of song acquisition, during the first months of their lives (Kroodsma and Pickert, 1980; Marler and Peters, 1987). Certain neural structures, including song nuclei that are only found in birds that learn their songs, develop in parallel with this sensitive period and are thought to enable and then restrict vocal model input (Bottjer, 2004; Konishi and Akutagawa, 1985; Nottebohm et al., 1976).

Model acquisition can also be shaped significantly by birds' social interactions (Beecher and Burt, 2004; Beecher et al., 2007; Nelson, 1997; Nordby et al., 2007; West and King, 1988). Zebra finches, for instance, prefer to learn songs from their own fathers or other similarly plumaged males (Clayton, 1988; Mann and Slater, 1995), whereas birds such as the song sparrow (*Melospiza melodia*) and chipping sparrow *(Spizella passerina)* tend to learn their songs from males that are nearby (Beecher et al., 1994; Liu and Kroodsma, 2006). In some species, males copy a single tutor among several available singers (e.g., zebra finches, Mann and Slater, 1995), whereas in other species males integrate elements of several tutors into their final songs (e.g., savannah sparrows, *Passerculus sandwichensis*, Wheelwright et al., 2008; nightingales, Hultsch and Todt, 1989). Birds reared by heterospecific tutors may copy the songs of their foster parents (Baptista and Petrinovitch, 1984).

These and parallel lines of evidence suggest that birds possess innate neural representations or "templates" that target specific tutor songs for acquisition, and which can be shaped by social influences (Adret, 2004; Marler, 1976, 1997). The neural template is presumably crystallized in the first few months of a bird's life, at least in "age-limited" or "closed-ended" learners (Marler and Peters, 1987). By contrast, some species, for example, European starlings (*Sturnus vulgaris*) and Northern mockingbirds, retain the ability to memorize new songs throughout their lives. Some species that were traditionally classified as close-ended learners now appear, according to recent evidence, to be able to learn new song material as adults, at least under specific social contexts (Brenowitz and Beecher, 2005). We revisit this topic in the final section.

B.   SENSORIMOTOR LEARNING

Often after a winter of silence, during which time memorized songs are neither heard nor practiced, birds gradually translate memorized model songs into vocal output (Marler and Peters, 1982a,b). At first, birds produce sounds that are relatively indistinct and not clearly related to any model song. This has been called "subsong" and is analogous to human infant babbling. Subsequently, birds produce structurally deficient yet recognizable versions of memorized song, called "plastic song," which over time increasingly resemble memorized model songs. This process involves auditory feedback, such that birds hear their own vocal output, compare this output to stored representations of song models, and refine their vocalizations accordingly (Brumm and Hultsch, 2001; Margoliash, 2002; Marler, 1997; Slater, 1989). After a month or two of practice, songs "crystallize" into a sterotypic form, which then changes very little if at all across the remainder of a bird's life (Marler and Peters, 1982a).

A key role for auditory feedback in sensorimotor learning was first demonstrated in studies in which young birds were deafened after the memorization phase. Birds that cannot hear themselves practice are found to produce very different songs than do unimpaired birds—their vocal output is comparatively variable, lispy, and lacks the clear tonality of normal songs (Konishi, 1965a,b). These sounds do retain some structural features of normal song, to an extent that some species-specific aspects of song can be recognized (Marler and Sherman, 1983; Nottebohm, 1972). By contrast, if birds are deafened after songs have crystallized, they continue to sing virtually normal songs (Nottebohm, 1968). This indicates that the role of auditory feedback is much less pronounced after songs achieve their final form. These experiments together demonstrate that birds' own vocal output, and the perception of that output, is central to the process by which model songs are converted into accurate imitations during sensorimotor learning (Brainard and Doupe, 2000). There is also evidence that sensorimotor learning involves specialized neural circuitry in the forebrain, which is to some extent integrated with circuitry that mediates song perception and adult vocal motor control (Aronov et al., 2008; Brainard and Doupe, 2002).

Sensorimotor learning also appears to provide birds with opportunities for distilling larger repertoires of memorized models into smaller subsets of copies to be crystallized (Beecher and Brenowitz, 2005; Nelson, 1992). Birds sometimes practice more song types earlier in development than they will eventually crystallize, and appear to retain those song types that will be most useful in social interactions. In field sparrows (*Spizella pusilla*), for instance, males settling on a territory initially sing multiple song types (Nelson, 1992). Following a series of interactions with neighboring males, however, individuals typically delete all song types but one from their repertoires. The song type that remains usually matches the song of a neighbor, and is sung by the individual for the rest of his life (Nelson, 1992). Song sparrows undergo a similar process, in which song types that poorly match neighbors are deleted during the selective attrition process (Nordby et al., 2007).

Overall, sensorimotor learning contributes significantly to the plasticity of birds' songs and song repertoires. Sometimes birds introduce "innovations," that is, structural variations or modifications of model songs, and other times introduce "inventions," that is, novel elements that bear no relationship to individual model songs (Hughes et al., 2002; Janik and Slater, 2000). Innovations and inventions are presumably shaped during sensorimotor ontogeny, and are crystallized as permanent features of song. One putative function for innovation has been identified in song sparrows. As mentioned above, song sparrows selectively delete songs from their repertoires that poorly match neighboring males, reflecting the importance of song matching in this species (Nordby et al., 2007). However, before crystallization, some songs have been observed to be modified to be less similar to the neighbor songs they match. The interpretation here is that song matching is important, but that individual recognition may be important as well, with birds rendering their songs increasingly distinctive (yet still recognizable to song type) gaining advantages in individual recognition (Nordby et al., 2007).

IV. VOCAL PERFORMANCE AND SENSORIMOTOR LEARNING

A. THE DEVELOPMENT OF MOTOR PROFICIENCY

As outlined above, sensorimotor learning encompasses a number of related processes that underlie the translation of memorized songs into vocal output, and the crystallization of vocal structure from variable to stereotyped form. The challenges inherent in these processes are often framed in neural terms, and rightly so. Vocal models are initially imprinted into a neural template (Marler, 1976; Slater, 1989; see above), and neural mechanisms presumably enable access to this template, guiding the development and refinement of additional neural circuits that come to control vocal output. Much remains to be learned about the interplay of neural circuits that guide song perception, memorization, production, and motor refinement (e.g., Aronov et al., 2008; Brainard and Doupe, 2002; Jarvis, 2004; Zeigler and Marler, 2008).

We hypothesize that young birds face additional challenges during sensorimotor development that relate specifically to vocal performance. Young birds presumably need to learn how to correctly operate the multiple motor systems involved in singing, and to coordinate them in a manner that enables successful vocal output. The challenges in doing this can be daunting even for simple songs, and it seems unlikely that birds possess requisite vocal abilities upon hatching. Rather, vocal motor competency likely develops gradually, in tandem with the development of neural competency. The need to develop motor competency is one potential adaptive explanation for the protracted nature of sensorimotor learning.

Empirical data on the development of vocal motor competency, which could be used to evaluate the above hypothesis, are relatively few and far between. Descriptive studies that focus solely on developmental changes in song structure (e.g., Marler and Peters, 1982a,b) do not necessarily provide insight into performance constraints or biases *per se*, because specific developmental milestones might be achieved principally through the refinement of relevant neural mechanisms, as is generally assumed in discussions of template theory. For instance, the increasingly precise coordination of vocal motor systems is achieved in part via maturation of the neural circuits that link these systems (Wild, 1997). More informative are studies that observe and measure motor correlates of vocal ontogeny. A study of cardinals showed that young birds at the subsong stage of vocal development lack the ability to precisely coordinate expiratory breathing with syringeal activation, as determined through simultaneous recording and measures of respiratory airflow (Suthers, 2004). This lack of coordination potentially explains abrupt onsets and offsets of notes that characterize subsong. Similarly, young song sparrows were shown to introduce vocal tract modulations only during late stages of song ontogeny, after note structure had developed near-crystallized form (Podos et al., 1995). Increasing application of vocal tract modulations resulted in songs with increasing tonal purity and may have been delayed in development so as allow birds to match learned patterns of syringeal output.

A complementary approach for assessing the development of motor competency is experimental, involving the presentation of probe training models to young birds and then tracking subsequent patterns of learning. Probe training models typically possess some conspecific song features, to ensure their viability as models, yet vary in other parameters that allow tests of the learning capacity of interest. Here we describe two sets of such studies. The first focused on the development of pure-tonal vocal structure in song sparrows (Nowicki et al., 1992; Peters and Nowicki, 1996). Songbirds of this and other species typically produce songs that are highly pure-tonal, meaning that little energy is expressed in harmonic overtones (Nowicki and Marler, 1988). In the two focal studies, young birds were presented with training models in which notes expressed typical phonological structure yet contained artificially high levels of energy in harmonic overtones (achieved by recording birds as they sang in a helium-enriched environment, see Nowicki, 1987). Presentation of "harmonic" models enabled a test of the hypothesis that pure-tonal structure is learned, as might be expected given the key role of learning in the development of many other vocal parameters. However, birds were found to reproduce harmonic models mostly without harmonic content, thus arguing against the imitative learning hypothesis. These data instead suggest that song sparrows possess an innate propensity to develop songs with pure-tonal structure, which in turn might be shaped by an innate bias to produce songs using vocal tract postures that enhance tonal purity (Peters and Nowicki, 1996). This motor bias likely emerges gradually during the sensorimotor phase (Podos et al., 1995), supporting the hypothesis that sensorimotor learning functions in part to enable motor as well as neural refinement of the vocal mechanism.

The second set of experimental studies speaks more directly to the development of vocal proficiency in the face of performance challenges. These studies, described earlier, involved presentation of unusually rapid trills to young swamp sparrows and mockingbirds (Podos, 1996; Zollinger and Suthers, 2004). Young birds of both species proved unable to accurately reproduce rapid models, in directions that suggested that birds encountered performance limits during development. An important limitation of both of these sets of studies, however, is that they revealed only the end-product of vocal motor development. By contrast they did not document the time courses or developmental trajectories over which motor biases were expressed.

B. Unfolding of Motor Biases

Perhaps the most direct method for documenting the influence of performance biases on song development would combine the above approaches, meeting three criteria: (1) documenting motor correlates of vocal ontogeny, for example, through direct studies of syringeal, respiratory, or vocal tract motor pattern development (e.g., Suthers, 2004); (2) training birds with song models modified to exhibit nontypical performance levels, in order to initiate modifications to song models to match birds' individual levels of vocal proficiency (e.g., Podos, 1996); and (3) tracking patterns of song ontogeny, in order to determine the sequence and timing of changes imposed on song models (e.g., Marler and Peters, 1982a). We know of no study that has met all three criteria, although one study, which we now discuss, has met the latter two criteria (Podos et al., 2004b). In this study, young swamp sparrows were presented three classes of song models: normal songs (as controls), songs with rapid trill rates, and songs with normal trill rates yet constructed with broken syntax, that is, with pauses interspersed between multisyllable segments (as described in Podos et al., 1999). Rapid trill models were expected to be difficult or impossible to reproduce in their original forms, because of performance limitations, whereas broken syntax models were anticipated to be unusually easy to reproduce, because of the presence of pauses between multisyllable segments. Of greater interest for our purposes was how and when birds would introduce modifications to memorized song models. Two contrasting scenarios for the expression of motor biases were envisioned. On the one hand, birds might have recognized early on, while acquiring and memorizing experimental models, that these experimental models did not match their own vocal capabilities, being either unusually difficult to produce or unusually easy to produce. According to this scenario, birds might have modified their song templates during the memorization process, well before they had any significant vocal experience. Modifications would thus have been purely neural in nature. On the other hand, birds memorizing models might be unable to anticipate future difficulties (or unusual ease of production) they would encounter later in model reproduction. According to this scenario, birds would only introduce modifications to memorized songs during sensorimotor ontogeny, as they discovered mismatches between their own vocal abilities and those required for accurate model reproduction. Tracking of song copies during ontogeny provided strong support for the latter scenario (Podos et al., 2004b). Birds were observed to employ a number of tentative motor solutions before settling on solutions that defined the crystallized copies, for example, broken syntax for copies of rapid trill models or removal of pauses from within copies of broken syntax models (Podos et al., 2004b).

It thus appears that swamp sparrows possess the ability to calibrate the final structure of memorized models to better suit their own levels of vocal proficiency, and that this calibration begins and then ends during sensorimotor learning (Podos et al., 2004b). Conclusions about the broader relevance of this "calibration hypothesis" await parallel studies in additional species. Nevertheless it seems timely to speculate on the significance of this proposed link between performance biases and sensorimotor learning. One area of particular relevance, to which our attention now turns, concerns the "developmental stress" hypothesis.

V. VOCAL PERFORMANCE AND DEVELOPMENTAL STRESS

A. THE DEVELOPMENTAL STRESS HYPOTHESIS: OVERVIEW

In most songbird species, songs are produced by males and are used primarily for two functions: to repel territorial male rivals, and to attract potential mates. Towards these ends, songs of many species have evolved certain characteristics including high levels of complexity (Kroodsma and Byers, 1991; Searcy and Andersson, 1986; Searcy and Yasukawa, 1996), song patterns typical of local versus distant populations (e.g., Baker and Cunningham, 1985; Podos and Warren, 2007; Searcy et al., 2002), and high levels of performance (reviewed here). Why should receivers respond deferentially (males) or preferentially (females) to singers that produce songs with these characteristics—or, in more expansive terms, to singers that are able to successfully learn and reproduce songs with these characteristics?

The developmental stress hypothesis provides one possible answer to this question. In songbirds, aspects of song that reliably indicate singer quality are presumably of interest to both sexes. For females, choosing a high-quality mate might ensure direct benefits such as territory quality, or indirect benefits in the form of good genes for her offspring. For males, evaluation of singer quality might provide useful information about whether to escalate or withdraw from impending territorial conflicts. In support of these expectations, a number of studies have identified correlations between male quality and song features (Searcy and Yasukawa, 1996). For example, one measure of song complexity, repertoire size, has been shown to correlate with reproductive success in several bird species including song sparrows (Hiebert et al., 1989), great reed warblers (*Acrocephalus arundinaceus*; Hasselquist, 1998; Hasselquist et al., 1996), and great tits (Lambrechts and Dhondt, 1986; McGregor et al., 1981). Similarly, birds sometimes gain higher reproductive success by singing songs with features typical of local versus distant dialects (e.g., MacDougall-Shackleton et al., 2002; Stewart and MacDougall-Shackleton, 2008). High-performance songs might also contribute to enhanced reproductive success (reviewed above). These kinds of observations do not, however, necessarily pinpoint mechanisms by which song features could become reliable (Maynard Smith and Harper, 2003; Searcy and Nowicki, 2005). From a proximate perspective, what would keep lower quality males from producing songs with more effective features? What costs or developmental constraints would curtail this kind of deception?

Nowicki et al. (1998, 2002a) proposed that learned song features attain reliability because song learning occurs during a restricted time window, when birds are young and confront severe stresses associated with nutritional needs. Altricial juvenile songbirds are completely dependent on their parents for food, and large percentages of young birds indeed die because of an inability of parents to provide sufficient food (O'Connor, 1984; Ricklefs and Peters, 1981). Although body growth in young songbirds is typically rapid, the development of brain regions integral to the acquisition and production of song unfolds over a protracted time period, coinciding with when birds are likely to experience nutritional stress. Because of the dependence of nutrition on successful brain development, adult song structure may thus provide receivers with reliable information about singers' early nutritional history (Nowicki et al., 1998, 2002a). Song structure may also reveal variation among singers in the quality of genes underlying phenotypic outcomes such as brain development or body condition. Moreover, to the extent that parental care is heritable, song structure may inform females about the quality of paternal care prospective mates could provide, because males raised by well-provisioning fathers are more likely to become good caregivers themselves.

As an aside, it is useful to note that young birds face additional stresses beyond poor nutrition—for example, in fighting parasitic infection—which has led to adoption of the more general term for the developmental stress hypothesis (e.g., Buchanan et al., 2003). It is also useful to view developmental stresses within the broader context of life history theory (e.g., Gustafsson and Sutherland, 1988). In a general sense, stresses might introduce constraints on signal development without tapping into highly specified developmental pathways, or might impose incidental consequences of the complex relationships between developmental timing, ecological resource availability, and life history stages (e.g., Krause et al., 2009). However, the elaborate neural circuitry that mediates song learning and development does provide a specific mechanism on which developmental stresses can act, and thus through which individual variation in singer quality might manifest (Nowicki et al., 1998).

B. The Developmental Stress Hypothesis: Evidence

Experimental tests of the developmental stress hypothesis for bird song learning have generally proceeded by manipulating a source of stress—food availability (by limited feeding or by brood size manipulation), parasite load, stress hormone levels, or social context—and then measuring the resulting effect on song features and song-system brain nuclei, particularly HVc and RA, which appear to develop only through about day 50, at least in zebra finches (reviewed by Nowicki et al., 1998). The volume of these song nuclei is known to correlate with repertoire size (Brenowitz and Kroodsma, 1996; Kroodsma and Canady, 1985), and likely mediates the expression of other song features as well (Vu et al., 1994; Yu and Margoliash, 1996). Zebra finches raised under developmental stress conditions show reductions in HVc size (Buchanan et al., 2004; but see Gil et al., 2006). In song sparrows, song nuclei growth is affected by developmental stress even before the onset of song learning; three song nuclei were measured at day 23–26 posthatch, and HVc in both sexes was found to be significantly smaller in nutritionally stressed birds than in control birds (MacDonald et al., 2006).

Developmental stresses may compromise a broad array of adult song features. Initial experimental work focused on the potential effect of developmental stress on song learning accuracy. Nowicki and colleagues (2002a) raised swamp sparrows collected between days 4 and 7 posthatch. From the time of collection to 28 days of age, birds in a control group were fed until satiation, whereas birds in an experimental group were fed only 70% of the average control group food intake. Despite remaining healthy, experimental birds proved to be significantly poorer learners, copying song models with reduced accuracy. Experimental groups also differed in the onset of sensorimotor development, such that experimental birds began practicing earlier. As expected, nutritional stress profoundly affected brain structure; both HVc and RA were significantly smaller in the nutritionally stressed birds. Results of similar studies on zebra finches have yielded mixed results. Gil et al. (2006) raised zebra finches in either large or small broods, thereby manipulating food availability, and found no effect on song features or on the size of song nuclei. Zann and Cash (2008) similarly found no effect of nutritional stress on song learning accuracy. A study by Holveck et al. (2008) controlled for the potentially confounding effects of sibling learning and tutor song quality. While the number of copied song elements did not vary between groups, element transitions were copied with significantly less accuracy by birds raised in large broods.

Another song feature that has drawn interest in the developmental stress literature is repertoire size. An observational study of great tit populations inhabiting areas of varying heavy metal pollution reported striking variations in repertoire size, with males at the highly polluted site having significantly smaller repertoires, as compared to males at two other sites (Gorissen et al., 2005). Another observational study, in song sparrows, compared repertoire size to HVc volume and levels of stress (Pfaff et al., 2007). These researchers found that song sparrows with large repertoires were in relatively good condition, exhibited less physiological stress (measured by heterophil to lymphocyte ratios), and had more robust immune systems (measured by lymphocytes per red blood cell). In an experimental study of canaries, Spencer et al. (2005a) found that birds infected with malaria showed reduced HVc volume, smaller repertoires, and lower levels of song complexity. Soma et al. (2006) found that brood size manipulations had a pronounced effect on body size and song complexity, measured by both numbers of notes and syntactical complexity. To date, most experimental tests of developmental stress have focused on bird species with relatively limited note or song repertoire sizes—zebra finches, canaries, and Bengalese finches (*Lonchura striata*), and swamp sparrows. More definitive inferences about the relationship between developmental stress and repertoire size await experimental studies in species with larger repertoires.

Song learning accuracy and repertoire size are not the only song features that appear to be influenced by developmental stress. In the Zann and Cash (2008) study mentioned above, developmental stress led to reductions in syllable rate and maximum syllable frequency. And in the Holveck et al. (2008) study above, nutritionally stressed finches sang song bouts with less temporal consistency, as measured by inter-motif duration. Buchanan et al. (2003) raised European starlings with either unpredictable food supplies or with *ad libitum* food availability, and found that birds in the former condition later sang less in terms of bout numbers, time spent singing, and song duration. Adult barn swallows (*Hirundo rustica*) infected with Newcastle-disease virus produced one song feature, the rattle, with shortened duration, but were able to maintain other song features at control levels (Dreiss et al., 2008). Finally, in the Gorissen et al. (2005) study mentioned above, birds from a polluted site, which presumably experienced greater levels of developmental stress, sang at lower rates.

A number of studies suggest that song features influenced by developmental stress are attended to in social interactions. Nowicki et al. (2002b) played songs of developmentally stressed and nonstressed males to wild-caught female song sparrows from the same population. These songs differed in the accuracy with which they had been learned. Females were found to give significantly more copulation solicitation displays in response to accurately learned songs than to poorly learned songs. In another study of female choice, Spencer et al. (2005b) presented female zebra finches with songs from males raised with limited food, or with corticosterone injections, or under nonstress control conditions. When given a choice, females perched more often and for longer periods of time near playback of control songs than near playback of experimental songs, thus indicating preferences for songs of unstressed males. By contrast, Naguib et al. (2008a) found only minor effects of brood size manipulation on male songs, and no female preference for unstressed males. In starlings, song duration is a trait that is both negatively affected by nutritional stress (Buchanan et al., 2003) and discriminated against by females (Eens et al., 1991; Mountjoy and Lemon, 1996).

C.   Adult Song as an Indicator of Sensorimotor-Phase Stresses?

The studies reviewed above indicate that developmental stress can impede the expression of a diverse array of vocal parameters. Some of these parameters, especially repertoire size and song learning accuracy, seem particularly likely to be influenced by early brain development and sensory learning, in accordance with original predictions of the developmental stress hypothesis. Other impacted parameters, however, such as song output and element duration, seem more likely to be shaped by birds' vocal performance capacities. Of key relevance here is emerging evidence that stressed birds appear to develop songs with lower levels of performance, for example, lower song output, reduced note or song duration, or lower consistency (Buchanan et al., 2003; Dreiss et al., 2008; Gorissen et al., 2005; Holveck et al., 2008; Zann and Cash, 2008). What would lead stressed birds to develop songs with lower levels of performance?

One possible answer to this question concerns singer condition. Perhaps birds that suffer stress as juveniles retain poor condition into adulthood and are thus unable to reproduce song models with baseline performance levels. Empirical evidence to date, however, suggests that birds stressed as juveniles typically recover baseline body size and condition as adults (e.g., Nowicki et al., 2002a). A more plausible answer to the question posed focuses on the learning process, and more specifically on the proposed relationship between vocal performance and sensorimotor learning.

Consider young birds that face stresses during their first weeks of life. As predicted by the developmental stress hypothesis, birds might fail to develop functional brain nuclei with sufficient robustness, and thus be unable to develop large repertoires or to reproduce model songs with accuracy. However, if the effects of stress extend into the sensorimotor period, additional negative impacts on song ontogeny might manifest in the realm of vocal performance. For instance, birds recovering from early stress might lack baseline abilities to reproduce challenging vocal features such as rapid trills or notes of extended duration, and thus crystallize songs with low performance levels. In the final accounting, songs would thus indicate not only bird's neural capacities as they existed during sensory learning, but also their performance capacities as they existed during sensorimotor learning.

This proposed extension of the developmental stress hypothesis is mostly speculative at the present time. It is virtually unknown as to whether the performance variables highlighted earlier in this chapter—duration, consistency, and trill structure—are indeed influenced by variation in developmental stress. For example, do stressed birds develop song repertoires with relatively poor consistency (Byers, 2007) or with fewer broadband trills (e.g., Kunc et al., 2006; Schimidt et al., 2006)? Do stressed birds develop trills with poorer consistency in note frequencies (Lambrechts, 1997), with narrowed frequency bandwidths (e.g., Podos, 1997) or with lower relative amplitudes (Forstmeier et al., 2002)? In addressing these types of questions it would seem especially useful to combine experimental manipulations of developmental stress with profiles of sensorimotor ontogeny, in order to attempt to document any resultant calibration of performance (Podos et al., 2004b).

VI. FUTURE DIRECTIONS

The connections we have drawn in this chapter between vocal performance and sensorimotor learning suggest at least three avenues for further exploration. First, much remains to be learned about how individuals vary in their vocal performance abilities, and about how this variation might contribute to vocal signal evolution. Empirical studies of performance, as reviewed above, will continue to be invaluable in this regard. However, advances of a conceptual nature are also needed, particularly in terms of documenting how vocal performance contributes to overall patterns of signal evolution (Podos et al., 2004a). One challenge is in defining "performance," which in its broadest sense can refer to actions that animals employ using available mechanisms. We recommend adopting a more restricted definition of vocal performance, in line with its standard usage in the fields of ecological morphology and biomechanics. This definition would meet three criteria: (i) vocal performance is receiver-independent, that is, based solely on physiological, metabolic, biomechanical, cognitive, motor, or other proximate properties of the signal producer; (ii) performance maxima in vocal expression are reached when animals encounter upper limits in the attributes listed above; and (iii) resulting variations in vocal parameters enhance signal reliability, insofar as these vocal parameters are uncheatable (Maynard Smith and Harper, 2003).

In some species, performance variations may be found to bear only minimally on patterns of vocal evolution, particularly for species or populations that sing below maximum performance capacities. A possible example of this is Slabbekoorn and Smith's (2000) study of African black-bellied seed-crackers (*Pyrenestes ostrinus*), for which marked beak size variation appears to have no influence on patterns of vocal evolution. More commonly, vocal performance variation will likely impose a detectable yet only partial impact on vocal evolution. The evolution of trilled vocal parameters, for instance, has been shown to be shaped not only by vocal performance (receiver-independent limitations) but also by how these signals are learned, perceived, and influenced by the acoustic transmission properties of the environment (e.g. Hansen, 1979; Nelson and Poesel, 2007; Podos, 1997; Wiley, 1991). This point is nicely reinforced in Naguib et al.'s (2008b) study of signal transmission in nightingales. These authors demonstrated that broadband trills, the presence of which reliably reflects male pairing success (Schmidt et al., 2006, 2008), experience substantial reductions of frequency bandwidth over relatively short distances, because of frequency-dependent signal attenuation.

A second avenue for further exploration concerns the potential role of vocal morphology in shaping song production. Vocal signals are known to be circumscribed by morphological parameters, and some vocal phenotypes made possible by specific morphological adaptations. An elegant example of this is provided in Fitch's (1999) study of tracheal elongation, a phenomenon in which tracheae are longer than they would appear to need be, sometimes coiled repeatedly in birds' sterna. Tracheal elongation has evolved repeatedly in diverse avian taxa and has now been linked to a specific acoustic phenomenon called formant frequency dispersion. In brief, birds with longer effective tracheae are able to produce calls in which acoustic energy achieves greater separation among vocal harmonics (Fitch, 1999, 2004). This appears to exaggerate birds' size, and thus may have evolved as an adaptive ploy for circumventing signal reliability with respect to information transmitted about body size (Fitch and Hauser, 2003). For this and parallel examples that do not involve imitative learning (e.g., *Thamnophilidae*; Seddon, 2005), mapping of vocal output to vocal morphology presumably occurs with little or no auditory feedback, and vocal output presumably emerges mostly as a consequence of birds' vocal apparati. However, how does this mapping unfold in birds that learn their songs, and who thus have the opportunity to calibrate song structure during sensorimotor ontogeny? Might the timing and trajectory of this mapping provide reliable information about male developmental histories?

Consider the songs of Darwin's finches of the Galápagos Islands. Darwin's finches are typical close-ended learners, insofar as they copy songs from adults during their early lives and then retain song structure intact for the remainder of their lives (Bowman, 1983; Grant and Grant, 1996, 1997). Variation in beak morphology has been recently identified as a possible factor in shaping vocal evolution, particularly within the ground finches (*Geospiza* spp.). More specifically, birds with large beaks, adapted for applying strong crushing forces to food items, appear to face limits in the velocity of vocal tract modulations they can employ, thus possibly explaining the lower-performance songs these birds produce (Herrel et al., 2009; Huber and Podos, 2006; Podos, 2001). Might sensorimotor learning influence the expression of morphology-dependent performance limits in this system? Consider, to illustrate, a young finch that learns to sing by copying an adult with comparatively inferior vocal performance capacities, perhaps with the adult tutor possessing a beak larger than that of the learner. In this situation, two contrasting developmental scenarios can be envisioned. First, the young finch might copy the adult song accurately in all parameters. Accuracy in the reproduction and delivery of individual song types might be favored in species with small repertoires, such as the Darwin's finches, for which a vast majority of birds sing only a single song type. In this scenario, the bird would sing below his vocal potential, thus obscuring the relationship between vocal morphology and realized performance. At the other extreme, the developing bird might adjust his vocal output to capitalize on his superior vocal potential, for example, by augmenting trill rate or frequency bandwidth. Such calibration would enhance the relationship between vocal morphology and realized performance. At least two lines of evidence support the latter scenario. First, comparisons of songs from tutors and tutees indicate low levels of imitative accuracy (e.g., Grant and Grant, 1996, their Figs. 7 and 8). Plasticity in song transmission might arise in part from birds' abilities to calibrate their output to individual vocal performance capacities. Second, within one species with wide-ranging beak variation, correlations between beak morphology and vocal performance are quite strong (Huber and Podos, 2006; Podos, 2001). To the extent that the second scenario is valid, adult songs would thus reflect the singer's vocal performance capacities, as well as his success in developing vocal morphology, at the time of sensorimotor learning—consistent with our proposed expansion of the developmental stress hypothesis.

A third avenue for further exploration concerns the diversity of learning programs birds express in nature. In strictly close-ended or "age-limited" learners, the crystallization process might act to preserve, for the life of an individual, information about his condition or performance abilities as they were manifest during sensorimotor learning. However, an array of songbird species acquire new songs well into adulthood, and thus undergo life long learning. In such "open-ended" learners, opportunities abound for recalibration to current performance limitations. For example, Botero et al. (2009) recently demonstrated that tropical mockingbirds (*Mimus gilvus*) sing learned syllable types with greater structural consistency as they age, perhaps because they achieve greater vocal proficiency with experience. Opportunities for postlearning recalibration may occur in species that do not have obviously open-ended learning programs. Some species that appear to be close-ended have recently been shown to retain the ability to learn some new songs later in life (e.g., Todt and Geberzahn, 2003), or to be able to adjust the structure of crystallized songs to a minor degree (e.g., Ballentine, 2009; Dalziell and Cockburn, 2008; de Kort et al., 2008; DuBois et al., 2009; Sakata et al., 2008;). Each year, males of many species sing plastic song before the breeding season, coinciding in time with the regrowth of song nuclei (Brenowitz et al., 1991; Meitzen et al., 2009; Nelson, 2000b; Nottebohm et al., 1986). Perhaps, in some species, this annual process allows birds to recalibrate their songs to current performance levels. Insights into how different species align with the different possibilities raised here will await further empirical study.

VII. SUMMARY

This chapter addresses the interplay of vocal performance, sensorimotor learning, and vocal evolution in songbirds. Vocal performance is increasingly recognized as an influential factor in song evolution, particularly with respect to vocal output, song consistency, and trill structure. We argue here that a comprehensive understanding of vocal performance requires attention to sensorimotor learning, a developmental phase during which birds attempt to reproduce song models memorized earlier in life. New research indicates that birds calibrate song structure during sensorimotor ontogeny in order to best match their own vocal performance capacities. Because of this relationship, performance-related features may provide reliable indicators of male quality as manifest during sensorimotor learning. We review evidence in support of the "developmental stress" hypothesis, and propose that this hypothesis be expanded to also consider vocal features crystallized during sensorimotor learning. We suggest avenues for future research that document relationships between vocal performance, morphology, and song learning programs.

Acknowledgments

We thank Vincent Janik, Nicola Clayton, Klaus Zuberbühler, and Marc Naguib for inviting this contribution. A subsong-level version of this chapter was presented by JP at the 2008 International Conference on Vocal Communication in Birds, at St Andrews University, Scotland, held in honor of Peter Slater on his retirement. Hats off to Peter! We thank Marc Naguib, Bruce Byers, and an anonymous reviewer for feedback on a plastic song-level version of the manuscript. Any failure to achieve high intellectual performance or to articulate a crystallized argument is purely our own. The authors were supported by NSF grant 0347291 (to J.P.), and by the Biology department and the graduate program in Organismic and Evolutionary Biology (OEB) at the University of Massachusetts Amherst.

References

Adret, P., 2004. In search of the song template. Ann. NY Acad. Sci. 1016, 303–324.
Alatalo, R.V., Glynn, C., Lundberg, A., 1990. Singing rate and female attraction in the pied flycatcher: an experiment. Anim. Behav. 39, 601–603.
Arnold, S.J., 1983. Morphology, performance, and fitness. Am. Zool. 23, 347–361.
Aronov, D., Andalman, A.S., Fee, M.S., 2008. A specialized forebrain circuit for vocal babbling in the juvenile songbird. Science 320, 630–634.
Arvidsson, B.L., Neergaard, R., 1991. Mate choice in the willow warbler: a field experiment. Behav. Ecol. Sociobiol. 29, 225–229.
Baker, M.C., Cunningham, M.A., 1985. The biology of bird-song dialects. Brain Behav. Sci. 8, 85–100.
Ballentine, B., 2006. Morphological adaptation influences the evolution of a mating signal. Evolution 60, 1936–1944.
Ballentine, B., 2009. The ability to perform physically challenging songs predicts age and size in male swamp sparrows, *Melospiza georgiana*. Anim. Behav. 77, 973–978.
Ballentine, B., Hyman, J., Nowicki, S., 2004. Vocal performance influences female response to male bird song: an experimental test. Behav. Ecol. 15, 163–168.
Baptista, L.F., Petrinovich, L., 1984. Social interaction, sensitive phases and the song template hypothesis in the white-crowned sparrow. Anim. Behav. 32, 172–181.
Beckers, G.J.L., Suthers, R.A., ten Cate, C., 2003. Pure-tone birdsong by resonance filtering of harmonic overtones. Proc. Natl. Acad. Sci. USA 100, 7372–7376.
Beebee, M.D., 2004. Variation in vocal performance in the songs of a wood warbler: evidence for the function of distinct singing modes. Ethology 110, 531–542.
Beecher, M.D., Brenowitz, E.A., 2005. Functional aspects of song learning in songbirds. Trends Ecol. Evol. 20, 143–149.

Beecher, M.D., Burt, J.M., 2004. The role of social interaction in bird song learning. Curr. Dir. Psychol. Sci. 13, 224–228.

Beecher, M.D., Campbell, S.E., Stoddard, P.K., 1994. Correlation of song learning and territory establishment strategies in the song sparrow. Proc. Natl. Acad. Sci. USA 91, 1450–1454.

Beecher, M.D., Burt, J.M., O'Loghlen, A.L., Templeton, C.N., Campbell, S.E., 2007. Bird song learning in an eavesdropping context. Anim. Behav. 73, 929–935.

Bennett-Clark, H.C., 1987. The tuned singing burrow of mole crickets. J. Exp. Biol. 128, 383–409.

Botero, C.A., Rossman, R.J., Caro, L.M., Stenzler, L.M., Lovette, I.J., de Kort, S.R., Vehrencamp, S.L., 2009. Syllable type consistency is related to age, social status and reproductive success in the tropical mockingbird. Anim. Behav. 77, 701–706.

Bottjer, S.W., 2004. Developmental regulation of basal ganglia circuitry during the sensitive period for vocal learning in songbirds. Ann. NY Acad. Sci. 1016, 395–415.

Bowman, R.I., 1983. The evolution of song in Darwin's finches. In: Bowman, R.I., Berson, M., Leviton, A.E. (Eds.), Patterns of Evolution in Galápagos Organisms. American Association for the Advancement of Science, Pacific Division, San Francisco, CA, pp. 237–537.

Braaten, R.F., Reynolds, K., 1999. Auditory preference for conspecific song in isolation-reared zebra finches. Anim. Behav. 58, 105–111.

Bradbury, J.W., Vehrencamp, S.L., 1998. Principles of Animal Communication. Sinauer Associates, Sunderland, MA.

Brainard, M.S., Doupe, A.J., 2000. Auditory feedback in learning and maintenance of vocal behaviour. Nat. Rev. Neurosci. 1, 31–40.

Brainard, M.S., Doupe, A.J., 2002. What songbirds teach us about learning. Nature 417, 351–358.

Brenowitz, E.A., Beecher, M.D., 2005. Song learning in birds: diversity and plasticity, opportunities and challenges. Trends Neurosci. 28, 127–132.

Brenowitz, E.A., Kroodsma, D.E., 1996. The neuroethology of birdsong. In: Kroodsma, D.E., Miller, E.H. (Eds.), Ecology and Evolution of Acoustic Communication in Birds. Cornell University Press, Ithaca, NY, pp. 285–304.

Brenowitz, E.A., Nalls, B., Wingfield, J.C., Kroodsma, D.E., 1991. Seasonal-changes in avian song nuclei without seasonal-changes in song repertoire. J. Neurosci. 11, 1367–1374.

Brumm, H., Hultsch, H., 2001. Pattern amplitude is related to pattern imitation during the song development of nightingales. Anim. Behav. 61, 747–754.

Brumm, H., Slater, P.J.B., 2006. Ambient noise, motor fatigue, and serial redundancy in chaffinch song. Behav. Ecol. Sociobiol. 60, 475–481.

Buchanan, K.L., 2000. Stress and the evolution of condition-dependent signals. Trends Ecol. Evol. 15, 156–160.

Buchanan, K.L., Leitner, S., Spencer, K.A., Goldsmith, A.R., Catchpole, C.K., 2004. Developmental stress selectively affects the song control nucleus HVC in the zebra finch. Proc. Roy. Soc. Lond. B. 271, 2381–2386.

Buchanan, K.L., Spencer, K.A., Goldsmith, A.R., Catchpole, C.K., 2003. Song as an honest signal of past developmental stress in the European starling (*Sturnus vulgaris*). Proc. Roy. Soc. Lond. B 270, 1149–1156.

Byers, B.E., 2007. Extrapair paternity in chestnut-sided warblers is correlated with consistent vocal performance. Behav. Ecol. 18, 130–136.

Cardoso, G.C., 2008. On the performance of brown skua, *Catharacta antarctica*, vocalizations. Anim. Behav 76, e1–e2.

Cardoso, G.C., Atwell, J.W., Ketterson, E.D., Price, T.D., 2007. Inferring performance in the songs of dark-eyed juncos (*Junco hyemalis*). Behav. Ecol. 18, 1051–1057.

Catchpole, C.K., Slater, P.J.B., 2008. Bird Song: Biological Themes and Variations, second ed Cambridge University Press, Cambridge, UK.

Chai, P., Dudley, R., 1995. Limits to vertebrate locomotor energetics suggested by hummingbirds hovering in heliox. Nature 377, 722–725.

Chew, S.J., Mello, C., Nottebohm, F., Jarvis, E., Vicario, D.S., 1995. Decrements in auditory responses to a repeated conspecific song are long-lasting and require two periods of protein synthesis in the songbird forebrain. Proc. Natl. Acad. Sci. USA 92, 3406–3410.

Christie, P.J., Mennill, D.J., Ratcliffe, L.M., 2004. Pitch shifts and song structure indicate male quality in the dawn chorus of black-capped chickadees. Behav. Ecol. Sociobiol. 55, 341–348.

Clayton, N.S., 1988. Song discrimination learning in zebra finches. Anim. Behav. 36, 1016–1024.

Collins, S., 2004. Vocal fighting and flirting: the functions of birdsong. In: Marler, P., Slabbekoorn, H. (Eds.), Nature's Music: The Science of Birdsong. Elsevier Academic Press, San Diego, CA, pp. 39–79.

Cramer, E.R.A., Price, J.J., 2007. Red-winged blackbirds *Ageliaus phoeniceus* respond differently to song types with different performance levels. J. Avian Biol. 38, 122–127.

Cresswell, W., 1994. Song as a pursuit deterrent signal, and its occurrence relative to other anti-predation behaviors of skylark (*Alauda arvensis*) on attack by merlins *(Falco columbarius)*. Behav. Ecol. Sociobiol. 34, 217–223.

Dalziell, A.H., Cockburn, A., 2008. Dawn song in superb fairy-wrens: a bird that seeks extrapair copulations during the dawn chorus. Anim. Behav. 75, 489–500.

de Kort, S.R., Bohman, E., Valderrama, S., Botero, C., Vehrencamp, S., 2008. Song consistency reflects age in banded wrens. Abstract from "Vocal Communication in Birds and Mammals" International Conference, St. Andrews, Scotland UK.

de Kort, S.R., Eldermire, E.R.B., Cramer, E.R.A., Vehrencamp, S.L., 2009. The deterrent effect of bird song in territory defense. Behav. Ecol. 20, 200–206.

Dooling, R., Searcy, M., 1980. Early perceptual selectivity in the swamp sparrow. Devel. Psychobiol. 13, 499–506.

Doupe, A.J., 1997. Song- and order-selective neurons in the songbird anterior forebrain and their emergence during vocal development. J. Neurosci. 17, 1147–1167.

Doutrelant, C., Leitao, A., Giorgi, M., Lambrechts, M., 1999. Geographical variation in blue tit song, the result of an adjustment to vegetation type? Behaviour 136, 481–493.

Draganoiu, T.I., Nagle, L., Kreutzer, M., 2002. Directional female preference for an exaggerated male trait in canary (*Serinus canaria*) song. Proc. Roy. Soc. Lond. B. 269, 2525–2531.

Dreiss, A.N., Navarro, C., de Lope, F., Moller, A.P., 2008. Effects of an immune challenge on multiple components of song display in barn swallows *Hirundo rustica*: implications for sexual selection. Ethology 114, 955–964.

DuBois, A.L., Nowicki, S., Searcy, W.A., 2009. Swamp sparrows modulate vocal performance in an aggressive context. Biol. Lett. 5, 163–165.

Eens, M., Pinxten, R., Verheyen, R.F., 1991. Male song as a cue for mate choice in the European starling. Behaviour 116, 210–238.

Fitch, W.T., 1999. Acoustic exaggeration of size in birds via tracheal elongation: comparative and theoretical analyses. J. Zool. 248, 31–48.

Fitch, W.T., 2004. Acoustic exaggeration of size by tracheal elongation. In: Marler, P., Slabbekoorn, H. (Eds.), Nature's Music: The Science of Birdsong. Elsevier Academic Press, San Diego CA, p. 326.

Fitch, W.T., Hauser, M.D., 2003. Unpacking "honesty": vertebrate vocal production and the evolution of acoustic signals. In: Simmons, A.M., Popper, A.N., Fay, R.R. (Eds.), Acoustic Communication. Springer, New York, NY, pp. 65–137.

Forstmeier, W., Kempenaers, B., Meyer, A., 2002. A novel song parameter correlates with extra-pair paternity and reflects male longevity. Proc. Roy. Soc. Lond. B 269, 1479–1485.

Garland Jr., T., Losos, J.B., 1994. Ecological morphology of locomotor performance in squamate reptiles. In: Wainwright, P.C., Reilly, S.M. (Eds.), Ecological Morphology: Integrative Organismal Biology. University of Chicago Press, Chicago, IL, pp. 240–302.

Gerhardt, H.C., 1994. The evolution of vocalization in frogs and toads. Ann. Rev. Ecol. Syst. 25, 293–324.

Gil, D., Gahr, M., 2002. The honesty of bird song: multiple constraints for multiple traits. Trends Ecol. Evol. 17, 133–141.

Gil, D., Naguib, M., Riebel, K., Rutstein, A., Gahr, M., 2006. Early condition, song learning, and the volume of song brain nuclei in the zebra finch (Taeniopygia guttata). J. Neurobiol. 66, 1602–1612.

Gillis, G. B, Bonvini, L., Irschick, D.J., 2009. Losing stability: tail loss and jumping in the arboreal lizard Anolis carolinensis. J. Exp. Biol. 212, 604–609.

Goller, F., Larsen, O.N., 1997. A new mechanism of sound generation in songbirds. Proc. Natl. Acad. Sci. USA 94, 14787–14791.

Gorissen, L., Snoeijs, T., Van Duyse, E., Eens, M., 2005. Heavy metal pollution affects dawn singing behaviour in a small passerine bird. Oecologia 145, 504–509.

Grant, B.R., Grant, P.R., 1996. Cultural inheritance of song and its role in the evolution of Darwin's finches. Evolution 50, 2471–2487.

Grant, P.R., Grant, B.R., 1997. Hybridization, sexual imprinting, and mate choice. Am. Nat. 149, 1–28.

Greenewalt, C., 1968. Bird Song: Acoustics and Physiology. Smithsonian Institution Press, Washington, DC.

Gustafsson, L., Sutherland, W.J., 1988. The costs of reproduction in the collared flycatcher Ficudela albicollis. Nature 335, 813–815.

Hansen, P., 1979. Vocal learning: its role in adapting sound structures to long-distance propagation, and a hypothesis on its evolution. Anim. Behav. 27, 1270–1271.

Hartley, R.S., Suthers, R.A., 1989. Airflow and pressure during canary song: evidence for mini-breaths. J. Comp. Physiol. A. 165, 15–26.

Hasselquist, D., 1998. Polygyny in great reed warblers: a long-term study of factors contributing to male fitness. Ecology 79, 2376–2390.

Hasselquist, D., Bensch, S., von Schantz, T., 1996. Correlation between male song repertoire, extra-pair paternity and offspring survival in the great reed warbler. Nature 381, 229–232.

Hauser, M.D., 1993. The evolution of nonhuman primate vocalizations: effects of phylogeny, body weight, and social context. Am. Nat. 142, 528–542.

Herrel, A., Podos, J., Vanhooydonck, B., Hendry, A.P., 2009. Force-velocity trade-off in Darwin's finch jaw function: a biomechanical basis for ecological speciation? Funct. Ecol. 23, 119–125.

Hiebert, S.M., Stoddard, P.K., Arcese, P., 1989. Repertoire size, territory acquisition and reproductive success in the song sparrow. Anim. Behav. 37, 266–273.

Hoese, W.J., Podos, J., Boetticher, N.C., Nowicki, S., 2000. Vocal tract function in birdsong production: experimental manipulation of beak movements. J. Exp. Biol. 203, 1845–1855.

Hofstad, E., Espmark, Y., Moksnes, A., Haugan, T., Ingebrigtsen, M., 2002. The relationship between song performance and male quality in snow buntings (Plectrophenax nivalis). Can. J. Zool. 80, 524–531.

Holveck, M.J., de Castro, A.C.V., Lachlan, R.F., ten Cate, C., Riebel, K., 2008. Accuracy of song syntax learning and singing consistency signal early condition in zebra finches. Behav. Ecol. 19, 1267–1281.

Huber, S.K., Podos, J., 2006. Beak morphology and song features covary in a population of Darwin's finches (*Geospiza fortis*). Biol. J. Linn. Soc. 88, 489–498.

Hughes, M., Hultsch, H., Todt, D., 2002. Imitation and invention in song learning in nightingales (*Luscinia megarhynchos* B., Turdidae). Ethology 108, 97–113.

Hultsch, H., Todt, D., 1989. Memorization and reproduction of songs in nightingales (*Luscinia megarhynchos*): evidence for package formation. J. Comp. Physiol. A 165, 197–203.

Illes, A.E., Hall, M.L., Vehrencamp, S.L., 2006. Vocal performance influences male receiver response in the banded wren. Proc. Roy. Soc. Lond. B. 273, 1907–1912.

Irschick, D.J., 2003. Measuring performance in nature: implications for studies of fitness within populations. Integr. Comp. Biol. 43, 396–407.

Irschick, D.J., Garland Jr., T., 2001. Integrating function and ecology in studies of adaptation: investigations of locomotor capacity as a model system. Ann. Rev. Ecol. Syst. 32, 367–396.

Irschick, D.J., Meyers, J.J., Le Galliard, J.F., 2008. How does selection operate on whole-organism functional performance capacities? A review and synthesis. Evol. Ecol. Res. 10, 177–196.

Janata, P., Margoliash, D., 1999. Gradual emergence of song selectivity in sensorimotor structures of the male zebra finch song system. J. Neurosci. 19, 5108–5118.

Janicke, T., Hahn, S., 2008. On the performance of brown skua, *Catharacta antarctica*, vocalizations: reply. Anim. Behav. 76, e3–e5.

Janicke, T., Hahn, S., Ritz, M.S., Peter, H.-U., 2008. Vocal performance reflects individual quality in a nonpasserine. Anim. Behav. 75, 91–98.

Janik, V.M., Slater, P.J.B., 2000. The different roles of social learning in vocal communication. Anim. Behav. 60, 1–11.

Jarvis, E.D., 2004. Brains and birdsong. In: Marler, P., Slabbekoorn, H. (Eds.), Nature's Music: The Science of Birdsong. Elsevier Academic Press, San Diego CA, pp. 226–271.

Jayne, B.C., Ellis, R.V., 1998. How inclines affect the escape behavior of a dune dwelling lizard. *Uma scoparia*. Anim. Behav. 55, 1115–1130.

Kempenaers, B., Verheyren, G.R., Dhondt, A.A., 1997. Extrapair paternity in the blue tit (*Parus caeruleus*): female choice, male characteristics, and offspring quality. Behav. Ecol. 8, 481–492.

Konishi, M., 1965a. Effects of deafening on song development in two species of juncos. Condor 66, 85–102.

Konishi, M., 1965b. The role of auditory feedback in the control of vocalization in the white-crowned sparrow. Z. Tierpsychol. 22, 770–783.

Konishi, M., Akutagawa, E., 1985. Neuronal growth, atrophy and death in a sexually dimorphic song nucleus in the zebra finch brain. Nature 315, 145–147.

Krause, E.T., Honarmand, M., Naguib, M., 2009. Early fasting is long lasting: differences in early nutritional conditions reappear under stressful conditions in adult female zebra finches. PloS One 4, e5015.

Kroodsma, D.E., Byers, B.E., 1991. The function(s) of bird song. Am. Zool. 31, 318–328.

Kroodsma, D.E., Canady, R.A., 1985. Differences in repertoire size, singing behavior, and associated neuroanatomy among marsh wren populations have a genetic basis. Auk 102, 439–446.

Kroodsma, D.E., Pickert, R., 1980. Environmentally dependent sensitive periods for avian vocal learning. Nature 288, 477–479.

Kunc, H.P., Amrhein, V., Naguib, M., 2006. Vocal interactions in nightingales (*Luscinia megarhynchos*): more aggressive males have higher pairing success. Anim. Behav. 72, 25–30.

Lambrechts, M.M., 1996. Organization of birdsong and constraints on performance. In: Kroodsma, D.E., Miller, E.H. (Eds.), Ecology and Evolution of Acoustic Communication in Birds. Cornell University Press, Ithaca, NY, pp. 305–320.

Lambrechts, M.M., 1997. Song frequency plasticity and composition of phrase versions in great tits *Parus major*. Ardea 85, 99–109.

Lambrechts, M.M., Dhondt, A.A., 1986. Male quality, reproduction, and survival in the great tit (*Parus major*). Behav. Ecol. Sociobiol. 19, 57–63.

Lambrechts, M.M., Dhondt, A.A., 1988. The anti-exhaustion hypothesis: a new hypothesis to explain song performance and song type switching in the great tit. Anim. Behav. 36, 327–334.

Liu, W.C., Kroodsma, D.E., 2006. Song learning by chipping sparrows: when, where, and from whom. Condor 108, 509–517.

Liu, I.A., Lohr, B., Olsen, B., Greenberg, R., 2008. Macrogeographic vocal variation in subspecies of swamp sparrow. Condor 110, 102–109.

Lucas, J.R., Schraeder, A., Jackson, C., 1999. Carolina chickadee (Aves, Paridae, *Poecile carolinensis*) vocalization rates: effects of body mass and food availability under aviary conditions. Ethology 105, 503–520.

MacDonald, I.F., Kempster, B., Zanette, L., MacDougall-Shackleton, S.A., 2006. Early nutritional stress impairs development of a song-control brain region in both male and female juvenile song sparrows (*Melospiza melodia*) at the onset of song learning. Proc. Roy. Soc. Lond. B. 273, 2559–2564.

MacDougall-Shackleton, E.A., Derryberry, E.P., Hahn, T.P., 2002. Nonlocal male mountain white-crowned sparrows have lower paternity and higher parasite loads than males singing local dialect. Behav. Ecol. 13, 682–689.

Mann, N.I., Slater, P.J.B., 1995. Song tutor choice by zebra finches in aviaries. Anim. Behav. 49, 811–820.

Margoliash, D., 2002. Evaluating theories of bird song learning: implications for future directions. J. Comp. Physiol. A 188, 851–866.

Marler, P., 1957. Specific distinctiveness in the communication signals of birds. Behaviour 11, 13–39.

Marler, P., 1970. A comparative approach to vocal learning: song development in white-crowned sparrows. J. Comp. Physiol. Psychol. 71, 1–25.

Marler, P., 1976. Sensory templates in species-specific behavior. In: Fentress, J.C. (Ed.), Simpler Networks and Behavior. Sinauer Press, Sunderland, MA, pp. 314–329.

Marler, P., 1997. Three models of song learning: evidence from behavior. J. Neurobiol. 33, 501–516.

Marler, P., Peters, S., 1977. Selective vocal learning in a sparrow. Science 198, 519–521.

Marler, P., Peters, S., 1982a. Structural changes in song ontogeny in the swamp sparrow *Melospiza georgiana*. Auk 99, 446–458.

Marler, P., Peters, S., 1982b. Subsong and plastic song: their role in the vocal learning process. In: Kroodsma, D.E., Miller, E.H. (Eds.), Acoustic Communication in Birds. Academic Press, New York, pp. 25–50.

Marler, P., Peters, S., 1987. A sensitive period for song acquisition in the song sparrow, *Melospiza melodia*: a case of age-limited learning. Ethology 76, 89–110.

Marler, P., Sherman, V., 1983. Song structure without auditory feedback: emendations of the auditory template hypothesis. J. Neurosci. 3, 517–531.

Marler, P., Slabbekoorn, H., 2004. Nature's Music: The Science of Birdsong. Elsevier Academic Press, San Diego, CA.

Maynard-Smith, J., Harper, D., 2003. Animal Signals. Oxford University Press, Oxford, UK.

McGregor, P.K., Krebs, J.R., Perrins, C.M., 1981. Song repertoires and lifetime reproductive success in the great tit (*Parus major*). Am. Nat. 118, 149–159.

Meitzen, J., Thompson, C.K., Choi, H., Perkel, D.J., Brenowitz, E.A., 2009. Time course of changes in Gambel's white-crowned sparrow song behavior following transitions in breeding condition. Horm. Behav. 55, 217–227.

Mountjoy, D.J., Lemon, R.E., 1996. Female choice for complex song in the European starling: a field experiment. Behav. Ecol. Sociobiol. 38, 65–71.

Naguib, M., Heim, C., Gil, D., 2008a. Early developmental conditions and male attractiveness in zebra finches. Ethology 114, 255–261.

Naguib, M., Schmidt, R., Sprau, P., Roth, T., Florcke, C., Amrhein, V., 2008b. The ecology of vocal signaling: male spacing and communication distance of different song traits in nightingales. Behav. Ecol. 19, 1034–1040.

Nelson, D.A., 1992. Song overproduction and selective attrition lead to song sharing in the field sparrow (*Spizella pusilla*). Behav. Ecol. Sociobiol. 30, 415–424.

Nelson, D.A., 1997. Social interaction and sensitive phases for song learning: a critical review. In: Snowdon, C.T., Hausberger, M. (Eds.), Social Influences on Vocal Development. Cambridge University Press, Cambridge, MA, pp. 318–342.

Nelson, D.A., 2000a. A preference for own-subspecies' song guides vocal learning in a song bird. Proc. Natl. Acad. Sci. USA 97, 13348–13353.

Nelson, D.A., 2000b. Song overproduction, selective attrition and song dialects in the white-crowned sparrow. Anim. Behav 60, 887–898.

Nelson, D.A., Poesel, A., 2007. Segregation of information in a complex acoustic signal: individual and dialect identity in white-crowned sparrow song. Anim. Behav. 74, 1073–1084.

Nelson, D.A., Marler, P., Palleroni, A., 1995. A comparative approach to vocal learning: intraspecific variation in the learning process. Anim. Behav. 50, 83–97.

Nordby, J.C., Campbell, S.E., Beecher, M.D., 2007. Selective attrition and individual song repertoire development in song sparrows. Anim. Behav. 74, 1413–1418.

Nottebohm, F., 1968. Auditory experience and song development in the chaffinch *Fringilla coelebs*. Ibis 110, 549–568.

Nottebohm, F., 1971. Neural lateralization of vocal control in a passerine bird. I. Song. J. Exp. Zool. 177, 229–262.

Nottebohm, F., 1972. The origins of vocal learning. Am. Nat. 106, 116–140.

Nottebohm, F., Stokes, T.M., Leonard, C.M., 1976. Central control of song in the canary, *Serinus canarius*. J. Comp. Neurol. 165, 457–486.

Nottebohm, F., Nottebohm, M., Crane, L., 1986. Developmental and seasonal changes in canary song and their relation to changes in the anatomy of song-control nuclei. Behav. Neural. Biol. 46, 445–471.

Nowicki, S., 1987. Vocal tract resonances in oscine bird sound production: evidence from birdsongs in a helium atmosphere. Nature 325, 53–55.

Nowicki, S., Capranica, R.R., 1986. Bilateral syringeal interaction in vocal production of an oscine bird sound. Science 231, 1297–1299.

Nowicki, S., Marler, P., 1988. How do birds sing? Music Percept 5, 391–426.

Nowicki, S., Marler, P., Maynard, A., Peters, S., 1992. Is the tonal quality of birdsong learned? Evidence from song sparrows. Ethology 90, 225–235.

Nowicki, S., Peters, S., Podos, J., 1998. Song learning, early nutrition, and sexual selection in songbirds. Am. Zool. 38, 179–190.

Nowicki, S., Searcy, W.A., Peters, S., 2002a. Brain development, song learning and mate choice in birds: a review and experimental test of the "nutritional stress hypothesis" J. Comp. Physiol. A. 188, 1003–1014.

Nowicki, S., Searcy, W.A., Peters, S., 2002b. Quality of song learning affects female response to male bird song. Proc. Roy. Soc. Lond. B. 269, 1949–1954.

Nystrom, K.G.K., 1997. Food density, song rate, and body condition in territory-establishing willow warblers (*Phylloscopus trochilus*). Can. J. Zool. 75, 47–58.

Oberweger, K., Goller, F., 2001. The metabolic cost of birdsong production. J. Exp. Biol. 204, 3379–3388.

O'Connor, R.J., 1984. The Growth and Development of Birds. John Wiley and Sons, New York.

Otter, K., Chruszcz, B., Ratcliffe, L., 1997. Honest advertisement and song output during the dawn chorus of black-capped chickadees. Behav. Ecol. 8, 167–178.

Peters, S., Nowicki, S., 1996. Development of tonal quality in birdsong: further evidence from song sparrows. Ethology 102, 323–335.

Pfaff, J.A., Zanette, L., MacDougall-Shackleton, S.A., MacDougall-Shackleton, E.A., 2007. Song repertoire size varies with HVC volume and is indicative of male quality in song sparrows (*Melospiza melodia*). Proc. Roy. Soc. Lond. B. 274, 2035–2040.

Pinxten, R., Eens, M., 1998. Male starlings sing most in the late morning, following egg-laying: a strategy to protect their paternity? Behaviour 135, 1197–1211.

Podos, J., 1996. Motor constraints on vocal development in a songbird. Anim. Behav. 51, 1061–1070.

Podos, J., 1997. A performance constraint on the evolution of trilled vocalization in a songbird family (Passeriformes: Emberizidae). Evolution 51, 537–551.

Podos, J., 2001. Correlated evolution of morphology and vocal signal structure in Darwin's finches. Nature 409, 185–188.

Podos, J., Nowicki, S., 2004. Performance limits on birdsong. In: Marler, P., Slabbekoorn, H. (Eds.), Nature's Music: The Science of Birdsong. Elsevier Academic Press, San Diego, CA, pp. 318–342.

Podos, J., Warren, P.S., 2007. The evolution of geographic variation in birdsong. Adv. Study Behav. 37, 403–458.

Podos, J., Sherer, J.K., Peters, S., Nowicki, S., 1995. Ontogeny of vocal tract movements during song production in song sparrows. Anim. Behav. 50, 1287–1296.

Podos, J., Nowicki, S., Peters, S., 1999. Permissiveness in the learning and development of song syntax in swamp sparrows. Anim. Behav. 58, 93–103.

Podos, J., Huber, S.K., Taft, B., 2004a. Bird song: the interface of evolution and mechanism. Ann. Rev. Ecol. Evol. Syst. 35, 55–87.

Podos, J., Peters, S., Nowicki, S., 2004b. Calibration of song learning targets during vocal ontogeny in swamp sparrows, *Melospiza georgiana*. Anim. Behav. 68, 929–940.

Poesel, A., Dabelsteen, T., 2006. Three vocalization types in the blue tit *Cyanistes caeruleus*: a test of the different signal-value hypothesis. Behaviour 143, 1529–1545.

Poesel, A., Foerster, K., Kempenaers, B., 2001. The dawn song of the blue tit *Parus caeruleus* and its role in sexual selection. Ethology 107, 521–531.

Price, J.J., Lanyon, S.M., 2004. Patterns of song evolution and sexual selection in oropendolas and caciques. Behav. Ecol. 15, 485–497.

Ricklefs, R.E., Peters, S., 1981. Parental components of variance in growth rate and body size of nestling European starlings (*Sturnus vulgaris*) in eastern Pennsylvania. Auk 98, 39–48.

Riede, T., Suthers, R.A., Fletcher, N.H., Blevins, W.E., 2006. Songbirds tune their vocal tract to the fundamental frequency of their song. Proc. Natl. Acad. Sci. USA 103, 5543–5548.

Ryan, M.J., Brenowitz, E.A., 1985. The role of body size, phylogeny, and ambient noise in the evolution of bird song. Am. Nat. 126, 87–100.

Sakata, J.T., Hampton, C.M., Brainard, M.S., 2008. Social modulation of sequence and syllable variability in adult birdsong. J. Neurophysiol. 99, 1700–1711.

Schmidt, R., Kunc, H.P., Amrhein, V., Naguib, M., 2006. Responses to interactive playback predict future mating status in nightingales. Anim. Behav. 72, 1355–1362.

Schmidt, R., Kunc, H.P., Amrhein, V., Naguib, M., 2008. Aggressive responses to broadband trills are related to subsequent pairing success in nightingales. Behav. Ecol. 19, 635–641.

Searcy, W.A., Andersson, M., 1986. Sexual selection and the evolution of song. Ann. Rev. Ecol. Syst. 17, 507–533.

Searcy, W.A., Nowicki, S., 2000. Male-male competition and female choice in the evolution of vocal signaling. In: Espmark, Y., Rosenqvist, G. (Eds.), Animal Signals: Signalling and Signal Design in Animal Communication. Tapir Academic Press, Trondheim, Norway, pp. 301–315.

Searcy, W.A., Nowicki, S., 2005. The Evolution of Animal Communication: Reliability and Deception in Signalling Systems. Princeton University Press, Princeton, NJ.

Searcy, W.A., Yasukawa, K., 1996. Song and female choice. In: Kroodsma, D.E., Miller, E.H. (Eds.), Ecology and Evolution of Acoustic Communication in Birds. Cornell University Press, Ithaca, NY, pp. 454–473.

Searcy, W.A., Nowicki, S., Hughes, M., Peters, S., 2002. Geographic song discrimination in relation to dispersal distances in song sparrows. Am. Nat. 159, 221–230.

Seddon, N., 2005. Ecological adaptation and species recognition drives vocal evolution in Neotropical suboscine birds. Evolution 59, 200–215.

Slabbekoorn, H., Smith, T.B., 2000. Does bill size polymorphism affect courtship song characteristics in the African finch *Pyrenestes ostrinus?* Biol. J. Linn. Soc. 71, 737–753.

Slater, P.J.B., 1989. Bird song learning: causes and consequences. Ethol. Ecol. Evol. 1, 19–46.

Slater, P.J.B., Eales, L.A., Clayton, N.S., 1988. Song learning in zebra finches (*Taeniopygia guttata*): progress and prospects. Adv. Study Behav. 18, 1–34.

Soha, J.A., Marler, P., 2000. A species-specific acoustic cue for selective song learning in the white-crowned sparrow. Anim. Behav. 60, 297–306.

Soha, J.A., Marler, P., 2001. Vocal syntax development in the white-crowned sparrow (*Zonotrichia leucophrys*). J. Comp. Psychol. 115, 172–180.

Soma, M., Takahasi, M., Ikebuchi, M., Yamada, H., Suzuki, M., Hasegawa, T., Okanoya, K., 2006. Early rearing conditions affect the development of body size and song in Bengalese finches. Ethology 112, 1071–1078.

Spencer, K.A., Buchanan, K.L., Leitner, S., Goldsmith, A.R., Catchpole, C.K., 2005a. Parasites affect song complexity and neural development in a songbird. Proc. Roy. Soc. Lond. B. 272, 2037–2043.

Spencer, K.A., Wimpenny, J.H., Buchanan, K.L., Lovell, P.G., Goldsmith, A.R., Catchpole, C. K., 2005b. Developmental stress affects the attractiveness of male song and female choice in the zebra finch (*Taeniopygia guttata*). Behav. Ecol. Sociobiol. 58, 423–428.

Stewart, K.A., MacDougall-Shackleton, E.A., 2008. Local song elements indicate local genotypes and predict physiological condition in song sparrows, *Melospiza melodia*. Biol. Lett. 4, 240–242.

Suthers, R.A., 1990. Contributions to birdsong from the left and right sides of the intact syrinx. Nature 347, 473–477.

Suthers, R.A., 2004. How birds sing and why it matters. In: Marler, P., Slabbekoorn, H. (Eds.), Nature's Music: The Science of Birdsong. Elsevier Academic Press, San Diego, CA, pp. 272–295.

Suthers, R.A., Goller, F., 1997. Motor correlates of vocal diversity in songbirds. In: Nolan Jr., E., Ketterson, E., Thompson, C.F. (Eds.), Current Ornithology, vol. 14. Plenum Press, NY, pp. 235–288.

ten Cate, C., 2004. Birdsong and evolution. In: Marler, P., Slabbekoorn, H. (Eds.), Nature's Music: The Science of Birdsong. Elsevier Academic Press, San Diego, CA, pp. 296–317.

Thomas, R.J., 1999. The effect of variability in the food supply on the daily singing routines of European robins: a test of a stochastic dynamic programming model. Anim. Behav. 57, 365–369.

Thorpe, W.H., 1958a. The learning of song patterns by birds, with especial reference to the song of the chaffinch, *Fringilla coelebs*. Ibis 100, 535–570.

Thorpe, W.H., 1958b. Further studies on the process of song learning in the chaffinch (*Fringilla coelebs gengleri*). Nature 182, 554–557.

Thorpe, W.H., Lade, B.I., 1961. The songs of some families of the Passeriformes: II. The songs of the buntings (emberizidae). Ibis 103, 246–259.

Todt, D., Geberzahn, N., 2003. Age-dependent effects of song exposure: song crystallization sets a boundary between fast and delayed vocal imitation. Anim. Behav. 65, 971–979.

Trillo, P.A., Vehrencamp, S.L., 2005. Song types and their structural features are associated with specific contexts in the banded wren. Anim. Behav. 70, 921–935.

Vallet, E., Beme, I., Kreutzer, M., 1998. Two-note syllables in canary songs elicit high levels of sexual display. Anim. Behav. 55, 291–297.

Vallet, E., Kreutzer, M., 1995. Female canaries are sexually responsive to special song phrases. Anim. Behav. 49, 1603–1610.

Vehrencamp, S.L., 2001. Is song-type matching a conventional signal of aggressive intentions? Proc. Roy. Soc. Lond. B. 268, 1637–1642.

Vu, E.T., Mazurek, M.E., Kuo, Y.C., 1994. Identification of a forebrain motor programming network for the learned song of zebra finches. J. Neurosci. 14, 6924–6934.

Wainwright, P.C., 1994. Functional morphology as a tool in ecological research. In: Wainwright, P.C., Reilly, S.M. (Eds.), Ecological Morphology: Integrative Organismal Biology. University of Chicago Press, Chicago, IL, pp. 42–59.

West, M.J., King, A.P., 1988. Female visual displays affect the development of male song in the cowbird. Nature 334, 244–246.

Westneat, M.W., Long, J.H., Hoese, W., Nowicki, S., 1993. Kinematics of birdsong: functional correlation of cranial movements and acoustic features in sparrows. J. Exp. Biol. 182, 147–171.

Wheelwright, N.T., Swett, M.B., Levin, I.I., Kroodsma, D.E., Freeman-Gallant, C.R., Williams, H., 2008. The influence of different tutor types on song learning in a natural bird population. Anim. Behav. 75, 1479–1493.

Wild, J.M., 1997. Neural pathways for the control of birdsong production. J. Neurobiol. 33, 653–670.

Wiley, R.H., 1991. Associations of song properties with habitats for terrestrial oscine birds of eastern North America. Am. Nat. 138, 973–993.

Yu, A.C., Margoliash, D., 1996. Temporal hierarchical control of singing in birds. Science 273, 1871–1875.

Zann, R., Cash, E., 2008. Developmental stress impairs song complexity but not learning accuracy in non-domesticated zebra finches (*Taeniopygia guttata*). Behav. Ecol. Sociobiol. 62, 391–400.

Zeigler, H.P., Marler, P., 2008. Neuroscience of Birdsong. Cambridge University Press, Cambridge, UK.

Zollinger, S.A., Suthers, R.A., 2004. Motor mechanisms of a vocal mimic: implications for birdsong production. Proc. Roy. Soc. Lond. B 271, 483–491.

Song and Female Mate Choice in Zebra Finches: A Review

KATHARINA RIEBEL

BEHAVIORAL BIOLOGY GROUP, INSTITUTE OF BIOLOGY, LEIDEN UNIVERSITY,
SYLVIUS LABORATORY, 2300 RA LEIDEN, THE NETHERLANDS

I. INTRODUCTION

Successful reproduction in sexually reproducing organisms depends on finding a suitable mate. Finding a partner to mate with requires locating, recognizing, and eventually choosing a mate—a process that crucially depends on mate advertising signals. In its simplest case, a mating signal conveys nothing more than the information needed for species recognition. However, mating is nonrandom within many species, and partner choice is often based on signals that reliably convey aspects of the sender's quality (Andersson, 1994; Johnstone, 1995).

Song in songbirds is a multifaceted signal which functions in intrasexual competition for mates and resources and as an important signal in mate attraction and stimulation (Andersson, 1994; Catchpole and Slater, 2008). Like many sexually selected traits, singing behavior is usually sexually dimorphic. Males are typically the advertising and females the choosing sex. In some species, such as the zebra finch, females do not sing at all, whereas in other species, such as the stripe-headed sparrow (*Aimophila r. ruficauda*), they might sing as much as or more than males (Illes and Yunes-Jimenez, 2009). In common with males, females can use song for mate advertising or resource defense (Hall, 2009; Langmore, 1998). Both inter- and intrasexual selection processes have been suggested to have contributed to the great complexity of birdsong and the extensive vocal learning abilities of oscines as highly conducive to this complexity (Beecher and Brenowitz, 2005; Catchpole and Slater, 2008; Searcy and Yasukawa, 1996). To understand this phenotypic variation in song, we need to study its condition dependency as well as individual learning and the cultural transmission processes (Lachlan and Slater, 1999; Nowicki and Searcy, 2005).

197

0065-3454/09 $35.00
DOI: 10.1016/S0065-3454(09)40006-8

In a mate choice context, song is addressed to receivers of the opposite sex. Here, I shall argue that a full understanding of the birdsong signaling system requires knowledge of the culture and condition dependency not only of the senders' song but also of receiver's preference. I shall illustrate this point using studies on the zebra finch in which these issues have been relatively well studied.

Zebra finches are small granivorous, sexually dimorphic, and socially monogamous estrilid finches occurring in Australia (*Taeniopygia g. castanotis*) and the Lesser Sunda Islands (*Taeniopygia g. guttata*) of Indonesia (for a comprehensive review of zebra finch biology, see Zann, 1996). They are very social and both sexes are highly vocal and call frequently, but only males produce mate advertising song. A typical zebra finch song begins with a few introductory notes and is then followed by a variable number of repeats of the so called 'motif' or 'phrase' motif (see Fig. 1). Each male has a unique song motif (Fig. 2). Pair bonds are long lasting and song is heard all year round, and

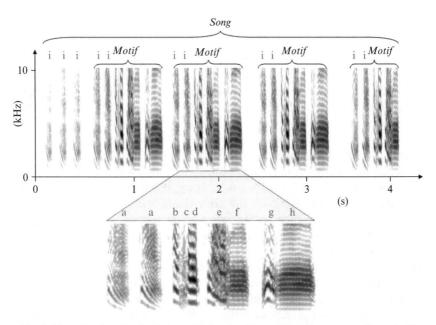

FIG. 1. Example of a zebra finch song with four motif repetitions. Songs generally start with a variable number of introductory notes ("i") which are followed by a (variable) number of repetitions of the motif. Motifs consist of syllables composed of elements (smallest units defined by being separated in time and/or structure) which are indicated by letters a–h in the lower panel. Because two introductory notes occur with every repetition of the motif they are here considered as part of the motif (labeled "a" in the lower panel).

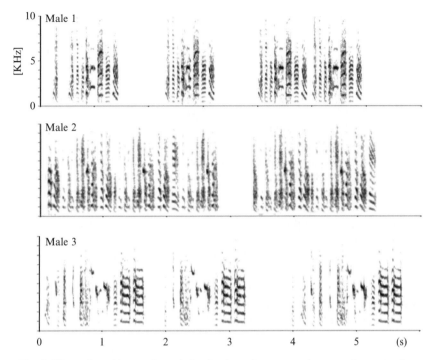

FIG. 2. Illustration of intermale variation in phonetic syntax and temporal aspects of song delivery.

breeding will start as soon as the unpredictable rainfalls begin (Immelmann, 1962; Zann, 1996). The absence of seasonality and territoriality greatly facilitate breeding in captivity. This in combination with a fast development of only about 100 days makes this species so suitable for the study of behavioral development. Male zebra finches have been instrumental in the study of avian vocal learning and its neurobiological bases (for review see, e.g., Brainard and Doupe, 2002; Slater et al., 1988; Zann, 1996) and female zebra finches have been similarly important in studying mate choice in the laboratory (Collins and ten Cate, 1996; Forstmeier and Birkhead, 2004; Rutstein et al., 2007; ten Cate and Mug, 1984). However, the two fields have not been integrated very much until recently. Song acquisition learning has been predominantly studied in male birds, quite understandably given that females do not produce any song. However, the zebra finch was one of the first species where experimental evidence for female song preference learning was reported (Clayton, 1988; Miller, 1979b; reviewed in Riebel, 2003a). Since then, a large number of studies have shown the importance of learning processes in shaping adult female song preferences. In stark contrast, the great majority of mate choice studies have focused on visual rather than acoustic cues or have restricted themselves to testing the quantity of song output ("song rate") rather than its quality (reviews in Collins and ten Cate, 1996; Forstmeier and Birkhead, 2004).

In this chapter, I shall start by briefly reviewing some key studies, that highlight the important role song plays in finding and choosing a partner. Having established this, and in keeping with the chronology of the field, I shall review the studies that set out to identify what makes a zebra finch song attractive, before reflecting on why this approach has not led to a catalog of "attractiveness traits" that determine the attractiveness of a zebra finch song. I shall ask what we might learn from recent experiments on the interaction between song learning and condition, before turning to the important question of female preference learning and whether the sole focus on male song might have been the cause of failing in identifying what makes a song attractive. To do so, this review provides a synthesis of the accumulating evidence that song preferences result from complex developmental processes on the female's side. In the last section, I shall summarize our current insights on culture and condition affecting zebra finch song and how this should guide future research integrating development and function of variation in trait and preference.

II. How Important is Song in Zebra Finch Mate Choice?

Song plays an important role in mate choice in oscine birds (Searcy and Yasukawa, 1996) but in many species mate advertising is a combination of song, morphological signals (i.e., sexual ornaments), and courtship displays. Zebra finch courtship is no exception to this (Morris, 1954; Williams, 2001). As a general rule, vocal signals often span longer distances and are thus thought more suitable for mate attraction and territory defense, especially in dense habitats (Bradbury and Vehrencamp, 1998), while visual signals are thought to be more important at closer distance and hence at a later stage in courtship. If sexual signaling involves more than one modality, for example, acoustic and visual signals, these can back up or enhance each other (if they contain the same information), or can convey multiple messages (if they contain different information; Candolin, 2003). In songbirds, song, morphological traits, and the performance of the courtship display often act in concert, and the relative importance of these signal components might depend on the species, population, or context. Zebra finches are not territorial and their song does not carry a very long distance, which might be the reason that there have been regular discussions on whether visual or acoustic cues are more important in female zebra finch mate choice.

The problems arising from such an approach are perhaps best illustrated by the discussion that tried to establish the relative importance of bill color versus song rate (for critical review, see Collins and ten Cate, 1996). Moreover, some of the confusion has arisen from referring to song as the quantity of song output only (for discussion, see Section III.B.1). In the next paragraph, I shall briefly review a few very convincing cases that demonstrate that song in zebra finches, as in other songbirds, plays a key role in recognizing, localizing, and eventually choosing a mate.

To test the importance of song versus visual cues in species recognition, Brazas and Shimizu (2002) gave female zebra finches the choice to approach either a Bengalese Finch or a zebra finch male, each located at the end of a y-shaped choice chamber. If they could hear and see the males, females preferentially approached males of their own species. If auditory cues were masked by noise, however, females' preference for zebra finches over Bengalese finches disappeared. This was not an effect of noise *per se*, as the same observations were made when female zebra finches could choose between an experimentally muted zebra finch and a singing Bengalese finch male (ten Cate and Mug, 1984). Conversely, Brazas and Shimizu (2002) found that if zebra finch song and calls were played back the preference for zebra finch males was reinstalled, even if the location of the playback did not match the stimulus birds' locations. This suggests that song needs to be present to make the visual cues salient. Song also seems to mediate subspecies recognition. Cross-fostering the morphologically and acoustically distinctive subspecies *T. g. guttata* and *T. g. castanotis*, Clayton showed that cross-fostered females preferred individuals singing the song of their foster subspecies independent of whether their morphology matched their own or their foster parents' morphological traits (Clayton, 1990a,c, 1991). Moreover, these preferences were concordant in playback, mate choice, and pair formation trials (Clayton, 1990b,c,d; for review, see Clayton, 1990a).

Thus, song plays an important role in species and subspecies recognition, but how important is it in influencing females' choices once a male has been identified and located this way? Choosing between songs of different males from the same colony predicts females' preferences for live males in choice chambers (Holveck and Riebel, 2007), which in turn predicts pair formation in aviaries (e.g., Clayton, 1990c; Tomaszycki and Adkins-Regan, 2005). A rather drastic, but very convincing demonstration of the importance of song in pair formation stems from an experiment where males were arbitrarily changed into good or bad singers by reversible surgery. Males' song deteriorated temporarily after air sac puncture or syrinx denervation but neither treatment affected the amount of courtship and singing, morphology, or condition. Females strongly preferred control over treated males in choice chambers and in pair formation trials in aviaries (Tomaszycki and

Adkins-Regan, 2005). Song is a necessary prerequisite in choosing extra-pair males too: in a study involving multiple trials for more than a hundred females, only singing males were chosen for extra-pair copulations although within the design the males were highly visible and at close distance throughout (Forstmeier, 2007).

The studies mentioned above illustrate the importance of song at several stages during the mate choice process: as a species recognition mechanism, but also for female choice of a social or extra-pair mate. This begs the question of what makes a song attractive to females (reviewed in Section III), which song attributes will reliably inform females on aspects of male quality (Section IV), and how females' development contributes to variation in song preferences (Section V).

III. Which Song Characteristics are Attractive?

A. Song Structure

1. Differences Between Learned and Untutored Song

Male song develops with or without exposure to an adult male that can function as song tutor (Immelmann, 1969; Slater et al., 1988; Zann, 1996). However, in comparison with males that were exposed to adult song when young, the song motifs of untutored males will show unusual note structure, an overall reduced element/syllable variety, less complex and longer syllables, resulting also in an overall slower tempo (element/s: 6.1 vs. 14.1 Immelmann, 1969). Untutored song can also contain more high-frequency elements and call notes, as well as inconsistent frequency modulations (Eales, 1987; Jones et al., 1996; Morrison and Nottebohm, 1993; Price, 1979; Williams et al., 1993). Moreover, syllables are not only of longer duration but their sequential arrangement (consistency of syllable transitions) is less consistent than in socially tutored birds (Volman and Khanna, 1995). This seems to be a genuine difference in sequential patterning because the occurrence of alterations, deletions, insertions, and repetitions were reported to be equally frequent in tutored and isolated birds (Helekar et al., 2000). The differences between isolate and tutored song does matter to females because the untutored males were the last to be paired in an aviary study (Williams et al., 1993). A potentially confounding variable could be the observation that isolate-reared males also seem to fail in directing song to females (Sturdy et al., 2001). However, females also preferentially approached loudspeakers playing back tutored versus untutored song in the absence of behavioral cues (Lauay et al., 2004; Svec and Wade, 2009). This preference depends on early song exposure of the females, because untutored females were equally attracted to tutored and nontutored song (Lauay et al., 2004), although they preferred conspecific over heterospecific song, as do tutored females.

2. Geographic Variation and Domestication

There is substantial geographical variation in song across the different Australian mainland populations (Zann, 1993b), but its salience to female receivers has as yet not been studied. More detail on both male song development and female song preference is available for the two zebra finch subspecies. Timor zebra finches, *T. g. guttata*, have longer motifs, more elements, and sing at higher pitch than mainland zebra finches *T. g. castanotis* (Clayton et al., 1991). Females discriminate between these two and prefer their own subspecies. Cross-fostering experiments, showed this to be a culturally transmitted preference (see Section IV.B).

A special form of geographic variation might arise from the isolation of captive populations. The only study comparing wild and domesticated song did find a wild, a recent captive and two captive domesticated populations to differ in some song parameters but it is currently unclear whether these differences are due to the domestication process *per se* or a result of genetic and cultural drift between populations (Slater and Clayton, 1991). The same question holds for differences in song structure reported among wild (Clayton et al., 1991; Zann, 1993b) or captive colonies (Sturdy et al., 1999). Although behavior and morphology have been reported to differ between wild and domesticated stock (e.g. Rutstein et al., 2007; Slater and Clayton, 1991; Sossinka, 1970; Tschirren et al., 2009), these studies are not conclusive with respect to the effect of domestication on song (or any other trait), because generally only one population of each wild and domesticated stock is compared. This makes it difficult to separate effects of geographic isolation from domestication. Moreover, rearing and housing conditions could potentially be confounding variables, they significantly affect physiology, mass, and condition on a short-term (10 days) and long-term (four generations) scale (Ewenson et al., 2001) which means that they could also affect song. This is highly relevant where wild caught birds are compared with aviary reared birds for any trait (e.g., Rutstein et al., 2007). Moreover, maternal effects might affect their offspring (Gil, 2008; Groothuis et al., 2005). Returning to the issue at hand, clearly, more studies comparing the same song parameters across several wild and domesticated colonies are needed to separate possible effects of domestication on song and mating preferences from random cultural and genetic drift. Reassuringly, domesticated populations differ from each other genetically, and so do wild populations and the variation seems continuous (Forstmeier et al., 2007). Despite general differences in morphology (such as a larger body size), domesticated and wild stock showed similar patterns of developmental reaction norms for several morphological and behavioral traits (Sossinka 1970; Tschirren et al., 2009). The heterogeneity of founder population size of colonies, and age and outbreeding status (including backcrosses with wild birds) of the existing colonies suggests that perhaps "the" domesticated zebra finch does not exist. It seems prudent to assume where their song and behavior are concerned that there might be differences between different domesticated colonies and between different wild populations. For the purpose of this review, I will treat laboratory and wild populations as samples from a continuum of populations of different size, isolation, and inbreeding rather than two homogenous and to be contrasted categories. This seems to fit the available genetic (Forstmeier et al., 2007), observational (e.g., on song Slater and Clayton, 1991; or beak color Burley et al., 1992), and experimental data to date (Rutstein et al., 2007; Tschirren et al., 2009).

3. Motif and Song Duration

Motif duration varies geographically, interindividually (e.g., Clayton et al., 1991; Gil et al., 2006; Zann, 1993b), and between directed and undirected singing (Sossinka and Böhner, 1980). Motif and song duration will be treated within the same section, because they are not independent of each other. Although males occasionally sing single motifs, songs normally consist of several motifs strung together. Unless longer motifs are repeated less often within a song than short motifs, there will generally be a positive association between motif and song duration. This might be worth quantifying in order to test for trade-offs between the two, but I am not aware of any data set testing this quantitatively for a larger set of males.

There is some evidence for condition dependency of motif duration (see Section III.C.3 and Table IV), but the evidence for a female preference for longer motifs per se is rather mixed. Although two studies showed directional preference for long versus short songs (Clayton and Pröve, 1989; Neubauer, 1999), other studies did not find motif duration a good explanatory variable for female song preference (Holveck and Riebel, 2007; Leadbeater et al., 2005; Riebel et al., prov. accept.; Vyas et al., 2009). The variation in results may be due to the fact that both studies that did find a preference for longer motifs used extreme differences in stimulus duration, and it is perhaps not surprising that results obtained in this way cannot be generalized to more natural variation. Two studies that used more natural differences between song stimuli found no female preference for long over short single song motifs (Leadbeater et al., 2005), or long over short songs consisting of four repeats of short or long motifs, respectively (Riebel et al., prov. accept.). Moreover, two other recent studies present correlational and experimental evidence that the difference in syllable repertoires is, indeed, a confounding variable (Holveck and Riebel, 2007; Vyas et al., 2009).

4. (Syllable) Repertoire Size

Repertoire size is generally assumed to be a sexually selected trait in songbirds (Searcy and Yasukawa, 1996). In zebra finches, differences in repertoire size have generally been assessed measuring the number of different elements or syllables within a males' motif. Clayton and Pröve (1989) reported that in their preference tests for "longer songs," the song duration was positively correlated with the total number of different elements/syllables, although it should be noted that shorter motifs do not necessarily consist of fewer different syllables (e.g., Spencer et al., 2003).

Female song preferences in an operant and phonotaxis setup were better explained by relative differences in the number of different syllables than song duration (Holveck and Riebel, 2007). This was confirmed by tests of a stimulus array that was constructed to disentangle the effects of duration from complexity which revealed stronger behavioral female responses toward complex rather than longer songs (Vyas et al., 2009). Summarizing the current and previous section: variation in song duration per se within the natural range might be less important in determining female preferences in zebra finches than previously thought, and earlier reports indicating a preference for longer songs may have been confounded by syllable repertoire size (for corroborating experimental evidence in the chaffinch (*Fringilla coelebs*), see Leitão et al., 2006). Further in line with this is the observation that females preferred edited motifs with a large number of different syllables (GHJKLMNE) over equally long songs with a smaller number of syllables (ABCDABCDE, Neubauer, 1999). However, these songs differ not only in syllable number but also in syntax—there is a predictable pattern of repetition within a motif that is absent in the other test stimulus. Do such syntactical differences matter to females?

5. Syntax

I will use the term "phonetic syntax" here to refer to rules with which the different units within the motifs and songs are arranged. Element sequencing seems to follow certain rules, call notes for example tend to occur at the end, and high notes in the middle of a song (Williams and Staples, 1992; Zann, 1993a,b, 1996). However, with the possible exception of the introductory elements, no position seems really fixed for a particular category of elements (but see Lachlan et al., in press). However, there are associations of subgroups of notes ("chunks") that are preferentially copied together (Williams and Staples, 1992). Breathing patterns also group several adjacent notes, a feature that is copied along with the song and suggest some possible production constraints on element sequencing (Franz and Goller, 2002).

Although zebra finches can discriminate between songs that differ in the position of one element only (Verzijden et al., 2007), this does not necessarily influence their preferences (Riebel, 2000). In a validated phonotaxis setup, neither song experienced nor song isolate females preferred regular forward versus reversed song (Lauay et al., 2005), which suggests that female receivers might be quite permissive with respect to the ordering of song elements. However, the relative freedom of rules for the sequencing of element categories within an individual motif allows no prediction regarding the importance of stereotypy versus variability in the delivery of this motif. In the next paragraph, I will explore whether closed versus open-ended variability of motifs has any signal value in zebra finches.

Male zebra finches do not sing each rendition of their motif with the exact same sequencing of the elements/syllables making up the motif, either because there is more than one preferred note order, or because of occasional changes in sequencing, deletions, insertions, and repetitions of notes (Helekar et al., 2000; Sturdy et al., 1999). The observation that there is substantial in-between male variation in this parameter, make it worth asking whether it matters to female receivers. To capture this variation, quite a few authors have used the linearity and consistency index introduced by Scharff and Nottebohm (1991) or slight variations thereof (e.g., Holveck et al., 2008). Song "linearity" corresponds to the number of different notes divided by the number of different transitions. Song consistency is the number of typical transitions divided by the total transitions. Males differ in how stereotyped their song motif is sequenced. Some of this seems to be a practice effect, the amount of singing during plastic song seems to have an effect on the stereotypy of sequencing (Johnson et al., 2002; Pytte and Suthers, 2000; Slater and Jones, 1998). A recent study suggests this to be a condition-dependent parameter (Holveck et al., 2008) which raises the intriguing and experimentally testable idea that poor juvenile condition might restrict practice time and thus leads to poorer performance in this parameter in adulthood.

Another intriguing question for future research is how female preference for variability and stereotypy can be balanced within the same song to attain maximum attractiveness. In the related Bengalese finch, the degrees of freedom in fixed sequencing of a fixed element repertoire alter how stimulating a particular song is to females (Okanoya, 2004). In zebra finches, females preferred to listen to songs where the syllables of the motif were rearranged in four different sequential sequences over four sequentially identical repetitions (Collins, 1999). This might be interpreted as a preference for variability, or for a repertoire as the same preference was found for a song made up of four motifs from four (related) males (Collins, 1999). However, these results viewed in combination with the results showing preferences for heterogeneous motif structure (Neubauer, 1999; Vyas et al., 2009) raise the question of how future experiments should test variability versus stereotypy of syntax, a question that has not been addressed systematically in zebra finches or other species. Moreover, this aspect of variability between males has not been captured well by those stimulus preparations consisting of one song per male only.

6. Special Elements

In a number of song bird species, the presence of particular phonetic structures enhances song attractiveness to females, for example, a particular trill type in the canary (Vallet and Kreutzer, 1995; Vallet et al., 1998) or the buzzy high-amplitude elements of the terminal flourish in chaffinches (Leitão and Riebel, 2003; Riebel and Slater, 1998). In zebra finches, high notes are notes very prominent high frequency and high amplitude. Some of these high notes are part of a special element class of inspiratory syllables requiring unusual motor coordination (Goller and Daley, 2001). Songs containing such syllables showed longer motif duration and syllable rate (Leadbeater et al., 2005), suggesting that they might be an indicator of a higher singing performance and motor control, but songs with such inspiratory notes were not preferred by females in operant song preference tests.

The absence of high notes and combination notes (Tomaszycki and Adkins-Regan, 2005) was the main effect of tracheosyringeal nerve transsection on male song quality. These songs were less attractive to females, although they did not differ in length or syllable repertoire from control songs. However, the overall spectral quality of all elements was clearly affected but whether this caused the reduced attractiveness remains to be tested with experimentally manipulated songs.

On the whole, no study to date has systematically tested the songs that were edited to contain specific syllables or syllable combinations, so for the time being, the existence of especially attractive elements in zebra finch song remains an open question.

7. Spectral Characteristics

Zebra finches (males and females) are very apt in discriminating differences in the harmonic spectrum between sounds; they can do so between syllables differing only in relative amplitude of just one harmonic only (Cynx et al., 1990). The fundamental frequency must in some way reflect male testosterone levels, because it can be lowered further with testosterone implants (Cynx et al., 2005), but to my knowledge the effect of fundamental frequency on song attractiveness has not been specifically tested. Songs with noisier elements are less attractive than those with a better defined harmonic spectrum (Tomaszycki and Adkins-Regan, 2005). Aspects of timbre resulting from reinforcing or filtering particular parts of the spectrum are learned (Goller and Cooper, 2004; Williams et al., 1989). Spectral characteristics have been shown to become more consistent with age up until 15 months of age, suggesting an effect of practice long after song crystallization which takes place when males are approximately 100 days old (Pytte et al., 2007). Variation in the fundamental frequencies of syllables with harmonic stacks was correlated with song preference strength in a phonotaxis test (Woolley and Doupe, 2008). These findings, in combination with the long development of stereotypy of spectral parameters, suggest that these parameters ought to be tested as possible correlates of male quality and female mating preferences.

B. SONG PERFORMANCE

1. *Song Rate (Amount or Duration of Song Motifs Per Unit Time)*

In zebra finches (and songbirds in general), interindividual differences in song output have received much attention as a potential indicator of male quality (Gil and Gahr, 2002; Searcy and Yasukawa, 1996). In zebra finches, different authors have defined and measured the song rate either as the total duration of song, the total number of motifs, or the total number of songs per unit time (most frequently number of songs/min). Time spent singing is thought to be costly both in terms of conspicuousness and the time lost for other activities (Gil and Gahr, 2002). Moreover, there are likely to be direct energetic costs too. Song production slightly increases oxygen consumption over presong level in zebra finches, suggesting some metabolic cost to song (Franz and Goller, 2003). In line with this, in the wild, the quantity of undirected song decreases after low overnight temperatures (Dunn and Zann, 1996b) and in the laboratory the daily song output decreased immediately after food deprivation (Johnson and Rashotte, 2002; Rashotte et al., 2001) while song rates could be sustained at energetically demanding colder temperatures provided sufficient food was available (Johnson and Rashotte, 2002; Rashotte et al., 2001). At least two feedback mechanisms seem to exist between nutrition and (undirected) song: both the unpredictability of food as well as the availability of carbohydrate metabolites affect the quantity of undirected song on a short-term basis (Cappendijk and Johnson, 2005; Johnson and Rashotte, 2002).

This suggests that the quantity of undirected song could inform a female of a male's current nutritional state and foraging success. However, I could find only one study comparing whether the amount of directed and undirected song was correlated within an individual and that was not the case (Caryl, 1981), and none that tested whether levels in daily song output (or the peak singing times) affected a male's attractiveness to a female.

a. Song rate during directed singing: Cause or effect of choice? Although the above section suggests that daily song output could indicate a male's condition, a quick glance at Table I shows that in the vast majority of studies song rate has been quantified in the context of a staged encounter with a novel female and is often not measured for longer than the first 5 or 10 min after the introduction of the female. This procedure is generally justified by the earlier finding that this period was most predictive of choice and that song rate dropped afterwards (ten Cate and Mug, 1984). It is important to stress that song rate, measured this way, is the "song rate" parameter in most mate choice studies (see Table II). However, increased song rate in this context is as much cause as effect of male and female preferences. Song rate predicts male mate choice (ten Cate, 1985) but female behavior elicits an increase in song rate (Collins, 1994; Rutstein et al., 2007; ten Cate and Mug, 1984). Moreover, effects of female identity on song rate have been reported too (e.g., Gil et al., 2006), highlighting the fact that song rate is also the outcome of an interaction and not only an isolated male trait. The most convincing argument against song rate being the parameter females base their choices on is the observation that during mate choice trials females' initial choice (at a stage where differences in male display rate and intensity have as yet not become apparent) is predictive of the total time she will spent in front of a male (Collins, 1994; Rutstein et al., 2007).

b. Song rate and male phenotypic quality Directed song rate during 5 min encounters has been reported to be repeatable (Birkhead and Fletcher, 1995; Forstmeier et al., 2004; Tschirren et al., 2009) and a number of studies reported positive associations between this measure of song rate and female preference in mate choice trials (Collins et al., 1994; Houtman, 1992). Although this might suggest that this parameter has some information on male quality, it does not solve the question whether song rate is the cause or consequence of female mate choice. An attractive male could be more likely to get encouraged to sing repeatedly by different females.

As discussed above, song rate might be a suitable indicator of short-term condition, but it looks like undirected song over a longer period of time rather than the high-performance intensive phase of courtship display ought to be measured. Table I suggests that short-term measures of song rate of directed song are not a good condition indicator and there is non-conclusive evidence as to how song rate measured this way responds to condition. More puzzling still, song rate measured this way is sometimes

TABLE I

CONTEXT AND CONDITION DEPENDENCY OF MALE ZEBRA FINCH SONG RATE

Time	♀	Finding related to song rate (SR)	Effect[a]	N	References
40'	✓	SR low > high condition males	(+)	20	Wynn and Price (1993)
5×5'	✓	SR large broods > small broods, repeatable	+	45	Tschirren et al. (2009)
2×9×20'	✓	SR small broods > large broods	+	52	de Kogel and Prijs (1996)
2×10'	✓	Juvenile food restriction or corticosterone treatment	−	69	Spencer et al. (2003)
5×5'	✓	SR uncorrelated with sperm quality; repeatable	−	10	Birkhead and Fletcher (1995)
5×5'	✓	SR not affected by rearing diet	−	20	Birkhead et al. (1999a)
5×5'	✓	SR - '' - flying exercise regime	−		Birkhead et al. (1999b)
8×5'	✓	Repeatable 1st vs. 2nd four trials ($R = 0.75 \pm 0.04$) and across 8 trials ($R = 0.59$)	+	104[b]	Forstmeier (2004); Forstmeier and Birkhead (2004); Forstmeier et al. (2004)
		Maternal effect on song rate	−		
		Laying or hatching order, brood size	−		
		Influenced by female ID	F		
		Unrelated to mass, beak color, aggression	−		
30'		SR unrelated to weight at independence (brothers)	−	18	Kilner (1998)
45'	✓	Brood size manipulation	−	45	Gil et al. (2006)
		Effect female ID	F		
30'	✓	Undirected song rate positively correlated with age	+	24	Dunn and Zann (1997)
		Undirected song rate lower in female and male company	M		
		Undirected song rate higher when mated female in sight	F		

Time	Type	Evidence factor affecting male song rate[a]	Evidence	n	Study
5'	Field	Low overnight temperatures reduced male song	+		Dunn and Zann (1996b)
180'	✓	SR down with increased foraging time for chick raising males	+		Brumm et al. (2009)
30', 15'	✓	Undirected and directed song rate uncorrelated	M	18	Caryl (1981)
15'	✓	Correlated with beak color, heritable	+	22(24)	Houtman (1992)
	✓	Effect of female preference on SR	F	8	Collins et al. (1994)
3×30'	✓	More song with female in adjacent part of test cage	M	25	ten Cate and Mug (1984)
		SR increased immediately before and even more after arrival of female, SR decreased after 8.6 s with female nearby	F		
3×30'	✓	SR predicts male mate choice (after heterospecific imprinting)	+	19	ten Cate (1985)
5' 6d	–	Monopolization nestboxes (12 males, 6 boxes per aviary)	+, M	36	Ratcliffe and Boag (1987)
5' 7d	✓	Successful pairing or color ring (12 males, 6 nestboxes, 6 females)	–		
5'[c]	Field	Undirected SR near the nest not affected by wheather, day time, season	–	17	Dunn and Zann (1996a)
		Not correlated with mate guarding (male following female)	–		

Time, number and duration of song rate measurement (e.g., $5 \times 5' = 5$ times 5 min); ♂, if this column is ticked, then a female was present for the recording.

[a] Evidence factor affecting male song rate: +, evidence; –, no evidence; M, motivation or context; F, effect of female.

[b] Same males in all three studies.

[c] 5 min *ad libitum* sampling in the field.

TABLE II

SONG RATE AND FEMALE BEHAVIOR

Source	FP	Song rate (SR)	♂♂	Test	(min)	♂/♀
ten Cate and Mug (1984)	i	SR slightly higher before and much higher after arrival female	2	LM	40'	25
Houtman (1992)	+	Correlated with time choosing	2	LM	15'	25/29
	+	EPC's	1	EPC	30'	18/18
Collins et al. (1994)	+	SR more important than (manipulation) beak colour	2	LM	40'; 50'	8/8; 10/10
Collins (1994)	−	SR effect not cause of preference	2	LM	10'	8/8
Collins (1995)	+	Effect of recent experiences with high/low display-ing males on initial preferences	2	LM	30'	14/15
Balzer and Williams (1998)	+	SR first 10' correlated with preference	6	LM	30'	33/33
Forstmeier et al. (2004)	−	Maternal effect on female preference	4	LM	3 h	104/103
Forstmeier (2004)	−	Female responsiveness, copulation rates	1	M	5'	- "_[b]
Forstmeier and Birkhead (2004)	i	SR in 8×5' encounters explained 9% variance female choice in LM test	4	LM	3 h	- "_[b]
		SR (7×10' observations) in 8males and 8 female housing not predictive of choice				
Forstmeier (2007)	−	Probability EPC	1	EPC	5'	63[c]/63[b]
Rutstein et al. (2007)	−	Females' choice before apparent SR differences	2	LM	15'	64/64[a]
	i	Female responsiveness affects SR	1	M	5×5'	- " -
Naguib et al. (2008)	−	SR covaried with brood size, but no preference	2	LM	20'	

FP Female preference (+, positive; −, negative; F, female cause of increase song rate; i, inconclusive with respect to song rate and female preference).

♂♂ Males simultaneously present during the preference test.

♂/♀ Sample sizes for males and females.

LM, live male tests in choice chambers or choice arenas; EPC, extra live male introduced into breeding cage; M, "NoChoice"-test: 1 live male introduced into female's home cage; AV, aviary.

[a]Half the sample was domesticated stock, the other wild caught birds.

[b]Same individuals in all three studies.

[c]At least 63.

even higher in males of low rather than high phenotypic quality in both domesticated and wild stock (Tschirren et al., 2009; Wynn and Price, 1993). It seems worth exploring in the future whether differences in song rate result from interactions between male condition and motivation and whether this is a cause or consequence of state-dependent mating strategies (McNamara and Houston, 1996).

c. *Song rate: Summary and conclusions* To summarize, the short-term measurements of song rate during (novel) mate encounters are likely to reflect male differences in courting motivation and/or his attractiveness, as well as a mutual interest of the male and female. The repeatability values for song rate found across several such tests could then reflect either male motivation or his attractiveness. Experimental studies using acoustic stimuli where this parameter has been manipulated in isolation are missing as yet. Daily song output has been shown to respond directly to experimental manipulation of males' energy budgets, suggesting that song output measured over longer units of time is a reliable indicator of current condition and nutritional state.

2. Temporal Performance (Within Motifs or Songs)

Aspects of temporal performance within a song are the consistency with which the stereotypy in element sequencing might be matched by the stereotypy in timing, the amount of sound versus silence delivered within a motif or song, and syllable rate. The proportion of sound versus silence within a song seem to go some way in explaining variation in female preference in two recent studies (Holveck and Riebel, 2007; Leadbeater et al., 2005). Interestingly, the consistency of this parameter seems also to signal male early condition (Holveck et al., 2008). Syllable rate was also found to be affected in adult birds that were raised under a food-restricted regime (Zann and Cash, 2008). This seems a promising parameter for further study.

3. Amplitude

Amplitude is an important performance parameter known to influence mate choice in various taxa, but this parameter is perhaps the least studied and understood in avian mate choice (for discussion, see Brumm and Slater, 2006; Searcy, 1996; Searcy and Yasukawa, 1996). In zebra finches, it has been shown that the amplitude of calls and both directed and undirected song is dependent on social context (Cynx and Gell, 2004). Females call louder if they can hear but not see another zebra finch (be it male or female) than when alone or in company. In contrast, males' calling amplitude is independent of social context, but song amplitude increases significantly in male and female company. Moreover, the rate of increase varies depending on distance to the female (Brumm and Slater, 2006). These studies do as yet not provide an answer to the question whether amplitude increased the effectiveness or attractiveness of the signal, but in terms of mate choice either mechanism would lead to more attention by listening females and thereby can increase males' mating chances. This seems worthwhile to test in view of the observation that there is substantial interindividual variation in song amplitude (15 db median range, for $N = 18$ males; Brumm and Slater, 2006).

4. Directed Versus Undirected Song

Zebra finches, like most estrilid finches, show two modes of singing: directed (or courtship) song and undirected (or solitary) song (Sossinka and Böhner, 1980). The two singing modes were initially defined by context of usage and the differences in posture by the singing bird (Morris, 1954), and have since been shown to be different motivational states (Caryl, 1981) triggered by the presence (not view) of the female (Hara et al., 2009) with different neuroendocrine control (Jarvis et al., 1998; Walters et al., 1991). Although the same motif is sung in both contexts, directed song shows overall higher performance levels. Directed song is delivered with more repetitions of the introductory notes, more motif repetitions per song, a faster element rate, and reduced spectral variability than undirected song (see Table III). While this means that the distinction of these two singing modes is likely justified, the meaning of either singing mode to female receivers and the function of these two singing modes in a sexual selection context is less well understood.

Although the general assumption is that these two singing modes have different roles in courtship, there has only been one direct experimental test regarding the salience of the differences between directed and undirected song to females (Woolley and Doupe, 2008). In a phonotaxis experiment, females preferred their mate's directed over his undirected song. The authors also conducted detailed song analyses. Only (low) variability in the fundamental frequency of notes with harmonics stacks covaried with female preference strength. Although the analyses of the test songs confirmed earlier findings on the differences between the two singing modes (see Table III), none of these parameters were related to female preference strength. This experiment is very important, as it shows for the first time that the differences between the two singing modes are detected and relevant to females. However, they do not allow conclusions regarding the role of undirected song in mate attraction or stimulation.

In the field and in the laboratory, mated males continue to spend a substantial time singing undirected song even after mating (Dunn and Zann, 1996a,b; ten Cate, 1982; Woolley and Doupe, 2008). There is little

TABLE III

DIFFERENCES BETWEEN DIRECTED AND UNDIRECTED SONG

Song parameter	Directed	Undirected	Source
Introductory notes	>		1, 2, 3
#Motifs/song	>		1, 3
#Motifs/song	$\approx^{a,b}$		2
Duration of 1st motif	$\approx^{a}$		2
Regularity sequence	>		1
Variability F_0	>		3
Syllable stereotypy[c]	=		3
Speed	>		1, 3, 4, 5
Spectral variability	<		5, 6, 7

Sources: 1 (Sossinka and Böhner, 1980); 2 (Bischof et al., 1981); 3 (Woolley and Doupe, 2008); 4 (Cooper and Goller, 2006); 5 (Kao and Brainard, 2006); 6 (Olveczky et al., 2005); 7 (Teramitsu and White, 2006).

[a]Measured in 4 contexts: female, stuffed female, plaster model, without stimulus.

[b]No clear differences between female, stuffed, and undirected but lower towards plaster model than without stimulus.

[c]A parameter in the Sound Analysis Pro (SAP) software.

song just after the young fledge, but from day 9 onwards, undirected singing becomes much more frequent again, and the predominant singing of mated males (ten Cate, 1982). Directed song activity is only high on the first day with a new female, and the decline thereafter is due to familiarity effects, not changes in hormonal status as a new female will recover high rates of directed singing (Caryl, 1976). Removing male or female companions will increase undirected singing, with a male's own female in sight more so than in any other condition (Dunn and Zann, 1997).

In the wild, undirected song is, by far, the more frequent of the two singing modes (Dunn and Zann, 1996b). Undirected singing activity peaks during nest building and laying stage and then dramatically drops again with the onset of incubation (Dunn and Zann, 1996b). During nesting, most undirected song is given near the nest and when the female is inside, with more undirected song when the females stay inside for longer (Dunn and Zann, 1996a). When females were removed from their mates in the field during the nonbreeding season, the rate of undirected singing went up and males quickly repaired (Dunn and Zann, 1996b). The amount of directed singing toward a male's partner is not correlated with the amount of undirected song. On the contrary, paired males with higher rates of undirected singing also showed higher rates of extra-pair directed singing (Dunn and Zann, 1996a). Such a potential mate attracting function of undirected song is line with the observations that undirected song is attractive to females in phonotaxis tests and operant setups (Collins, 1999; Riebel, 2000; Riebel and Smallegange, 2003; Riebel et al., 2002). Moreover, the males' whose undirected songs females preferred in operant tasks or in a phono-taxis setup, are the males they prefer when tested in binary association tests with live males (Holveck and Riebel, 2007).

5. Female Preference: Cause or Effect of Difference in Male Performance?

This is a rather neglected issue, despite substantial evidence that female presence changes male song output (as most apparent in the switch from undirected to directed song, see above). And, as discussed, females' pre-ferences can have an effect on song rate, which in the past has often been measured as a male secondary trait. In addition, there are several observa-tions that suggest that females might influence male song acquisition. Male song learning from an adult male tutor is improved if they are housed with a female (Adret, 2004) and poorer when they are housed with a deafened female (Williams, 2004). Females' song experiences before they are cohoused with young males seem to have some influence on which elements of two different tutors these young males retain in their crystallized song motif (Jones and Slater, 1993). Even adult male singing, that is generally supposed to be stereotyped, is malleable: females' calling behavior can induce motif stops and alter the frequency of certain motif variants in a male's performance (Williams, 2004). Clearly, this field deserves more study, espe-cially in view of the well-documented role in male song "tutoring" by nonsinging females in another songbird species, the cowbird, *Molothrus ater* (West and King, 1988).

C.   SONG AS INDICATOR TRAIT AND CONDITION DEPENDENCY OF MALE SONG

1.   Song as Age Indicator?

There is evidence from quite a few species that parameters like repertoire size (Gil and Gahr, 2002) and also aspects of song performance like the spectral and temporal consistency of trill delivery (de Kort et al., 2009) might be the reliable age indicators. In zebra finches, little attention has been given to this question. I found two studies addressing this issue in wild zebra finches. Song output (undirected song) in the feeding flock was not age correlated ($N = 15$ males; Dunn and Zann, 1996b), but the rate of undirected song when males were isolated from conspecifics was positively correlated with age in F1 laboratory-bred wild males ($N = 24$ males; Dunn and Zann, 1997). The work on age effects on song in the laboratory has centered around identifying the neurobiological substrate involved in maintaining stereotypy, mostly by experimentally inducing changes in stereotypy at different ages (reviewed in Pytte et al., 2007). Pytte et al. (2007) conducted a very detailed longitudinal song analysis and concluded that both temporal and spectral aspects of syllables within stereotyped motifs kept on moving toward more stereotypy across the recording sessions at 4, 9, and 15 months of age, and motifs tended to get slightly shorter, mostly as a consequence of a decrease in syllable duration. Comparable effects were found by Jones et al. (1996) who reported these types of changes most pronounced in initially untutored, poorly singing birds. No such changes were found if songs of birds older than 37 months were compared across similar recording intervals (Pytte et al., 2007). Thus, song does not only signal a male's maturity but, in addition, also contains information on whether a male is relatively young or rather older (and supposedly experienced). However, whether this information is used in mate choice is not known, since no data are available on female preference regarding the song of older versus younger males or on songs that systematically differ in the above-described parameters.

2. Hormonal State

In zebra finches, like in other vertebrates, male sexual behavior is dependent on androgens. Castration of adult males, or pharmaceutical blocking of testosterone production, leads to the loss of directed song and greatly reduces undirected song (Pröve, 1974; Pröve and Immelmann, 1982), but both directed and undirected song can be restored with testosterone replacement treatment (Pröve, 1974). The conversion of androgens to estrogen is a necessary precondition for the production of directed (but not undirected) song (Walters et al., 1991). Testosterone mediates the transition from plastic to fully crystallized song and is implicated in maintaining adult song stereotypy (Williams et al., 2003). Experimental manipulation of adult males' testosterone titers decreases the fundamental frequency of males' song and the latency to first song upon introduction of a female (Cynx et al., 2005). Song rate and androgen titers are positively correlated (Pröve, 1978). Social conditions during rearing can influence plasma T: it is higher in birds from large than small broods (Naguib et al., 2004). Postfledging social conditions, like single and mixed sex group housing led to lower plasma T in young zebra finches than in isolation kept or female housed individuals (Pröve, 1981). How and when these interindividual differences at this early age might affect song development and aspects of adult song needs further study.

3. Condition Dependency of Song and Song Learning

Zebra finch song learning has been studied intensively and is an important model in behavioral development and vocal learning (reviewed in, e.g., Bolhuis and Gahr, 2006; Brainard and Doupe, 2002; Slater et al., 1988; Tchernichovski et al., 2001). However, the question of whether learned song variation could be an indicator of a male's condition (Buchanan et al., 2003; Nowicki et al., 1998) has only received attention after the publication of the "nutritional stress hypothesis" (Nowicki et al., 1998, 2002). This hypothesis proposed that learned song features could be indicators of male condition because the development of (supposedly costly) brain structures mediating song learning and production occurs during the period of fastest development, that is, when young birds are most vulnerable to environmental stressors (see also Buchanan et al., 2003). Table IV shows that a wide variety of approaches have been taken to manipulate juvenile condition and to capture the various dimensions of song that might be affected by suboptimal development. While this heterogeneity hampers comparisons somewhat at this stage, this diversity may also help to identify suitable designs and song measures that covary with condition. Remarkably, regardless of approach, the song features traditionally implied in female mate choice, namely song rate and the number of different syllables, were not affected at all in any study and there were rather mixed results for motif duration. Two studies reported an effect of juvenile condition on adult motif duration (Spencer et al., 2003; Zann and Cash, 2008), three did not (Brumm et al., 2009; Gil et al., 2006; Holveck et al., 2008), another three reported substantial influence of tutor-ID on motif song duration (Gil et al., 2006; Tchernichovski and Nottebohm, 1998; Zann and Cash, 2008). However, there were no treatment effects on the number of different syllables. Unless the differences are due to differences in how the motif was measured (not all authors clearly stated how they dealt with the problem of variable numbers of introductory notes), males must have either sung longer elements, or must have increased the number of element repetitions, or the intervals between motifs. This issue clearly warrants further study. Quite remarkably, across the various studies, a number of parameters that have not routinely measured previously are reported to covary with juvenile condition. For example, the consistency of temporal patterning (i.e., sound vs. silence within a song) and the accuracy with which element sequences are learned from the tutor (Brumm et al., 2009; Holveck et al., 2008). Moreover, the latter is the only parameter that was affected by more than one type of treatment (brood size manipulation and parental feeding restriction) and seems to be robust with respect to undirected and directed singing. Female appreciation of accurate learning has been demonstrated by experimental breeding with good and bad learners (Tchernichovski and Nottebohm, 1998). Hatching order affects the

TABLE IV
Evidence of Effects of Rearing or Adult Condition(s) on Male Song (Learning) in the Zebra Finch and Related Estrild Finches

Reference	Factor affecting condition *other variable affecting song*	Song rate	Motif (ms)	# syl	#dif syl	# syl learned	Other affected song parameters	Song sample
Zebra finch								
de Kogel and Prijs (1996)	Brood size	✓down						D
Tchernichovski and Nottebohm (1998)	Hatching order					✓		
Birkhead et al. (1999a)	Food quality	No						D
Spencer et al. (2003)	Food availability or Corticosterone[a]	No	✓	✓	No		✓ max. frequency	D
Gil et al. (2006)	Brood size—35d	No	No	No	No	No		D
	TutorID 35–100d	✓	✓					
Zann and Cash (2008)	Food availability		✓up	No	No		No effect learning accuracy *✓syllable rate* *✓f at max. amplitude*	D
	Tutor ID			✓	✓			
	Season (winter vs. fall)			✓	✓			
Holveck et al. (2008)	Brood size		No	No	No	No	✓syntax copying accuracy ✓consistency of timing	UD
Tschirren et al. (2009)	Brood size	✓up						D
Brumm et al. (2009)	Food availability		No	No	No	No	✓syntax copying accuracy	D
Bengalese finch								
Soma et al. (2006)	Brood size[b]		✓	(✓)	(✓)[c]		✓syntactical complexity	UD
Soma et al. (2009)	Laying order		No	No	No	No	✓syntactical complexity	UD

syl, total number of syllables (elements)/motif; #dif syl, total number of different syllable (element) types; # syl learned, number of syllables (elements) learned; f, frequency.

[a]Treatments pooled for analyses; D, directed song, UD, undirected song.

[b]Natural, not manipulated brood size.

[c]Brood size × sex ratio interaction.

accuracy of song imitation. The last male to hatch generally showed the best imitation and induced higher reproductive performance in females (Tchernichovski and Nottebohm, 1998).

Performance rather than repertoire-related variables were also identified to be linked to male adult condition in a correlative study (Holveck and Riebel, 2007). Songs with a higher syllable rate, a higher proportion of motif duration per song (i.e., lower proportion of intermotif silences), and a higher intramotif sound density predicted larger beak length, beak upper area, and mass. Likewise, songs with higher stereotypy were sung by males with longer and larger beaks. Concurrent song preference tests showed that female choice covaried with some of the performance-related parameters (Holveck and Riebel, 2007). Moreover, preference tests with male song from males with known rearing conditions showed that variation in female song preferences mapped onto variation in male rearing condition (zebra finches: Tchernichovski and Nottebohm, 1998; Spencer et al., 2005; and song sparrows, *Melospiza melodia*; Nowicki et al., 2002). However, the question whether females' base their choices on the song parameters that our song analyses found to covary with juvenile condition will need further study, for example, with edited songs systematically varying the parameters in question.

Song is perhaps an indicator of cross-domain competences: male zebra finches with a larger syllable repertoire were those that learned a new foraging task more quickly (Boogert et al., 2008). If there is a positive link between song complexity and other cognitive domains, the question as to how interindividual (learned and condition dependent) differences in song map on personality and behavioral syndromes (Sih and Bell, 2008) might be worth exploring in future studies.

4. Song Rate During Song Development

High song output during plastic song (not crystallization) leads to more consistent song patterns (Johnson et al., 2002; Pytte and Suthers 2000; Slater and Jones, 1998). It might be worth testing whether the amount of practice, that is, the song rate during development is condition dependent, which would provide a possible mechanism by which differences in juvenile condition could lead to differences in adult song stereotypy.

IV. FEMALE ONTOGENY AND VARIATION IN SONG PREFERENCES

Birdsong is an important model for cultural transmission processes in animals (Lynch, 1996; Slater and Ince, 1979) and there is substantial evidence that (learned) geographic variation in song influences female mating preferences (Searcy and Yasukawa, 1996). Despite the wide recognition that song learning processes contribute to variation in the male signal, the study of female preference learning has only been slowly forthcoming but not for want of evidence (for review and discussion, see Riebel, 2003b; Riebel et al., 2005). In zebra finches, song is an extreme behavioral sexual dimorphism and the sex differences in the anatomy of the forebrain song system are the most extreme of the species studied to date (MacDougall-Shackleton and Ball, 1999; Wade and Arnold, 2004). This section will show that this is no hindrance to song preference learning—rather not surprising given that males' (learned) songs are intended for female receivers. Perhaps counter intuitively, I will start my review on song preference learning by asking whether there is any evidence for unlearned biases. This is for two reasons: (1) Song learning is a so-called "channeled" learning process where unlearned biases guide what is learned (Riebel, 2003a; ten Cate et al., 1993). (2) For our understanding of the evolutionary dynamics between senders and receivers, we need to know which aspects of female preference are robust and which are plastic with respect to females' individual learning experiences and developmental background.

A. WHAT EVIDENCE IS THERE FOR UNLEARNED BIASES?

Females reared without exposure to adult male song show clear preferences for conspecific over heterospecific song upon first exposure as juveniles (Braaten and Reynolds, 1999) or adults (Lauay et al., 2004). However, only song experienced females prefer tutored over untutored male song (Lauay et al., 2004; Williams et al., 1993) and show repeatable preferences for variants of conspecific song (Riebel, 2000). Such learned rather than unlearned biases also mediate subspecies recognition. Despite the substantial macrostructural differences in male song, cross-fostered females of either subspecies prefer the singing style matching their foster father rather than their genetic father (Clayton, 1990b,d). This finding and the fact that the above tests on own-species bias have to date only been conducted with spectrally and structurally very different song of European starlings, *Sturnus vulgaris*, raises the question of how own-species specific these biases really are. For this, we need more tests involving the songs of other estrilid species as well (Campbell and Hauser, 2009; Campbell et al., 2009), but at the onset of the song acquisition phase or in untutored females.

With respect to within species variation in song, sexual selection pressures have often proven to lead to trait exaggeration, but for research on sensitive preferences one should be careful to avoid reversing the argument, namely to implicitly assume that biases for extreme trait values are a population wide norm. To illustrate this caveat: in zebra finches, syllable repertoire size and motif duration have been implicated in female choice, but both preferences for longer and more heterogeneous songs are experi-ence-dependent (Neubauer, 1999). Untutored females do not prefer longer or short motifs (Neubauer, 1999) or songs with larger syllable diversity (cf. this with the lack of preference for tutored song Lauay et al., 2004). To conclude, there seems little evidence for specific unlearned biases be-yond crude species recognition, which seem to map unto the unlearned aspects of male song. Whether this is indeed so and which song character-istics (if any) guide song acquisition on top of the social interactions with conspecifics are questions for future study. A number of relatively straight forward behavioral assays that allow testing of unlearned biases in young birds should help to tackle these questions (e.g., calling assays Clayton, 1988; or phonotaxis and operant approaches, e.g., Adret, 1993; Braaten and Reynolds, 1999; Houx and ten Cate, 1999; Nelson et al., 1997; Tchernichovski et al., 2001).

B.   EARLY SENSORY LEARNING GUIDING ADULT SONG PREFERENCES

1.   Learned Preferences for Specific Song Variants

The zebra finch was one of the first species for which experimental evidence for female song preference learning was reported (Clayton, 1988; Miller, 1979a,b; reviewed in Riebel, 2003b). After the initial report of adult females preferentially approaching their father's song in phono-taxis test over an unfamiliar song (Miller, 1979b), more detailed studies on the timing of this process (Clayton, 1988) and generalization of specific learned song preferences to population-specific song properties followed (Clayton, 1990a). Since then, the importance of subadult song experiences in shaping adult preferences has been well demonstrated and further spe-cified (see Table V). There is now experimental evidence showing that female zebra finches prefer the song they heard when young over unfamil-iar songs, be it the father's, foster father's, or unrelated adult male's song (Clayton, 1988, 1990d; Miller, 1979b; Riebel et al., 2002; Riebel et al., prov. accept.), the song of an additional later, live tutor next to the father (Clayton, 1988), or a song they heard from tape only (Riebel, 2000). Song preference learning in females like in juvenile males seems to have a sensitive phase, however, its exact nature and timing needs further study (for review and discussion, see Riebel, 2003a). Despite the pronounced sex differences in song production learning, the combined evidence to date makes it worthwhile asking how similar the acquisition or sensory learning phase is between the two sexes (e.g., Riebel et al., 2002; Tomaszycki et al., 2006). As in juvenile male birds (Jones et al., 1996; Volman and Khanna, 1995),

Experimental treatment	Groups	Age (days) exposure	Preference test	Categories of song stimuli used in preference tests with adult females	Preference	Source
Song learning						
Mate of 6–24 months	I	>120	Phonotaxis	Mate vs. male from neighboring cage	✓	[1]Miller (1979a)
Father	I	0–35	Phonotaxis	Father vs. unfamiliar similar and dissimilar	✓	[2]Miller (1979b)
Father	I	0–25	Phonotaxis	Father vs. unfamiliar	No	[1]Clayton (1988)
	II	0–35			✓	
	III	0–35		All 3 tests: father vs. unfamiliar	✓	
+ Tutor 1		35–70		1st tutor vs. unfamiliar	✓	
+ Tutor 2		120–180		2nd tutor vs. unfamiliar	✓	
Foster father followed by tutor 1	I	0–35 35–70	CSD-e	Two unfamiliar songs: test for generalization of foster vs. own subspecies (*T.g. guttata, castanotis*)	✓	[2,3]Clayton (1990d)
Aviary reared	I	0–70	Phonotaxis	Long "supernormal" vs. normal songs	I: ✓	[1]Neubauer (1999)
Late isolates	II	0–35		"	II: ✓ III: no	
Early isolates	III	0–25		"	I: ✓	
Individual tape tutoring	I	35–65	Operant	Tutor vs. unfamiliar	II: no	[1]Riebel (2000)
Isolation	II	35–65		"		
2nd tape tutoring	I + II	145–148		"	I+II: no	
Father	I		Operant	Father over unfamiliar	✓	[1]Riebel et al. (2002)
Father	I	0–75	Operant	Unfamiliar brother vs. unfamiliar nonkin	no	[1]Riebel and Smalle-gange (2003)

(*Continued*)

TABLE V (Continued)

Experimental treatment	Groups	Age (days) exposure	Preference test	Categories of song stimuli used in preference tests with adult females	Preference	Source
Foster father followed by unrelated tutor	I	2–35 35–100	Operant	Tutor vs. unfamiliar	✓	[4]Riebel et al. (prov. accept.)
Tutor Isolate	I II		Phonotaxis	Social vs. social isolate song	I ✓ II no	[1]Lauay et al. (2004)
Foster father Zf Foster father Bf	I II		Phonotaxis	Zebra finch vs. other estrilid finches' song	✓	[1]Campbell and Hauser (2009)
Unlearned biases						
Isolates	I	–	Operant	Zebra finch vs. heterospecific song[a]	✓	[1]Braaten and Reynolds (1999)
Condition						
Foster father Nonrelated tutor	III	3–35 35–65	Operant	Rearing condition affects preference strength for unfamiliar songs, but not tutor song	✓	[4]Riebel et al. (prov. accept.)

CSD, copulation solicitation displays during song playback (CSD-e: with estradiol implants).
[1]Domesticated *Taniopygia guttata*;
[2]wild stock *Taniopygia g. guttata*; or
[3]*T. g. castanotis*.
[4]*Taniopygia g. guttata* F$_4$-offspring wild stock.
[a]This preference test was conducted with juvenile birds (28–44 days).

absence of a male tutor can lead to learning from peers instead resulting in preference for their subadult peers song over unfamiliar song in adult females (Honarmand, 2009).

2. Generalization Processes

Generalization is an important aspect of learning—it is the process by which a learned response influences an animal's response to novel stimuli either along the same gradient of a single dimension stimulus or to stimuli sharing some features in the case of multidimensional stimuli (Ghirlanda and Enquist, 2003). The section above provided good experimental evidence for female learning of specific songs, and proof of principle that learning influences female song preferences and mate choice. However, outside a laboratory setting, female zebra finches are unlikely to mate with the male(s) they learned their songs from as juveniles. Dispersal, high mortality, and stable pair bonds, make it unlikely that young birds will mate with exact the same adult males whose songs they were exposed too. Clayton's work (1990a) on zebra finch subspecies recognition learning provides solid experimental evidence how a learned preference for a specific song (the foster father) is generalized to other unfamiliar (foster) subspecies songs (Clayton, 1990d). This raises the question whether specific features of the song or its overall *gestalt* were generalized. Two other studies tested whether females' preference strength for their fathers' song would be less pronounced if the unfamiliar song was structurally very similar to it than when the unfamiliar song was very dissimilar, but this was not the case (Clayton, 1988; Miller, 1979b). These results are hard to interpret, because "similarity" had not been established along dimensions known to influence song preferences, but based on overall similarity of the spectrograms of the motifs to human observers. Moreover, generalization might not be observed as long as the preferred original stimulus is present and potentially interfering individual recognition processes are possible. Females showed no preferences for the songs of unfamiliar brothers over songs from other males of the colony either (Riebel and Smallegange, 2003). These males had learned their songs from the preferred father, but in an earlier or later breeding round than the tested females. However, the study involved rather few families (and hence stimuli) and song learning from the father might differ substantially between subsequent broods (e.g., Spencer et al., 2003; Zann and Cash, 2008) or be influenced by the number of male siblings in the nest (Tchernichovski et al., 1998). From the four quoted studies, it becomes apparent that these questions need more attention, and that there are likely to be complex interactions between general sensory and individual and kin recognition learning processes, all likely bearing on female evaluation of male song.

3. How Much is Learned When and from Whom?

The experiments on female song preference learning to date (Section IV and Table V) have provided good proof of principle that the rearing environment can contribute to variation in female preferences. They also provide us with good working hypotheses regarding the timing of the process (Riebel, 2003a). However, the social environment in the laboratory lacks the great complexity and instability of the fission–fusion dynamics observed in wild populations (Zann, 1996). The experiments to date have not been designed to tell us from which or from how many male(s) females learned their preferences in the wild (for the discussion of this issue regarding male song learning, see Slater and Mann, 1990). However, future experimental studies can build on the current findings to ask how song preference acquisition occurs in socially more complex settings, where females are exposed to several or a succession of males and where a juvenile family phase is followed by a subadult phase in species-specific or mixed species flocks. We can then test whether females exposed to a greater variety of song learn to prefer colony-specific features or every individual song of males they interacted within the colony. Discrimination tests have shown that a great number of songs heard early in life can be remembered (Braaten et al., 2008), but it is unclear whether all of them would be preferred to unfamiliar songs or influence mating preferences.

C. ADULT LEARNING

Preference learning seems to take place in adulthood too. Both Clayton and Miller report that females preferred the song of a male that they were housed with much later in life namely after 120 days (Clayton, 1988) or that they were mated to (Miller, 1979a) without losing the initially learned preference for the father's or foster father's song. Generally, females prefer their mate's versus unfamiliar song even when paired up experimentally which suggests that the song preference for their mate's song is a consequence of pair formation not its cause (Clayton, 1988; Miller, 1979a; Swaddle and Page, 2007; Woolley and Doupe, 2008). However, not all song exposure in adulthood leads to a preference. A familiarization with a novel song played back from tape for 3 days did not make this song more attractive than an unfamiliar song (Riebel, 2000). Whether this was because of exposure for a briefer period or not combined with social or visual stimulation than in those cases, where adult females acquired a preference for a specific song in adulthood (Clayton, 1988; Miller, 1979a) remains to be tested. What is important to note though is that as yet there are no documented cases of a later acquired preference affecting the original preference. A stable preference for early learned song as well as adult learning of specific preferences have also been reported in female canaries, *Serinus canaria* (Nagle and Kreutzer, 1997a,b). However, whether there are any interactions between early and adult learning has to the best of my knowledge not been addressed in female songbirds as yet. This is, however, very likely; as subadult song experiences seem to have permanent effects on female perception above and beyond the song-specific preferences documented above as the following paragraph will show.

D. EFFECTS ON SONG PERCEPTION BEYOND SPECIFIC PREFERENCES

Early exposure to song has more consequences than just the acquisition of specific song preferences. The latter is just one observable effect on a sensory system that we ought to consider developmentally plastic. Lack of exposure to adult song models results in weaker performance in frequency range and frequency ratio discrimination tasks (Sturdy et al., 2001). Such effects could arise both from the lack of song experience only or the lack of song experience in social interactions with singing conspecifics. This is an important question to address in the future. However, just being exposed to song contributes to fine-tuning females' perception. Tape tutoring induced stable and repeatable song preferences that were absent in song of isolation-reared females (Riebel, 2000). Preferences for supernormal song length are only expressed by aviary or bird-room raised females but not females deprived of male song after 25 days (Neubauer, 1999). An interesting question following from this is whether exposure to one male's song is sufficient to enable females to judge these differences or whether they need exposure to several different songs to learn about "average song length" to perceive unusually long songs as more attractive.

Female song preference learning as documented here is a learned receiver bias. Other than receiver biases arising from peripheral and primary properties of the sensory system with little developmental plasticity, "learning-based biases" are characterized by changes in central information processing as a consequence of individual learning processes (ten Cate and Rowe, 2007). Skews arising from learned receiver biases might play an important role in the dynamics of signal evolution (ten Cate and Rowe, 2007). For example, zebra finches sexually imprint on the opposite sex parent's beak color and adult preferences are shifted toward stimuli that have more extreme trait values than the originally learned parental beak colors (ten Cate et al., 2006). Such a preference for stimuli that show a more extreme trait value than an original positive and negative stimulus in discrimination learning is the result of peak shift and this phenomenon can also occur in song discrimination learning (Verzijden et al., 2007). It is too early days to draw any firm conclusions, but as the previous sections have shown, there is enough evidence, the theoretical framework and testing paradigms to tackle these issues for song preference learning.

E. LEARNING IN THE BRAIN

Is there any evidence for the above-mentioned changes in central information processing required for learning-based receiver biases? The literature on this subject has been growing rapidly recently and deserves a review on its own. For now, it is important to mention that the behavioral differences between tutored and untutored females are reflected in neuroanatomical, electrophysiological, and genomic changes in the brain. Electrophysiological measures in the auditory area (field L) show that song experienced versus untutored females show different tuning to conspecific song (Hauber et al., 2007) and song isolate females show spine deficits in the NCM an auditory area involved in song perception (Lauay et al., 2005). Upon exposure to various categories of song stimuli, tutored and untutored females show differential immediate early gene (IEG) expression patterns in auditory perceptual areas upon exposure to conspecific song as early as 45 days (Tomaszycki et al., 2006). These responses can be as specific as to pertaining to specific song types: for example, the early tutor song (Terpstra et al., 2006), a females' mate's song (Woolley and Doupe, 2008), or her mate's call (Vignal et al., 2008) all leading to a higher activation in the auditory forebrain areas than an unfamiliar conspecific vocalization.

V. CONCLUSIONS

Song plays a crucial role in zebra finch mate choice. It functions as a species recognition mechanism and plays a role in choosing social and extra-pair mates. Female mating preferences in zebra finches do not result from strong directional preferences for long songs *per se* and high (directed) song rates. Instead, the current evidence indicates that syllable diversity and male performance parameters in the temporal and spectral domain, in concert with female learned preferences, are better predictors of which songs a female will find attractive. Although song output is condition-related, song rates during brief episodes of directed singing are not reliable indicators of male condition, but instead are the product of male and female mutual mating preferences.

Female song preferences show substantial phenotypic plasticity, much of which is mediated by subadult sensory learning. This is a young but growing field of research, and there is now good experimental evidence that the type of song(s) a female hears when subadult will affect her adult mating preferences. Exposure to adult song at the subadult stage also plays an important role in perceptual fine-tuning and in the development of receiver competence. The evidence that only tutored females appreciate tutored song, suggests that male and female song learning needs to be considered by theoretical models of nongenetic transmission processes affecting trait or preference variation (Beltman et al., 2003; Lachlan and Slater, 1999; Laland, 1994; Ritchie et al., 2008). However, much is still to be discovered on this issue, for example, how condition (Riebel et al., prov. accept.) and context (Tchernichovski et al., 1998) interact with learned preferences. To this end, studies in the laboratory are likely to continue to provide important insights into the underlying mechanisms and development of female preference, and a challenge for the future will be to design and conduct appropriate field studies to better understand the function of this plasticity in female mating preferences. One of the main messages of this review is that to this end the development of trait and preference have to be studied in concert. There is substantial condition dependency of male song, also for a number of traits that were not previously implied in female mate choice. Some concern aspects of song structure that females can perhaps detect without prior knowledge of a specific song, such as the stability of temporal patterning. Others, like copying accuracy of the tutor's element sequencing seem at first sight to require female knowledge of the model song, which makes them unlikely candidates for mate choice in a natural setting. However, more accurate copying of the tutor may indicate better motor control, and correlated song stereotypy is the underlying perceptually relevant parameter. If males grow up in poor environmental conditions, so will females of the same generation. How the development of female song preferences is affected by her condition deserves more attention for two reasons. Firstly, in a culturally transmitted mating signal the receivers should be able to track cultural change including confounds by condition (Ritchie et al., 2008). Secondly, state-dependent mate choice theory predicts that a female's condition may affect her optimal mating preferences (Cotton et al., 2006; McNamara and Houston, 1996). Against this background, a better understanding of the development of female mating preferences is paramount, but just a first step. The real challenge will be to develop a research program that integrates the study of the development and function of variation in male signaling and female preferences, as our only access to decoding this complex communication system.

Acknowledgments

I thank Nicky Clayton, Vincent Janik, and Klaus Zuberbühler for organizing the symposium on "Acoustic Communication in Birds and Mammals" in honor of Peter Slater's retirement and for their invitation to speak at the symposium and to contribute to this volume.

Carel ten Cate, Simon Verhulst, and two anonymous referees provided important and much appreciated comments on an earlier manuscript version.

References

Adret, P., 1993. Operant conditioning, song learning and imprinting to taped song in the zebra finch. Anim. Behav. 46, 149–159.

Adret, P., 2004. Vocal imitation in blindfolded zebra finches (*Taeniopygia guttata*) is facilitated in the presence of a non-singing conspecific female. J. Ethol. 22, 29–35.

Andersson, M., 1994. Sexual Selection. Princeton University Press, Princeton.

Balzer, A.L., Williams, T.D., 1998. Do female zebra finches vary primary reproductive effort in relation to mate attractiveness? Behaviour 135, 297–309.

Beecher, M.D., Brenowitz, E.A., 2005. Functional aspects of song learning in songbirds. Trends Ecol. Evol. 20, 143–149.

Beltman, J.B., Haccou, P., ten Cate, C., 2003. The impact of learning foster species' song on the evolution of specialist avian brood parasitism. Behav. Ecol. 14, 917–923.

Birkhead, T.R., Fletcher, F., 1995. Male phenotype and ejaculate quality in the zebra finch *Taeniopygia guttata*. Proc. R. Soc. Lond. B 262, 329–334.

Birkhead, T.R., Fletcher, F., Pellatt, E.J., 1999a. Nestling diet, secondary sexual traits and fitness in the zebra finch. Proc. R. Soc. Lond. B 266, 385–390.

Birkhead, T.R., Fletcher, F., Pellatt, E.J., 1999b. Sexual selection in the zebra finch *Taeniopygia guttata*: condition, sex traints and immune capacity. Behav. Ecol. Sociobiol. 44, 179–191.

Bischof, H.J., Böhner, J., Sossinka, R., 1981. Influence of external stimuli on the quality of the song of the zebra finch (*Taeniopygia guttata castanotis* Gould). Z. Tierpsychol. 57, 261–267.

Bolhuis, J.J., Gahr, M., 2006. Neural mechanisms of birdsong memory. Nat. Rev. Neurosci. 7, 347–357.

Boogert, N.J., Giraldeau, L.-A., Lefebvre, L., 2008. Song complexity correlates with learning ability in zebra finch males. Anim. Behav. 76, 1735–1741.

Braaten, R.F., Reynolds, K., 1999. Auditory preference for conspecific song in isolation-reared zebra finches. Anim. Behav. 58, 105–111.

Braaten, R.F., Miner, S.S., Cybenko, A.K., 2008. Song recognition memory in juvenile zebra finches: effects of varying the number of presentations of heterospecific and conspecific songs. Behav. Process. 77, 177–183.

Bradbury, J.W., Vehrencamp, S.L., 1998. Principles of Animal Communication. Sinauer, Sunderland.

Brainard, M.S., Doupe, A.J., 2002. What songbirds teach us about learning. Nature 417, 351–358.

Brazas, M.L., Shimizu, T., 2002. Significance of visual cues in choice behavior in the female zebra finch (*Taeniopygia guttata castanotis*). Anim. Cogn. 5, 91–95.

Brumm, H., Slater, P.J.B., 2006. Animals can vary signal amplitude with receiver distance: evidence from zebra finch song. Anim. Behav. 72, 699–705.

Brumm, H., Zollinger, S.A., Slater, P.J.B., 2009. Developmental stress affects song learning but not song complexity and vocal amplitude in zebra finches. Behav. Ecol. Sociobiol. 62, 1387–1395.

Buchanan, K.L., Spencer, K.A., Goldsmith, A.R., Catchpole, C.K., 2003. Song as an honest signal of past developmental stress in the European starling (*Sturnus vulgaris*). Proc. R. Soc. Lond. B 270, 1149–1156.

Burley, N.T., Price, D.K., Zann, R.A., 1992. Bill color, reproduction and condition effects in wild and domesticated zebra finches. Auk 109, 13–23.

Campbell, D.L.M., Hauser, M.E., 2009. Cross-fostering diminishes song discrimination in zebra finches (*Taeniopygia guttata*). Anim. Cogn. 12, 481–490.

Campbell, D.L.M., Shaw, R.C., Hauber, M.E., 2009. The strength of species recognition in captive female zebra finches (*Taeniopygia guttata*): a comparison across estrildid heterospecifics. Ethology 115, 23–32.

Candolin, U., 2003. The use of multiple cues in mate choice. Biol. Rev. 78, 575–595.

Cappendijk, S.L.T., Johnson, F., 2005. Inhibitors of carbohydrate metabolism reduce undirected song production at doses that do not alter food intake in singly housed male zebra finches. Behav. Brain Res. 159, 51–54.

Caryl, P.G., 1976. Sexual behavior in zebra finch *Taeniopygia guttata*—response to familiar and novel partners. Anim. Behav. 24, 93–107.

Caryl, P.G., 1981. The relationship between the motivation of directed and undirected song in the zebra finch. Z. Tierpsychol. 57, 37.

Catchpole, C.K., Slater, P.J.B., 2008. Bird Song: Biological Themes and Variations. Cambridge University Press, Cambridge.

Clayton, N.S., 1988. Song discrimination learning in zebra finches. Anim. Behav. 36, 1016–1024.

Clayton, N.S., 1990a. Assortative mating in zebra finch subspecies *Taeniopygia guttata guttata* and *T. g. castanotis*. Philos. Trans. R. Soc. Lond. B 330, 351–370.

Clayton, N.S., 1990b. The effects of cross-fostering on assortative mating between zebra finch subspecies. Anim. Behav. 40, 1102–1110.

Clayton, N.S., 1990c. Mate choice and pair formation in Timor and Australian mainland zebra finches. Anim. Behav. 39, 474–480.

Clayton, N.S., 1990d. Subspecies recognition and song learning in zebra finches. Anim. Behav. 40, 1009–1017.

Clayton, N.S., Pröve, E., 1989. Song discrimination in female zebra finches and Bengalese finches. Anim. Behav. 38, 352–354.

Clayton, N.S., Hodson, D., Zann, R.A., 1991. Geographic variation in zebra finch subspecies. Emu 91, 2–11.

Collins, S.A., 1994. Male displays: cause or effect of female preference? Anim. Behav. 48, 371–375.

Collins, S.A., 1995. The effect of recent experience on female choice in zebra finches. Anim. Behav. 49, 479–486.

Collins, S.A., 1999. Is female preference for male repertoires due to sensory bias? Proc. R. Soc. Lond. B 266, 2309–2314.

Collins, S.A., ten Cate, C., 1996. Does beak colour affect female preference in zebra finches? Anim. Behav. 52, 105–112.

Collins, S.A., Hubbard, C., Houtman, A.M., 1994. Female mate choice in the zebra finch—the effect of male beak colour and male song. Behav. Ecol. Sociobiol. 35, 21–25.

Cooper, B.G., Goller, F., 2006. Physiological insights into the social-context-dependent changes in the rhythm of the song motor program. J. Neurophysiol. 95, 3798–3809.

Cotton, S., Small, J., Pomiankowski, A., 2006. Sexual selection and condition-dependent mate preferences. Curr. Biol. 16, R755–R765.

Cynx, J., Gell, C., 2004. Social mediation of vocal amplitude in a songbird, *Taeniopygia guttata*. Anim. Behav. 67, 451–455.

Cynx, J., Williams, H., Nottebohm, F., 1990. Timbre discrimination in zebra finch (*Taeniopygia guttata*) song syllables. J. Comp. Psychol. 104, 303–308.

Cynx, J., Bean, N.J., Rossman, I., 2005. Testosterone implants alter the frequency range of zebra finch songs. Horm. Behav. 47, 446–451.

de Kogel, C.H., Prijs, H.J., 1996. Effects of brood size manipulations on sexual attractiveness of offspring in the zebra finch. Anim. Behav. 51, 699–708.

de Kort, S.R., Eldermire, E.R.B., Veldarrama, S., Botero, C.A., Vehrencamp, S.L., 2009. Trill consistency is an age-related assessment signal in banded wrens. Proc. R. Soc. Lond. B 276, 2315–2321.

Dunn, A.M., Zann, R.A., 1996a. Undirected song encourages the breeding female zebra finch to remain in the nest. Ethology 102, 540–548.

Dunn, A.M., Zann, R.A., 1996b. Undirected song in wild zebra finch flocks: contexts and effects of mate removal. Ethology 10, 529–539.

Dunn, A.M., Zann, R.A., 1997. Effects of pair bond and presence of conspecifics on singing in captive zebra finches. Behaviour 134, 127–142.

Eales, L.A., 1987. Song learning in female-raised zebra finches; another look at the sensitive phase. Anim. Behav. 35, 1356–1365.

Ewenson, E.L., Zann, R.A., Flannery, G.R., 2001. Body condition and immune response in wild zebra finches: effects of capture, confinement and captive-rearing. Naturwissenschaften 88, 391–394.

Forstmeier, W., 2004. Female resistance to male seduction in zebra finches. Anim. Behav. 68, 1005–1015.

Forstmeier, W., 2007. Do individual females differ intrinsically in their propensity to engage in extra-pair copulations? PLoS ONE 2, e952.

Forstmeier, W., Birkhead, T.R., 2004. Repeatability of mate choice in the zebra finch: consistency within and between females. Anim. Behav. 68, 1017–1028.

Forstmeier, W., Coltman, D.W., Birkhead, T.R., 2004. Maternal effects influence the sexual behavior of sons and daughters in the zebra finch. Evolution 58, 2574–2583.

Forstmeier, W., Segelbacher, G., Mueller, J.C., Kempenaers, B., 2007. Genetic variation and differentiation in captive and wild zebra finches (*Taeniopygia guttata*). Mol. Ecol. 16, 4039–4050.

Franz, M., Goller, F., 2002. Respiratory units of motor production and song imitation in the zebra finch. J. Neurobiol. 51, 129–141.

Franz, M., Goller, F., 2003. Respiratory patterns and oxygen consumption in singing zebra finches. J. Exp. Biol. 206, 967–978.

Ghirlanda, S., Enquist, M., 2003. A century of generalization. Anim. Behav. 66, 15–36.

Gil, D., 2008. Hormones in avian eggs: physiology, ecology and behavior. Adv. Study Behav. 38, 337–398.

Gil, D., Gahr, M., 2002. The honesty of bird song: multiple constraints for multiple traits. Trends Ecol. Evol. 17, 133–141.

Gil, D., Naguib, M., Riebel, K., Rutstein, A.N., Gahr, M., 2006. Early condition, song learning and the volume of song brain nuclei in the zebra finch (*Taeniopygia guttata*). J. Neurobiol. 66, 1602–1612.

Goller, F., Cooper, B.G., 2004. Peripheral motor dynamics of song production in the zebra finch. Ann. N. Y. Acad. Sci. 1016, 130–152.

Goller, F., Daley, M.A., 2001. Novel motor gestures for phonation during inspiration enhance the acoustic complexity of birdsong. Proc. R. Soc. Lond. B 268, 2301–2305.

Groothuis, T.G.G., Muller, W., von Engelhardt, N., Carere, C., Eising, C., 2005. Maternal hormones as a tool to adjust offspring phenotype in avian species. Neurosci. Biobehav. Rev. 29, 329–352.

Hall, M.L., 2009. A review of vocal duetting in birds. Adv. Stud. Behav. 40, 67–121.

Hara, E., Kubikova, L., Hessler, N.A., Jarvis, E.D., 2009. Assessing visual requirements for social context-dependent activation of the songbird song system. Proc. R. Soc. Lond. B 276, 279–289.

Hauber, M.E., Woolley, S.M.N., Theunissen, F.E., 2007. Experience-dependence of neural responses to social versus isolate conspecific songs in the forebrain of female zebra finches. J. Ornithol. 148, S231–S239.

Helekar, S.A., Marsh, S., Viswanath, N.S., Rosenfield, D.B., 2000. Acoustic pattern variations in the female-directed birdsongs of a colony of laboratory-bred zebra finches. Behav. Process. 49, 99–110.

Holveck, M.-J., Riebel, K., 2007. Preferred songs predict preferred males: consistency and repeatability of zebra finch females across three test contexts. Anim. Behav. 74, 297–309.

Holveck, M.-J., Vieira de Castro, A.C., Lachlan, R.F., ten Cate, C., Riebel, K., 2008. Accuracy of song syntax learning and singing consistency signal early condition in zebra finches. Behav. Ecol. 19, 1267–1281.

Honarmand, M., 2009. Eating like a bird: long term effects of nutritonal stress in zebra finches. [PhD Thesis]. Bielefeld, Germany: University Bielefeld.

Houtman, A.M., 1992. Female zebra finches choose extra-pair copulations with genetically attractive males. Proc. R. Soc. Lond. B 249, 3–6.

Houx, B.B., ten Cate, C., 1999. Song learning from playback in zebra finches: is there an effect of operant contingency? Anim. Behav. 57, 837–845.

Illes, A.E., Yunes-Jimenez, L., 2009. A female songbird out-sings male conspecifics during simulated territorial intrusions. Proc. R. Soc. Lond. B 276, 981–986.

Immelmann, K., 1962. Beiträge zur einer vergleichen Biologie australischer Prachtfinken (Spermestidae). Zool. Jahrb. (Syst.) 90, 1–196.

Immelmann, K., 1969. Song development in the zebra finch and other estrildid finches. In: Hinde, R.A. (Ed.), Bird Vocalizations. Cambridge University Press, Cambridge, pp. 61–74.

Jarvis, E.D., Scharff, C., Grossman, M.R., Ramos, J.A., Nottebohm, F., 1998. For whom the bird sings: context-dependent gene expression. Neuron 21, 775–788.

Johnson, F., Rashotte, M.E., 2002. Food availability but not cold ambient temperature affects undirected singing in adult male zebra finches. Physiol. Behav. 76, 9–20.

Johnson, F., Sonderstrom, K., Whitney, O., 2002. Quantifying song bout production during zebra finch sensory-motor learning suggests a sensitive period for vocal practice. Behav. Brain Res. 131, 57–65.

Johnstone, R.A., 1995. Sexual selection, honest advertisement and the handicap principle— reviewing the evidence. Biol. Rev. 70, 1–65.

Jones, A.E., Slater, P.J.B., 1993. Do young male zebra finches prefer to learn songs that are familiar to females with which they are housed? Anim. Behav. 46, 616–617.

Jones, A.E., ten Cate, C., Slater, P.J.B., 1996. Early experience and plasticity of song in adult male zebra finches (Taeniopygia guttata). J. Comp. Psychol. 110, 354–369.

Kao, M.H., Brainard, M.S., 2006. Lesions of an avian basal ganglia circuit prevent context-dependent changes to song variability. J. Neurophysiol. 96, 1441–1455.

Kilner, R., 1998. Primary and secondary sex ratio manipulation by zebra finches. Anim. Behav. 56, 155–164.

Lachlan, R.F., Slater, P.J.B., 1999. The maintenance of vocal learning by gene-culture interaction: the cultural trap hypothesis. Proc. R. Soc. Lond. B 266, 701–706.

Lachlan, R.F., Verhagen L., Peters S., ten Cate, C., in press. Are there species-universal categories in bird song phonology and syntax? J. Comp. Psychol.

Laland, K.N., 1994. On the evolutionary consequences of sexual imprinting. Evolution 48, 477–489.

Langmore, N.E., 1998. Functions of duet and solo songs of female birds. Trends Ecol. Evol. 13, 136–140.

Lauay, C., Gerlach, N.M., Adkins-Regan, E., Devoogd, T.J., 2004. Female zebra finches require early song exposure to prefer high-quality song as adults. Anim. Behav. 68, 1249–1255.

Lauay, C., Komorowski, R.W., Beaudin, A.E., DeVoogd, T.J., 2005. Adult female and male zebra finches show distinct patterns of spine deficits in an auditory area and in the song system when reared without exposure to normal adult song. J. Comp. Neurol. 487, 119–126.

Leadbeater, E., Goller, F., Riebel, K., 2005. Unusual phonation, covarying song characteristics and song preferences in female zebra finches. Anim. Behav. 70, 909–919.

Leitão, A., Riebel, K., 2003. Are good ornaments bad armaments? Male chaffinch perception of songs with varying flourish length. Anim. Behav. 66, 161–167.

Leitão, A., ten Cate, C., Riebel, K., 2006. Within song complexity in a songbird is meaningful both to male and female receivers. Anim. Behav. 71, 1289–1296.

Lynch, A., 1996. The population memetics of birdsong. In: Kroodsma, D.E., Miller, E.H. (Eds.), Ecology and Evolution of Acoustic Communication in Birds. Comstock Publishing Associates, Ithaca and London, pp. 181–197.

MacDougall-Shackleton, S.A., Ball, G.F., 1999. Comparative studies of sex differences in the song-control system of songbirds. Trends Neurosci. 22, 432–436.

McNamara, J.M., Houston, A.I., 1996. State-dependent life histories. Nature 380, 215–221.

Miller, D.B., 1979a. The acoustic basis for mate recognition by female zebra finches (*Taeniopygia guttata*). Anim. Behav. 27, 376–380.

Miller, D.B., 1979b. Long-term recognition of father's song by female zebra finches. Nature 280, 389–391.

Morris, D., 1954. The reproductive behaviour of the zebra finch (*Poephila guttata*), with special reference to pseudomale behaviour an displacement activities. Behaviour 6, 271–322.

Morrison, R.G., Nottebohm, F., 1993. Role of a telencephalic nucleus in the delayed song learning of socially isolated zebra finches. J. Neurobiol. 24, 1045–1064.

Nagle, L., Kreutzer, M.L., 1997a. Adult female domesticated canaries can modify their song preferences. Can. J. Zool. Rev. Can. Zool. 75, 1346–1350.

Nagle, L., Kreutzer, M.L., 1997b. Song tutoring influences female song preferences in domesticated canaries. Behaviour 134, 89–104.

Naguib, M., Riebel, K., Marzal, A., Gil, D., 2004. Nestling immunocompetence and testosterone covary with brood size in a songbird. Proc. R. Soc. Lond. B 271, 833–838.

Naguib, M., Heim, C., Gil, D., 2008. Early developmental conditions and male attractiveness in zebra finches. Ethology 114, 255–261.

Nelson, D.A., Marler, P., Soha, J.A., Fullerton, A.L., 1997. The timing of song memorization differs in males and females: a new assay for avian vocal learning. Anim. Behav. 54, 587–597.

Neubauer, R.L., 1999. Super-normal length song preferences of female zebra finches (*Taeniopygia guttata*) and a theory of the evolution of bird song. Evol. Ecol. 13, 365–380.

Nowicki, S., Searcy, W.A., 2005. Song and mate choice in birds: how the development of behavior helps us understand function. Auk 122, 1–14.

Nowicki, S., Peters, S., Podos, J., 1998. Song learning, early nutrition and sexual selection in songbirds. Am. Zool. 18, 179–190.

Nowicki, S., Searcy, W.A., Peters, S., 2002. Brain development, song learning and mate choice in birds: a review and experimental test of the "nutritional stress hypothesis" J. Comp. Physiol. A 188, 1003–1014.

Okanoya, K., 2004. Song syntax in bengalese finches: proximate and ultimate analyses. Adv. Study Behav. 34, 297–346.

Olveczky, B.P., Andalman, A.S., Fee, M.S., 2005. Vocal experimentation in the juvenile songbird requires a basal ganglia circuit. PLoS Biol. 3, 902–909.

Price, P.H., 1979. Developmental determinants of structure in zebra finch song. J. Comp. Physiol. Psychol. 93, 260–277.

Pröve, E., 1974. Der Einfluß von Kastration und Testosteronsubstitution auf das Sexualverhalten männlicher Zebrafinken *Taeniopygia guttata castanotis* Gould. J. Ornithol. 115, 338–347.

Pröve, E., 1978. Quantitative Untersuchungen zu Wechselbeziehungen zwischen Balzaktivität und Testosterenontitern bei männlichen Zebrafinken (*Taeniopygia guttata castanotis* Gould). Z. Tierpsychol. 48, 47–67.

Pröve, E., 1981. Der Einfluß sozialer Haltungsbedingungen auf die Balzaktivität und Androgentiter männlicher Zebrafinken (*Taeniopygia guttata castanotis* Gould). In: Verh. Dtsch. Zool. Ges.. Gustav Fischer Verlag, Stuttgart, p. 255.

Pröve, E., Immelmann, K., 1982. Behavioral and hormonal responses of male zebra finches to antiandrogens. Horm. Behav. 16, 121–131.

Pytte, C.L., Suthers, R.A., 2000. Sensitive period for sensorimotor integration during vocal motor learning. J. Neurobiol. 42, 172–189.

Pytte, C.L., Gerson, M., Miller, J., Kirn, J.R., 2007. Increasing stereotypy in adult zebra finch song correlates with a declining rate of adult neurogenesis. Dev. Neurobiol. 67, 1699–1720.

Rashotte, M.E., Sedunova, E.V., Johnson, F., Pastukhov, I.F., 2001. Influence of food and water availability on undirected singing and energetic status in adult male zebra finches (*Taeniopygia guttata*). Physiol. Behav. 74, 533–541.

Ratcliffe, L.M., Boag, P.T., 1987. Effects of color bands on male competition and sexual attractiveness in zebra finches (*Poephila guttata*). Can. J. Zool. Rev. Can. Zool. 65, 333–338.

Riebel, K., 2000. Early experience leads to repeatable preferences for male song in female zebra finches. Proc. R. Soc. Lond. B 267, 2553–2558.

Riebel, K., 2003a. Developmental influences on auditory perception in female zebra finches—is there a sensitive phase for song preference learning? Anim. Biol. 53, 73–87.

Riebel, K., 2003b. The 'mute' sex revisited: vocal production and perception learning in female songbirds. Adv. Study Behav. 33, 49–86.

Riebel, K., Naguib, M., Gil, D. (prov. accept.). Experimental manipulation of the rearing environment influences adult female zebra finch song preferences. Anim. Behav. (prov. acceptance).

Riebel, K., Slater, P.J.B., 1998. Testing female chaffinch song preferences by operant conditioning. Anim. Behav. 56, 1443–1453.

Riebel, K., Smallegange, I.M., 2003. Does zebra finch preference for the (familiar) father's song generalize to the songs of unfamiliar brothers? J. Comp. Psychol. 117, 61–66.

Riebel, K., Smallegange, I.M., Terpstra, N.J., Bolhuis, J.J., 2002. Sexual equality in zebra finch song preference: evidence for a dissociation between song recognition and production learning. Proc. R. Soc. Lond. B 269, 729–733.

Riebel, K., Hall, M.L., Langmore, N.E., 2005. Female songbirds still struggling to be heard. Trends Ecol. Evol. 20, 419–420.

Ritchie, G.R.S., Kirby, S., Hawkey, D.J.C., 2008. Song learning as an indicator mechanism: modelling the developmental stress hypothesis. J. Theor. Biol. 251, 570–583.

Rutstein, A.N., Brazill-Boast, J., Griffith, S.C., 2007. Evaluating mate choice in the zebra finch. Anim. Behav. 74, 1277–1284.

Scharff, C., Nottebohm, F., 1991. A comparative study of the behavioral deficits following lesions of various parts of the zebra finch song system: implications for vocal learning. J. Neurosci. 11, 2896–2913.

Searcy, W.A., 1996. Sound pressure levels and song preferences in female red-winged blackbirds (*Agelaius phoeniceus*) (Aves, Emberizidae). Ethology 102, 187–196.

Searcy, W.A., Yasukawa, K., 1996. Song and female choice. In: Kroodsma, D.E., Miller, E.H. (Eds.), Ecology and Evolution of Acoustic Communication in Birds. Comstock Publishing Associates, Ithaca, pp. 454–473.

Sih, A., Bell, A.M., 2008. Insights for behavioral ecology from behavioral syndromes. Adv. Study Behav. 38, 227–281.

Slater, P.J.B., Clayton, N.S., 1991. Domestication and song learning in zebra finches *Taeniopygia guttata*. Emu 91, 126–128.

Slater, P.J.B., Ince, S.A., 1979. Cultural evolution in chaffinch song. Behaviour 71, 146–166.

Slater, P.J.B., Jones, A.E., 1998. Practice and song development in zebra finches. Behaviour 135, 1125–1136.

Slater, P.J.B., Mann, N.I., 1990. Do male zebra finches learn their fathers' songs? Trends Ecol. Evol. 5, 415–417.

Slater, P.J.B., Eales, L.A., Clayton, N.S., 1988. Song learning in zebra finches: progress and prospects. Adv. Study Behav. 18, 1–34.

Soma, M., Takahasi, M., Ikebuchi, M., Yamada, H., Suzuki, M., Hasegawa, T., et al., 2006. Early rearing conditions affect the development of body size and song in Bengalese finches. Ethology 112, 1071–1078.

Soma, M., Hiraiwa-Hasegawa, M., Okanoya, K., 2009. Early ontogenetic effects on song quality in the Bengalese finch (*Lonchura striata var. domestica*): laying order, sibling competition, and song syntax. Behav. Ecol. Sociobiol. 63, 363–370.

Sossinka, R., 1970. Domestikationserscheinungen beim Zebrafinken. Zool. Jahrb. 97, 455–521.

Sossinka, R., Böhner, J., 1980. Song types in the zebra finch. Z. Tierpsychol. 53, 123–132.

Spencer, K.A., Buchanan, K.L., Goldsmith, A.R., Catchpole, C.K., 2003. Song as an honest signal of developmental stress in the zebra finch (*Taeniopygia guttata*). Horm. Behav. 44, 132–139.

Spencer, K.A., Wimpenny, J.H., Buchanan, K.L., Lovell, P.G., Goldsmith, A.R., Catchpole, C.K., 2005. Developmental stress affects the attractiveness of male song and female choice in the zebra finch (*Taeniopygia guttata*). Behav. Ecol. Sociobiol. 58, 423–428.

Sturdy, C.B., Phillmore, L.S., Weisman, R.G., 1999. Note types, harmonic structure, and note order in the songs of zebra finches (*Taeniopygia guttata*). J. Comp. Psychol. 113, 194–203.

Sturdy, C.B., Phillmore, L.S., Sartor, J.J., Weisman, R.G., 2001. Reduced social contact causes auditory perceptual deficits in zebra finches, *Taeniopygia guttata*. Anim. Behav. 62, 1207–1218.

Svec, L.A., Wade, J., 2009. Estradiol induces region-specific inhibition of ZENK but does not affect the behavioral preference for tutored song in adult female zebra finches. Behav. Brain Res. 199, 298–306.

Swaddle, J.P., Page, L.C., 2007. High levels of environmental noise erode pair preferences in zebra finches: implications for noise pollution. Anim. Behav. 74, 363–368.

Tchernichovski, O., Nottebohm, F., 1998. Social inhibition of song imitation among sibling male zebra finches. Proc. Natl. Acad. Sci. USA 95, 8951–8956.

Tchernichovski, O., Schwabl, H., Nottebohm, F., 1998. Context determines the sex appeal of male zebra finch song. Anim. Behav. 55, 1003–1010.

Tchernichovski, O., Mitra, P.P., Lints, T., Nottebohm, F., 2001. Dynamics of the vocal imitation process: how a zebra finch develops its song. Science 291, 2564–2569.

ten Cate, C., 1982. Behavioural differences between zebra finch and Bengalese finch (foster) parents raising zebra finch offspring. Behaviour 81, 152–172.

ten Cate, C., 1985. Directed song of male zebra finches as a predictor of intra- and inter-specific social behaviour and pair formation. Behav. Process. 10, 369–374.

ten Cate, C., Mug, G., 1984. The development of mate choice in zebra finch females. Behaviour 90, 125–150.

ten Cate, C., Rowe, C., 2007. Biases in signal evolution: learning makes a difference. Trends Ecol. Evol. 22, 380–387.

ten Cate, C., Vos, D.R., Mann, N., 1993. Sexual imprinting and song learning: two of one kind? Neth. J. Zool. 43, 34–45.

ten Cate, C., Verzijden, M.N., Etman, E., 2006. Sexual imprinting can induce sexual preferences for exaggerated parental traits. Curr. Biol. 16, 1128–1132.

Teramitsu, I., White, S.A., 2006. FoxP2 regulation during undirected singing in adult songbirds. J. Neurosci. 26, 7390–7394.

Terpstra, N.J., Bolhuis, J.J., Riebel, K., van der Burg, J.M.M., den Boer-Visser, A.M., 2006. Localized brain activation specific to auditory memory in a female songbird. J. Comp. Neurol. 494, 784–791.

Tomaszycki, M.L., Adkins-Regan, E., 2005. Experimental alteration of male song quality and output affects female mate choice and pair bond formation in zebra finches. Anim. Behav. 70, 785–794.

Tomaszycki, M.L., Sluzas, E.M., Sundberg, K.A., Newman, S.W., DeVoogd, T.J., 2006. Immediate early gene (ZENK) responses to song in juvenile female and male zebra finches: effects of rearing environment. J. Neurobiol. 66, 1175–1182.

Tschirren, B., Rutstein, A.N., Postma, E., Mariette, M., Griffith, S.C., 2009. Short- and long-term consequences of early developmental conditions: a case study on wild and domesticated zebra finches. J. Evol. Biol. 22, 387–395.

Vallet, E., Kreutzer, M., 1995. Female canaries are sexually responsive to special song phrases. Anim. Behav. 49, 1603–1610.

Vallet, E., Beme, I., Kreutzer, M., 1998. Two-note syllables in canary songs elicit high levels of sexual display. Anim. Behav. 55, 291–297.

Verzijden, M.N., Etman, E., van Heijningen, C., van der Linden, M., ten Cate, C., 2007. Song discrimination learning in zebra finches induces highly divergent responses to novel songs. Proc. R. Soc. Lond. B 274, 295–301.

Vignal, C., Bouchut, C., Mathevon, N., 2008. Sound-induced brain activity depends on stimulus subjective salience in female zebra finches. C. R. Biol. 331, 347–356.

Volman, S.F., Khanna, H., 1995. Convergence of untutored song in group-reared zebra finches (*Taeniopygia guttata*). J. Comp. Psychol. 109, 211–221.

Vyas, A., Harding, C., Borg, L., Bogdan, D., 2009. Acoustic characteristics, early experience, and endocrine status interact to modulate female zebra finches' behavioral responses to songs. Horm. Behav. 55, 50–59.

Wade, J., Arnold, A.P., 2004. Sexual differentiation of the zebra finch song system. Behav. Neurobiol. Birdsong 1016, 540–559.

Walters, M.J., Collado, D., Harding, C.F., 1991. Oestrogenic modulation of singing in male zebra finches: differential effects on directed and undirected songs. Anim. Behav. 42, 445–452.

West, M.J., King, A.P., 1988. Female visual displays affect the development of male song in the cowbird. Nature 334, 244–246.

Williams, H., 2001. Choreography of song, dance and beak movements in the zebra finch (*Taeniopygia guttata*). J. Exp. Biol. 204, 3497–3506.

Williams, H., 2004. Birdsong and singing behavior. Ann. N. Y. Acad. Sci. 1016, 1–30.

Williams, H., Staples, K., 1992. Syllable chunking in zebra finch (*Taeniopygia guttata*) song. J. Comp. Psychol. 106, 278–286.

Williams, H., Cynx, J., Nottebohm, F., 1989. Timbre control in zebra finch (*Taeniopygia guttata*) song syllables. J. Comp. Psychol. 103, 366–380.

Williams, H., Kilander, K., Sotanski, M.L., 1993. Untutored song, reproductive success and song learning. Anim. Behav. 45, 695–705.

Williams, H., Connor, D.M., Hill, J.W., 2003. Testosterone decreases the potential for song plasticity in adult male zebra finches. Horm. Behav. 44, 402–412.

Woolley, S.C., Doupe, A.J., 2008. Social context-induced song variation affects female behavior and gene expression. PLoS Biol. 6, 525–537.

Wynn, S.E., Price, T., 1993. Male and female choice in zebra finches. Auk 110, 635–638.

Zann, R., 1993a. Structure, sequence and evolution of song elements in wild Australian zebra finches. Auk 110, 702–715.

Zann, R., 1993b. Variation in song structure within and among populations of Australian zebra finches. Auk 110, 716–726.

Zann, R.A., 1996. The Zebra Finch: A Synthesis of Field and Laboratory Studies. Oxford University Press, Oxford.

Zann, R., Cash, E., 2008. Developmental stress impairs song complexity but not learning accuracy in non-domesticated zebra finches (*Taeniopygia guttata*). Behav. Ecol. Sociobiol. 62, 391–400.

Plasticity of Communication in Nonhuman Primates

CHARLES T. SNOWDON

DEPARTMENT OF PSYCHOLOGY, UNIVERSITY OF WISCONSIN, MADISON,
WISCONSIN 53706, USA

I. INTRODUCTION

Many taxa display impressive communicative abilities. From the wonderfully diverse patterns of song seen across the range of songbirds to the songs of humpback whales and other cetaceans to the highly coordinated duetting of gibbons and siamangs, nature provides us with many examples of impressive vocal complexity and vocal variability. Songbirds also provide us with an important model of vocal development that has been offered as a model for understanding the ontogeny of speech and language (e.g., Marler, 1970). Except for the songs of gibbons and siamangs, nonhuman primates, the closest relatives of humans, appear to have superficially simple vocal repertoires and none of the striking virtuosity of a tiny songbird. There does not appear to be much direct evidence of vocal learning (Hammerschmidt and Fischer, 2008; Janik and Slater, 1997, 2000) although there are many examples suggestive of learning.

Why do most nonhuman primates show so little diversity and complexity in their calls? One potential explanation is that those taxa with the greatest communicative virtuosity and ability to learn signals are species that are highly mobile. Many birds migrate and may return with a very different set of companions than from the previous year and so the ability to adjust vocal patterns to fit in with those of the neighbors may be important. Even nonmigratory birds have the ability to move across several home ranges to find mates and establish territories. Cetaceans and other sea mammals as well as bats can also cover long distances and encounter individuals from many other locations. In contrast, most terrestrial mammals including nonhuman primates do not travel far, with dispersal in nonhuman primates rarely going more than two or three home ranges from the natal group (Pusey and Packer, 1987). Thus nonhuman primates are unlikely to encounter individuals from other populations and this may militate against vocal learning as

239

0065-3454/09 $35.00
DOI: 10.1016/S0065-3454(09)40007-X

adaptive. Another explanation for the complexity of birdsong is its role in sexual selection whereas in many nonhuman primates sexually selected traits are more often represented by morphological patterns.

A significant problem in studying the possibility of vocal learning in nonhuman primates is that few animal ethics committees today would approve the isolation rearing of nonhuman primates that has provided unequivocal evidence of vocal learning in birds. A few early studies suggest that isolate-reared squirrel monkeys (*Saimiri sciureus*) have a complete vocal repertoire along with appropriate usage (Herzog and Hopf, 1983, 1984; Winter et al., 1973) whereas isolate-reared rhesus macaques (*Macaca mulatta*) show only minor deficits in vocal signals (Newman and Symmes, 1974). Different inferential methods are needed to replace isolation rearing in order to determine if primates are capable of vocal learning.

Song is but one of many signals used by birds and relatively little is known about the ontogeny of other signals in birds. In contrast, research on nonhuman primates has focused on multiple signal types that may not meet the strict criteria of Janik and Slater in terms of vocal learning but are, nonetheless, used in complex, subtle, and innovative ways. The more interesting results from nonhuman primates may not be in vocal production, *per se*, but rather in how calls are used and understood by others.

In reviewing developmental studies on nonhuman primates, Seyfarth and Cheney (1997) noted that there was little evidence for plasticity in vocal production in nonhuman primates, but considerable evidence for plasticity in comprehension and in usage of calls. Subsequent research has been expanded on the notions of plasticity in all three dimensions: production, usage, and responses to calls. In this chapter, I will review some of this recent work and in addition look at the role of communication signals in facilitating social learning. Birdsong is socially learned, but do signals themselves influence social learning in primate species?

II. Plasticity of Production

Janik and Slater (2000) proposed a strict definition of production learning that requires a demonstration that vocal structure is changed as a result of social interaction with others. Many of the examples that follow cannot be explained in terms of the strong inference methods required to demonstrate that call structures are changed only through direct contact with others. Hence, I will use the term "plasticity" to indicate evidence of change that appears to be possibly due to social interactions but where strong evidence for vocal learning is not available.

A. POPULATION DIFFERENCES

Contrary to strong views that primate vocal structures are basically hard wired and consistent within a species, there are several examples of signals that show systematic variation in different populations. Green (1975) first reported that different populations of Japanese macaques (*Macaca fuscata*) produced different variations of food vocalizations when a caretaker approached to provision them. He, thus, hypothesized that these population-specific calls came about through conditioning by caretakers, but the same calls were heard in unprovisioned groups so the argument for learning was hypothetical. Masataka (1992) conditioned two infant Japanese macaque females to respond to their names. Each time they gave a vocal response to a human calling their name the monkeys received a food reward. Over a 4-week training period, the monkeys increased their rate of vocalization in response to hearing their names and each monkey produced a coo call variant that was idiosyncratic to each individual, suggesting conditioning of vocal production and the ability of monkeys to alter vocal structure within the parameters of a call already in their repertoire.

In other studies on Japanese macaques, Tanaka et al. (2006) described the differences in the structure of coo calls of two populations that had arisen from the same population but had been separated for more than 30 years. Coo structures differed significantly at all ages except for very young animals, suggesting that the "dialects" of the two populations were learned early in life.

Different populations of wild chimpanzees (*Pan troglodytes*) have different versions of pant-hoots, a long distance vocalization. The first reports illustrated differences in structure between chimpanzees at Gombe National Park and those at Mahale Mountains National Park, both in Tanzania (Mitani and Brandt, 1994; Mitani et al., 1992), although the Gombe calls were not recorded contemporaneously with those at Mahale, so differences may represent historic drift. Mitani et al. (1999) compared contemporaneous recordings made at Mahale and Kibale National Park in Uganda and found quantitative differences in structure between the two populations. They suggested that these were due to genetic drift, differences in habitat acoustics, or ambient noise spectra, but did not do simultaneous measurements of habitat acoustics or ambient noise spectra.

Marshall et al. (1999) found significant differences in pant-hoot structure between two captive populations of chimpanzees in the United States and argued that since the males within each group had come from different origins, the common theme to each group must have been due to learning after the males joined each group to allow the development of group-specific variants.

Crockford et al. (2004) reported differences in pant-hoot structure in males from three contiguous populations of chimpanzees in Tai Forest, Ivory Coast using discriminant function analysis. They found no differences between these contiguous populations and a fourth distant population, suggesting that vocal divergence may be important to distinguish local populations from each other. They also reported no correlation between acoustic differences and genetic differences in pairs of animals. They suggested that there should be little variation in habitat among the areas of the three populations, but they did not directly evaluate habitat acoustics. Based on the lack of relationship of acoustic variation and genetic variation and the assumption of no differences in habitat acoustics, they suggested that the differences in pant-hoot structure must be due to social learning.

Fischer et al. (1998) recorded shrill bark vocalizations of two populations of captive Barbary macaques (*Macaca sylvanus*) to the presence of a dog and reported distinct population differences in the structure of shrill barks on the basis of discriminant function analysis. They also played back calls of the same population and calls of the other population to both and found a slight (ca. 1 s), but significant, increase in looking time to calls from the other population. Both groups had been from the same founder population and the study was done approximately 20 years after each group had been established, making it unlikely that the differences were genetic.

De la Torre and Snowdon (2009) studied five populations of the pygmy marmoset (*Callithrix (Cebuella) pygmaea*) in Ecuador. Pygmy marmosets have two types of vocalizations exchanged between group members at close distances, the Trill and the J-call. The five populations spanned an east–west transect of about 300 km and a north–south transect of about 100 km, De la Torre and Snowdon (2009) studied the adult male and female from two to three separate groups and found that within each population there were significant individual differences. However, after controlling for individual variation, there were clear differences in both the trill and the J-call across populations using both discriminant function analyses and testing individual call variables. For trills, rate of frequency modulation, minimum frequency, and call duration were the main contributors to the discriminant analysis and calls were classified correctly 71.4 % of the cases compared with an expected value of 20%. For J-calls, maximum frequency and duration were the main variables with 78.6% of cases being correctly classified. Based on the analyses of individual variables, each population differed from each other population on at least one acoustic variable.

De la Torre and Snowdon (in preparation) also measured the spectrum of ambient noise and the degree of reverberation in each habitat and found significant differences between habitats. Whereas some of the acoustic differences in call structure could be interpreted as adaptations to local acoustic environment, other differences could not be explained on the basis of habitat differences. Because rivers serves as barriers to dispersal in the Amazon, it is possible that the differences are due to genetic drift leading to population differences, but as captive pygmy marmosets quickly change vocal structure in response to social changes (Elowson and Snowdon, 1994; Snowdon and Elowson, 1999), we cannot rule out the possibility of some form of vocal learning.

Interestingly, we found parallel differences in the same five populations in the tree species used for exudates feeding. Each population had a preferred tree species, but the preferences were not based on the relative abundance of the preferred tree species in that habitat (Yepez et al., 2005), suggesting that the five different populations vary not only in vocal structure but in foraging choices as well.

In summary, there are some examples of population differences in vocal structure across a broad taxonomic range of primates. However, only in Japanese macaques there is clear experimental evidence of vocal change at an individual level. All other claims for vocal learning are at present inferential and in the absence of genetic analyses and careful measurements of habitat acoustics, current field data do not support that vocal learning occurs using the criteria of Janik and Slater (2000).

B. Environmental Influences

Ey et al. (2009) studied grunt vocalizations of wild olive baboons in a forest and in an open habitat and found that grunts given in the forest population were longer and had a lower fundamental frequency and/or lower emphasized harmonic than the baboons in the open habitat as expected if vocal structure was adapted to habitat acoustics. As predicted, forest-living baboons also produced contact calls at a higher rate than those in an open habitat.

The Lombard effect is the increase in amplitude of speech that occurs when background ambient noise is increased. Two Old World monkeys, a male long-tailed macaque (*Macaca fascicularis*) and a female pig-tailed macaque (*Macaca nemestrina*) increased the amplitude of their vocalizations when presented with increased levels of ambient noise in the range of their own vocalizations (masking). They showed no change in amplitude to increases in high-frequency ambient noise (nonmasking). Amplitude of vocalizations tended to increase with increased amplitude of masking noise (Sinnott et al., 1975). Common marmosets (*Callithrix jacchus*) also increased the amplitude of their twitter calls with increasing amplitude of ambient noise and they also increased the duration of individual units within their twitter calls (Brumm et al., 2004). Using a different methodology involving a burst of white noise in the middle of an on-going long call in cotton-top tamarins (*Saguinus oedipus*), Miller et al. (2003) found that this noise would interrupt the production of long calls with the call terminating after completion of the syllable that was interrupted. Egnor et al. (2006) expanded on this paradigm and found that white noise bursts during long call production lead to shorter notes and calls with higher amplitude and longer interpulse intervals consistent with the idea that tamarins can adjust calling facultatively to environmental noise. Both the Lombard effect and the truncation of a call in response to a burst of white noise imply that these nonhuman primates must have some degree of control over the structure of their vocalizations. Vocalizations are not simply due to fixed motor control systems.

C. Social Influences

Another approach to understanding variation in primate communication involves natural or experimental changes in social status or social housing of animals. Fischer et al. (2004) studied the "wahoo" calls of wild baboons (*Papio cynocephalus ursinus*) in Botswana. Among other contexts, wahoos are given in aggressive interactions between males. High ranking males produce wahoos at higher rates and for longer duration bouts than subordinate males, and call structure changes with rank as well. Both fundamental frequency and call duration are positively correlated with male rank. The finding of higher fundamental frequency with increased rank is different from the expectation of studies in other species that low-frequency calls are markers of dominance. More energy may be required to sustain a higher pitched call over the longer bouts of dominant males and this may be an honest indicator of male quality. In support of this, Fischer et al. (2004) found that fundamental frequency of wahoos decreased as males aged and lost dominance status. However, neither dominance nor higher pitched wahoos are age-determined since subordinate males of the same age as dominants did not have increased fundamental frequencies. This study suggests that male baboons can manipulate the fundamental frequency of wahoos to reflect their dominance status.

In cotton-top tamarins, Roush and Snowdon (1999) noted that food-associated calls of young monkeys were not as consistent and well-formed as those of breeding adults and that young monkeys also inserted many other call types into feeding bouts. Curiously, there appeared to be no maturation of call structure over a broad age range with even postpubertal monkeys still producing immature forms of food calls. Since tamarins are cooperative breeders with older individuals often caring for infants rather than breeding themselves, one hypothesis is that older individuals use infant versions of food vocalizations to communicate a subordinate status to reproductively dominant animals. If this hypothesis is true, then when the social status of tamarins is changed, call structure should change as well. Postpubertal, sexually mature animals were recorded in feeding contexts in their natal groups and then they were paired and housed in a different colony room. Within 3 weeks of pairing, tamarins no longer produced other forms of calls when feeding and within 6 weeks they were producing adult-typical forms of food calls. Different animals were paired at different ages so the results are not due to age, but must be related to change in social status.

Changing the social group of animals and evaluating vocal behavior before and after the social change has been an effective experimental method for showing vocal plasticity (e.g., Boughman, 1998 in greater spear-nosed bats). A few studies on marmosets have demonstrated vocal plasticity. Elowson and Snowdon (1994) used the opportunity of bringing two different colonies of pygmy marmosets together in one colony room to examine the structures of trill vocalization before and after the change. Groups within each colony remained in the same social groups as before; the only difference was that two previously unfamiliar groups were housed in the same space. Animals from both populations increased the bandwidth and peak frequency over the first 10 weeks after the animals were housed in the same room. Subsequently, Snowdon and Elowson (1999) measured parameters of trills in individual marmosets before pairing with a new mate, during the first 6 weeks after pairing, and 3 years later. In the pairs with individuals that differed significantly prior to pairing, there were significant changes in call structure in at least one of the animals leading to a convergence in call structure between pair members. Although many of the acoustic parameters had changed over the course of 3 years, the pairs still maintained very similar call structure.

In a similar study on Wied's black tufted-ear marmosets (*Callithrix kuhlii*), Ruckstalis et al. (2003) found stability in phee call structure over several weeks of baseline, but when some monkeys were moved and housed adjacent to novel conspecifics, the discriminant function that had success-fully identified each individual was no longer accurate, suggesting that the monkeys that had been moved had significantly altered the structure of their phees. In contrast, for monkeys that remained in a stable social environment, the discriminant functions that had successfully assigned calls to individuals in the baseline condition were still successful in assigning calls recorded after the baseline to appropriate individuals.

Mitani and Gros-Louis (1998) found convergence in the structure of chimpanzee pant-hoot vocalizations when they were given in choruses and by examining the structures of calls given alone and in choruses, they concluded that chimpanzees actively altered the structure of their calls to accommodate the calls of the individual(s) with which they were currently chorusing.

Lemasson and colleagues (Lemasson and Hausberger, 2004; Lemasson et al., 2005) have described similarities in calls of individual captive Campbell's monkeys (*Cercopithecus campbelli*) that were closely affiliated. Call structure changed over time and was especially labile when social disruptions occurred. Different captive groups had different call variants suggesting group-specific call variants. Japanese macaques also appeared to match the acoustic features of the coo vocalizations of familiar group members when these were played back, suggesting that Japanese macaques could adjust the fine structure of their calls to match those of the specific caller they heard (Sugiura, 1998). Koda (2004) reported that Japanese monkeys altered the structure of coo calls depending on whether the first call in a sequence elicits a response from others. When a call fails to elicit a response, the second call is higher in pitch and has a longer duration. In playback studies, monkeys responded more often to the playback of the second call than to the first suggesting that monkeys adjust their call structure to increase the likelihood of response by others.

In summary, with the precision of digital analysis methods that can detect subtle changes in vocal structure, it is clear that vocalizations can change within individual monkeys as a function of changes in social status or social companions in both wild and captive populations. Furthermore, the changes can take place very quickly (within a period of a few minutes in short-term vocal accommodation or over a few weeks in terms of developing longer term social relationships) and vocalizations also show drift over time. Primate vocalizations are not as precise and stereotyped as once thought and manipulation of social status or social partners is a valuable experimental method for studying vocal plasticity.

D.   DEVELOPMENTAL INFLUENCES

Early isolation-rearing studies of squirrel monkeys found no impairments in vocal production (Winter et al., 1973) and even though Newman and Symmes (1974) noted pathologies in the vocalizations of isolate-reared rhesus macaques, these were found in only one type of vocalization, the coo. Hybridization between two species of squirrel monkeys with two very different forms of isolation calls led to offspring displaying the form of isolation peep appropriate for their mothers (Newman and Symmes, 1982). Studies of hybrid gibbons (Geissmann, 1984) found that hybrid songs had elements of calls of each parent. Since mothers are the only caretakers of squirrel monkeys and both parents stay together during the development of gibbons, the apparent genetic results from hybridization may be due to the experience an infant gains from hearing its parent(s).

One way of avoiding this confounding variable is to cross-foster animals between species. Thus, an infant of one species will be exposed only to the signals of its foster parent. When Japanese macaques were cross-fostered to rhesus macaques and vice versa, there was no evidence that the fostered infants showed any ability to acquire the calls of their foster parents indicating no social influence on vocal production (Owren et al., 1993). These results do not conflict with those of Sugiura (1998) previously described. Although many species of nonhuman primates appear capable of making minor changes in call structure in response to social companions, they do not appear to have the capacity to learn to produce calls of another species.

Several studies have recorded calls from monkeys across early development. Lieblich et al. (1980) followed the development of isolation peeps in infant squirrel monkeys and found that the species-typical structure was present in the earliest recordings with the only changes being an increase in call duration which could be related to physical maturation. Similarly, Hammerschmidt et al. (2000) recorded coo vocalizations from rhesus macaque infants over the first 5 months and found that adult-like structure was present at the first week with the only changes being reduced fundamental frequency and decreased variability in calls. In contrast to the earlier results of Newman and Symmes (1974), Hammerschmidt et al. (2000) found no differences in structure between mother-reared and peer-reared monkeys.

Vervet monkeys (*Chlorocebus pygerythrops* formerly *Cercopithecus aethiops*) have a suite of alarm calls specific to different types of predators and young monkeys produce alarm calls that are very similar to those produced by adults, but for grunts, a series of calls involved in social interactions, young vervet monkeys did not display adult structure until adolescence (Seyfarth and Cheney, 1986).

Stephan and Zuberbühler (2008) compared a population of Diana monkeys exposed to leopard predation with a population that did not have leopards as predators. Both populations produced similar calls to playback of leopard growls and leopard alarm calls of other Diana monkeys responding to leopards, suggesting an innate response to cues associated with leopards. However, alarms from the leopard-free population were acoustically more complex and also were used in response to general disturbance compared with the population that had leopards present. This suggests some ontogenetic modification of alarm call structure.

Marmosets and tamarins appear to develop their call repertoires more slowly. Cotton-top tamarins have eight chirp-like vocalizations that are each specific to a different context (mobbing, alarm, food, territorial defense, cohesion; Cleveland and Snowdon, 1982). Castro and Snowdon (2000) experimentally induced several of these chirp types in adult animals. They subsequently did the same manipulations on groups with infants present over the first 5 months of infant development. Although infants produced sounds that could be identified as chirps, they typically produced them in series of two or three calls with descending pitch. In contrast, adult chirps were not produced in series and the call structure was precise and appropriate for the experimental manipulation. It is possible that infants do not have the vocal control to allow them to produce calls with the same precision as adults, but there may also be an interaction with maturation of physical control and learning to know which specific structures to use in specific contexts. In a detailed study of the ontogeny two of the chirp types (C and D chirps) used in feeding contexts, Roush and Snowdon (1994) found that calls of immature animals were consistently less "well-formed" than adult chirps.

The pygmy marmoset is unusual among nonhuman primates in that infants engage in long repetitive bouts of vocalization that can go for minutes (Elowson et al., 1998). These bouts contain many of the vocalizations that are part of the adult repertoire, but the same call types are repeated frequently and different call types are temporally associated that in adults would be seen in specific and different contexts. Thus, an infant might produce two or three contact calls followed immediately by some threat vocalizations followed by some alarm calls and so on. This "babbling" is highly energetic with infants producing up to three calls per second and continuing for as long as 6 min. Most of the call structures were similar to those seen in the adult repertoire with only 2 of 16 call types being unique to infants. This vocal activity is superficially similar to the subsong and plastic song of birds which has been labeled as analogous to human babbling. But pygmy marmosets show three important exceptions. Unlike birds, pygmy marmosets begin their vocal activity as infants and it is not a function of puberty. Both male and female marmosets engage in this behavior whereas in many songbirds only the male sings. Finally, song is but one part of the vocal repertoire of birds whereas marmosets produce 70% of adult call types in their "babbling" vocalizations. For these reasons, this complex vocal behavior of pygmy marmosets may be more relevant than birdsong as a model of human vocal development. However, it is unclear why this complex vocal behavior is seen only in pygmy marmosets. The author has observed similar behavior in wild infant common marmosets (unpublished observations).

What are the possible functions of this complex infant vocal behavior? It is not an artifact of captivity since we have observed it in the field (De la Torre and Snowdon, unpublished observations) where infant vocalizations can help us to locate a group. The behavior is energetically costly to infants and by making their location easily identified can also increase vulnerability to predators. The vocal behavior does draws the attention of adults and "babbling" infants are more likely to be subsequently involved in social interactions than a quiet infant (Elowson et al., 1998). Thus, this complex vocal behavior may lead to parental contact much as crying does for human infants and the vigor of calling may communicate to parents about the health of offspring and guide parental investment (Snowdon and Elowson, 2001).

But is there any effect of this babbling behavior on vocal development? Since subsong and plastic song seem to be critical to a bird developing a normal adult song, and babbling appears important in human vocal development, could the complex vocal behavior of young pygmy marmosets also be involved in developing adult vocal skills? As infant pygmy marmosets mature, they showed a decrease in bout length, but continued to show babbling behavior through puberty. There was a reduced frequency of infant vocal types and adult-variant calls with a corresponding increase in calls that matched adult acoustic parameters. Peripubertal monkeys acquired the long call which had not been observed in any of the infant babbling bouts (Snowdon and Elowson, 2001). We selected the call type most commonly found in babbling and most commonly used by adult marmosets, the trill, and examined changes in structure with age and as a function of variation in infant babbling. Infants that exhibited greatest diversity of calls in infancy had better formed trills in the fifth month than infants with less call diversity in their bouts ($R_S = 0.714$) and infants that produced a greater number of calls when babbling displayed a greater change in trill structure ($R_S = 0.857$). Thus, the diversity and amount of vocal activity in infancy predicted the quality and amount of change in trill structure in 5-month-old marmosets.

Trill structure did not reach final form until adulthood. Infant trills were shorter, more asymmetric in structure and rarely displayed a constant frequency range within the call. Prepubertal juveniles produced calls that were of normal duration and had a constant center frequency, but they continued to produce asymmetric calls (Fig. 1, Snowdon and Elowson, 2001). These results suggest that different components of adult call structure appear at different developmental ages and thus could be due to maturation of motor control systems. At the same time, there is also an apparent effect of vocal practice on the rate at which marmosets develop adult features of trills.

In summary, the preponderance of evidence supports the notion that vocal learning is not involved in vocal production of nonhuman primates. At the same time, it is also clear that infant primates are not born with the ability to produce the complete adult vocal repertoire. In many species,

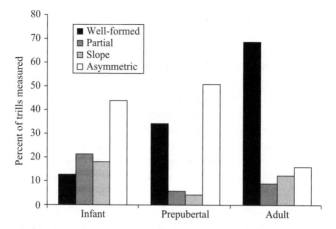

FIG. 1. Proportion of trills that are well-formed, partial (short duration), sloped (central frequency increasing or decreasing), or asymmetric (variable bandwidth) in pygmy marmosets studied in infant, prepubert, and adult stages. The percentage of well-formed trills increased significantly over age (Freidman Anova, $P = 0.005$), partial trills decreased from infant to prepubertal (Friedman Anova, $P = 0.005$) and the percentage of asymmetric trills decreased significantly between infant and prepubertal levels to adult levels (Friedman Anova, $P < 0.01$). (Adapted from Snowdon and Elowson, 2001.)

physical maturation leading to lower fundamental frequency and to improved breath control to produce longer vocalizations and greater motor control could account for the variation in structure that is seen developmentally. Vocal practice may be important in developing motor skills. At the same time, some calls such as the long call of pygmy marmosets, used mainly in territorial interactions do not appear until relatively late in development meaning either that the appropriate contexts for the calls are not experienced by young monkeys or that these calls are acquired late in development.

E. SUMMARY

The structural plasticity of primate vocalizations is much less than that found in bird song. Nonetheless, primates do not show completely stereotyped vocalizations, but are able to adjust subtle aspects of call structure to different social and environmental circumstances and group-typical and pair-typical call structures do emerge. In some cases, conditioning can change the structure of calls. Developmental studies suggest that call structure undergoes modification with practice and physical maturation being the most likely mechanisms. The overall result is that despite little direct evidence of vocal learning, nonhuman primates do exhibit some ability to control vocal production and that practice and maturation may both be critical in vocal ontogeny.

III. PLASTICITY IN USAGE

A. DEVELOPMENTAL INFLUENCES

We next look at plasticity in how calls are used by primates, where there is much more evidence of flexibility in communication. Many primates are able to use their signals in a variety of contexts, suggesting that there is not a one-to-one mapping between a call and how it is used. However, early results on development suggested that call usage might be innate. Herzog and Hopf (1984) reported that isolate-reared squirrel monkeys produced alarm vocalizations when first presented with a naturally threatening stimulus. Miller (1967) also reported that isolate-reared rhesus macaques in a fear conditioning paradigm produced facial expressions to a stimulus predicting a shock that allowed a typically reared monkey to respond to avoid the shock to both animals. Seyfarth and Cheney (1986) reported that young vervet monkeys produced appropriate type of predator alarm calls in generally appropriate contexts (i.e., an "eagle" alarm was restricted to some aerial stimulus such as a bird of any type or a leaf falling from a tree and a "snake" alarm to objects on the ground). Young vervet monkeys eventually became very precise in their use of specific predator alarms to specific predators, but even in infancy they appeared to have a general concept of what calls should be used in what contexts.

In contrast to these results, Koda et al. (2008) studied two different populations of Japanese macaques that lived in habitats differing in visibility. Call rates during feeding and moving were greater in adults in the visually restricted habitat compared to adults in the more open habitat and this difference in call rate emerged developmentally, suggesting the authors that some learning process is involved in call usage.

Young captive cotton-top tamarins do not appear to distinguish between contexts in call usage. As noted earlier, Castro and Snowdon (2000) developed experimental manipulations to elicit specific chirp variants from adults. When the same manipulations were presented to families over the first 5 months of infant life, the most common reaction from infants was to produce a sequence of chirps that was not related in structure to the forms adults used. Some, but not all, infants did produce an appropriate form of chirp on at least one trial over the 5 months, but no one chirp type was produced in the appropriate context by all infants, and no single infant produced each of the five chirp types that could be elicited in adults. Furthermore, if an infant did produce an appropriate chirp in an appropriate context, it was unlikely to produce that chirp again in the same context. The one exception was a chirp type used in feeding and, as we will see later, adults provide infants with considerable experience with these call types during food transfers. Interestingly, however, the infants inhibited calling in contexts eliciting alarm and mobbing. Possibly alarm, mobbing, and territorial calls are dangerous for infants to practice in contrast to food and affiliative calls. Thus, captive infant tamarins do not appear to be able to use calls in appropriate contexts.

As noted earlier in the description of babbling in pygmy marmosets, a characteristic of this vocal behavior was the juxtaposition of calls used by adults in a wide variety of contexts, suggesting that the connection between context and call type is something that both tamarins and marmosets need to acquire through some development process. In addition, we noted in both captivity (Snowdon and Elowson, 2001) and in the wild (de la Torre, unpublished observations) that adult marmosets occasionally showed babbling behavior, typically in the context of a subordinate reacting to aggressive behavior from another. Thus, babbling behavior is not restricted to infants but can be used by adults in response to conspecific aggression.

B. AUDIENCE EFFECTS AND CALL INHIBITION

If primates modify their vocalizations as a function of whether or not other individuals or which specific individuals are present, then the audience is influencing call usage. The ability of animals to inhibit call production is another index of vocal control. Several examples show that primates are sensitive to the audience they have.

Wich and de Vries (2006) found that Thomas langur males only gave alarm calls when other group members were present, and that a male initiating alarm calling continued to call until all other group members in his group had given at least one alarm call, suggesting that the initiating male was keeping track of each individual in the group. Papworth et al. (2008) found that blue monkeys produced significantly more eagle alarm calls (hacks) in response to playbacks when other group members were close to the playback location, than when they were further away, suggesting sensitivity to the danger experienced by other group members.

Slocombe and Zuberbühler (2007) found that the structure of chimpanzee agonistic screams varied as a function of the severity of aggression received by the caller, but victims produced scream structures that exaggerated the degree of aggression they had experienced when there was at least one group member present that was of higher rank than the aggressor.

Zuberbühler et al. (1999) have shown that Diana monkeys (*Cercopithecus diana*) have specific alarm calls for aerial predators and for leopards, but they do not vocalize when they hear chimpanzees. Leopard alarm calls deter leopards from attacking, but a group of chimpanzees will use the calls of Diana monkeys to localize them and attack. Thus, inhibition of calling to predators is adaptive with certain predators.

Food-associated vocalizations have been a curious category of communication. What does it benefit an animal to communicate when it has found food, when that signal can recruit others to compete over food? Hauser and Wrangham (1987) studied food calls in chimpanzees in response to varying amounts of food and found that chimpanzees did not respond to small amounts of food, but only vocalized when large amounts of food were available. Subsequently, Hauser et al. (1993) presented chimpanzees with a watermelon cut into several pieces versus a single, intact watermelon and found food-related vocalizations only to the multiple pieces of melon. These results suggest that chimpanzees can control the production of food vocalizations according to whether the resource can be shared or not.

Rhesus macaques also produce food-related vocalizations and here there is evidence of punishment of group members that fail to give food calls when discovering food (Hauser, 1992). Interestingly, punishment is reserved for group members that fail to call and not for solitary animals that do not belong to a group.

Pollick et al. (2005) found that brown capuchin monkeys were more likely to give food vocalizations when other group members were present. Subordinate monkeys were more likely to call than dominants, but as audience size increased, even dominant monkeys gave food calls.

Female chimpanzees in Budongo Forest in Uganda often give copulation calls while mating, but the production of calls is not correlated with female reproductive cycle but rather with having a high ranking male as a partner. Interestingly, females inhibited copulation calls if higher ranking females were nearby, indicating an ability to control calling as a function of social environment (Townsend et al., 2008).

In contrast to these studies, Roush and Snowdon (2000) failed to find any audience effects in food calling in cotton-top tamarins. Pairs of tamarins were separated from their mates and were either in visual contact or visually isolated. Rates of food calling did not differ as a function of whether the mate was visible or not.

C. CAPTIVITY AS NOVEL ECOLOGICAL NICHE

Captivity can be conceptualized as a novel ecological niche and can be used to ask questions about flexibility of usage. Studies that we have done on cotton-top tamarins have indicated that they show little initial alarm response to the presentation of a large boa constrictor, which is a natural predator (Campbell and Snowdon, 2009; Hayes and Snowdon, 1990). Captive tamarins never display mobbing responses to a live snake in their cage (although wild tamarins have been observed to mob snakes), and we have been unable to condition a fear response to snakes using playbacks of mobbing vocalizations (Campbell and Snowdon, 2009). Captive-reared tamarins react no differently to a live snake than they do to a laboratory rat, reacting to both with curiosity and mild arousal. In contrast, captive tamarins do react with mobbing behavior to caretakers dressed in garb to capture monkeys and, curiously, to a bright blue duster used in cage cleaning (Campbell and Snowdon, 2007) and to caretakers wearing unfamiliar shoes (Neuburg and Snowdon, unpublished data). For captive tamarins, mobbing vocalizations and mobbing behavior was elicited not by natural predators but by unfamiliar and unusual objects in their captive environment. These objects may represent danger in the context of captivity and hence ecologically appropriate for mobbing calls. In another study, we adulterated a familiar, highly preferred food with white pepper and animals that tasted this adulterated food for the first time produced alarm calls, a totally novel context from even their prior captive experience (Snowdon and Boe, 2003).

D. CALL VARIATION RELATED TO DISTANCE

Captivity is not the only place where one can see flexibility in usage. Pygmy marmosets have four different call types that appear to be used in contexts involving maintaining vocal contact with group members (quiet trill, trill, J-call, and long call from Pola and Snowdon, 1975). Two separate studies in the Western Amazon have shown that monkeys use different forms of these vocalizations as a function of how far apart they are from other conspecifics. In the first study, done in Peru, Snowdon and Hodun (1981) argued on the basis of acoustic cues for sound localization that quiet trills would be most difficult to localize, and J-calls had many more cues for sound localization. If marmosets could systematically vary call structure according to distance from others, then they would be expected to use more cryptic calls when close to other animals and more easily detected calls when they were farther apart. Snowdon and Hodun found that most quiet trills were given when animals were within 5 m of each other, other trills at distances up to 15 m and J-calls were exclusively used beyond 15 m.

In a follow-up and extension, de la Torre and Snowdon (2002) studied marmosets in Ecuador and compared trills, J-calls, and long calls. They studied call degradation as a function of habitat and found that trills degraded rapidly (due to both reverberation that made distinction of temporal features difficult as well as decrease of high-frequency components due to excess attenuation) whereas the long call was less affected over the same distances. They also recorded the distance between animals when each call type was given and found that most trills were given within 10 m of another animal, J-calls within the range of 10–20 m, and long calls given at distance of 15 m or more from the caller (Fig. 2). Both studies also measured the ambient noise spectrum and found that most of the acoustic energy was at frequencies above most of the ambient noise. Thus, marmosets in the wild appear to use different call types flexibly adjusting call type to the distance between themselves and their neighbors.

E. FOOD-RELATED VOCALIZATIONS

Food-related calls are not automatically produced in response to food. In cotton-top tamarins, the rate of food calling was proportional to the preference that an individual had for a particular food type (Elowson et al., 1991). Tamarins produced more food calls to foods that the individuals

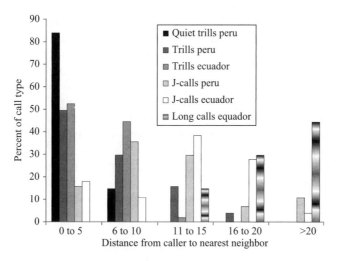

FIG. 2. Call types produced by pygmy marmosets as a function of distances (m) from nearest neighbors. (Peru data adapted from Snowdon and Hodun, 1981; Ecuador data adapted from de la Torre and Snowdon, 2002.)

preferred most. Clay and Zuberbühler (2009) found that bonobos produce five different call types during interactions with food and these call types are produced in long sequences. The authors established individual food preferences for 10 individuals and, like Elowson et al. (1991), found that call types conveyed information about each individual's food preferences.

Slocombe and Zuberbühler (2005, 2006) showed that chimpanzees produce "rough grunts" in feeding contexts. Variants of these grunts reliably corresponded to differences in food quality and in playback experiments, chimpanzees responded readily to a location with high-quality food after playbacks of grunts given to it than to grunts indicating a low-quality food. These results from captive chimpanzees were not replicated in analyses of calls from wild chimpanzees, suggesting that the differentiation of food calls to different quality foods may be an adaption to the ecology of captivity.

Chapman and Lefebvre (1990) studied wild spider monkeys (*Ateles* sp.) and also found that food-related calls were given only at food patches with high-quality fruit. The production of food calls appears to be paradoxical in the context of primates feeding on live prey that might be able to hear the calls and avoid predation. We found that pygmy marmosets, like tamarins chimpanzees, bonobos, and spider monkeys, tended to produce more food calls with more preferred foods. However, when live prey was presented the animals were silent (Snowdon, unpublished observations). Gros-Louis (2004) reported a similar result for wild white-faced capuchin monkeys (*Cebus capucinus*) where calls were produced to fruits but not to animate prey. These examples of food calling indicate contextual influences on call usage. Food calls are not given at all times when food is available but rather calling is related to both food quality and to whether it is animate or not.

Addington (1998) studied vocalizations in the context of feeding in captive pygmy marmosets and identified a call that occurred regularly in feeding contexts. However, some individuals combined the food call with the long call used in long distance communication. In almost every case when the two vocalizations occurred together as a single call, the caller was an unmated animal. The function of the combined call might be to communicate to a potential mate that the caller had sharable food. For the current purposes, the example serves to illustrate the ability of monkeys to create novel call combinations.

F. SUMMARY

Many nonhuman primates display plasticity in how they use vocalizations. Although there is some evidence that isolate-reared animals or very young wild animals appear to use calls in generally appropriate contexts. Other species appear to acquire appropriate usage of calls over a relatively long developmental period and call usage may be related to social status. Captive animals provide an interesting example of how communication is affected in a novel ecological niche and many animals respond to the features of captive environments in ecologically appropriate ways that are unrelated to natural conditions. Monkeys can adjust call structure to the distance from other conspecifics, adding features to make calls more detectable as distance between caller and other conpecifics increases. Many species produce calls in feeding contexts but call rate is adjusted to food quality and quantity and also whether foods are animate or inanimate. All of these examples support the notion of signal usage as highly variable and plastic in many species of nonhuman primates.

IV. PLASTICITY IN COMPREHENSION

It is in how nonhuman primates comprehend or respond to signals when the clearest evidence of plasticity in communication occurs with examples of cross-species comprehension of signals and signals having differential effects as a result of differing social status or life history.

A. DEVELOPMENT

As with each of the previous sections, early studies suggest that isolation rearing has a major influence on how monkeys interpret responses. The data are conflicting. Herzog and Hopf (1983, 1984) argued that isolate-reared squirrel monkeys responded appropriately to playbacks of species-typical calls including alarm calls and more affiliative vocalizations. In contrast, Miller (1967) used a fear conditioning paradigm where one rhesus monkey could see the stimulus predicting shock, but the monkey that controlled the response to avoid the shock could only see the face of the first monkey. Isolate-reared monkeys were quite good in producing the signals, but when they were in the role of responding to fear cues in another monkey, they were unable to respond to its signals of fear. As noted earlier, captive-born cotton-top tamarins did not respond to live snakes in their cage nor to playback of predator cues (Campbell and Snowdon, 2009; Friant et al., 2008; Hayes and Snowdon, 1990) although they produce alarm calls and mobbing calls in other contexts.

B. CROSS-SPECIES COMPREHENSION

The strongest evidence for primate flexibility in comprehension of communication signals comes from studies of cross-species communication. Vervet monkeys in Kenya learn to respond to the alarm calls of an avian species, the superb starling (Cheney and Seyfarth, 1985; Hauser, 1988) and in habituation–dishabituation studies that involved habituation to alarm calls of one species with transfer tests to calls of the other species, vervet monkeys appear to categorize starling aerial alarms in similar fashion to their own aerial alarm calls. Starlings were less specific in the targets to which they gave terrestrial alarm calls and vervet monkeys were less specific in their reactions to these calls (Seyfarth and Cheney, 1990).

Oda and Masataka (1996) showed that ring-tailed lemurs would respond appropriately to playback of alarm calls of Verraux's sifakas, Diana monkeys in areas where they are sympatric with Campbell's monkeys respond to the eagle and leopard alarm calls of Campbell's monkeys as strongly as to the playbacks of calls of the actual predators (Zuberbühler, 2000a). However, Diana monkeys responded to the leopard alarm calls of chimpanzees but only if they share a home range with chimpanzees (Zuber-bühler, 2000b). In a reversal of the study with vervet monkeys responding to alarms of superb starlings Rainey, Zuberbühler and Slater (2004) found that yellow-casqued hornbills responded to playbacks of Diana monkey aerial alarm calls though not to Diana monkey leopard alarm calls, as would be expected since leopards could not prey upon hornbills.

As mentioned earlier, the cross fostering of Japanese macaques with rhesus macaques did not show any evidence of changes in vocal structure in the cross-fostered infants (Owren et al., 1993). However, the foster mothers of these infants responded more readily to food calls and play calls typical of their foster infant than they did to playbacks of calls of infants of their own species, clearly indicating that foster mothers have learned the vocal characteristics of their foster infants and respond appropriately to them (Seyfarth and Cheney, 1997). If mothers have the capacity to be flexible in response to infant vocalizations, then there may be no selective pressure for offspring to be flexible in their vocal production.

C.   PARENTAL STATUS AFFECTS RESPONSES

Although the primary focus of this chapter has been on vocal communication to this point, I would like to make a brief digression to olfactory signals as a way to illustrate how parental status can affect responses to signals. Olfactory cues can have important influences on reproduction. We have shown using functional magnetic resonance imaging methods that presenting a male common marmoset with the odor of a novel, ovulating female produced increased neural activation in the anterior hypothalamus and medial preoptic areas, parts of the brain known to be involved in male sexual arousal (Ferris et al., 2001). Activation of these areas also activates the pituitary gland to secrete gonadotrophins that in turn activate the gonads. We, subsequently, were interested in behavioral and hormonal responses to odors of novel, ovulating females and predicted that marmoset males would increase several behaviors relating to scent exploration and reproduction. We also predicted that testosterone levels would be increased after exposure to the odor of a novel female. Indeed, many males had significant increases in erections and in sniffing and licking at the stimulus. The same males also displayed a significant increase in testosterone levels within 30 min of exposure to the odor (Ziegler et al., 2005). However, there was a class of males that did not respond to odors of novel ovulating females—those who were fathers currently active in infant care. Fathers were not interested in exploring the scent stimulus and they showed no change in testosterone levels after exposure to odors from novel females.

In a subsequent study, in marmoset, we presented fathers and nonfathers with either a live infant in an adjacent cage or the vocalizations of an infant. All fathers responded rapidly to both a live infant and the playback of a live infant, and they responded equally to both their own infants and unrelated, unfamiliar infants. Nonfathers did not respond to live infants or their vocalizations (Zahed et al., 2008). Do fathers have different hormonal responses than nonfathers? Adult males were presented with odors of an infant versus the vehicle control and fathers, but not nonfathers, displayed a significant reduction in testosterone levels to infant odors compared to the vehicle (Prudom et al., 2008). This, the identical olfactory stimulus, elicits different behavioral and hormonal responses in male marmosets dependent on whether or not they were fathers.

In cotton-top tamarins, we have seen a sequence of changes in hormones in males during the last half of their mate's pregnancy with increases in testosterone, estrogens, and prolactin. But these changes are seen only in experienced fathers and not in first time fathers (Ziegler et al., 2004). The proximate cause appears to be the increased secretion of glucocorticoids by mothers at the midpoint of pregnancy, likely due to the maturation of the fetal adrenal gland. Within a week of this increase in excretion, experienced father began the sequence of hormonal changes, but first time fathers do not. Since all females exhibit the midpregnancy change in glucocorticoid excretion, the most likely explanation for the differences between first time and experienced fathers is experience. Thus, parental status is an important social variable that can influence response to communication.

D. Summary

Nonhuman primates are quite flexible in their responses to signals from both their own species and those of other species. Of course, many birds are able to respond to alarm and mobbing calls of other species but this could be due to the convergence in vocal structure typical for each type of call (Marler, 1955). However, Magrath et al. (2009) showed that birds responding to heterospecific alarm calls did not have similar call structure and they responded to another species alarm call only when the species were sympatric implying that the birds learn each other's alarm calls and there is no convergence of call structure. Some primate species born and reared in captivity do not respond to visual or auditory cues from nature but do respond to cues appropriate to captivity. Cross-species reactions to alarm calls cannot simply be explained by convergence in signal structure, since the alarm calls of, say superb starlings and hornbills are quite different from those of the primates responding to them. This flexibility of response in captive-reared or cross-fostered animals and the responses to calls of other species in wild populations suggest some form of learning about signals is important to nonhuman primates. Finally, there is flexibility in how animals respond to signals, both behaviorally and hormonally as a function of parental status.

V. COMMUNICATION SIGNALS AND SOCIAL LEARNING AND TEACHING

There has been much interest in recent years in understanding the potential of nonhuman primates for social learning with considerable debate about whether nonhuman primates have a capacity for imitation and emulation. There have been some impressive demonstrations especially in great apes with considerably less success seen with monkeys (Visalberghi and Fragaszy, 1990). Nonetheless, results with cooperatively breeding primates have been more impressive with evidence of imitation (e.g., Völkl and Huber, 2000) and other forms of social learning. One hypothesis for the abilities of cooperatively breeding primates to learn from others is that this breeding system leads to greater tolerance and closer coordination between individuals than other types of breeding systems (Cousi Korbel and Fragaszy, 1995). An additional hypothesis may be due to frequent communication between animals to manage coordination or greater sensitivity by recipients to signals from others. Here, we look at some examples of how communication may affect social learning in both positive and negative ways and examine the possibility of teaching in cooperatively breeding animals.

A. AVOIDING NOXIOUS FOOD

Galef and Giraldeau (2001) reviewed the studies of social influences on foraging behavior in a wide array of species and noted the lack of evidence in nonhuman primates for socially learning to avoid toxic or unpalatable foods. In one study, Visalberghi and Addessi (2000) presented capuchin monkeys with mozzarella cheese adulterated with ground white pepper and found no evidence that capuchin monkeys learned socially to avoid the distasteful food. Rather each individual learned when the food was distasteful and when it was palatable again. In a study of similar design, Snowdon and Boe (2003) presented groups of cotton-top tamarins with tuna fish, a highly preferred food that all animals ate readily, that was adulterated with white pepper. In contrast to the capuchin monkeys, cotton-top tamarins readily learned from others to avoid the adulterated food. Only one-third of animals ever sampled the foods and when nonadulterated food was returned, a minority of monkeys continued to avoid eating tuna fish, some for months and even years later even though they had not been the individuals who had sampled the food (Fig. 3). What could account for the species differences in learning to avoid a noxious food? One major difference was the presence of communicative signals in the tamarins. Tamarins that sampled the adulterated tuna gave fewer than normal food-related vocalizations and instead produced alarm calls (Fig. 4). They also gave facial expressions of disgust—chin wiping, retching, etc. No such signals were reported in the study on capuchin monkeys.

B. FOOD TRANSFERS AND TEACHING

Caro and Hauser (1992) set three criteria for determining whether nonhuman animals exhibited teaching behavior: the demonstrator had to engage the learner; there was a cost to the demonstrator; and the learner's

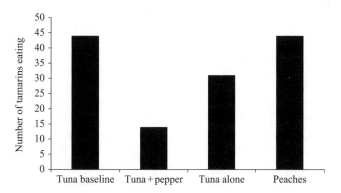

FIG. 3. Number of cotton-top tamarins responding (out of 44) to tuna presented in baseline, tuna adulterated with white pepper, restoration of normal tuna and to peaches (used as a palatable control food). (Adapted from Snowdon and Boe, 2003.)

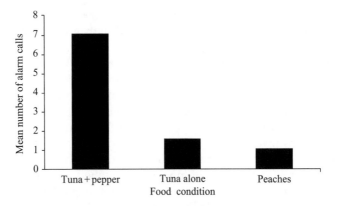

FIG. 4. Number of alarm calls by cotton-top tamarins given to pepper adulterated tuna, to tuna without pepper and to peaches (Wilcoxon $T = 4$, $P < 0.05$ between tuna + pepper and tuna alone and peaches). (Adapted from Snowdon and Boe, 2003.)

subsequent behavior was affected by the interactions. Although teaching is often thought to require a theory of mind, the operational definition of Caro and Hauser (1992) allows examination of possible cases of teaching without requiring demonstration of a theory of mind.

Rapaport and Brown (2008) noted that in great apes and most monkeys, there was little evidence of teaching foraging skills to the young. Rather, young primates acquired skills by closely watching a demonstrator. Rapaport and Brown noted, however, that food transfers commonly seen in cooperatively breeding primates appeared to be an exception where adult transfers of food to infants appeared to be a good nonhuman primate example of teaching behavior. Food transfers from adults, often animals other than the mother, are seen in many species of marmosets and tamarins and are usually characterized by specific vocalizations given in feeding contexts. In cotton-top tamarins, these vocalizations are similar in structure to individual calls given by adults when encountering food. However, in the context of food transfers to infants, the calls are given in a rapid sequence and higher amplitude not observed in feeding contexts among adults (Joyce and Snowdon, 2007). Infants frequently beg for food but only when adults produce the intensified form of food vocalizations will the infants be successful in obtaining food (Fig. 5, Joyce and Snowdon, 2007; Roush and Snowdon, 2001). Furthermore, infants that are involved at an earlier age with food transfers eat independently and produce food vocalizations sooner than those for whom food transfers began at a later age. This is most striking in comparing twin infants with singletons (Fig. 6). Family members engaged in food transfers and associated vocalizations with twin

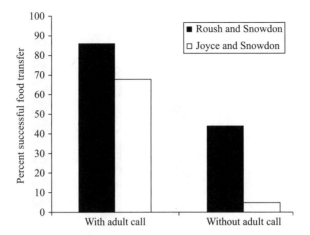

FIG. 5. Percentage successful food transfers to cotton-top tamarin infants as a function of whether adults gave rapid series of food calls or not (chi-square, $P < 0.001$). (Adapted from Joyce and Snowdon, 2007; Roush and Snowdon, 2001.)

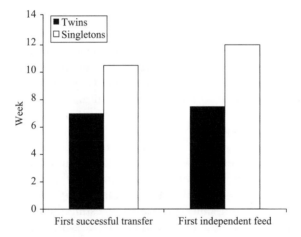

FIG. 6. Mean age at first food transfer and first independent feed for twin and singleton infant cotton-top tamarins (twins earlier than singletons on both measures, U's = 0, $P < 0.05$). (Drawn from data in Joyce and Snowdon, 2007.)

infants significantly earlier than with singletons and twins eat independently significantly sooner as well (Joyce and Snowdon, 2007). Adults also phased out food transfers and vocalizing to infants as the infants began to forage on their own (Fig. 7).

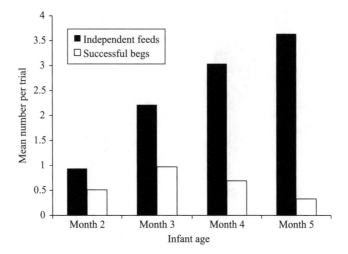

Fɪɢ. 7. Relationship between successful begs and independent feeding in infant cotton-top tamarins (independent feeds—Months 3, 4, and 5 > Month 2, Month 5 > Month 3) Wilcoxon T's < 2, P's < 0.01; Successful Begs Month 3 > Months 4 and 5 Wilcoxon T's = 0, P's < 0.01). (Adapted from Joyce and Snowdon, 2007.)

Food transfers in marmosets and tamarins appear to meet the criteria of teaching. Adults share a preferred resource and have special forms of vocalizations used only with infants. The infants are attracted to the vocalizing adult and are able to receive solid food and this, in turn, leads to development of independent foraging behavior and production of food vocalizations in the young.

Whether information about food quality or novelty is also transmitted has led to conflicting results. Working with captive lion tamarins (*Leontopitechus* spp.), Rapaport (1999) found that adults were more likely to transfer food that was unfamiliar to the infant (but not to the adult) as well as food that was difficult to process suggesting that the lion tamarins understood something about the knowledge base of the infants. In contrast, Brown et al. (2005) did not find evidence that common marmosets were more willing to transfer novel food or food that was difficult to obtain.

In field studies of golden lion tamarins in Brazil, Rapaport noted that animate prey were extremely difficult for juvenile monkeys to obtain and that adults frequently vocalized in the presence of animal prey and transferred them to juveniles but did not otherwise transfer food (Rapaport, 2006; Rapaport and Ruiz-Miranda, 2006). In addition, she noted that tamarins often showed "scaffolding" behavior. That is, an adult would give food transfer vocalizations and the juvenile would approach and located near the vocalizing adult was a prey item that the juvenile captured and ingested (Rapaport and Ruiz-Miranda (2002). As juveniles gained more skill in foraging on their own, adults gave fewer food transfer calls and transferred food less often (Figs. 8 and 9).

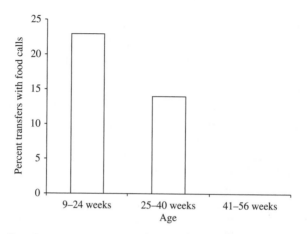

FIG. 8. Decline of adult food vocalizations to young golden lion tamarins at different ages ($F(1,18) = 8.462$, $P = 0.009$). (Adapted from Rapaport and Ruiz-Miranda, 2006.)

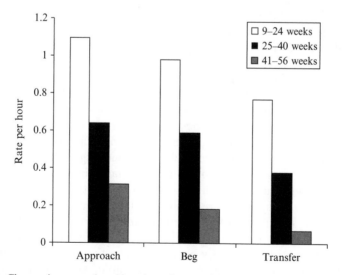

FIG. 9. Changes in approach and begs by and successful food transfers to young golden lion tamarins decline as a function of age (approaches $F(2,10) = 17.56$, $P < 0.0001$), begs $F(2,16) = 83.30$, $P < 0.001$, transfers $F(2,16) = 122.89$, $P < 0.00001$). (Adapted from Rapaport and Ruiz-Miranda, 2006.)

We developed a laboratory analogue of foraging using an apparatus with two possible solutions and we trained one parent on each solution (Humle and Snowdon, 2008). Highly preferred food was hidden in Styrofoam dishes suspended by a string in two opaque cylinders and one parent was trained to obtain food by reaching from a perch underneath to obtain food and the other parent was trained to pull the string up hand over hand from the ceiling. Following training, one parent was tested with each twin juvenile. Testing was not started until all of the juveniles were routinely foraging on their own with no evidence of food transfers from parents. In control trials, we did not observe food transfers between parents and juveniles, but in the test trials, juveniles frequently emitted food begging vocalizations to adults who had food from the foraging apparatus, and adults would give food transfer calls and often transfer food. Paradoxically, the adults that transferred food to begging juveniles most frequently had the least successful offspring. A possible reason for this is that adults frequently took the food to another part of the cage and so food transfers were done at a distance from the apparatus, possibly not allowing the recipient of food transfers to make the connection between the apparatus and the food. In this case, vocalizations and food transfers inhibited learning in juveniles in contrast to the data from the field on lion tamarins (Rapaport, 2006). One other intriguing result was that as soon as a juvenile successfully solved the task, the parents no longer vocalized with food or allowed those young to beg successfully (Fig. 10, Humle and Snowdon, 2008). Thus, these parents rapidly adjusted their vocal and food transfer behavior when a juvenile successfully solved the foraging task. Furthermore, in this context, greater parental response to juvenile vocal begging led to less success in learning the novel task.

In contrast to the helpfulness of tamarin parents to offspring in learning about food and foraging techniques is the absence of such support in chimpanzees. The chimpanzees at Bossou in Guinea engage in ant-dipping behavior, placing sticks into the nests or in columns of driver ants and then as the ants bite on to the stick the chimpanzees pick up the sticks and ingest the ants. The ants produce severe bites and one might expect that adults would provide some sort of guidance to infants in this context where foraging could be quite painful. However, in a longitudinal study of infant and juvenile chimpanzees there was no evidence of maternal assistance in helping young offspring to find the right size stick or develop the proper skills to minimize the likelihood of being bitten by ants. Instead, each individual learned in its own by observing its mother and other adults, but there was none of the vocal or visual communication seen in tamarin parents (Humle et al., in press).

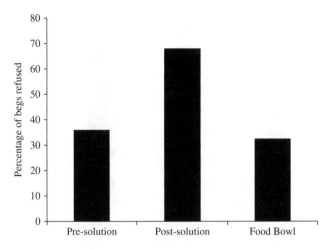

FIG. 10. Percentage of juvenile begs rejected in cotton-top tamarins by adult demonstrators as before and after the juvenile had successfully solved the novel foraging task. Food bowl is control condition requiring no task solution (presolution differs from postsolution, $t(7) = 3.91$, $P = 0.006$). (Adapted from Humle and Snowdon, 2008.)

C. COOPERATION AND DONATION BEHAVIOR

One more example illustrates the negative role of vocal signals in a social task. Several recent studies on chimpanzees (e.g., Silk et al., 2005; Vonk et al., 2008) find that when chimpanzees have the opportunity to provide food for a companion at no cost to themselves (by choosing a tray that has food rewards for both versus a food reward for themselves alone), they do not pull the two reward trays more often when a partner is present to receive the food. In contrast, cotton-top tamarins rapidly learn to cooperate with each other when both must act simultaneously to obtain a food reward (Cronin et al., 2005) and tamarins will continue to cooperate even when only one individual at a time is rewarded showing reciprocity over a period of days (Cronin and Snowdon, 2008). It seemed logical to expect that tamarins would succeed at the food donation task where chimpanzees had failed. Burkart et al. (2007) found that common marmosets were successful at an even more stringent task of pulling a tray that provided food only to the partner and not to itself. This donation behavior occurred between unrelated as well as related animals. We completed an almost identical test using pairs of tamarins that had lived together for long periods of time. To our surprise, the tamarins failed to donate food to their partners and more strikingly, there was a decrease in donating to the mate on trials where the mate was observed to give food vocalizations and/or to reach for the food (Fig. 11, Cronin et al., 2009), indicating that tamarins are attending to

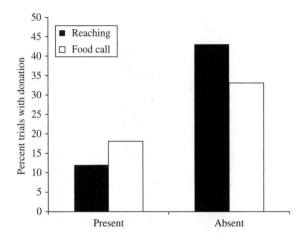

FIG. 11. Proportion of trials where mate donated food to its partner as a function of whether the partner gave food calls or not and reached toward food or not. (food calls $t(12) = 2.147$, $P = 0.053$; reaches $t(10) = 6.340$, $P = 0.001$). (Adapted from Cronin et al., 2009.)

the signals of their mates and adjusting behavior even if it is not in the expected direction. Lakshminarayanan and Santos (2008) reported that capuchin monkeys would provide food for a companion. The positive results with capuchin monkeys and common marmosets contrasting with the negative results with chimpanzees and cotton-top tamarins suggest that neither phylogeny nor cooperative breeding are adequate explanations for prosocial behavior.

D. SUMMARY

The role of communication signals in social learning and teaching is not consistent and varies between tasks. Aversive signals such as alarm calls and visual disgust responses appear to help tamarins learn to avoid adulterated food and may explain why such social learning has not been seen in other species where such communication is not present. Specialized versions of food vocalizations are given by adult tamarins that are willing to transfer food to infants and in wild tamarins these signals continue to be used with juveniles in the context of feeding on animal prey, the food most difficult for young tamarins to acquire on their own. Similar food transfers are seen in captive tamarins when their juveniles are faced with a novel foraging task. In both cases, adults appear to reduce their vocalizations and food transfers as the young acquire more skills. Offspring of parents that do not withdraw support are less likely to learn foraging skills. Finally, in studies where tamarins can donate food to a long time mate, the donors are less likely to provide food if the recipient mate has shown any interest by food calling or reaching toward the food.

VI. Long-Term Memory

Relatively little work has been done to explore the limits of memory in nonhuman primates. However, long-term memory would appear to be valuable in foraging in the wild where fruit resources may be available only at certain time of the year. Long-term memory for communication signals may also be useful to prevent inbreeding after animals have dispersed. We have examples of long-term memory for vocalizations in captive tamarins and Campbell's monkeys.

In one study, we collected long call vocalizations from many colony members and then played back the calls of (1) the subject's current mate, (2) a former family member from which the subject had been separated in a different colony room for periods ranging from 6 months to 5.5 years, and (3) the call of an unfamiliar animal, which had always been in a different colony room. Monkeys reacted with a high level of arousal to the call of the unfamiliar animals and showed very little reaction to the calls of their mates. When the calls of a formerly familiar animal (parent, offspring, or sibling) were played back, the subjects responded with few alerting and orienting behaviors similar to the response to calls of their mates, indicating a memory for the calls of familiar animals. This result held no matter how long had been the separation (Matthews and Snowdon, unpublished data).

Lemasson et al. (2005) found that adult female Campbell's monkeys will alter the structure of calls that they use in vocal exchanges over time. Playbacks of current variants elicited significant responses in other monkeys within a minute of playback. Playbacks of formerly used variants (from 4 years earlier) as well as calls of strange females did not elicit any vocal responses from others. However, playback of former variants of current group members did lead to a significant reduction in call rate over 10 min whereas neither the current variant nor the call of a stranger affected call rate over 10 min. Long-term memory for calls of former relatives would be adaptive to avoid inbreeding after animals have dispersed form their natal groups.

VII. Overall Summary and Conclusions

I have tried to provide evidence in this chapter that communication behavior in nonhuman primates is more complex and flexible than the earlier views that have been presented. Since the review by Seyfarth and

Cheney (1997) which concluded there was evidence of limited plasticity in vocal production, but increased plasticity in signal usage and responses to signals, many new studies have shown that primates can control vocal output in response to environmental and social changes and there is increasing evidence of local and population variation in call structure. Developmentally, young tamarins do not produce context-appropriate adult calls and pygmy marmosets engage in long bouts of vocal behavior with calls structurally similar to adult calls but not given in appropriate contexts. Production of the full adult repertoire develops slowly and may involve practice, physical maturation and, possibly, imitation, for full development. None of these new results suggest that primates will soon challenge songbirds for vocal virtuosity, but nonetheless the accumulation of results suggests a much greater degree of vocal control and flexibility of production than previously thought. However, direct evidence in controlled studies for vocal learning is still rare.

In both the usage of calls and how primates respond to calls, more recent findings support the conclusions of Seyfarth and Cheney (1997). Considering captivity as an ecological niche allows examination of how primates can use and respond to signals in novel ways that would not be possible in field studies. Thus, captive primates respond to people in veterinary garb and to cleaning apparatus with mobbing calls and apply alarm calls to novel situations such as discovering familiar food that has been made unpalatable.

Changes in social status also provide tools for examining plasticity in communication. As male baboons attain dominance status they change the structure of their calls and as tamarins move from being alloparents to breeding adults, they also change the structure of some calls. These changes cannot simply be due to age or physical maturation. Social status also affects response to signals with some of the strongest evidence emerging in how fatherhood in marmosets alters not only behavioral but neuroendocrine response to some signals as well.

Social learning may be facilitated by use of communication signals in avoiding noxious food or learning how to forage in a novel task, but communication does not always facilitate social learning and can even reduce food provisioning behavior in the case of cotton-top tamarins. The role of plasticity in communication becomes clearest in the teaching behavior of tamarins. In both wild lion tamarins and captive cotton-top tamarins, adults adjust their communication signals according to the skill levels of their infants and juveniles, with withdrawal of signals as young animals acquire skills or using signals in different contexts to help older offspring succeed. Finally, there is evidence in tamarins of long-term memory for calls of socially important individuals as well as memory for foraging tasks.

I have focused here on the structure, usage, and response to signals and have not dealt with any of the cognitive components of primate communication. The chapter by Zuberbühler provides clear evidence of cognitive abilities. Taken together, these chapters provide an impressive documentation of the plasticity and cognitive skills of nonhuman primates. Although few primates can sing like birds or humpback whales, they still show impressive sophistication in their production, use, and interpretation of communication signals.

References

Addington, R.A., 1998. Social foraging in captive pygmy marmosets (*Cebuella pygmaea*): effects of food characteristics and social context on feeding competition and vocal behavior. Unpublished Ph.D. dissertation, University of Wisconsin, Madison.

Boughman, J.W., 1998. Vocal learning by greater spear-nose bats. Proc. R. Soc. Lond. Ser. B. 265, 227–233.

Brown, G.R., Almond, R.E.A., Bates, N.J., 2005. Adult–infant food transfer in common marmosets: an experimental study. Am. J. Primatol. 65, 301–312.

Brumm, H., Voss, K., Köllmer, I., Todt, D., 2004. Acoustic communication in noise: regulation of call characteristics in a New World monkey. J. Exp. Biol. 207, 443–448.

Burkart, J.M., Fehr, E., Efferson, C., van Schaik, C.P., 2007. Other-regarding preferences in a non-human primate: common marmosets provision food altruistically. Proc. Natl. Acad. Sci. USA 104, 19762–19766.

Campbell, M.W., Snowdon, C.T., 2007. Vocal response of captive-reared *Saguinus oedipus* during mobbing. Int. J. Primatol. 28, 257–270.

Campbell, M.W., Snowdon, C.T., 2009. Can auditory playback condition predator mobbing in captive-reared cotton-top tamarins? Int. J. Primatol. 30, 93–102.

Caro, T.M., Hauser, M.D., 1992. Is there teaching in nonhuman animals? Q. Rev. Biol. 67, 151–174.

Castro, N.A., Snowdon, C.T., 2000. Development of vocal responses in infant cotton-top tamarins. Behaviour 137, 629–646.

Chapman, C.A., Lefebvre, L., 1990. Manipulating foraging group size: spider monkey food calls at fruit trees. Anim. Behav. 39, 891–896.

Cheney, D.L., Seyfarth, R.M., 1985. Social and nonsocial knowledge in vervet monkeys. Philos. Trans. R. Soc. Lond. B 308, 187–201.

Clay, Z., Zuberbühler, K., 2009. Food-associated calling sequences in bonobos. Anim. Behav. 77, 1387–1396.

Cleveland, J., Snowdon, C.T., 1982. The complex vocal repertoire of the adult cotton-top tamarin (*Saguinus oedipus oedipus*). J. Tierpsychol. 58, 231–270.

Cousi Korbel, S., Fragaszy, D.M., 1995. On the relation between social dynamics and social learning. Anim. Behav. 50, 1441–1453.

Crockford, C., Herbinger, I., Vigilant, L., Boesch, C., 2004. Wild chimpanzees produce group-specific calls: a case for vocal learning? Ethology 110, 221–243.

Cronin, K.A., Snowdon, C.T., 2008. The effects of unequal reward distributions on cooperative problem solving by cottontop tamarins (*Saguinus oedipus*). Anim. Behav. 75, 245–257.

Cronin, K.A., Kurian, A.V., Snowdon, C.T., 2005. Cooperative problem solving in a cooperatively-breeding primate, the cotton-top tamarin (*Saguinus oedipus*). Anim. Behav. 69, 133–142.

Cronin, K.A., Schroeder, K.K., Rothwell, E.D., Silk, J.A., Snowdon, C.T., 2009. Cooperatively breeding cottontop tamarins (*Saguinus oedipus*) do not preferentially donate rewards to their long-term mates. J. Comp. Psychol.

De la Torre, S., Snowdon, C.T., 2002. Environmental correlates of vocal communication f wild pygmy marmosets, *Cebuella pygmaea*. Anim. Behav. 63, 847–856.

De la Torre, S., Snowdon, C.T., 2009. Dialects in pygmy marmosets? Population variation in call structure. Am. J. Primatol. 71, 333–342.

Egnor, S.E.R., Iguina, C., Hauser, M.D., 2006. Perturbation of auditory feedback causes systematic perturbation in vocal structure in adult cotton-top tamarins. J. Exp. Biol. 209, 3652–3663.

Elowson, A.M., Snowdon, C.T., 1994. Pygmy marmosets, *Cebuella pygmaea*, modify vocal structure in response to changed social environment. Anim. Behav. 47, 1267–1277.

Elowson, A.M., Tannenbaum, P.L., Snowdon, C.T., 1991. Food-associated calls correlate with food preferences in cotton-top tamarins. Anim. Behav. 42, 931–937.

Elowson, A.M., Snowdon, C.T., Lazaro-Perea, C., 1998. Infant "babbling" in a nonhuman primate: complex vocal sequences with repeated call types. Behaviour 135, 643–664.

Ey, E., Rahn, C., Hammerschmidt, K., Fischer, J., 2009. Wild female olive baboons adapt their grunt vocalizations to environmental conditions. Ethology 118, 493–503.

Ferris, C.F., Snowdon, C.T., King, J.A., Duong, T.Q., Ziegler, T.E., Ugurbil, K., et al., 2001. Functional imaging of brain activity in conscious monkeys responding to sexually arousing cues. NeuroReport 12, 2231–2236.

Fischer, J., Hammerschmidt, K., Todt, D., 1998. Local variation in Barbary macaque shrill barks. Anim. Behav. 56, 623–629.

Fischer, J., Kitchen, D.M., Seyfarth, R.M., Cheney, D.L., 2004. Baboon loud calls advertise male quality: acoustic features and their relation to rank, age and exhaustion. Behav. Ecol. Sociobiol. 56, 140–148.

Friant, S.C., Campbell, M.A., Snowdon, C.T., 2008. Captive-born cotton-top tamarins (*Saguinus oedipus*) respond similarly to vocalizations of predators and non-predators. Am. J. Primatol. 70, 707–710.

Galef, B.G., Giraldeau, L.A., 2001. Social influences on foraging in vertebrates: causal mechanisms and adaptive functions. Anim. Behav. 61, 3–15.

Geissmann, T., 1984. The inheritance of song parameters in the gibbon song analysed in two hybrid gibbons (*Hylobates pileatus X Hylobates lar*). Folia. Primatol. 42, 216–235.

Green, S., 1975. Dialects in Japanese macaques: vocal learning and cultural transmission of locale-specific behavior. Z. Tierpsychol. 38, 304–314.

Gros-Louis, J., 2004. The function of food associated calls in white faced capuchins, *Cebus capucinus*, from the perspective of the signaler. Anim. Behav. 67, 431–440.

Hammerschmidt, K., Fischer, J., 2008. Constraints on primate vocal production. In: Oller, D.K., Griebel, U. (Eds.), Evolution of Communicative Flexibility. MIT Press, Cambridge, MA, pp. 93–119.

Hammerschmidt, K., Newman, J.D., Champoux, M., Suomi, S.J., 2000. Changes in rhesus macaque vocalizations during early development. Ethology 106, 873–886.

Hauser, M.D., 1992. Costs of deception: cheaters are punished by rhesus monkeys (*Macaca mulatta*). Proc. Natl. Acad. Sci. USA 89, 12137–12139.

Hauser, M.D., 1988. How infant vervet monkeys learn to recognize starling alarm calls: the role of experience. Behaviour 105, 187–201.

Hauser, M.D., Wrangham, R.W., 1987. Manipulation of food calls in captive chimpanzees. Folia Primatol. 48, 207–210.

Hauser, M.D., Teixidor, P., Field, L., Flaherty, R., 1993. Food-elicited calls in chimpanzees: effects of food quantity and divisibility. Anim. Behav. 45, 817–819.

Hayes, S.L., Snowdon, C.T., 1990. Predator recognition in cotton-top tamarins (*Saguinus oedipus*). Am. J. Primatol. 20, 283–291.

Herzog, M., Hopf, S., 1983. Effects of species-specific vocalizations on the behavior of surrogate reared squirrel monkeys. Behaviour 86, 197–214.

Herzog, M., Hopf, S., 1984. Behavioral responses to species-specific warning calls in infant squirrel monkeys reared in social isolation. Am. J. Primatol. 7, 99–106.

Humle, T., Snowdon, C.T., 2008. Socially biased learning in the acquisition of a complex foraging task in juvenile cottontop tamarins (*Saguinus oedipus*). Anim. Behav. 75, 267–277.

Humle, T., Snowdon, C.T., Matsuzawa, T. (in press). Social influences on the acquisition of ant dipping among the wild chimpanzees (*Pan troglodytes verus*) of Bossou, Guinea, West Africa. Anim. Cogn.

Janik, V.M., Slater, P.J.B., 1997. Vocal learning in mammals. Adv. Study Behav. 26, 59–99.

Janik, V.M., Slater, P.J.B., 2000. The different roles of social learning in vocal communication. Anim. Behav. 60, 1–11.

Joyce, S.M., Snowdon, C.T., 2007. Developmental changes in food transfers in cotton-top tamarins (*Saguinus oedipus*). Am. J. Primatol. 28, 257–270.

Koda, H., 2004. Flexibility and context-sensitivity during the vocal exchange of coo calls in wild Japanese macaques (*Macaca fuscata yakui*). Behaviour 141, 1279–1296.

Koda, H., Shimooka, Y., Sugiura, H., 2008. Effects of caller activity and habitat visibility on contact call rate of wild Japanese macaques (*Macaca fuscata*). Am. J. Primatol. 70, 1055–1063.

Lakshminarayanan, V.R., Santos, L.R., 2008. Capuchin monkeys are sensitive to other's welfare. Curr. Biol. 18, R999–R1000.

Lemasson, A., Hausberger, M., 2004. Patterns of vocal sharing and social dynamics in a captive group of Campbell's monkeys (*Cercopithecus campbelli campbelli*). J. Comp. Psychol. 118, 347–359.

Lemasson, A., Hausberger, M., Zuberbühler, K., 2005. Socially meaningful vocal plasticity in Campbell's monkeys (*Cercopithecus campbelli*). J. Comp. Psychol. 119, 220–229.

Lieblich, A.K., Symmes, D., Newman, J.D., Shapiro, M., 1980. Development of the isolation peep in laboratory bred squirrel monkeys. Anim. Behav. 28, 1–9.

Magrath, R.D., Pitcher, B.J., Gardner, J.L., 2009. Recognition of other species' alarm calls: speaking the same language or learning another. Proc. R. Soc. Lond. B 276, 769–774.

Marler, P., 1955. Characteristics of some animal calls. Nature 176, 6–8.

Marler, P., 1970. Bird song and speech development: could there be parallels? Am. Sci. 58, 669–673.

Marshall, A.J., Wrangham, R.W., Clark, A.P., 1999. Does learning affect the structure of vocalizations in chimpanzees? Anim. Behav. 58, 825–830.

Masataka, N., 1992. Attempts by animal caretakers to condition Japanese macaque vocalizations result inadvertently in individual-specific calls. In: Nishida, T., McGrew, W.C., Marler, M., Pickford, M., de Waal, F.B.M. (Eds.), Topics in Primatology 1: Human Origins. University of Tokyo Press, Tokyo, pp. 271–278.

Miller, R.E., 1967. Experimental approaches to the physiological and behavioral concomitants of affective communication in rhesus monkeys. In: Altmann, S.A. (Ed.), Social Communication Among Primates. University of Chicago Press, Chicago, pp. 125–134.

Miller, C.T., Flusberg, S., Hauser, M.D., 2003. Interruptibility of long call production in tamarins: implications for vocal control. J. Exp. Biol. 206, 2629–2639.

Mitani, J.C., Brandt, K., 1994. Social factors influence the acoustic variability in the long-range distance calls of male chimpanzees. Ethology 96, 233–252.

Mitani, J.C., Gros-Louis, J., 1998. Chorusing and call convergence in chimpanzees: tests of three hypotheses. Behaviour 135, 1041–1064.

Mitani, J.C., Hasegawa, T., Gros-Louis, J., Marler, P., Byrne, R., 1992. Dialects in wild chimpanzees? Am. J. Primatol. 27, 233–243.

Mitani, J.C., Hunley, K.L., Murdoch, M.E., 1999. Geographic variation in the calls of wild chimpanzees: a reassessment. Am. J. Primatol. 47, 133–151.

Newman, J.D., Symmes, D., 1974. Vocal pathology in socially-deprived monkeys. Dev. Psychobiol. 7, 351–358.

Newman, J.D., Symmes, D., 1982. Inheritance and experience in the acquisition of primate acoustic behavior. In: Snowdon, C.T., Brown, C.H., Petersen, M.R. (Eds.), Primate Communication. Cambridge University Press, Cambridge, pp. 259–278.

Oda, R., Masataka, N., 1996. Interspecies responses of ring-tailed lemurs to playback of antipredator alarm calls given by Verraux's sifakas. Ethology 102, 441–453.

Owren, M.J., Dieter, J.A., Seyfarth, R.M., Cheney, D.L., 1993. Vocalizations of rhesus (*Macaca mulatta*) and Japanese (*M. fuscata*) macaques cross-fostered between species show evidence of only limited modification. Dev. Psychobiol. 26, 389–406.

Papworth, S., Böse, A.-S., Barker, J., Schel, A.M., Zuberbühler, K., 2008. Male blue monkeys call in response to danger experienced by others. Biol. Lett. 4, 472–475.

Pola, Y.V., Snowdon, C.T., 1975. The vocalizations of the pygmy marmoset (*Cebuella pygmaea*). Anim. Behav. 23, 826–842.

Pollick, A.S., Gouzoules, H., de Waal, F.B.M., 2005. Audience effects on food calls in brown capuchin monkeys, *Cebus apella*. Anim. Behav. 70, 1273–1281.

Prudom, S.L., Broz, C.A., Schultz-Darken, N., Ferris, C.T., Snowdon, C.T., Ziegler, T.E., 2008. Exposure to infant scent lowers serum testosterone in father common marmosets, (*Callithrix jacchus*). Biol. Lett. 4, 603–605.

Pusey, A.E., Packer, C., 1987. Dispersal and philopatry. In: Smuts, B.B., Cheney, D.L., Seyfarth, R.M., Wrangham, R.W., Struhsaker, T.T. (Eds.), Primate Societies. University of Chicago Press, Chicago IL, pp. 250–266.

Rainey, H.G., Zuberbuhler, K., Slater, P.J.B., 2004. Hornbills can distinguish between primate alarm calls. Proc. Roy. Soc. Lond. B. 271, 755–759.

Rapaport, L.G., 1999. Provisioning of young in golden lion tamarins (Callitrichidae, *Leontopithecus rosalia*): a test of the information hypothesis. Ethology 105, 619–636.

Rapaport, L.G., 2006. Provisioning in wild golden lion tamarins (*Leontopithecus rosalia*): benefits to omnivorous young. Behav. Ecol. 17, 212–221.

Rapaport, L.G., Brown, G.R., 2008. Social influences on foraging behavior in young nonhuman primates. Evol. Anthropol. 17, 189–201.

Rapaport, L.G, Ruiz-Miranda, C.R., 2002. Tutoring in wild golden lion tamarins. Int. J. Primatol. 23, 1063–1070.

Rapaport, L.G., Ruiz-Miranda, C.R., 2006. Ontogeny of provisioning in two populations of wild golden lion tamarins (*Leontopithecus rosalia*). Behav. Ecol. Sociobiol. 60, 724–735.

Roush, R.S., Snowdon, C.T., 1994. Ontogeny of food associated calls in cotton-top tamarins. Anim. Behav. 47, 263–273.

Roush, R.S., Snowdon, C.T., 1999. The effects of social status on food associated calls in captive cotton-top tamarins. Anim. Behav. 58, 1299–1305.

Roush, R.S., Snowdon, C.T., 2000. Quality, quantity, distribution and audience effects on food calling in cotton-top tamarins. Ethology 106, 673–690.

Roush, R.S., Snowdon, C.T., 2001. Food transfer and development of feeding behavior and food-associated vocalizations in cotton-top tamarins. Ethology 107, 415–429.

Ruckstalis, M., Fite, J.E., French, J.A., 2003. Social change affects vocal structure in a Callitrichid primate (*Callithrix kuhlii*). Ethology 109, 327–340.

Seyfarth, R.M., Cheney, D.L., 1986. Vocal development in vervet monkeys. Anim. Behav. 34, 1640–1656.

Seyfarth, R., Cheney, D., 1990. The assessment by vervet monkeys of their own and other species' alarm calls. Anim. Behav. 40, 754–764.

Seyfarth, R.M., Cheney, D.L., 1997. Vocal development in nonhuman primates. In: Snowdon, C.T., Hausberger, M. (Eds.), Social Influences on Vocal Development. Cambridge University Press, Cambridge, pp. 249–273.

Silk, J.B., Brosnan, S.F., Vonk, J., Henrich, J., Povinelli, D.J., Richardson, A.S., et al., 2005. Chimpanzees are indifferent to the welfare of unrelated group members. Nature 437, 1357–1359.

Sinnott, J.M., Stebbins, W.C., Moody, D.B., 1975. Regulation of voice amplitude by the monkey. J. Acoust. Soc. Am. 58, 412–414.

Slocombe, K.E., Zuberbühler, K., 2005. Functionally referential communication in a chimpanzee. Curr. Biol. 15, 1779–1784.

Slocombe, K.E., Zuberbühler, K., 2006. Food-associated calls in chimpanzees: responses to food types or food preferences? Anim. Behav. 72, 989–999.

Slocombe, K.E., Zuberbühler, K., 2007. Chimpanzees modify recruitment screams as a function of audience composition. Proc. Natl. Acad. Sci. USA 104, 17228–17233.

Snowdon, C.T., Boe, C.Y., 2003. Social communication about unpalatable foods in tamarins (Saguinus oedipus). J. Comp. Psychol. 117, 142–148.

Snowdon, C.T., Elowson, A.M., 1999. Pygmy marmosets modify vocal structure when paired. Ethology 105, 893–908.

Snowdon, C.T., Elowson, A.M., 2001. 'Babbling' in pygmy marmosets: development after infancy. Behaviour 138, 1235–1248.

Snowdon, C.T., Hodun, A., 1981. Acoustic adaptations in pygmy marmoset contact calls: locational cues vary with distances between conspecifics. Behav. Ecol. Sociobiol. 9, 295–300.

Stephan, C., Zuberbühler, K., 2008. Predation increases acoustic complexity in alarm calls. Biol. Lett. 4, 641–644.

Sugiura, H., 1998. Matching of acoustic features during the vocal exchange of coo calls by Japanese macaques. Anim. Behav. 55, 673–687.

Tanaka, T., Sugiura, H., Masataka, N., 2006. Cross-sectional and longitudinal studies of the development of group differences in acoustic features of coo calls of two groups of Japanese macaques. Ethology 112, 7–21.

Townsend, S.W., Deschner, T., Zuberbühler, K., 2008. Female chimpanzees use copulation calls flexibly to prevent social competition. PLoS ONE 3, e2431.

Visalberghi, E., Addessi, E., 2000. Response to changes in food palatability in tufted capuchin monkeys, Cebus apella. Anim. Behav. 59, 231–238.

Visalberghi, E., Fragaszy, D.M., 1990. Do monkeys ape? In: Parker, S.T., Gibson, K.R. (Eds.), "Language" and Intelligence in Monkeys and Apes. Cambridge University Press, Cambridge, pp. 247–275.

Völkl, B., Huber, l., 2000. True imitation in marmosets. Anim. Behav. 60, 195–202.

Vonk, J., Brosnan, S.F., Silk, J.B., Henrich, J., Richardson, A.S., Lambeth, S.P., et al., 2008. Chimpanzees do not take advantage of very low cost opportunities to deliver food to unrelated group members. Anim. Behav. 75, 1757–1770.

Wich, S.A., de Vries, H., 2006. Male monkeys remember which group members have given alarm calls. Proc. R. Soc. Lond. B 273, 735–740.

Winter, P., Hanley, P., Ploog, D., Schott, D., 1973. Ontogeny of squirrel monkey calls under normal conditions and under acoustic isolation. Behaviour 47, 230–239.

Yepez, P., de la Torre, S., Snowdon, C.T., 2005. Interpopulation differences in exudate feeding of pygmy marmosets in Ecuadoran Amazon. Am. J. Primatol. 66, 145–158.

Zahed, S.R., Prudom, S.L., Snowdon, C.T., Ziegler, T.E., 2008. Male parenting and response to infant stimuli in the common marmoset (*Callithrix jacchus*). Am. J. Primatol. 70, 84–92.

Ziegler, T.E., Washabaugh, K.F., Snowdon, C.T., 2004. Responsiveness of expectant male cotton-top tamarins, *Saguinus oedipus*, to mate's pregnancy. Horm. Behav. 45, 84–92.

Ziegler, T.E., Schultz-Darken, N.J., Scott, J.J., Snowdon, C.T., Ferris, C.F., 2005. Neuroendocrine response to female ovulatory odors depends upon social condition in male common marmosets, *Callithrix jacchus*. Horm. Behav. 47, 56–64.

Zuberbühler, K., 2000a. Interspecies semantic communication in two forest primates. Proc. R. Soc. Lond. B 267, 713–718.

Zuberbühler, K., 2000b. Causal knowledge of predators' behavior in wild Diana monkeys. Anim. Behav. 59, 209–220.

Zuberbühler, K., Jenny, D., Bshary, R., 1999. The predator deterrence function of primate alarm calls. Ethology 105, 477–490.

Survivor Signals: The Biology and Psychology of Animal Alarm Calling

Klaus Zuberbühler

SCHOOL OF PSYCHOLOGY, UNIVERSITY OF ST ANDREWS, ST ANDREWS
KY16 9JP, SCOTLAND, UNITED KINGDOM

I. Introduction

Many social species produce specific vocalizations when threatened or startled by a predator or some other significant disturbance. These signals are usually termed "alarm calls" (from old Italian "all' arme" meaning "to arms" on the approach of an enemy), but "distress," "alert," or "mobbing calls" are also common, usually in cases where the calls are given in conjunction with some specific antipredator behavior. Although many authors treat mobbing calls as functionally distinct from alarm calls, this distinction is not always useful. For example, many forest primates produce acoustically distinct alarm calls to ground predators, such as leopards, but these calls are often accompanied by mobbing behavior (e.g., Zuberbühler et al., 1997). In this chapter, I will therefore treat mobbing calls as a subtype of alarm calls, one that is linked with relatively specific antipredator behavior.

Alarm calls have long been of interest to researchers and they have continued to bewilder and fascinate, for a number of reasons. A first one is merely practical. When working with free-ranging animals, it is often difficult to divide the continuous stream of behavior into discrete and meaningful units that can be studied systematically. Alarm calls are a rare exception. They are structurally and perceptually unique, which facilitates identification and systematic study considerably.

Second, alarm calls are a particularly useful tool for studying cognitive mechanisms, often providing a rare window into an animal's mind. Diurnal life and sociality are strongly associated with whether or not a species produces alarm calls (Shelley and Blumstein, 2005) and individual callers often require a specific audience (Zuberbühler, 2008). Because of these social dimensions, alarm calls are interesting for a number of scientific

277

0065-3454/09 $35.00
DOI: 10.1016/S0065-3454(09)40008-1

disciplines. Key problems are what features of the event alarm calls convey, whether callers have a targeted audience and are aware of their situation, and whether receiver responses are driven directly by the calls or whether they are linked to specific mental representations that relate to the associated events. In this context, eavesdropping is increasingly recognized as an important process as most species live in relatively complex systems where they share some of their predators with other species (e.g., McGregor and Dabelsteen, 1996). Research on alarm calls has also helped to clarify a number of theoretical concepts, such as the nature of referential signaling, and the relation between animal signals and human communication (Tomasello, 2008; Zuberbühler, 2003).

Third, it has long been recognized that alarm calls pose somewhat of a conundrum to evolutionary theory (Maynard-Smith, 1965). In many species, alarm calls are amongst the most noticeable signals in a species' vocal repertoire, which is paradoxical as this is likely to reveal the presence and location of the caller to the predator. Why is such seemingly maladaptive behavior common in animal communication? What selection processes have provided an advantage to individuals that behave conspicuously in the presence of a predator? Much of the earlier research has focused on the impact of kin selection, but more recent studies emphasize the different ways by which callers can benefit more directly.

The objective of this review is not so much to provide a systematic overview of the alarm calling behavior in the various taxonomic groups, but to generate progress with regard to these theoretical issues, for which studies of the alarm calling have turned out to be particularly useful. A special focus will be on nonhuman primates, simply because much work has been carried out with these species especially with regard to cognitive questions, but various examples from nonprimate species will also be discussed.

II. The Evolution of Alarm Calls

Three main groups of evolutionary hypotheses have been put forward to explain why animals produce conspicuous vocalizations in the presence of a predator. Firstly, they can provide a selective advantage to the signaler if they increase the survival chances of closely related kin, the kin selection hypothesis (Maynard-Smith, 1965). Calling may be costly to the signaler and increase the predation risk but under this hypothesis this is all outweighed by the benefits of increased survival of recipients who carry a proportion of the caller's genes.

Secondly, alarm calling is beneficial to a signaler if it increases the reproductive success of the caller, the sexual selection hypothesis (Darwin, 1871). This may go by the way of receivers preferring individuals as mating partners that are more willing to produce risky alarm calls in the presence of predators, compared to more reluctant individuals. In some primates, there are considerable sexual dimorphisms in alarm calling: male calls are usually more conspicuous than female calls, suggesting that sexual selection has acted upon male callers (Zuberbühler, 2006).

Thirdly, the alarm calling is directly beneficial for the caller, if it elicits behavior in others that decreases the vulnerability of the caller, the individual selection hypothesis. Here, two main scenarios have been distinguished (Zuberbühler, 2006). A first one draws on the effects of alarm calling on other potential prey animals, usually group members, in terms of their antipredator responses. In many cases, the initial costs of alarm calling are quickly outweighed by other individuals' antipredator responses. A good example is the turmoil caused by escaping birds when hearing an alarm call, creating a cloud of confusion for the predator from which the caller can benefit (the "prey manipulation hypothesis"; Charnov and Krebs, 1975). Callers also benefit if this initiates a subsequent group effort to get rid of the predator, as for instance, in predator mobbing (the "cooperative defense hypothesis"; Curio, 1978). However, sometimes animals give alarm calls to a predator in the absence of an audience, suggesting that the behavior has evolved for other purposes. A popular idea here is that some predators are affected by the alarm calls directly and without the intermediate step of other prey behavior (the "perception advertisement" hypothesis; Bergstrom and Lachmann, 2001). This is especially the case for predators that depend on surprising their prey, which may give up hunting once detected. In the following, selected empirical findings that support one or several of the proposed selective forces underlying the evolution of alarm calling are discussed.

A. KIN SELECTION

A first solution to the apparent paradox is that individuals give alarm calls preferentially when close genetic relatives are nearby. Kin selection theory can explain the evolution of conspicuous signaling in the presence of predators, if alarm calling improves the survival of individuals that share a certain proportion of the caller's own genes (Sherman, 1977). Individuals prevented from reproduction should be especially susceptible. Another testable prediction is that the number of close relatives in the audience should impact on an individual's willingness to produce risky alarm calls. The empirical evidence for the kin selection hypothesis is strongest for the parent–offspring relation (e.g., Blumstein et al., 1997) and alarm calling in this context may be conceptualized as a form of altruistic parental care. In great gerbils (*Rhombomys opimus*), adults alarm call more often when pups are present, while solitary individuals seldom give alarms, suggesting that alarm calls primarily function to warn vulnerable offspring (Randall et al., 2000). In socially living Siberian jays (*Perisoreus infaustus*), alpha females alarm call more frequently when accompanied by offspring than by unrelated immigrants, even if they are already independent. In contrast, alpha males call indiscriminately, suggesting that they are affected by different factors (Griesser and Ekman, 2004). In gray-cheeked mangabeys (*Lophocebus albigena*) of Kibale National Park, Uganda, adult males are most active in defense but also overrepresented in the prey spectrum of crowned eagles, demonstrating the high costs of antipredator behavior. High-ranking males are most likely to alarm call and attack the eagles, suggesting that they are more motivated to secure the survival of offspring (Arlet and Isbell, 2009).

An empirically more challenging endeavor has been to explain alarm calling with the presence of nondescendent kin, such as brothers and sisters. If kin selection operates at this level to provide indirect fitness benefits, then individuals should be willing to engage in risky alarm call behavior if it increases the survival chances of closely related nondescendent kin, following Hamilton's rule (Hamilton, 1963). Considerable empirical effort has been devoted to this topic, particularly in various rodent species, but the overall picture is very inconsistent. Males and females often differ in terms of their alarm calling to the presence of nondescendent kin, suggesting that kin selection has affected individuals in sex-specific ways. For example, in Gunnison's prairie dogs (*Cynomys gunnisoni*), females with nondescendent kin call more often to a ground predator than females without nondescendent kin. Males are also keen alarm callers, but calling is unrelated to kinship of nearby listeners (Hoogland, 1996). A nondescendent kin audience can enhance alarm calling differently to aerial and ground predators. For example, Belding's ground squirrels (*Spermophilus beldingi*) show kin-sensitive responding to terrestrial predators, but in the case of aerial predators the caller's own exposure appears to be the main factor (Sherman, 1977, 1985). A study on Columbian ground squirrels (*Spermophilus columbianus*) found the opposite pattern (Macwhirter, 1992). In this species, females do not behave nepotistically toward other nondescendent kin in the presence of terrestrial predators, but do so in response to aerial predators.

Kin selection has also been put forward as an explanation for the evolution of alarm calls in nonhuman primates, but the overall evidence is even less strong. For example, spider monkeys alter their alarm call behavior as a function of the number of kin in the vicinity (Chapman et al., 1990) and gibbons produce calls than can be heard in neighboring home ranges, which are often occupied by the callers' close relatives, suggesting that these calls also warn kin (Clarke et al., 2006; Tenaza and Tilson, 1977). In Capuchin monkeys, alarm calling to vipers was consistent with the predictions of the kin selection hypothesis, but callers also benefited from attracting other conspecifics for cooperative defense (Wheeler, 2008).

In sum, alarm calling is probably widely affected by the presence of kin, but the strongest effects are found for descendents, and alarm calling may simply be one aspect of parental care. In some species, kin selection appears to have additionally favored alarm calling to benefit a nondescendent kin audience, but no clear and general patterns are visible. In cases where individuals alarm call to warn nondescendent relatives, kin selection appears to have acted in various idiosyncratic ways. Reviewing over 200 species of rodents, Shelley and Blumstein (2005) concluded that alarm signals evolved primarily to communicate to predators, but that nepotistic benefits can be important for maintaining alarm calling in a species.

B. Sexual Selection

Animals also give alarm calls when no kin is nearby, and this requires a very different set of evolutionary explanations. One is based on the idea of alarm calls as sexually selected behavior, produced by one sex as part of its attempts to increase reproductive success. Indirect evidence comes from the sexual dimorphisms in alarm call structure and usage seen in a number of species. In domestic chickens, for example, males are more likely to produce alarm calls while in the presence of unrelated females compared to other audiences (Evans et al., 1994), suggesting that alarm calls may be part of a mating strategy to enhance the caller's reproductive success. Similarly, male vervet monkeys (*Cercopithecus aethiops*) alarm call at higher rates in the presence of adult females than adult males (Cheney and Seyfarth, 1990).

In some primates, particularly the forest guenons, adult male alarm calls are structurally different from those of the adult females. The male calls are conspicuous loud signals given in response to predators and other circumstances, and they carry over remarkable distances (Gautier and Gautier, 1977). Research on West African Diana monkeys (*Cercopithecus diana*) and other forest primates has shown that these calls can function as predator alarm calls (Zuberbühler, 2003). These monkeys live in small stable social groups with one adult male and several adult females with their offspring (Uster and Zuberbühler, 2001). They are hunted by leopards (*Panthera pardus*) and crowned eagles (*Stephanoaetus coronatus*), and both the adult male and the females produce predator-specific alarm calls to these predators (Zuberbühler et al., 1997). However, the vocal behavior of the adult males consists of low-pitched high-amplitude calls given in long sequences, which carry over up to a kilometer through dense tropical forest habitat. Male–male competition is a likely candidate responsible for this structural specialization of male calls. In this case, sexual selection seems to have acted as a secondary evolutionary force on communication systems where alarm calls have already been present.

Polygynous social systems are notorious for sexually selected conspicuous male traits, including vocalizations (Clutton-Brock and Albon, 1979). In these social systems, male competition over females is especially high, which typically leads to the evolution of male traits that are useful in male–male competition or that females find attractive (Anderson, 1994). In polygynous monkeys, such as the Diana monkey, males typically try to take over a group of females and mate with them for some time until replaced by another male. If females are able to exert some choice over tenure length of a particular male, then one might expect to see a relation between female tolerance toward the male and how committed he is to engage in antipredator behavior, such as producing costly alarm calls in the presence of a predator (Eckardt and Zuberbühler, 2004). It is interesting to note that during puberty several developmental changes occur in the vocal behavior of male Diana monkeys and other guenons, specifically a drop in pitch and the loss of some of the juvenile vocal repertoire (Gautier and Gautier, 1977). Subadult male Diana monkeys go through a phase in which their alarm shows remnants of a female alarm call, but also the first emerging elements of a fully developed male loud call, suggesting that males go through a transition phase when their calls develop from female alarm calls to male loud calls (Zuberbühler, 2002a), a further sign that sexual selection has acted secondarily on the structure and usage of male monkey alarm calls.

Primates are not the only group of animals where sexual selection appears to have acted on alarm call behavior. In fowls (*Gallus gallus*), mating frequency and rate at which males produced alarm signals are related. Increased calling may result from recent mating success, a form of mate investment, but it is also possible that calling is attractive to females (Wilson and Evans, 2008). In roe deer (*Capreolus capreolus*), solitary individuals alarm call more frequently to predators than deer in groups, suggesting that the calls do not serve to warn conspecifics of potential danger, but to inform any potential predator that it has been identified. However, if a male's alarm calls are played from within a buck's territory, this provokes counter-barking or aggressive behavior, not antipredator behavior, suggesting that the male alarm calls possess a communication function in male–male competition (Reby et al., 1999).

According to Darwin (1859), sexual selection "... depends, not on the struggle for existence, but on a struggle between the males for possession of the females; the result is not death of the unsuccessful competitor, but few or no offspring." If alarm calls are unnecessarily conspicuous this could have been favored by the forces of sexual selection.

C. Individual Selection

Animals, sometime, give alarm calls in the absence of any apparent audience, suggesting that alarm calling can provide direct benefits to the caller. Two main evolutionary routes have been suggested for alarm calls to be favored by individual selection. Either the caller signals directly to the predator or it affects the behavior of other potential prey in a way that increases its own chances of survival.

1. Prey Manipulation and Cooperative Defense

Alarm calls are usually of great interest to other nearby individuals, especially if they share predators with the caller. If the alarm leads to chaotic movement, it can confuse or disorient a predator (the "prey manipulation" hypothesis, e.g., Charnov and Krebs, 1975). In starlings, for example, alarm calls trigger flock departures, thus reducing the probability of the initial caller being targeted. The alarm calling is more common when visibility is reduced, suggesting that calling has a cost to the producer (Devereux et al., 2008). In some cases, alarm calls attract other individuals to the site and this can lead to mobbing behavior, a phenomenon with its own literature (Curio, 1978). In meerkats (*Suricata suricatta*), mobbing is performed not only to deter predators but also to gather information and to allow young to learn about predators by observing adults, a hypothesis suggested on other occasions (Curio et al., 1978; Graw and Manser, 2007). In Siberian jays, kin groups mobbed predator models for longer and produced more alarm calls than nonkin groups, but predator type and the social position of the individual had further effects on mobbing behavior (Griesser and Ekman, 2005). Collective antipredator behavior can include multiple species but then this may be related to the degree of familiarity between individuals of the different species (Eckardt and Zuberbühler, 2004; Wolters and Zuberbühler, 2003). Brood parasites, such as cowbirds, can also elicit alarm calling, which then leads to mobbing to the benefit of the caller (e.g., Grim, 2008). In conclusion, if individuals share the same predator alarm calls often lead to joint antipredator behavior from which the caller can benefit in ways that would not be possible with solitary antipredator behavior.

2. Predator-Directed Signals

Alarm calls can interfere in various ways with a predator's hunting technique. One interesting example is the distress calls given by individuals when restrained by a predator. These calls often have a startling effect and appear to increase the chances of escape. However, predator-directed signals can also occur at earlier stages of a predation event. For example, if predators depend on unwary prey then alarm calling will signal detection and that further hunting is futile (the "perception advertisement" hypothesis, e.g., Bergstrom and Lachmann, 2001). Some primate alarm calls appear to function in this way, particularly to forest leopards (Zuberbühler and Jenny, 2002) and to some degree to crowned eagles (Shultz and Noë, 2002). Crowned eagles and leopards reliably elicited high rates of conspicuous alarm calls in Diana monkeys, while playbacks of two other equally dangerous predators, the chimpanzees (*Pan troglodytes*) and human poachers, never did, a pattern found in a number of species (Zuberbühler, 2003). Monkeys seem to be aware of the respective hunting strategies of these predators, and adjust their alarm calling behavior accordingly.

But are alarm calls effective in deterring predators? Results of a radio-tracking study showed that forest leopards hunt monkeys by approaching unwary groups and hiding in their vicinity, presumably to wait for individuals to descend to the ground (Zuberbühler and Jenny, 2002). The alarm calling monkeys reliably caused the leopard to abandon a hiding spot to move on and leave the area, strong evidence in support of the idea that alarm calling is directly beneficial for monkeys (Zuberbühler et al., 1999a; Fig. 1) and this is typically potentiated by the subsequent mobbing behavior of other prey animals. Bergstrom and Lachmann (2001) have generated a game-theoretical model, the watchful babbler game, aimed to explain why callers can benefit by signaling to a predator that it has been detected. The main finding was that willingness to signal increases with predator density, and increasing pursuit costs to the predator will allow for cheaper signals by the prey.

Perception advertisement is a relatively frequently encountered functional explanation of alarm calls in the recent literature, especially for primates. It has been suggested as a primary function of alarm calls in gray-cheeked mangabeys responding to crowned eagles (Arlet and Isbell, 2009) and in spectral tarsiers responding to snakes (Gursky, 2006). In capuchin monkeys, alarm calls to felids appear to be addressed to both predators and conspecifics; this can leads to cooperative defense behavior, which is also seen after alarm calls to raptors (Wheeler, 2008).

To conclude, individual selection is a powerful and ubiquitous force underlying the evolution of alarm calling in many species, but warning descendent kin and partners can also benefit callers. In many cases, it is

A

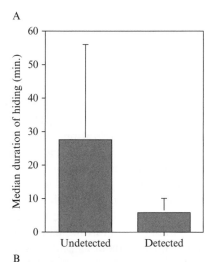

B

FIG. 1. The hunting behavior of forest leopards in the Taï Forest, Ivory Coast, is influenced by the alarm calling behavior of monkeys: (A) duration of hiding in the vicinity of a monkey group before and after detection; (B) a radio-collar is fitted to an anesthetized forest leopard to study the alarm call responses of forest monkeys to this predator (Zuberbühler et al., 1999b; photo: David Jenny).

difficult to tease apart the various possible functions, perhaps because multiple functions are present. This is well illustrated in cases where alarm calls are directly aimed at the predator. If callers enjoy a reasonable protection from being captured, other prey often joins in, leading to a cooperative effort.

III. ALARM CALL STRUCTURE

A. ACOUSTIC DIVERSITY

Many species possess a repertoire of acoustically distinct alarm calls (e.g., mammals and birds: Slobodchikoff et al., 1991; Blumstein and Arnold 1995; primates: Macedonia and Evans, 1993; Ouattara et al., 2009; Struhsaker, 1967; Birds: Gyger et al., 1987; Takahashi and Hasegawa, 2008). The diversity of calls can be the result of variation in temporal, spectral, and sequential call features. In white throated magpie-jays (*Calocitta formosa*), callers vary the temporal features of call production by altering call duration and intercall interval, and both parameters are perceptually salient to receivers (Ellis, 2008). A particularly remarkable example of alarm calling behavior is found in drongos, a family of small passerine tropical birds. In greater racket-tailed drongos (*Dicrurus paradiseus*) of Sri Lankan rainforests, callers learn to mimic alarm calls of other species and include them as part of their own alarm calling behavior (Goodale and Kotagama, 2006).

In primates, there are considerable differences in how species convey information about external events with vocal signals. A common finding is that one acoustically distinct alarm call type is given to a narrow range of aerial threats, while a second type is given to other types of danger, usually terrestrial predators or other disturbances. Capuchin monkeys, *Cebus capucinus*, produce two basic types of alarm calls, which can be separated further into different subtypes (Digweed et al., 2005). For the first call type, three subtypes could be distinguished given to aerial predators, humans (a terrestrial disturbance), and unfamiliar conspecifics. However, the second call type, given to snakes, caimans, terrestrial predators, and during aggressive interactions, revealed no clear context specificity and all acoustic variation appeared to be linked with changes in urgency, although this variable was not measured independently (Fichtel et al., 2005).

Some other primates convey information by assembling a small repertoire of calls into more complex sequences, as discussed later.

Another way to generate acoustic diversity is by modifying some of the acoustic features on a graded continuum. This type of alarm call system has been extensively studied in baboons. Female Chacma baboons (*Papio cynocephalus*) produce loud barks in response to predators but also when individuals seek to reestablish contact with other group members. The barks constitute a graded continuum, ranging from tonal to noisy-harsh. Tonal barks are given to seek contact, while harsh barks are given to mammalian carnivores and crocodiles (Fischer et al., 2001a). In playback experiments, individuals discriminated between the different bark variants, suggesting that they conveyed meaning using a graded calling system

(Fischer et al., 2001b). From about 6 months of age, infants begin to reliably discriminate between alarm and contact barks, demonstrating that call comprehension is learned (Fischer et al., 2000). Similarly, male baboons respond to predators with alarm "wahoos," but the same call type is also produced during male contests, and when a male has become separated from the group. Call variants given in these three contexts differ in a range of features, such as call rate, frequency characteristics, duration, and amplitude (Fischer et al., 2002). In playback experiments, females responded for significantly longer to alarm than to contest "wahoos" and only alarm "wahoos" caused females to flee (Kitchen et al., 2003). In Thomas langurs, males produce loud calls in a range of contexts, including to predators. The calls differed acoustically depending on context and receiver responses to the different variants suggested that they perceived the differences in loud call characteristics between the various contexts (Wich et al., 2003). In chimpanzees, finally, individuals produce screams when detecting a leopard (SOS scream, Goodall, 1986; Zuberbühler, 2000a; Fig. 2), but they also give screams during agonistic interactions (victim or aggressor screams: Slocombe and Zuberbühler, 2005a, 2007) and during social frustration (tantrum screams). Receivers are able to discriminate between the call variants, suggesting they can infer the most likely associated context (Slocombe et al., 2009; Zuberbühler, 2000a).

B. RECEIVER PSYCHOLOGY

Animal signals may have largely evolved in relation to the psychology of the targeted receivers, that is, what they find easy to detect, discriminate, and remember (Guilford and Dawkins, 1991; Klump and Shalter, 1984). One classic study is by Klump et al. (1986), who have compared the auditory sensitivity of a small songbird, the great tit, and its primary predator, the European sparrowhawk. To predators, the main demand of alarm calls is to interfere with their hunting technique. If predators spend large amounts of time observing their prey before attacking, alarm calls should be so that they can be detected easily, discriminated from other vocal signals, and remembered as a sign of a failed hunting attempt. In line with this, many species produce highly conspicuous calls to stalking predators. For example, chaffinches produce more alarm signals to models of cats than hawks (Jones and Whittingham, 2008). Many forest primates behave conspicuously to leopards, a ground predator that captures monkeys from concealed locations (Zuberbühler et al., 1999a).

Responses of monkeys to predatory chimpanzees, in contrast, are very different, reflecting the fact that their hunting behavior is not deterred by acoustic signals. To chimpanzees, monkeys escape silently to locations

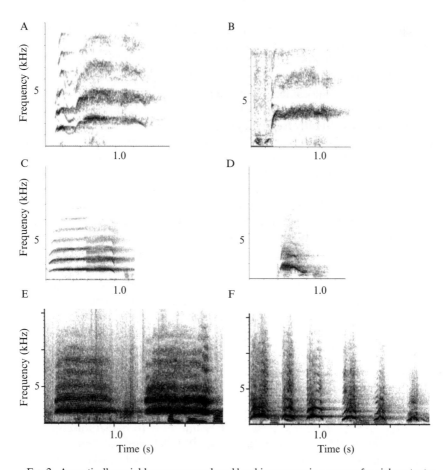

FIG. 2. Acoustically variable screams produced by chimpanzees in a range of social contexts: (A) victims screams, (B) SOS screams given to a leopard; (C) victim screams and (D) aggressor screams given during an agonistic interactions; (E) severe victim screams and (F) mild victim screams given during aggression. Chimpanzees and other primates can discriminate between the different scream variants (Slocombe et al., 2009; Zuberbühler, 2000a).

within the forest canopy where an encounter is less likely. Similarly, bird alarm calls to aerial predators are acoustically different from alarm calls to terrestrial predators, or calls given in distress or during mobbing. Marler (1955) suggested that the aerial alarm calls of birds were acoustically adapted to minimize the costs for the signaler by making localization more difficult for raptors. Many songbirds produce high-frequency "seet" calls when threatened by a raptor, a call that is difficult to locate and that also causes less interest in raptors (Jones and Hill, 2001; Jurisevic and

Sanderson, 1998). Here, natural selection appears to have favored an acoustic structure that makes perception and localization difficult, while keeping response motivation low. Aerial alarm calls are not specifically adapted to the perceptual capacities of raptors; other birds also find them hard to localize (Wood et al., 2000). When comparing the auditory sensitivity of three different songbirds, house sparrows, white-breasted nuthatches, and tufted titmice, all three species exhibited maximum sensitivity from 2.2 to 3.2 kHz, but in the high-frequency range, sensitivity varied with the maximum frequency of species-specific vocalizations (Henry and Lucas, 2008). In white-faced Capuchin monkeys, the acoustic structure of general alert calls are easier to localize than aerial alarm calls, allowing signalers to remain inconspicuous in the presence of raptors (Digweed et al., 2005).

It is very likely that predator-driven effects are modulated by habitat acoustics (see also chapter by Naguib and Brumm). If call production is tuned to receiver psychology, as argued earlier, then natural selection is likely to act on efficient signal transmission, with habitat acoustics as a key variable. In two species of whistling rats (*Parotomys brantsii* and *Parotomys littledalei*), the alarm calls consist of high-pitched vocalizations that are difficult to locate, but the lower pitched calls were produced by the species that lived in a more closed habitat, *P. littledalei*, suggesting that the transmission properties of the habitat have further shaped acoustic differences (le Roux et al., 2002). There was no evidence that alarm calls were adapted to the habitat in marmots (Blumstein, 1999).

C. INDIVIDUAL DIFFERENCES

Individual differences in vocalizations ("signatures") are reliably found across species and call types, particularly in calls given during social interactions. For example, chimpanzee calls, such as screams, copulation calls, or pant hoots, are individually distinct, allowing bystanders to assess the relevance of an ongoing social event and to locate a socially relevant partner (Slocombe and Zuberbühler, 2007; Townsend et al., 2008). The adaptive function of individual signatures in alarm calls, on the other hand, is more difficult to understand although this has been understand (e.g., Bayly and Evans, 2003; Yorzinski et al., 2006). Individual differences are likely to occur due to size and shape differences of the vocal tract, and the crucial question is whether such inevitable differences can be perceived by conspecifics. Alarm calls are a potentially attractive vehicle for dishonest signaling, suggesting that receivers benefit from an ability to recognize group members by their vocalizations. In mixed species bird flocks, where individuals do not interact repeatedly and probably do not know each other individually, deceptive alarm calling has been reported (Munn, 1986). In vervet monkeys, receivers are reluctant to respond to the alarm calls of juveniles, which often alarm call to disturbances that are not dangerous to anyone (Hauser, 1993; Seyfarth and Cheney, 1986). However, this age-effect is not universal. In yellow-bellied marmots (*Marmota flaviventris*), alarm calls of juveniles elicit greater vigilance than calls from adult females, suggesting that receivers perceive juveniles as especially vulnerable (Blumstein and Daniel, 2004). Alarm calls of adults are also individually distinct and when calls were broadcast and rerecorded over different distances, the acoustic variables that conveyed the caller's identity persisted (Blumstein and Munos, 2005). Individually distinct alarm calls have also been found in the great gerbil (*Rhombomys opinus*, Randall et al., 2005). In Belding's ground squirrels (*S. beldingi*), individually distinctive alarm calls were linked with the genetic similarity between callers, suggesting that the development of alarm call structure is under genetic control (McCowan and Hooper, 2002). Meerkats (*S. suricatta*) produce individually distinct alarm calls, but surprisingly in playback experiments, receivers failed to distinguish between different callers (Schibler and Manser, 2007). In this species, attending to individual differences may be irrelevant because unreliable callers are uncommon, and predation pressure is high.

Somewhat different results are obtained in primates. In putty-nosed monkeys, pyow (but not hack) alarm calls contain individually distinct acoustic features (Price et al., 2009). In playback experiments, females did not respond to the pyow-hack call sequences, indicating group travel, if they were produced by an unfamiliar male (Arnold and Zuberbühler, 2008), suggesting that this was because they attended to the acoustic features of the pyows. Individual differences in alarm calls have further been reported from baboons (Fischer et al., 2002), Thomas langurs (Wich et al., 2003), or cotton-top tamarins (Sproul et al., 2006).

D. POPULATION DIFFERENCES

Geographic variation in vocal behavior has been described in a wide range of species, but not normally in alarm calls. In golden-mantled ground squirrels (*Spermophilus laterialis* and *Spermophilus saturatus*), alarm calls to predatory wolves varied geographically, but this was not just due to genetic differences as changes were also observed between years (Eiler and Banack, 2004). Alarm calls of Gunnison's prairie dogs (*C. gunnisoni*) to humans differed between populations, with no differences between neighboring colonies (Slobodchikoff et al., 1998), which suggested that habitat differences could account for some of the effects (Perla and Slobodchikoff, 2002).

E. SEQUENTIAL ORGANIZATION

When responding to predators, many species respond with sequences of calls, and sometimes these calling bouts contain acoustically different call types. In fowls (*G. gallus*), males respond to raptors with distinctive aerial alarm calls, but there are significant changes throughout a sequence (Bayly and Evans, 2003). In Arabian babblers (*Turdoides squamiceps*), the first call is always a short, metallic-sounding "tzwick." In response to cats, babblers continue to use "tzwicks," but switch to long trills in response to owls (Naguib et al., 1999). Black-capped chickadees (*Poecile atricapilla*) produce significantly more chick-a-dee calls to near than distant predators, while the syllable composition also differed between the two conditions (Baker and Becker, 2002). In Carolina chickadees (*Poecile carolinensis*), the average number of note types and categories of note composition in a calling sequence was associated with the proximity of the signaler to the ground, the signaler's flight behavior, and the presence of an avian predator (Freeberg, 2008).

Richardson's ground squirrels (*Spermophilus richardsonii*) produce call sequences that consist of acoustically variable syllables. Sequences begin either with chirps or with a whistle followed by chucks. The production of chucks is related to the proximity to the disturbance and they increase vigilance in recipients (Sloan et al., 2005). Playback experiments showed that altering syllable order affected receiver responses, with the first syllable triggering strong responses regardless of their position within the (artificial) sequence (Swan and Hare, 2008a,b).

In primates, evidence for sequential signaling comes from observational work on Capuchin monkeys (*Cebus olivaceus*) (Robinson, 1984). A fraction of calls were given in sequences although it was not possible to link any of them with specific events. In Campbell's monkeys, males produce sequential signals to discriminate between different types of disturbances. One alarm call type is mainly given to crowned eagles, while another type is mainly given to leopards (Zuberbühler, 2001). If the disturbance is nonimminent, for example, if the caller heard distant alarm calls by other monkeys or if a large branch fell to the ground somewhere in the vicinity, the males reliably introduce loud calls by a pair of low-resounding "booms," followed by a 30 s period of silence, before they produced their loud calls. Playback experiments demonstrated that artificially adding booms to a loud call sequence altered the meaning of the calls for other monkeys. Nearby Diana monkeys largely ignored boom-introduced predator alarms by Campbell's monkeys, despite the fact that they normally responded very strongly if the same calls were played back without the booms (Zuberbühler, 2002a,b). Meaningful call combinations have also been found in Nigerian putty-nosed monkeys. Here, adult males produce two alarm call types to predators, "pyows" and "hacks." "Hacks" are reliably given to crowned eagles, "pyows" are given to leopards, although the match between predator category and call type is far from perfect (Arnold and Zuberbühler, 2006a), in contrast to other primates' alarm call system such as Diana or vervet monkeys (Seyfarth et al., 1980; Zuberbühler et al., 1997). One other surprising finding was that males often combined the two call types in context-specific ways (Arnold et al., 2008). One combination, some "pyows" followed by some "hacks," was highly specific, in the sense that it is a reliably predicted group movement both in predation and nonpredation situations (Arnold and Zuberbühler, 2006b). Subsequent playback experiments confirmed that it was the syntax of this call sequence, not the acoustic features of the individual components, which carried the crucial information for other group members (Arnold and Zuberbühler, 2008; Fig. 3). Black-and-white colobus monkeys possess an alarm call system that relies on the structural organization of call units, rather than just the acoustic features of individual calls, but this system differs from the ones discussed so far. Across sub-Saharan Africa, black-and-white colobus monkeys produce two basic call types, snorts and acoustically variable roars. In some areas, these calls are given before dawn, usually as part of a chorusing event involving many groups. However, the monkeys use the same basic calls also in response to predators. Field experiments have demonstrated that the syntax of these sequences is largely dependent on the external event, that is, whether callers respond to a neighbor's dawn calls or to the presence of a leopard or eagle (Schel et al., 2009). Similar to the Campbell's monkey calls, it is the sequential information that carries the bulk of the message to receivers (Candiotti et al., in preparation).

Fieldwork with free-ranging lar gibbons produced some evidence that call sequences in apes can also carry meaning. Using predator models, it could be demonstrated that both members of a pair readily produced songs in response to terrestrial predators, such as clouded leopards or tigers. These songs consisted of the same basic units as the duet songs, which are produced regularly in the morning, but the song units were arranged in different ways. Although the relevant playback experiments have yet to be carried out, some natural observations indicated that neighboring individuals (often close relatives of the callers) seemed to understand these syntactic nuances, because they responded with their own matching song type (Clarke et al., 2006).

IV. THE COGNITIVE BASES OF ALARM CALLS

A. ONTOGENY OF COMPETENCE

1. Signalers

An interesting question is whether animals have an experience-independent ability to identify their predators (Blumstein et al., 2008). In meerkats, captive-born individuals produce all alarm calls documented in the wild and

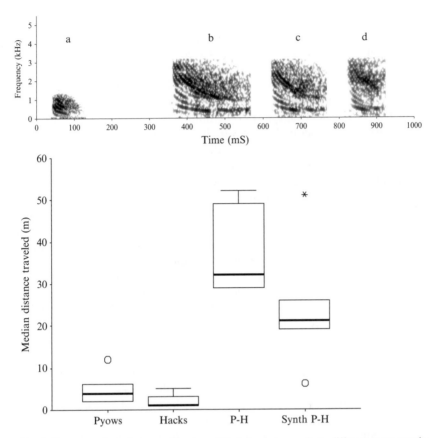

FIG. 3. Putty-nosed monkeys combine two of their loud alarm calls in different sequences in context-specific ways. Responses to crowned eagles typically consist of series of hacks and responses to leopards usually consist of series of pyows, and the two call sequences cause different responses in the group's females. If in addition the calling male is about to leave the area he combines hacks and pyows into a pyow-hack sequence, which triggers progression in listeners (Arnold and Zuberbühler, 2008). (a) hack, (b-d) pyows.

do so in similar contexts. In this species, predator recognition is strongly based on odors, which seems to be largely innate (Hollen and Manser, 2007b). Interactions with a predator, therefore, are not necessary for correct alarm-call usage in these animals. Compared to adults, however, young meerkats were less likely to give alarm calls overall, and more likely to do so to nonthreatening species, suggesting that some learning is necessary (Hollen et al., 2008). Focusing on ontogenetic patterns, one study found that the acoustic features linked to the urgency of the situation underwent developmental modification before the acoustic features linked with predator type (Hollen and Manser, 2007a).

Not much is known about how monkeys learn to use their alarm call repertoire (Janik and Slater, 2000). One core question is how a relationship between a particular alarm call and a corresponding external event is formed. Some observational data are available from free-ranging vervet monkeys. These monkeys come in contact with over 150 species of birds and mammals, and only a small proportion of them are posing a threat to them (Seyfarth and Cheney, 1997). Infant vervet monkeys do not apply their alarm calls randomly, however. Instead, they give eagle alarm calls only to birds and other objects in the air, but never to animals on the ground. Similarly, they give leopard alarm calls to a variety of species on the ground, most of which do not pose any danger to them, but then they learn to focus call usage to the relevant predator classes (Seyfarth and Cheney, 1997). Some studies have compared the alarm calling behavior of populations in which a particular predator was present or absent (e.g., Gil-da-Costa et al., 2003). In a recent one, the alarm calling response to leopards was compared between two populations of Guereza colobus monkeys in Uganda that differed in terms of their histories of leopard predation. Despite the fact that leopards had been locally extinct in one region for decades, colobus groups still responded to leopard models in largely the same way as groups from a neighboring region where leopards were common (Schel and Zuberbühler, in press). In a study on Diana monkeys, experience with leopards determined alarm calling, not in terms of the acoustic structure of alarm calls, but in how calls were produced in sequences (Stephan and Zuberbühler, 2008; Fig. 4).

A largely unexplored area of research is how social learning influences vocal behavior. In spectral tarsiers (*Tarsius spectrum*) on Sulawesi, Indonesia, infants gave alarm calls in response to all potential predator types. Infants and mothers produced a twittering alarm call to raptor models and repeated harsh loud alarm calls to snake models. Infants sometimes gave incorrect alarm calls and then, interestingly, mothers produced alarm calls at lower rates than if the infants gave correct alarm calls (Gursky, 2003).

2. Receivers

At the receiver side, the ontogenetic processes involved in acquiring adult competence are somewhat better understood (Janik and Slater, 2000). Learning appears to play a powerful role in most groups of animals. In white-browed scrubwrens (*Sericornis frontalis*), for example, fledglings respond to their parents' aerial alarm calls whereas nestlings fail to do so (Magrath et al., 2006). In contrast, nestlings responded to ground alarm calls from early on, while the response to aerial alarm calls emerged only toward the end of the nestling stage (Platzen and Magrath, 2005). In another study, nestlings did not show evidence of recognizing alarm

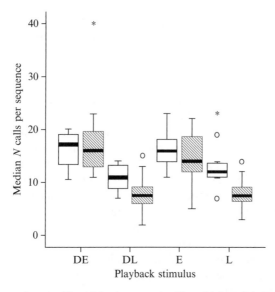

Fɪɢ. 4. Diana monkeys on Tiwai Island are not familiar with leopards but are exposed to crowned eagles, while Tai monkeys are hunted by both predators. Playback experiments have revealed differences in how callers of the two populations structure their calling behavior. Box plots indicate the median numbers of calls per sequence in Taï (hatched boxes) and Tiwai (open boxes). Diana monkeys to playbacks of eagle shrieks (E), leopard growls (L), male Diana alarm calls to eagles (DE), and male Diana alarm calls to leopards (DL). Box plots show median values, quartiles, range, and outliers. Circles and asterisks show extreme values, asterisks being more extreme (Stephan and Zuberbühler, 2008).

calls of parents until very late (Maurer et al., 2003). Yellow warblers (*Dendroica petechia*) produce "seet" calls to brood-parasitic brown-headed cowbirds (*Molothrus ater*) and "chip" calls toward mammalian and avian nest predators. Nestlings remained inactive for longer periods to chip than to seet alarm calls, suggesting that only chip calls were recognized as a source of danger (Gill and Sealy, 2003).

In laboratory rats, individuals produce ultrasonic alarm calls in the 22 kHz range, and naïve individuals are predisposed to associate these calls with aversive stimuli, which is subsequently difficult to extinguish (Endres et al., 2007). In Belding's ground squirrels (*S. beldingi*), responses to alarm calls are similar in free-living and captive juveniles, but captive individuals show more exaggerated and prolonged responses (Mateo and Holmes, 1999). In meerkats, infants initially respond to alarm calls indiscriminately by running to nearby adults. The probability of producing adult-like responses increases with age, with exposure to adult models explaining some of the observed variance in competence (Hollen and

Manser, 2006). Squirrel monkeys (*Saimiri sciureus*) appear to have an innate predisposition in order to respond to alarm peeps but require experience to associate them with the appropriate type of predatory threat (Herzog and Hopf, 1984). Infants, juveniles, and subadults responded more frequently to alarm peeps than adults, and responses changed with age. Adults responded more frequently to the alarm peeps of other adult than infants (McCowan et al., 2001).

Research on interspecies communication is another fruitful area to study how individuals come to understand alarm signals. For example, birds that migrate together respond to each other's alarm calls, but some of these calls are not universally recognized by other birds (Nocera et al., 2008). In Verreaux's sifakas (*Propithecus verreauxi*) of Madagascar, infants from about 6 months no longer run toward an adult but perform predator-specific escape responses to alarm calls of conspecifics and those of other species (Fichtel, 2008). In another study, captive and wild populations of sifakas produced the same acoustically distinct alarm calls to raptors and ground predators, but differences were found in usage and comprehension (Fichtel and van Schaik, 2006).

B. WHAT INFORMATION IS CONVEYED?

The alarm calling has been related to physiological stress responses, according to a study on yellow-bellied marmots (*M. flaviventris*) (Blumstein et al., 2006). What specific aspects of a predator encounter callers respond to (e.g., degree of threat or predator category), however, is a contentious issue.

1. Predator-Specific Alarm Calls

The classic study for predator-specific alarm calls was conducted on East African vervet monkeys. In this primate, individuals produce acoustically different alarm calls to at least five different types of predator: large terrestrial carnivores, eagles, snakes, baboons, and unfamiliar humans (Struhsaker, 1967). Some of these calls elicit antipredator responses in other monkeys that resemble their natural response to the corresponding predators. For example, playbacks of eagle alarm calls cause monkeys to look up into the air or run into a bush (Seyfarth et al., 1980). Similar findings have been reported from other monkey species. In Diana monkeys, when hearing a male's alarm calls nearby females respond with their own corresponding alarm calls, suggesting that the calls contain information about the type of predator present (Zuberbühler et al., 1997). Free-ranging saddleback and moustached tamarins (*Saguinus fuscicollis* and *Saguinus mystax*) in Peru each produce acoustically distinct alarm calls to aerial and terrestrial predators. Playbacks of conspecific and heterospecific alarm calls showed that receivers responded by looking into the direction from where the predator was most likely to be expected. The acoustic features of the calls, in other words, provided sufficient information about the predator type or the appropriate reaction (Kirchhof and Hammerschmidt, 2006). In a study on redfronted lemurs and white sifakas (*P. verreauxi*), gaze and escape directions corresponded to the hunting strategies of the two predator classes, suggesting that the corresponding vocalizations were categorized correctly. The terrestrial alarm call was less specific than the aerial alarm calls because it was also given to a range of other disturbances (Fichtel and Kappeler, 2002).

Birds have long been known to possess acoustically distinct alarm calls, typically in response to raptors and terrestrial predators (Curio, 1969). In pale-winged trumpeters (*Psophia leucoptera*), for example, adults produce a range of vocalizations, including alarm calls to raptors and terrestrial predator, but the terrestrial alarm call is also used for conspecific intruders. Receivers respond to these calls as to the corresponding event, suggesting that they denote meaning to the calls (Seddon et al., 2002). In yellow warblers (*D. petechia*), parents produce a "seet" alarm calls in response to brood-parasitic brown-headed cowbirds (*M. ater*) and chip alarm calls to nest predators and other intruders, but not cowbirds. In a population allopatric with cowbirds, seet calls were rarely produced in response to cowbird or avian nest predator models and never to seet playbacks, suggesting that the seet calls can take on a specific meaning (Gill and Sealy, 2004). In black-capped chickadees (*P. atricapilla*), the acoustic features of predator calls vary with the size of the predator, and receivers appear to understand the implications of the acoustic differences (Templeton et al., 2005).

In great gerbils, *R. opinus*, individuals produce acoustically distinct alarm calls to dogs, humans, and monitor lizards, with age, sex, and other individual factors explaining a further proportion of the acoustic variance (Randall et al., 2005). In Gunnison's prairie dogs (*C. gunnisoni*), as discussed earlier, individuals respond to live predators in a relatively specific ways, which are identical to their responses of the corresponding alarm calls (Kiriazis and Slobodchikoff, 2006). In addition, the acoustic structure of alarm calls to terrestrial predators varies as a function of stimulus silhouette (Ackers and Slobodchikoff, 1999), a finding also reported from black-tailed prairie dogs (*Cynomys ludovicianus*) (Frederiksen and Slobodchikoff, 2007).

2. Urgency-Related Alarm Calls

Alarm calls have been interpreted as threat- or urgency-related in a number of species. Empirically, this is mostly based on the finding that some structural aspect of the alarm signal changes with the distance between the caller and the predator. For example, reed warblers (*Acroce-phalus scirpaceus*) give the same alarm calls to common cuckoos (*Cuculus canorus*, a nest parasite), and sparrow hacks (*Accipiter nisus*, a predator), but call usage varies with distance from the nest (Welbergen and Davies, 2008). In great gerbils (*R. opimus*), three different alarm vocalizations can be discriminated but these calls are related to the distance of the predator and hence signaled urgency, and receiver responses mirrored this distance-related specificity (Randall and Rogovin, 2002). In three species of marmots, Olympic (*Marmota olympus*), hoary (*Marmota caligata*), and Vancouver Island marmots (*Marmota vancouverensis*), call structure also varied as a function of distance to and type of the disturbance. However, callers often changed calls within a calling bout and there were no call-specific responses observed in receivers (Blumstein, 1999). In primates, some studies have interpreted acoustic variables of alarm calls to vary with threat-related variables. In bonnet macaques (*Macaca radiata*), for instance, callers were exposed to models of leopards and pythons, but differences in alarm call structure were explained with the level of perceived threat, not predator type (Coss et al., 2007). In domestic chickens (*G. gallus*), cockerels produce acoustically distinct alarms to raptors and ground predators, suggesting that these alarm calls might function as labels for certain predator classes. However, experiments have shown that callers mainly respond to a predator's direction of attack, regardless of its biological class. For example, when a picture of a raccoon, a typical ground predator, is moved across an overhead video screen, cockerels respond with aerial alarm calls, which they normally give to raptors (Evans et al., 1994). Similarly, some species of squirrels produce acoustically distinct alarm calls, but they too do not appear to respond to the predator category *per se*, but to the relative distance and threat imposed by the predator (Leger et al., 1980).

Urgency is often expressed in the temporal features of an alarm call sequence. In Brants' whistling rat (*Parotomys branisii*), the duration of alarm calls is related to the threat of the situation, although this parameter did not affect receiver responses (Le Roux et al., 2001b). Richardson's ground squirrels (*S. richardsonii*) produce repetitive calls to predator models and call rates are inversely correlated with the distance between the caller and the disturbance. Receivers respond with increased vigilance as call rate goes up (Warkentin et al., 2001). Richardson's ground squirrels also produce alarm calls in the ultrasonic 48 kHz region; while the ratio of ultrasonic to audible 8 kHz alarm calls increases with increasing distance from the disturbance. Ultrasonic calls do not travel well in space, making them more suitable for close-range communication (Wilson and Hare, 2006).

In a playback study, the effects of call length and variation in intersyllable latency in repetitive alarm calls on the behavior of call recipients were examined and results showed that the length of calls had no significant effect but recipients showed greater vigilance after the playback of monotonous calls than after variable calls (Sloan and Hare, 2004).

The urgency of the situation may also become apparent for a receiver by focusing on the number of individuals producing alarm calls. In Richardson's ground squirrels, repetitive alarm calls of two juvenile callers, played from separate speakers, induced greater vigilance in adults, but not other juveniles than the calls of one juvenile caller only (Sloan and Hare, 2008).

3. Combined Messages

In some species, both predator type and urgency-related features appear to be encoded in the same utterance. For example, white-browed scrubwren (*S. frontalis*) produce a specific aerial trill alarm call, which consists of more elements and higher pitch if the predator is close, something that is recognized by listeners (Leavesley and Magrath, 2005). Meerkats produce acoustically distinct alarm calls to different predator types, but their call structure also varies depending on the level of urgency (Manser, 2001). In playback experiments, receivers responded differently to alarm calls given to snakes, and to aerial or terrestrial predators. Within the aerial alarm calls, however, responses differed depending on the level of urgency encoded in the calls (Manser et al., 2001), suggesting that some of their alarm calls simultaneously encode both predator type and the signaler's perception of urgency (Manser et al., 2002).

In primates, the typical finding is that individuals produce acoustically distinct calls to different types of disturbances, but other factors may also be at work in some species. In squirrel monkey (*S. sciureus*), responses to artificially modified mobbing calls increased with call frequency and amplitude (Fichtel and Hammerschmidt, 2003). Redfronted lemurs (*Eulemur fulvus*) give specific alarm calls only toward raptors, and another alarm call type to terrestrial predators, such as dogs, and during intergroup encounters, which differs in frequency depending on the two contexts. Altering the frequency or amplitude of the calls generated differences in the orienting response of receivers, demonstrating that individuals attended to these features (Fichtel and Hammerschmidt, 2002).

A difficult problem, rarely addressed in field studies, is to separate the effects of predator type from the threat exerted by the predator. In Diana monkeys, callers responded to predator type, while distance (and hence threat) had only minor effects within the different alarm calls

(Zuberbühler, 2000b; Fig. 5). Similar findings have also been reported from Campbell's monkeys, *Cercopithecus campbelli* (Zuberbühler, 2003), suggesting that nonhuman primates generally label the biological class of a predator, regardless of momentary discrepancies in degrees of threat.

4. The Evolution of Urgency and Predator-Related Signaling

What exactly has lead to the evolution of predator-related signaling has caused a lively debate. One idea is that the distinction between urgency and predator-related alarm calling has to do with the caller's habitat. For species inhabiting three-dimensional habitats, it may be more adaptive to produce signals that classify predator types, whereas those living in two-dimensional environments may benefit better from signaling the risk associated with a disturbance, especially if individuals rely on only one basic escape strategy. The hypothesis was addressed with a study on Brants' whistling rat (*P. brantsii*). Individuals were exposed to three predator types, human, raptor, and snake. Calls did not differ between predator types, but call duration varied positively with distance (Le Roux et al., 2001a). This hypothesis was challenged by a set of studies on Gunnison's prairie dogs. Here, individuals produced alarm calls to red-tailed hawks (*Buteo jamaicensis*), domestic dogs (*Canis familaris*), and coyotes (*Canis latrans*). Although the alarm calls produced to these predators were composed of the same structures, their relative distribution was predator-dependent (Slobodchikoff and Placer, 2006). Responses to the different alarm calls were compared with responses to the corresponding predators, and this did not reveal any differences (Kiriazis and Slobodchikoff, 2006). The habitat hypothesis also failed to explain the alarm calling behavior in suricates, despite the fact that they only have one escape response, to retreat to bolt holes (Manser et al., 2001).

Another hypothesis is that the range of predators, and the type of adaptive antipredator responses, may be more important than the habitat, as demonstrated in various monkey species. This idea has received support from game-theoretic modeling. It was found that when the number of alarm signals is limited, the evolutionary trend is to group together the situations, which require similar responses (Donaldson et al., 2007).

C. EAVESDROPPING

Eavesdropping is usually defined as the use of signal information by individuals other than the primary target. Who exactly the target of signaling event is can be difficult to decide, unless other species are involved. Eavesdropping, thus, is typically reported from studies on heterospecific interactions (e.g., Templeton and Greene, 2007). A general assumption is

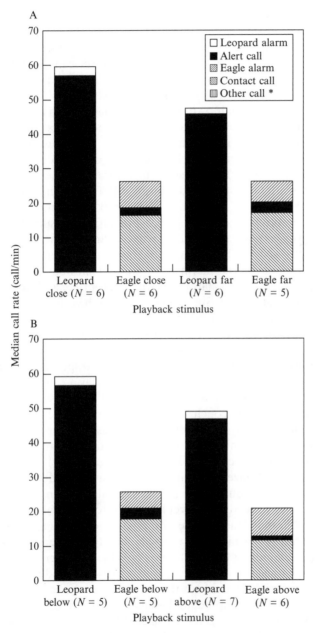

FIG. 5. The acoustic structure of Diana monkey alarm calls is mainly determined by the predator type present, while distance and direction of attack only have minor effects. Box plots depict female vocal behavior in response to leopards and crowned eagles as a function of (A) predator distance and (B) elevation. Bars represent the median number of calls produced in the first minute after onset of the playback stimulus (Zuberbühler, 2000d).

that individuals will benefit most from responding to the alarm signals of another species if they have similar predators, as the case, for instance, in mixed species bird flocks or polyspecific monkey groups.

In the Sri Lankan rainforest, the aerial alarm calls of Orange-billed Babbler (*Turdoides rufescens*) and Greater Racket-tailed Drongos (*D. paradiseus*) cause babblers to move quickly away from the playback speaker after hearing their own species' or drongo alarm calls, but drongos show no difference in response to any treatment (Goodale and Kotagama, 2008). Drongos are known to mimic a variety of sounds associated with danger, including the calls of alarm calls of other species in the forest (Goodale et al., 2008). It is possible, therefore, that they are better than other birds in attending to subtle acoustic differences, and thus recognized the playback stimuli as artificial. In another experiment, the aerial alarm calls of white-browed scrubwrens (*S. frontalis*) and superb fairy-wrens (*Malurus cyaneus*) were used as playback stimuli. The two species co-occur in mixed species flocks during the nonbreeding season, and produce acoustically similar aerial alarm calls. Results showed that both species responded to each other's alarm calls with appropriate antipredator behavior (Magrath et al., 2007). Subsequent research has shown, however, that the ability to eavesdrop on other species' alarm calls is entirely based on learning, even when the two species produce acoustically similar alarm calls to the same predator. Fairy-wrens responded to playback of the acoustically similar scrubwren aerial alarm calls only if the two species lived in sympatry. Moreover, fairy-wrens responded to aerial alarm calls of a honeyeater (*Phylidonyris novaehollandiae*), despite the fact that these calls were acoustically very different. In conclusion, in these birds call similarity is neither sufficient nor necessary for interspecific eavesdropping (Magrath et al., 2009). The idea of learning is further supported by the responses to alarm calls of black-capped chickadees (*Poecile atricapillus*) by resident and migrant birds in Belize. Familiarity with the chickadees alarm calling behavior was a prerequisite for proper responses, even if the calls were broadcast out of context at a novel location (Nocera et al., 2008).

It is possible that much of the observed eavesdropping is the result of simple associative learning. For example, in adult golden-mantled ground squirrels (*Spermophilus lateralis*) it was possible to associate a novel sound with the appearance of a predator, using a classical conditioning protocol. After repeated trials, individuals that experienced the tone paired with the hawk responded with antipredator behavior that was indistinguishable from responses to natural, conspecific alarm calls (Shriner, 1999). It is, therefore, not surprising perhaps that eavesdropping is by no means restricted to operating within particular groups of animals. For example, red squirrels (*Sciurus vulgaris*) and sympatric Eurasian jays (*Garrulus glandarius*) share the same predators, and red squirrels respond with antipredator behavior to playbacks of jay alarm calls, but not to control sounds (Randler, 2006). Similarly, eastern chipmunks respond to the alarm calls of eastern tufted titmice (Schmidt et al., 2008).

Although alarm calling is a typical feature of sociality, the ability to eavesdrop is not. In Gunther's dik-diks (*Madoqua guentheri*), a monogamous, territorial, and nonsocial miniature antelope with a simple vocal repertoire, individuals responded to playback of white-bellied go-away bird (*Corythaixoides leucogaster*) alarm calls by running to cover, decreasing their foraging activity, increasing their rate of head turning, and increasing their period of vigilance compared to control stimuli (Lea et al., 2008). A similar pattern emerged in a study on highly territorial zenaida doves (*Zenaida aurita*) that have no vocal alarm signals of their own. They often associate with Carib grackles (*Quiscalus lugubris*), which produce conspicuous alarm calls. Zenaida doves suppressed foraging, remained alert, and tail-flicked in response to grackle alarm calls (Griffin et al., 2005). In another study, it was found that a nonvocal reptile, the Galapagos marine iguana (*Amblyrhynchus cristatus*) eavesdrops on the alarm call of the Galapagos mockingbird (*Nesomimus parvulus*) and responds with antipredator behavior despite the fact that iguanas do not produce any acoustic signals themselves (Vitousek et al., 2007).

Primates are also highly attentive to the alarm calls of other species. Vervet monkeys (*C. aethiops*), for example, respond to superb starlings' (*Spreo superbus*) terrestrial and raptor alarm calls, and young vervet monkeys need several months to learn to recognize starling alarm calls (Hauser, 1988). Ring-tailed lemurs (*Lemur catta*) respond appropriately not only to their own alarm calls but also to playbacks of the alarm calls of sympatric sifakas (*P. verreauxi*, Oda and Masataka, 1996). The various monkey species living in the West African forests regularly forage in mixed species groups to improve their protection against predation, and it is, therefore, not surprising that individuals of mixed species groups respond to each other's alarm calls, such as in the case of the Diana monkey—Campbell's monkey association (Wolters and Zuberbühler, 2003). This ability, however, is not a uniquely primate capacity. Yellow-casqued and black-casqued hornbills readily distinguish between Diana monkey eagle and leopard alarm calls as well (Rainey et al., 2004a,b; Fig. 6).

What exactly receivers are able to extract from heterospecific alarm calls is a more demanding problem. Banded mongooses (*Mungos mungo*) respond to alarm calls of several sympatric plover species (*Vanellus* spp.). Plover alarms mainly encode the level of urgency experienced by the caller, but there was no evidence that the mongooses differentiated between calls given in high and low urgency situations (Muller and Manser, 2008).

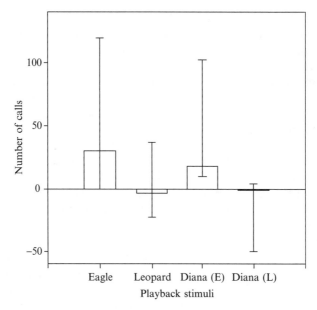

FIG. 6. Hornbills respond to Diana monkey alarm calls, provided they signal the presence of a crowned eagle, a predator shared by both species (Rainey et al., 2004).

D. COGNITION OF COMPREHENSION

What kinds of mental representations do individuals activate when hearing another individual's alarm calls? A cognitively simple model suggests that responses to alarm calls are based on superficial processing of the calls' physical features. Call comprehension, in this view, does not require any specialist cognitive equipment but can be handled by general associative learning mechanisms (Tomasello, 2008). Alternatively, alarm call processing might be more akin to that of linguistic information processing. In human language, speech sounds are not just processed at the peripheral acoustic level, but in relation to the types of cognitive structures they refer to, which are shared by both the signaler and the recipient (Yates and Tule, 1979). Under this model, alarm calls are processed by signalers accessing the meanings potentially associated with the calls, that is, the mental representation associated with the calls.

The notion that animals possess mental concepts, akin to ours, is not universally accepted, despite decades of research (Herrnstein and Loveland, 1964). One parsimonious hypothesis is that animals simply learn to generalize across stimuli, rather than forming mental concepts. For example, an individual may simply learn, over hundreds of exposures, to attend to the peripheral features common to a training set, rather than accessing the organizing principle. Using extensive conditioning paradigms can be problematic since the training experience itself can interfere with the mental concepts to be investigated. Evolutionary relevant mental concepts should reveal themselves unprompted and during natural acts of communication.

In one such study, Diana monkeys were exposed to typical vocalizations of their predators, crowned eagles or leopards, or the corresponding monkey alarm calls to them (Zuberbühler et al., 1999b). In each trial, the playback speaker was positioned in the vicinity of a Diana monkey group to play two stimuli, a prime and a probe, separated by 5 min of silence. Monkeys were primed with either a predator vocalization followed by the same predator vocalization (baseline condition) or alarm calls followed by the matching or nonmatching predator vocalization (test and control conditions). Results showed that the semantic content of the prime stimuli, not the acoustic features, explained the response patterns of the monkeys: Both eagle shrieks and leopard growls, two normally very powerful stimuli, lost their effectiveness in eliciting alarm calls in the test condition if subjects were primed first with the corresponding male alarm calls (Fig. 7).

In another experiment, the alarm calls of crested guinea fowls (*Guttera pucherani*), a gregarious ground-dwelling forest bird, to ground predators were investigated. When hearing these alarm calls, Diana monkeys respond as if a leopard were present, suggesting that the monkeys associate guinea fowl alarm calls with the presence of a leopard. However, crested guinea fowls sometimes give the same alarm calls to humans. For Diana monkeys, the best antipredator response to humans is to remain silent to avoid detection. In playback experiments, different groups of Diana monkeys were primed to the presence of a leopard or a human poacher, by playing back brief recordings of either leopard growls or human speech in the vicinity of a monkey group. After a 5-min period of silence, the same group was exposed to playbacks of guinea fowl alarm calls. Results revealed significant differences in the way leopard-primed and human-primed Diana monkey groups responded to guinea fowl alarm calls, suggesting that the monkeys' response was not driven by the guinea fowl alarm calls themselves, but by the type of predator most likely to have caused the birds' alarm calls (Zuberbühler, 2000c).

A similar problem exists when the monkeys are confronted with a nearby group of chimpanzees, a dangerous predator. Chimpanzees are occasionally attacked by leopards themselves (Zuberbühler and Jenny, 2002) and when this happens they give loud and conspicuous "SOS" screams (Goodall, 1986). When chimpanzee SOS screams were broadcast to different groups of Diana monkeys about half of all the groups switched from a

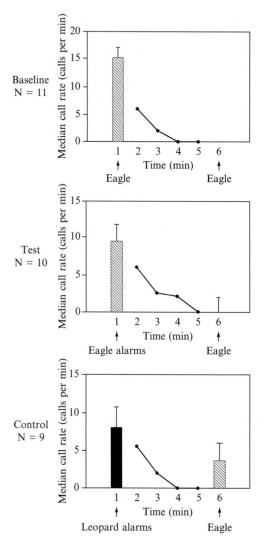

FIG. 7. Diana monkeys no longer respond to predator vocalizations if they have been warned by the corresponding alarm calls 5 min earlier (Zuberbühler et al., 1999a).

chimp-specific cryptic response to a leopard-specific conspicuous response, suggesting that in some groups individuals assumed the presence of a leopard when hearing the chimpanzee alarm screams. Interestingly, Diana monkey groups with a home range in the core area of a resident chimpanzee community were significantly more likely to do so than peripheral groups, which were more likely to respond cryptically, suggesting that Diana monkey groups differ in semantic knowledge of chimpanzee vocal behavior (Zuberbühler, 2000a).

Primates, in other words, process their own and other species' alarm calls on a conceptual-semantic rather than a perceptual-acoustic level. Whether this is true for other groups of animals is largely unknown.

E. AUDIENCE EFFECTS AND SOCIAL AWARENESS

Humans are generally aware of what their receivers understand and know about a situation, and human communication is heavily influenced by this factor. Meaning is shared between individuals. Human communication, hence, is more than the product of a mere stimulus-response contingency and involves signalers actively assessing receivers' mental states. Whether such social awareness is a uniquely human trait, or whether precursor abilities are also present in nonhuman animals is an open question. The literature on audience effects is relevant to this question. Audience effects have been observed widely, also in studies of alarm calling behavior. For example, the 22 kHz ultrasonic alarm calls of rats are dependent on conspecific presence and the caller's own assessment of safety (Litvin et al., 2007, but see Wohr and Schwarting, 2008). In yellow mongoose, individuals do not produce alarm calls when alone (Le Roux et al., 2008), and in Thomas langurs (*Presbytis thomasi*), males only emit alarm calls if they are with an audience (Wich and Sterck, 2003). Primates are also sensitive to the composition of their audience, particularly the presence of kin or mates (e.g., Cheney and Seyfarth, 1985), but an unresolved issue is whether callers can alter their calling behavior in systematic ways to affect the behavior of nearby individuals. In Thomas langurs, males continued to give alarm calls to a model predator until all other group members had given at least one alarm call themselves, as if the males were trying to keep track of which group members had and had not called (Wich and de Vries, 2006). Similarly, in a study on blue monkey alarm calls, adult mlaes were exposed to playbacks of a neighbor's eagle alarm calls. Results showed that male responded with significantly more eagle alarm calls if group members were close to the calling neighbor (and presumed eagle) compared to when they were further away, regardless of the calling male's own position (Papworth et al., 2008; Fig. 8). Nonhuman primates, and possibly other social mammals, it seems, exhibit a considerable amount of social awareness, although this ability has revealed itself more clearly in other contexts (Slocombe and Zuberbühler, 2007).

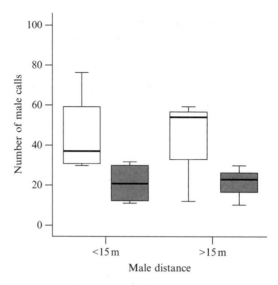

Fig. 8. Blue monkey males alarm call more if their group is close to a suspected eagle than if they are further away, regardless of their own position relative to the eagle. Box plots indicate male calling effort as a function of females' distance to the speaker. White boxes represent cases when the females were close (<15 m) and gray boxes when they were far from the stimulus (>15 m) (Papworth et al., 2008).

F. DECEPTION

Deceptive use of alarm calling has originally been observed in mixed species flocks of birds (Evans et al., 2004; Munn, 1986). More recently, similar observations have been made in mixed species associations between gork-tailed drongos (*Dicrurus adsimilis*) and pied babblers (*Turdoides bicolor*). When foraging alone drongos remain silent in the face of terrestrial predators, but when foraging with babblers they consistently produce alarm calls. Babblers respond to drongo alarm calls by fleeing to cover, providing drongos with opportunities to steal babbler food items by occasionally giving false alarm calls (Ridley et al., 2007).

Within conspecific social groups, deceptive alarm calling is not common (Wheeler, 2009). One potential strategy to minimize the costs of deception is for receivers to assess signalers in terms of their reliability. In Richardson's ground squirrels, for example, receivers discriminate between reliable and unreliable signalers, which is revealed in terms of their responsiveness (Hare and Atkins, 2001), a finding also reported from vervet monkeys (Cheney and Seyfarth, 1988). In yellow-bellied marmots (*M. flaviventris*), receivers assess the reliability of a caller based on which they decide how much time to allocate to vigilance (Blumstein et al., 2004).

V. CONCEPTUAL ISSUES

From a biological perspective, human language is just another example of the diverse ways by which mammals can communicate. Although human language is a complex and flexible behavior, it has shared most of its evolutionary past with other mammals. Only very recently, some hundred thousand years according to one theory (Enard et al., 2002), did humans begin to diverge significantly from the rest of the animal world in terms of their communication skills. This process coincided with other important changes, including a rapid increase in brain size, which makes it difficult to decide whether language is a specially adapted behavior, or the by-product of other transitions.

In language, speakers possess two main mechanisms to generate meaning. Either they can produce meaning through the semantic content encoded by an utterance or they generate nonencoded signals, such as pointing, changing the tone of voice, or gestures that are understood by both signaler and recipient (Tomasello, 2008). The compound meaning, therefore, is thus largely determined by the intentions with which speakers produce the utterance in a given context. Grice (1969) has argued that producing a meaningful utterance is thus equivalent with getting the recipient to recognize the intention of the utterance, a crucial feature of human communication. Whether or not the Grician approach has any heuristic value for studying animal communication is controversial, recent research on primate gestural communication has produced considerable progress in relation to the question of animal intentionality (Call and Tomasello, 2007).

A. REFERENCE, MEANING, AND AROUSAL

In the animal literature, referential communication is usually defined as "encoding information about environmental events" (external reference), which is distinguished from encoding individual attributes, such as species, size, or motivational state (internal reference) (Evans, 1997). Macedonia and Evans (1993) have produced a list of criteria required for demonstrating reference, in terms of production and perception criteria. First, a signal only qualifies as "referential" if its eliciting stimuli belong to a common category, for example, "leopard" or "ground predator." The "perception" criterion concerns the receivers. Here, the requirement is that a signal alone is sufficient to trigger appropriate responses, regardless of context, some-thing that is usually demonstrated with playback experiments. In Macedonia and Evans' view referential and context-dependent signaling are largely equivalent, provided the signaler reliably produces a particular signal in response to a specific event (=context), to which the receiver responds with an appropriate response.

The classic study for Macedonia and Evans-type animal referential commu-nication is the well-known field experiment with free-ranging vervet monkeys (Seyfarth et al., 1980). These monkeys produce a range of alarm calls to different predator types, and listeners respond to these calls in ways that suggest they are linked to mental representations of the corresponding preda-tor categories. A number of other studies have reported similar findings, although the evidence is usually stronger for the perception criterion. For example, chimpanzees produce rough grunts when encountering food, and the acoustic fine structure of these calls corresponds strongly with the perceived value of the food (Slocombe and Zuberbühler, 2005a,b). In playback experiments, it was possible to demonstrate that different rough grunt types conveyed information about food. In this study, the chimpanzees learned that two types of food, apple and bread, were consistently given at two different locations. When hearing the rough grunts given to bread, the subject was more likely to search at the bread location, than when hearing rough grunts to apples.

Although Macedonia and Evans' (1993) production and perception criteria are intuitively straightforward and widely used for referential communication in animal literature, a number of issues have emerged over the years. First, concerning the production criterion, if a signal is not stimulus specific, it must be explained in other terms, such as arousal, motivation, or response urgency. In long-term studies, instances of atypical call production usually accumulate, making it less and less likely that the production criterion can be fulfilled. For instance, putty-nosed monkeys typically give "hacks" to crowned eagles, but sometimes males produce the same calls to a falling branch. Of course, it is always possible that there are subtle differences between the hacks given to eagles and falling branches, which are meaningful to listeners, but it is equally possible that there are no unifying principles within the human conceptual system. The "production" criterion is anthropomorphic because it depends on finding a mental concept that encompasses all calling events, regardless of the psychological processes that take place in the animal. Concerning the perception criterion, one complication is that some primates are capable of invoking several meanings when hearing a particular call type, and subsequently use context to select among the semantic alter-natives. As mentioned before, in the absence of further evidence Diana monkeys respond to playbacks of guinea fowl alarm calls as if a leopard were present, but they alter their responses if the guinea fowls' alarm calls are caused by human presence (Zuberbühler, 2000c). Strictly speaking, these cases failed the perception criterion because listeners take the ongoing context into account if it is relevant and available.

It is also relevant that the term "reference" is used very differently in other literatures. Pointing, for instance, is widely considered to be referential, even though it fails Macedonia and Evans' (1993) production criterion. Pointing merely joins the attention of the signaler and recipient to an external referent, while the emerging meaning depends entirely on the knowledge and conventions shared by signaler and receiver (Tomasello, 2008). For example, by pointing to a snake a signaler can refer to its color, location, biological species, deadness, or request for it to be removed. The referent, in other words, has less to do with the specifics of the object, but with what assumptions signalers and receivers make about each other's intentions and world knowledge. These considerations take the quest for the mammalian origins of human language away from reference as conceptualized by Ogden and Richards (1923) referential triangle, toward an investigation of the biological roots of cooperative motivation and social awareness during the acts of communication.

B. THE EVOLUTION OF ARTICULATION

Alarm calls have also helped to clarify a number of problems concerning the basic biology of sound production in animals. Humans possess extraordinary motor control over their articulators, the physical basis of speech production, and alarm calls have been somewhat useful for understanding the origins of vocal flexibility. For mammals, the default assumption has long been that animal vocal tracts resemble a uniform tube with no relevant constrictions (Lieberman, 1968; Lieberman et al., 1969). In a uniform vocal tract, the resonance frequencies produced by the larynx will appear as evenly spaced multiples of the first resonance in the spectrogram. Frequency modulation, according to the uniform-tube idea is achieved at the level of the sound source, not due to vocal tract filtering (Riede and Zuberbühler, 2003a,b). Acoustic analyses have revealed that Diana monkey alarm calls contain two main and acoustically modulated formants, something that is not predicted under the uniform-tube hypothesis. Using lateral radiographs and postmortem dissection, Riede et al. (2005) determined the geometry of the Diana monkeys' vocal tract and identified a number of constrictions between vocal folds and lips (Fig. 9). Moreover, when responding to a leopard, forest guenons, such as Campbell's, Diana, or putty-nosed

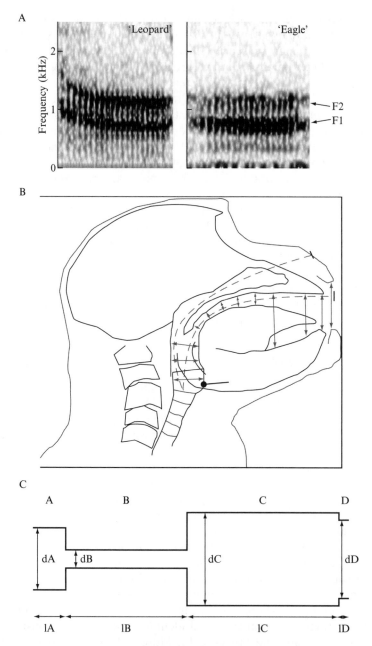

FIG. 9. Diana monkey vocal tracts contain constrictions that enable callers to produce formant frequencies, which can be modulated by mandible, lip, and larynx movements. (A) Male leopard and eagle alarm calls, (B) schematic representation of a Diana monkey vocal tract, and (C) three-tube model of a Diana monkey vocal tract capable of replicating the basic formant frequency patterns seen in natural calls (Riede et al., 2005).

monkeys, produce alarm calls with formants exhibiting a strong decrease in frequency. A study in Diana monkeys has shown that these modulations are not caused by changes at the level of the sound source, since very little variability in the fundamental frequency was observed. In sum, there is good evidence that nonhuman primates are able to constrict the pharynx and other regions of the vocal tract, during alarm call production, to achieve acoustic effects similar to those caused by tongue movements, the principle way of articulation in humans. Although sophisticated tongue movement can be observed in nonhuman primates, this is typically in the context of food transport. To what degree tongue movements play a role during vocal behavior in animals is still largely unknown.

VI. CONCLUSIONS

The alarm calling is found in a large number of species, demonstrating its adaptive value in predation avoidance. There is evidence that alarm calls are or have been under the influence of all major selective forces, that is, individual, kin, and sexual selection. In nonhuman primates, alarm calling is the result of complex cognitive processes. This is interesting because predation is an ecological force often thought to have lead to rather basic behavioral patterns, not higher cognitive abilities. Instead, complex cognitive processes, such as inference making, causal understanding, semantic and syntactic processing, and rapid association learning have also been reported. Alarm call studies have also been useful for addressing problems of how animals generate meaning, although many argue that the resemblance with human language is only superficial, mainly because there is no good evidence that signalers try to communicate their intentions, something that characterizes human language. Instead, callers respond to external events that often have direct survival consequences, and receivers are left on their own to make sense of these contingencies provided by the caller.

Acknowledgments

Much of the field research reviewed in this chapter was made possible by grants of the University of Pennsylvania, the US National Science Foundation, the Leakey Foundation, the National Geographic Society, the Max-Planck-Society, the Swiss National Science Foundation, the European Science Foundation (OMLL), the British Academy, the Leverhulme Trust, BBSRC, and EU FP6 Pathfinder Initiative. I am grateful to the Royal Zoological Society of Scotland for providing core support for the Budongo Conservation Field Station.

References

Ackers, S.H., Slobodchikoff, C.N., 1999. Communication of stimulus size and shape in alarm calls of Gunnison's prairie dogs, *Cynomys gunnisoni*. Ethology 105, 149–162.

Anderson, M., 1994. Sexual Selection. Princeton University Press, Princeton, NJ.

Arlet, M.E., Isbell, L.A., 2009. Variation in behavioral and hormonal responses of adult male gray-cheeked mangabeys (*Lophocebus albigena*) to crowned eagles (*Stephanoaetus coronatus*) in Kibale National Park, Uganda. Behav. Ecol. Sociobiol. 63, 491–499.

Arnold, K., Zuberbühler, K., 2006a. The alarm-calling system of adult male putty-nosed monkeys, *Cercopithecus nictitans martini*. Anim. Behav. 72, 643–653.

Arnold, K., Zuberbühler, K., 2006b. Semantic combinations in primate calls. Nature 441, 303.

Arnold, K., Zuberbühler, K., 2008. Meaningful call combinations in a non-human primate. Curr. Biol. 18, R202–R203.

Arnold, K., Pohlner, Y., Zuberbühler, K., 2008. A forest monkey's alarm call series to predator models. Behav. Ecol. Sociobiol. 62, 549–559.

Baker, M.C., Becker, A.M., 2002. Mobbing calls of black-capped Chickadees: effects of urgency on call production. Wilson Bull. 114, 510–516.

Bayly, K.L., Evans, C.S., 2003. Dynamic changes in alarm call structure: a strategy for reducing conspicuousness to avian predators? Behaviour 140, 353–369.

Bergstrom, C.T., Lachmann, M., 2001. Alarm calls as costly signals of antipredator vigilance: the watchful babbler game. Anim. Behav. 61, 535–543.

Blumstein, D.T., Arnold, W., 1995. Situational specificity in Alpine-marmot alarm communication. Ethology 100(1), 1–13.

Blumstein, D.T., 1999. Alarm calling in three species of marmots. Behaviour 136, 731–757.

Blumstein, D.T., Daniel, J.C., 2004. Yellow-bellied marmots discriminate between the alarm calls of individuals and are more responsive to calls from juveniles. Anim. Behav. 68, 1257–1265.

Blumstein, D.T., Munos, O., 2005. Individual, age and sex-specific information is contained in yellow-bellied marmot alarm calls. Anim. Behav. 69, 353–361.

Blumstein, D.T., Steinmetz, J., Armitage, K.B., Daniel, J.C., 1997. Alarm calling in yellow-bellied marmots: II. The importance of direct fitness. Anim. Behav. 53, 173–184.

Blumstein, D.T., Verneyre, L., Daniel, J.C., 2004. Reliability and the adaptive utility of discrimination among alarm callers. Proc. R. Soc. B 271, 1851–1857.

Blumstein, D.T., Patton, M.L., Saltzman, W., 2006. Faecal glucocorticoid metabolites and alarm calling in free-living yellow-bellied marmots. Biol. Lett. 2, 29–32.

Blumstein, D.T., Cooley, L., Winternitz, J., Daniel, J.C., 2008. Do yellow-bellied marmots respond to predator vocalizations? Behav. Ecol. Sociobiol. 62, 457–468.

Call, J., Tomasello, M., 2007. The Gestural Communication of Apes and Monkeys. Taylor and Francis, Lea, London.

Chapman, C.A., Chapman, L.J., Lefebvre, L., 1990. Spider monkey alarm calls: honest advertisement or warning kin. Anim. Behav. 39, 197–198.

Charnov, E.L., Krebs, J.R., 1975. Evolution of alarm calls: altruism or manipulation? Am. Nat. 109, 107–112.

Cheney, D.L., Seyfarth, R.M., 1985. Vervet monkey alarm calls: manipulation through shared information? Behaviour 94, 739–751.

Cheney, D.L., Seyfarth, R.M., 1988. Assessment of meaning and the detection of unreliable signals by vervet monkeys. Anim. Behav. 36, 477–486.

Cheney, D.L., Seyfarth, R.M., 1990. Attending to behaviour versus attending to knowledge: examining monkey's attribution of mental states. Anim. Behav. 40, 742–753.

Clarke, E., Reichard, U., Zuberbühler, K., 2006. The syntax and meaning of wild gibbon songs. PLoS ONE 1, e73.

Clutton-Brock, T.M., Albon, S.D., 1979. The roaring of red deer and the evolution of honest advertisement. Behaviour 69, 145–170.

Coss, R.G., McCowan, B., Ramakrishnan, U., 2007. Threat-related acoustical differences in alarm calls by wild Bonnet macaques (*Macaca radiata*) elicited by python and leopard models. Ethology 113, 352–367.

Curio, E., 1969. Funktionsweise und Stammesgeschichte des Flugfeinderkennens einiger Darwinfinken (Geospizinae). Zeitschrift für Tierpsychologie 26, 394–487.

Curio, E., 1978. The adaptive significance of avian mobbing: I. Teleonomic hypotheses and predictions. Z. Tierpsychol. 48, 175–183.

Curio, E., Ernst, U., Vieth, W., 1978. The adaptive significance of avian mobbing: II. Cultural transmission of enemy recognition in blackbirds: effectiveness and some constraints. Z. Tierpsychol. 48, 184–202.

Darwin, C., 1859. The Origin of Species. Random House, New York.

Darwin, C., 1871. The descent of man and selection in relation to sex. Murrey/Random House, London.

Devereux, C.L., Fernandez-Juricic, E., Krebs, J.R., Whittingham, M.J., 2008. Habitat affects escape behaviour and alarm calling in Common Starlings *Sturnus vulgaris*. Ibis 150, 191–198.

Digweed, S.M., Fedigan, L.M., Rendall, D., 2005. Variable specificity in the anti-predator vocalizations and behaviour of the white-faced capuchin, *Cebus capucinus*. Behaviour 142, 997–1021.

Donaldson, M.C., Lachmann, M., Bergstrom, C.T., 2007. The evolution of functionally referential meaning in a structured world. J. Theor. Biol. 246, 225–233.

Eckardt, W., Zuberbühler, K., 2004. Cooperation and competition in two forest monkeys. Behav. Ecol. 15, 400–411.

Eiler, K.C., Banack, S.A., 2004. Variability in the alarm call of golden-mantled ground squirrels (*Spermophilus lateralis* and *S. saturatus*). J. Mammal. 85, 43–50.

Ellis, J.M.S., 2008. Which call parameters signal threat to conspecifics in white-throated magpie-jay mobbing calls? Ethology 114, 154–163.

Enard, W., Przeworski, M., Fisher, S.E., Lai, C.S.L., Wiebe, V., Kitano, T., et al., 2002. Molecular evolution of FOXP2, a gene involved in speech and language. Nature 418, 869–872.

Endres, T., Widmann, K., Fendt, M., 2007. Are rats predisposed to learn 22 kHz calls as danger-predicting signals? Behav. Brain Res. 185, 69–75.

Evans, C.S., 1997. Referential signals. In: Owings, D.H., Beecher, M.D., Thompson, N.S. (Eds.), Perspectives in Ethology. Plenum, New York, pp. 99–143.

Evans, C.S., Evans, L., Marler, P., 1994. On the meaning of alarm calls: functional reference in an avian vocal system. Anim. Behav. 45, 23–38.

Evans, D.M., Ruxton, G.D., Ruxton, D.A., 2004. Do false alarm anti-predatory flushes provide a foraging benefit to subdominant species? Biologia 59, 675–678.

Fichtel, C., 2008. Ontogeny of conspecific and heterospecific alarm call recognition in wild Verreaux's sifakas (*Propithecus verreauxi verreauxi*). Am. J. Primatol. 70, 127–135.

Fichtel, C., Hammerschmidt, K., 2002. Responses of redfronted lemurs to experimentally modified alarm calls: evidence for urgency-based changes in call structure. Ethology 108, 763–777.

Fichtel, C., Hammerschmidt, K., 2003. Responses of squirrel monkeys to their experimentally modified mobbing calls. J. Acoust. Soc. Am. 113, 2927–2932.

Fichtel, C., Kappeler, P.M., 2002. Anti-predator behavior of group-living Malagasy primates: mixed evidence for a referential alarm call system. Behav. Ecol. Sociobiol. 51, 262–275.

Fichtel, C., van Schaik, C.P., 2006. Semantic differences in sifaka (*Propithecus verreauxi*) alarm calls: a reflection of genetic or cultural variants? Ethology 112, 839–849.

Fichtel, C., Perry, S., Gros-Louis, J., 2005. Alarm calls of white-faced capuchin monkeys: an acoustic analysis. Anim. Behav. 70, 165–176.

Fischer, J., Cheney, D.L., Seyfarth, R.M., 2000. Development of infant baboons' responses to graded bark variants. Proc. R. Soc. Lond. Ser. B-Biol. Sci. 267, 2317–2321.

Fischer, J., Hammerschmidt, K., Cheney, D.L., Seyfarth, R.M., 2001a. Acoustic features of female chacma baboon barks. Ethology 107, 33–54.

Fischer, J., Metz, M., Cheney, D.L., Seyfarth, R.M., 2001b. Baboon responses to graded bark variants. Anim. Behav. 61, 925–931.

Fischer, J., Hammerschmidt, K., Cheney, D.L., Seyfarth, R.M., 2002. Acoustic features of male baboon loud calls: influences of context, age, and individuality. J. Acoust. Soc. Am. 111, 1465–1474.

Frederiksen, J.K., Slobodchikoff, C.N., 2007. Referential specificity in the alarm calls of the black-tailed prairie dog. Ethol. Ecol. Evol. 19, 87–99.

Freeberg, T.M., 2008. Complexity in the Chick-a-Dee call of carolina chickadees (Poecile Carolinensis): associations of context and signaler behavior to call structure. Auk 125, 896–907.

Gautier, J.-P., Gautier, A., 1977. Communication in old world monkeys. In: Sebeok, T.A. (Ed.), How Animals Communicate. Indiana University Press, Bloomington, Indiana, pp. 890–964.

Gil-da-Costa, R., Palleroni, A., Hauser, M.D., Touchton, J., Kelley, J.P., 2003. Rapid acquisition of an alarm response by a neotropical primate to a newly introduced avian predator. Proc. R. Soc. Lond. Ser. B-Biol. Sci. 270, 605–610.

Gill, S.A., Sealy, S.G., 2003. Tests of two functions of alarm calls given by yellow warblers during nest defence. Can. J. Zool.-Rev. Can. Zool. 81, 1685–1690.

Gill, S.A., Sealy, S.G., 2004. Functional reference in an alarm signal given during nest defence: seet calls of yellow warblers denote brood-parasitic brown-headed cowbirds. Behav. Ecol. Sociobiol. 56, 71–80.

Goodale, E., Kotagama, S.W., 2006. Context-dependent vocal mimicry in a passerine bird. Proc. R. Soc. B-Biol. Sci. 273, 875–880.

Goodale, E., Kotagama, S.W., 2008. Response to conspecific and heterospecific alarm calls in mixed-species bird flocks of a Sri Lankan rainforest. Behav. Ecol. 19, 887–894.

Goodale, E., Salgado, A., Kotagama, S.W., 2008. Birds of a different feather. Nat. Hist. 117, 24–28.

Goodall, J., 1986. The chimpanzees of Gombe: patterns of behavior. Harvard University Press, Cambridge.

Graw, B., Manser, M.B., 2007. The function of mobbing in cooperative meerkats. Anim. Behav. 74, 507–517.

Grice, H.P., 1969. Utterers' meaning and intentions. Philos. Rev. 78, 147–177.

Griesser, M., Ekman, A., 2004. Nepotistic alarm calling in the Siberian jay, Perisoreus infaustus. Animal Behaviour 67, 933–939.

Griesser, M., Ekman, J., 2005. Nepotistic mobbing behaviour in the Siberian jay, *Perisoreus infaustus*. Anim. Behav. 69, 345–352.

Griffin, A.S., Savani, R.S., Hausmanis, K., Lefebvre, L., 2005. Mixed-species aggregations in birds: zenaida doves, *Zenaida aurita*, respond to the alarm calls of carib grackles, *Quiscalus lugubris*. Anim. Behav. 70, 507–515.

Grim, T., 2008. Are Blackcaps (*Sylvia atricapilla*) defending their nests also calling for help from their neighbours? J. Ornithol. 149, 169–180.

Guilford, T., Dawkins, M.S., 1991. Receiver psychology and the evolution of animal signals. Anim. Behav. 42, 1–14.

Gursky, S., 2003. Predation experiments on infant spectral tarsiers (Tarsius spectrum). Folia Primatol. 74, 272–284.

Gursky, S., 2006. Function of snake mobbing in spectral tarsiers. Am. J. Phys. Anthropol. 129, 601–608.

Gyger, M., Marler, P., Pickert, R., 1987. Semantics of an avian alarm call system: the male domestic fowl, G. domesticus. Behaviour 102, 15–40.

Hamilton, W.D., 1963. The evolution of altruistic behavior. Am. Nat. 97, 354–356.

Hare, J.F., Atkins, B.A., 2001. The squirrel that cried wolf: reliability detection by juvenile Richardson's ground squirrels (*Spermophilus richardsonii*). Behav. Ecol. Sociobiol. 51, 108–112.

Hauser, M.D., 1988. How infant vervet monkeys learn to recognize starling alarm calls: the role of experience. Behaviour 105, 187–201.

Hauser, M.D., 1993. Do vervet monkey infants cry wolf? Anim. Behav. 45, 1242–1244.

Henry, K.S., Lucas, J.R., 2008. Coevolution of auditory sensitivity and temporal resolution with acoustic signal space in three songbirds. Anim. Behav. 76, 1659–1671.

Herrnstein, R.J., Loveland, D., 1964. Complex visual concepts in the pigeon. Science 146, 549–551.

Herzog, M., Hopf, S., 1984. Behavioral responses to species-specific warning calls in infant squirrel monkeys reared in social isolation. Am. J. Primatol. 7, 99–106.

Hollen, L.I., Manser, M.B., 2006. Ontogeny of alarm call responses in meerkats, *Suricata suricatta*: the roles of age, sex and nearby conspecifics. Anim. Behav. 72, 1345–1353.

Hollen, L.I., Manser, M.B., 2007a. Motivation before meaning: motivational information encoded in meerkat alarm calls develops earlier than referential information. Am. Nat. 169, 758–767.

Hollen, L.I., Manser, M.B., 2007b. Persistence of alarm-call behaviour in the absence of predators: a comparison between wild and captive-born meerkats (*Suricata suricatta*). Ethology 113, 1038–1047.

Hollen, L.I., Clutton-Brock, T., Manser, M.B., 2008. Ontogenetic changes in alarm-call production and usage in meerkats (*Suricata suricatta*): adaptations or constraints? Behav. Ecol. Sociobiol. 62, 821–829.

Hoogland, J.L., 1996. Why do Gunnison's prairie dogs give anti-predator calls? Anim. Behav. 51, 871–880.

Janik, V.M., Slater, P.J.B., 2000. The different roles of social learning in vocal communication. Anim. Behav. 60, 1–11.

Jones, K.J., Hill, W.L., 2001. Auditory perception of hawks and owls for passerine alarm calls. Ethology 107, 717–726.

Jones, K.A., Whittingham, M.J., 2008. Anti-predator signals in the Chaffinch *Fringilla coelebs* in response to habitat structure and different predator types. Ethology 114, 1033–1043.

Jurisevic, M.A., Sanderson, K.J., 1998. Acoustic discrimination of passerine anti-predator signals by Australian raptors. Aust. J. Zool. 46, 369–379.

Kirchhof, J., Hammerschmidt, K., 2006. Functionally referential alarm calls in tamarins (*Saguinus fuscicollis* and *Saguinus mystax*)—evidence from playback experiments. Ethology 112, 346–354.

Kiriazis, J., Slobodchikoff, C.N., 2006. Perceptual specificity in the alarm calls of Gunnison's prairie dogs. Behav. Process. 73, 29–35.

Kitchen, D.M., Cheney, D.L., Seyfarth, R.M., 2003. Female baboons' responses to male loud calls. Ethology 109, 401–412.

Klump, G.M., Shalter, M.D., 1984. Acoustic behaviour of birds and mammals in the predator context. I: Factors affecting the structure of alarm signals. II: The functional significance and evolution of alarm signals. Z. Tierpsychol. 66, 189–226.

Klump, G.M., Kretzschmar, E., Curio, E., 1986. The hearing of an avian predator and its avian prey. Behav. Ecol. Sociobiol. 18, 317–323.

Lea, A.J., Barrera, J.P., Tom, L.M., Blumstein, D.T., 2008. Heterospecific eavesdropping in a nonsocial species. Behav. Ecol. 19, 1041–1046.
Leavesley, A.J., Magrath, R.D., 2005. Communicating about danger: urgency alarm calling in a bird. Anim. Behav. 70, 365–373.
Leger, D.W., Owings, D.H., Gelfand, D.L., 1980. Single note vocalizations of California ground squirrels: graded signals and situation—specificity of predator and socially evoked calls. Z. Tierpsychol. 52, 227–246.
Le Roux, A., Jackson, T.P., Cherry, M.I., 2001a. Does Brants' whistling rat (Parotomys brantsii) use an urgency-based alarm system in reaction to aerial and terrestrial predators? Behaviour 138, 757–774.
Le Roux, A., Jackson, T.P., Cherry, M.I., 2001b. The effect of changing call duration and calling bouts on vigilance in Brants' whistling rat, Parotomys brantsii. Behaviour 138, 1287–1302.
Le Roux, A., Jackson, T.P., Cherry, M.I., 2002. Differences in alarm vocalizations of sympatric populations of the whistling rats, Parotomys brantsii and P-littledalei (Rodentia: Muridae). J. Zool. 257, 189–194.
Le Roux, A., Cherry, M.I., Manser, M.B., 2008. The audience effect in a facultatively social mammal, the yellow mongoose, Cynictis penicillata. Anim. Behav. 75, 943–949.
Lieberman, P., 1968. Primate vocalizations and human linguistic ability. J. Acoust. Soc. Am. 44, 1574–1584.
Lieberman, P., Klatt, D.H., Wilson, W.H., 1969. Vocal tract limitations on the vowel repertoires of rhesus monkeys and other nonhuman primates. Science 164, 1185–1187.
Litvin, Y., Blanchard, D.C., Blanchard, R.J., 2007. Rat 22kHz ultrasonic vocalizations as alarm cries. Behav. Brain Res. 182, 166–172.
Macedonia, J.M., Evans, C.S., 1993. Variation among mammalian alarm call systems and the problem of meaning in animal signals. Ethology 93, 177–197.
Macwhirter, R.B., 1992. Vocal and escape responses of Columbian ground squirrels to simulated terrestrial and aerial predator attacks. Ethology 91, 311–325.
Magrath, R.D., Platzen, D., Kondo, J., 2006. From nestling calls to fledgling silence: adaptive timing of change in response to aerial alarm calls. Proc. R. Soc. B-Biol. Sci. 273, 2335–2341.
Magrath, R.D., Pitcher, B.J., Gardner, J.L., 2007. A mutual understanding? Interspecific responses by birds to each other's aerial alarm calls. Behav. Ecol. 18, 944–951.
Magrath, R.D., Pitcher, B.J., Gardner, J.L., 2009. Recognition of other species' aerial alarm calls: speaking the same language or learning another? Proc. R. Soc. B-Biol. Sci. 276, 769–774.
Manser, M.B., 2001. The acoustic structure of suricates' alarm calls varies with predator type and the level of response urgency. Proc. R. Soc. Lond. Ser. B-Biol. Sci. 268, 2315–2324.
Manser, M.B., Bell, M.B., Fletcher, L.B., 2001. The information that receivers extract from alarm calls in suricates. Proc. R. Soc. Lond. Ser. B-Biol. Sci. 268, 2485–2491.
Manser, M.B., Seyfarth, R.M., Cheney, D.L., 2002. Suricate alarm calls signal predator class and urgency. Trends Cogn. Sci. 6, 55–57.
Marler, P., 1955. Some characteristics of some animal calls. Nature 176, 6–8.
Mateo, J.M., Holmes, W.G., 1999. How rearing history affects alarm-call responses of Belding's ground squirrels (Spermophilus beldingi, Sciuridae). Ethology 105, 207–222.
Maurer, G., Magrath, R.D., Leonard, M.L., Horn, A.G., Donnelly, C., 2003. Begging to differ: scrubwren nestlings beg to alarm calls and vocalize when parents are absent. Anim. Behav. 65, 1045–1055.
Maynard-Smith, J., 1965. The evolution of alarm calls. Am. Nat. 99, 59–63.
McCowan, B., Hooper, S.L., 2002. Individual acoustic variation in Belding's ground squirrel alarm chirps in the High Sierra Nevada. J. Acoust. Soc. Am. 111, 1157–1160.
McCowan, B., Franceschini, N.V., Vicino, G.A., 2001. Age differences and developmental trends in alarm peep responses by Squirrel monkeys (Saimiri sciureus). Am. J. Primatol. 53, 19–31.

McGregor, P.K., Dabelsteen, T., 1996. Communication networks. In: Kroodsma, D.E., Miller, E.H. (Eds.), Ecology and Evolution of Acoustic Communication in Birds. Cornell University Press, Ithaca, New York, pp. 409–425.

Muller, C.A., Manser, M.B., 2008. The information banded mongooses extract from hetero-specific alarms. Anim. Behav. 75, 897–904.

Munn, C.A., 1986. Birds that "cry wolf" Nature 319, 143–145.

Naguib, M., Mundry, R., Ostreiher, R., Hultsch, H., Schrader, L., Todt, D., 1999. Cooperatively breeding Arabian babblers call differently when mobbing in different predator-induced situations. Behav. Ecol. 10, 636–640.

Nocera, J.J., Taylor, P.D., Ratcliffe, L.M., 2008. Inspection of mob-calls as sources of predator information: response of migrant and resident birds in the Neotropics. Behav. Ecol. Sociobiol. 62, 1769–1777.

Oda, R., Masataka, N., 1996. Interspecific responses of ringtailed lemurs to playback of antipredator alarm calls given by Verreaux's sifakas. Ethology 102, 441–453.

Ogden, C.K., Richards, I.A., 1923. The Meaning of Meaning. 8th Ed. New York, Harcourt, Brace & World, Inc.

Ouattara, K., Zuberbühler, K., N'goran, E.K., Gombert, J.-E., Lemasson, A., 2009. The alarm call system of female Campbell's monkeys. Anim. Behav. 78(1), 35–44.

Papworth, S., Böse, A.-S., Barker, J., Zuberbühler, K., 2008. Male blue monkeys alarm call in response to danger experienced by others. Biol. Lett. 4, 472–475.

Perla, B.S., Slobodchikoff, C.N., 2002. Habitat structure and alarm call dialects in Gunnison's prairie dog (Cynomys gunnisoni). Behav. Ecol. 13, 844–850.

Platzen, D., Magrath, R.D., 2005. Adaptive differences in response to two types of parental alarm call in altricial nestlings. Proc. R. Soc. B-Biol. Sci. 272, 1101–1106.

Price, T., Arnold, K., Zuberbühler, K., Semple, S., 2009. Pyow but not hack calls of the male putty-nosed monkey (Cercopithecus nictitans) convey information about caller identity. Behaviour 146(7), 871–888.

Rainey, H.J., Zuberbühler, K., Slater, P.J.B., 2004a. Hornbills can distinguish between primate alarm calls. Proc. R. Soc. Lond. Ser. B-Biol. Sci. 271, 755–759.

Rainey, H.J., Zuberbühler, K., Slater, P.J.B., 2004b. The responses of black-casqued hornbills to predator vocalisations and primate alarm calls. Behaviour 141, 1263–1277.

Randall, J.A., Rogovin, K.A., 2002. Variation in and meaning of alarm calls in a social desert rodent Rhombomys opimus. Ethology 108, 513–527.

Randall, J.A., Rogovin, K.A., Shier, D.M., 2000. Antipredator behavior of a social desert rodent: footdrumming and alarm calling in the great gerbil, Rhombomys opiums. Behav. Ecol. Sociobiol. 48, 110–118.

Randall, J.A., McCowan, B., Collins, K.C., Hooper, S.L., Rogovin, K., 2005. Alarm signals of the great gerbil: acoustic variation by predator context, sex, age, individual, and family group. J. Acoust. Soc. Am. 118, 2706–2714.

Randler, C., 2006. Red squirrels (Sciurus vulgaris) respond to alarm calls of eurasian jays (Garrulus glandarius). Ethology 112, 411–416.

Reby, D., Cargnelutti, B., Hewison, A.J.M., 1999. Contexts and possible functions of barking in roe deer. Anim. Behav. 57, 1121–1128.

Ridley, A.R., Child, M.F., Bell, M.B.V., 2007. Interspecific audience effects on the alarm-calling behaviour of a kleptoparasitic bird. Biol. Lett. 3, 589–591.

Riede, T., Zuberbühler, K., 2003a. Pulse register phonation in Diana monkey alarm calls. J. Acoust. Soc. Am. 113, 2919–2926.

Riede, T., Zuberbühler, K., 2003b. The relationship between acoustic structure and semantic information in Diana monkey alarm vocalization. J. Acoust. Soc. Am. 114, 1132–1142.

Riede, T., Bronson, E., Hatzikirou, H., Zuberbühler, K., 2005. Vocal production mechanisms in a non-human primate: morphological data and a model. J. Hum. Evol. 48, 85–96.

Robinson, J.G., 1984. Syntactic structures in the vocalizations of wedge-capped capuchin monkeys, Cebus olivaceus. Behaviour 90, 46–79.

Schel, A.M., Tranquilli, S., Zuberbühler, K., 2009. The alarm call system of black-and-white colobus monkeys. J. Comp. Psychol. 123, 136–150.

Schibler, F., Manser, M.B., 2007. The irrelevance of individual discrimination in meerkat alarm calls. Anim. Behav. 74, 1259–1268.

Schmidt, K.A., Lee, E., Ostfeld, R.S., Sieving, K., 2008. Eastern chipmunks increase their perception of predation risk in response to titmouse alarm calls. Behav. Ecol. 19, 759–763.

Seddon, N., Tobias, J.A., Alvarez, A., 2002. Vocal communication in the pale-winged trumpeter (Psophia leucoptera): repertoire, context and functional reference. Behaviour 139, 1331–1359.

Seyfarth, R.M., Cheney, D.L., 1986. Vocal development in vervet monkeys. Anim. Behav. 34, 1640–1658.

Seyfarth, R.M., Cheney, D.L., 1997. Behavioral mechanisms underlying vocal communication in nonhuman primates. Anim. Learn. Behav. 25, 249–267.

Seyfarth, R.M., Cheney, D.L., Marler, P., 1980. Vervet monkey alarm calls: semantic communication in a free-ranging primate. Anim. Behav. 28, 1070–1094.

Shelley, E.L., Blumstein, D.T., 2005. The evolution of vocal alarm communication in rodents. Behav. Ecol. 16, 169–177.

Sherman, P.W., 1977. Nepotism and the evolution of alarm calls. Science 197, 1246–1253.

Sherman, P.W., 1985. Alarm calls of Belding's ground squirrels to aerial predators: nepotism or self-preservation? Behav. Ecol. Sociobiol. 17, 313–323.

Shriner, W.M., 1999. Antipredator responses to a previously neutral sound by free-living adult golden-mantled ground squirrels, Spermophilus lateralis (Sciuridae). Ethology 105, 747–757.

Shultz, S., Noë, R., 2002. The consequences of crowned eagle central-place foraging on predation risk in monkeys. Proc. R. Soc. Lond. Ser. B-Biol. Sci. 269, 1797–1802.

Sloan, J.L., Hare, J.F., 2004. Monotony and the information content of Richardson's ground squirrel (Spermophilus richardsonii) repeated calls: tonic communication or signal certainty? Ethology 110, 147–156.

Sloan, J.L., Hare, J.F., 2008. The more the scarier: adult Richardson's ground squirrels (Spermophilus richardsonii) assess response urgency via the number of alarm signallers. Ethology 114, 436–443.

Sloan, J.L., Wilson, D.R., Hare, J.F., 2005. Functional morphology of Richardson's ground squirrel, Spermophilus richardsonii, alarm calls: the meaning of chirps, whistles and chucks. Anim. Behav. 70, 937–944.

Slobodchikoff, C.N., Placer, J., 2006. Acoustic structures in the alarm calls of Gunnison's prairie dogs. J. Acoust. Soc. Am. 119, 3153–3160.

Slobodchikoff, C.N., Kiriazis, J., Fischer, C., Creef, E., 1991. Semantic information distinguishing individual predators in the alarm calls of Gunnison's prairie dogs. Anim. Behav. 42, 713–719.

Slobodchikoff, C.N., Ackers, S.H., Van Ert, M., 1998. Geographic variation in alarm calls of Gunnison's prairie dogs. J. Mammal. 79, 1265–1272.

Slocombe, K.E., Zuberbühler, K., 2005a. Agonistic screams in wild chimpanzees (Pan troglodytes schweinfurthii) vary as a function of social role. J. Comp. Psychol. 119, 67–77.

Slocombe, K.E., Zuberbühler, K., 2005b. Functionally referential communication in a chimpanzee. Curr. Biol. 15, 1779–1784.

Slocombe, K.E., Zuberbühler, K., 2007. Chimpanzees modify recruitment screams as a function of audience composition. Proc. Natl. Acad. Sci. USA 104, 17228–17233.

Slocombe, K.E., Townsend, S.W., Zuberbühler, K., 2009. Wild chimpanzees (Pan troglodytes schweinfurthii) distinguish between different scream types: evidence from a playback study. Anim. Cogn. 12(3), 441–449.

Sproul, C., Palleroni, A., Hauser, M.D., 2006. Cottontop tamarin, *Saguinus oedipus*, alarm calls contain sufficient information for recognition of individual identity. Anim. Behav. 72, 1379–1385.

Stephan, C., Zuberbühler, K., 2008. Predation increases acoustic complexity in primate alarm calls. Biol. Lett. 4, 641–644.

Struhsaker, T.T., 1967. Auditory communication among vervet monkeys (*Cercopithecus aethiops*). In: Altmann, S.A. (Ed.), Social Communication Among Primates. University of Chicago Press, Chicago, pp. 281–324.

Swan, D.C., Hare, J.F., 2008a. The first cut is the deepest: primary syllables of Richardson's ground squirrel, *Spermophilus richardsonii*, repeated calls alert receivers. Anim. Behav. 76, 47–54.

Swan, D.C., Hare, J.F., 2008b. Signaler and receiver ages do not affect responses to Richardson's ground squirrel alarm calls. J. Mammal. 89, 889–894.

Takahashi, M., Hasegawa, T., 2008. Seasonal and diurnal use of eight different call types by Indian peafowl (*Pavo cristatus*). J. Ethol. 26, 375–381.

Templeton, C.N., Greene, E., 2007. Nuthatches eavesdrop on variations in heterospecific chickadee mobbing alarm calls. Proc. Natl. Acad. Sci. USA 104, 5479–5482.

Templeton, C.N., Greene, E., Davis, K., 2005. Allometry of alarm calls: black-capped chickadees encode information about predator size. Science 308, 1934–1937.

Tenaza, R.R., Tilson, R.L., 1977. Evolution of long-distance alarm calls in Kloss's gibbon. Nature 268, 233–235.

Tomasello, M., 2008. Origins of Human Communication. MIT Press, Cambridge, MA.

Townsend, S.W., Deschner, T., Zuberbühler, K., 2008. Female chimpanzees use copulation calls flexibly to prevent social competition. PLoS ONE 3, e2431.

Uster, D., Zuberbühler, K., 2001. The functional significance of Diana monkey 'clear' calls. Behaviour 138, 741–756.

Vitousek, M.N., Adelman, J.S., Gregory, N.C., St Clair, J.J.H., 2007. Heterospecific alarm call recognition in a non-vocal reptile. Biol. Lett. 3, 632–634.

Warkentin, K.J., Keeley, A.T.H., Hare, J.F., 2001. Repetitive calls of juvenile Richardson's ground squirrels (*Spermophilus richardsonii*) communicate response urgency. Can. J. Zool.-Rev. Can. De Zool. 79, 569–573.

Welbergen, J.A., Davies, N.B., 2008. Reed warblers discriminate cuckoos from sparrowhawks with graded alarm signals that attract mates and neighbours. Anim. Behav. 76, 811–822.

Wheeler, B.C., 2008. Selfish or altruistic? An analysis of alarm call function in wild capuchin monkeys, *Cebus apella nigritus*. Anim. Behav. 76, 1465–1475.

Wheeler, B.C., 2009. Monkeys crying wolf? Tufted capuchin monkeys use anti-predator calls to usurp resources from conspecifics. Proc. R. Soc. B. in press.

Wich, S.A., de Vries, H., 2006. Male monkeys remember which group members have given alarm calls. Proc. R. Soc. B-Biol. Sci. 273, 735–740.

Wich, S.A., Sterck, E.H.M., 2003. Possible audience effect in Thomas Langurs (Primates; *Presbytis thomasi*): an experimental study on male loud calls in response to a tiger model. Am. J. Primatol. 60, 155–159.

Wich, S.A., Koski, S., de Vries, H., van Schaik, C.P., 2003. Individual and contextual variation in Thomas langur male loud calls. Ethology 109, 1–13.

Wilson, D.R., Evans, C.S., 2008. Mating success increases alarm-calling effort in male fowl, *Gallus gallus*. Anim. Behav. 76, 2029–2035.

Wilson, D.R., Hare, J.F., 2006. The adaptive utility of Richardson's ground squirrel (*Spermophilus richardsonii*) short-range ultrasonic alarm signals. Can. J. Zool.-Rev. Can. De Zool. 84, 1322–1330.

Wohr, M., Schwarting, R.K.W., 2008. Ultrasonic calling during fear conditioning in the rat: no evidence for an audience effect. Anim. Behav. 76, 749–760.

Wolters, S., Zuberbühler, K., 2003. Mixed-species associations of Diana and Campbell's monkeys: the costs and benefits of a forest phenomenon. Behaviour 140, 371–385.

Wood, S.R., Sanderson, K.J., Evans, C.S., 2000. Perception of terrestrial and aerial alarm calls by honeyeaters and falcons. Aust. J. Zool. 48, 127–134.

Yates, J., Tule, N., 1979. Perceiving surprising words in an unattended auditory channel. Q. J. Exp. Psychol. 31, 281–286.

Yorzinski, J.L., Vehrencamp, S.L., Clark, A.B., McGowan, K.J., 2006. The inflected alarm caw of the American Crow: differences in acoustic structure among individuals and sexes. Condor 108, 518–529.

Zuberbühler, K., Noë, R., Seyfarth, R.M., 1997. Diana monkey long-distance calls: messages for conspecifics and predators. Anim. Behav. 53, 589–604.

Zuberbühler, K., 2000a. Referential labelling in Diana monkeys. Anim. Behav. 59, 917–927.

Zuberbühler, K., 2000b. Causal cognition in a non-human primate: field playback experiments with Diana monkeys. Cognition 76, 195–207.

Zuberbühler, K., 2000c. Causal knowledge of predators' behaviour in wild Diana monkeys. Anim. Behav. 59, 209–220.

Zuberbühler, K., 2000d. Interspecific semantic communication in two forest monkeys. Proc. R. Soc. Lond. Ser. B-Biol. Sci. 267, 713–718.

Zuberbühler, K., 2001. Predator-specific alarm calls in Campbell's guenons. Behav. Ecol. Sociobiol. 50, 414–422.

Zuberbühler, K., 2002a. Effects of natural and sexual selection on the evolution of guenon loud calls. In: Glenn, M.E., Cords, M. (Eds.), The Guenons: Diversity and Adaptation in African Monkeys. Plenum, New York, pp. 289–306.

Zuberbühler, K., 2002b. A syntactic rule in forest monkey communication. Anim. Behav. 63, 293–299.

Zuberbühler, K., 2003. Referential signalling in non-human primates: cognitive precursors and limitations for the evolution of language. Adv. Study Behav. 33, 265–307.

Zuberbühler, K., 2006. Alarm calls—evolutionary and cognitive mechanisms. In: Brown, K. (Ed.), Encyclopedia of Language and Linguistics. Elsevier, Oxford, pp. 143–155.

Zuberbühler, K., 2008. Audience effects. Curr. Biol. 18, R189–R190.

Zuberbühler, K., Jenny, D., 2002. Leopard predation and primate evolution. J. Hum. Evol. 43, 873–886.

Zuberbühler, K., Cheney, D.L., Seyfarth, R.M., 1999a. Conceptual semantics in a nonhuman primate. J. Comp. Psychol. 113, 33–42.

Zuberbühler, K., Jenny, D., Bshary, R., 1999b. The predator deterrence function of primate alarm calls. Ethology 105, 477–490.

Index

A

Acoustic communication, delphinids
  cognition, 146–147
  complexity and adaptation, 147–148
  evolutionary aspects, 146
  functions
    food-related calls, 143–145
    group and individual
      recognition, 140–142
    social contexts, 142–143
    sophisticated observation, 138–139
    species recognition, 139–140
  geographic variation and
    dialects, 133–135
  perception, 129–130
  ranges and strategies, 131–133
  signature whistle, 130
  vocal development and
    learning, 135–138
  vocalizations types
    frequency modulation
      complexity, 127
    sound production mechanisms and
      categorization, 126–127
    whistle types, 127–129
Acoustic signal production
  alarm calls structure, 286–287
  environmental acoustics
    (*see* Environmental acoustics,
    songbirds evolution)
  habitat adaptation, 37–38
  sensorimotor learning and vocal
    performance
    behavioral/evolutionary
      plasticity, 160–162
    performance concept, 161–162

vocal frequencies, 162–163
    signaler adaptations, 5
    vocal performance, 160–163
Adaptive hypotheses
  character displacement, 54, 59–60
  habitat adaptation, 56–57
  sexual selection
    latitude, 52–53
    midlatitude, 58–59
    size dimorphism, 48–49, 51–52,
      58–59
Alarm calls
  evolution
    individual selection, 283–285
    kin selection, 279–281
    sexual selection, 281–283
  structure
    acoustic diversity, 286–287
    individual differences, 289–290
    population differences, 290
    receiver psychology, 287–289
    sequential organization, 291–292
Avian duetting hypotheses, 99–100

B

Barbets duetting evolution, 96–97
Behavioral adaptations, 18–20
Bird song evolution and environmental
  acoustics
  adaptation hypothesis, 3
  ambient noise, 2–3
  receiver adaptations
    distance assessment, noise
      implications, 24–25
    noise signals, 21–24

Contents of Previous Volumes